Henry Eyster Jacobs

First Free Lutheran Diet in America, Philadelphia, December 27-28, 1877

The essays, debates and proceedings

Henry Eyster Jacobs

First Free Lutheran Diet in America, Philadelphia, December 27-28, 1877
The essays, debates and proceedings

ISBN/EAN: 9783337037222

Printed in Europe, USA, Canada, Australia, Japan

Cover: Foto ©ninafisch / pixelio.de

More available books at **www.hansebooks.com**

FIRST

FREE LUTHERAN DIET

IN AMERICA.

PHILADELPHIA DECEMBER 27-28, 1877.

THE ESSAYS, DEBATES

AND

PROCEEDINGS.

PHILADELPHIA
J. FREDERICK SMITH, PUBLISHER,
42 NORTH NINTH STREET.
1878.

PREFACE.

After the adjournment of the Diet, the secretaries divided the work assigned between them, Dr. Baum undertaking to secure a publisher, and the undersigned to collect the essays and remarks, and edit the book. The call (p. 10) specified as one of the rules of the Diet, that a synopsis of each speech in the discussion be furnished for publication. It was only, however, by a great deal of correspondence and delay, that the remarks here published were secured, with a very few exceptions, from the speakers themselves. Considerable delay has resulted also from the reading of the proof of each essay by its author.

The book, as it now appears, we believe, will be found by those who were present at the Diet, to faithfully reproduce everything of essential importance in its proceedings. We have endeavored, by means of a full table of contents and indexes, to render its many items of value readily accessible.

In addition to Dr. Baum, special acknowledgments are due Drs. Seiss, Krauth, Diehl and Valentine, for important services and suggestions connected with the editing of the volume.

H. E. JACOBS.

Gettysburg, March 23d, 1878.

CONTENTS.

	PAGE.
Call for the Diet	9
Members of Diet	11
Opening Remarks by Dr. Morris	13
FIRST PAPER: "The Augsburg Confession and the Thirty-Nine Articles of the Anglican Church," by Rev. J. G. Morris, D. D., LL. D.	15
SECOND PAPER: "The Relations of the Lutheran Church to the Denominations around us," by Rev. C. P. Krauth, D. D., LL. D.	27
Remarks of Rev. D. P. Rosenmiller	70
" " C. W. Schaeffer, D. D.	70
" " F. W. Conrad, D. D.	72
" " J. A. Brown, D. D.	73
" " C. P. Krauth, D. D., LL. D.	77
THIRD PAPER: "The Four General Bodies of the Lutheran Church in the United States: Wherein they agree, and wherein they might harmoniously coöperate," by Rev. J. A. Brown, D. D.	80
Remarks of Rev. D. P. Rosenmiller	96
" " W. J. Mann, D. D.	96, 98
" " Prof. V. L. Conrad	97, 99
" " F. W. Conrad, D. D.	99
" " A. C. Wedekind, D. D.	101
" " R. A. Fink, D. D.	102
" " W. S. Emery	103
" " J. A. Brown, D. D.	104
FOURTH PAPER: "The History and Progress of the Lutheran Church in the United States," by Rev. H. E. Jacobs, D. D.	107
Remarks of Rev. F. W. Conrad, D. D.	137
" " J. A. Brown, D. D.	139
" " C. P. Krauth, D. D., LL. D.	141
" " D. P. Rosenmiller	144
FIFTH PAPER: "Education in the Lutheran Church in the United States," by Rev. M. Valentine, D. D.	145
Remarks of Rev. C. A. Stork, D. D.	160
" " J. F. Reinmund, D. D.	163
" " A. Spaeth, D. D.	163
Note from M. Valentine, D. D.	164
SIXTH PAPER: "The interests of the Lutheran Church in America as affected by Diversities of Language," by D. Luther, M. D.	165

CONTENTS.

	PAGE.
Remarks of Rev. L. E. Albert, D. D.	171
" " J. K. Plitt	172
" " J. B. Rath	172
" " J. Kohler	174
" " W. J. Mann, D. D.	176
" " A. Spaeth, D. D.	176
" " D. Luther, M. D.	177

SEVENTH PAPER: "Misunderstandings and Misrepresentations of the Lutheran Church," by Rev. J. A. Seiss, D. D. ... 180
Remarks of Rev. C. W. Shaeffer, D. D. ... 194
    "   "   J. A. Brown, D. D. ... 195
    "   "   C. P. Krauth, D. D., LL. D. ... 199
    "   "   J. A. Seiss, D. D. ... 204

EIGHTH PAPER: "The Characteristics of the Augsburg Confession," by Rev. F. W. Conrad, D. D. ... 206
Remarks of Rev. C. P. Krauth, D. D., LL. D. ... 233
    "   "   J. A. Brown, D. D. ... 237
Note of Rev. C. P. Krauth, D. D., LL. D. ... 238

NINTH PAPER: "True and False Spirituality in the Lutheran Church," by Rev. E. Greenwald, D. D. ... 243

TENTH PAPER: "Liturgical Forms in Worship," by Rev. C. A. Stork, D.D. 257
Remarks of Rev. L. E. Albert, D. D. ... 272
    "   "   F. W. Conrad, D. D. ... 272
    "   "   J. A. Brown, D. D. ... 274

ELEVENTH PAPER: "Theses on the Lutheranism of the Fathers of the Church in this Country," by Rev. W. J. Mann, D. D. ... 276
Remarks of Rev. J. G. Morris, D. D., LL. D. ... 283, 284
    "   "   W. J. Mann, D. D. ... 284
    "   "   J. A. Brown, D. D. ... 284, 285
    "   "   C. P. Krauth, D. D., LL. D. ... 285, 289
    "   "   J. A. Seiss, D. D. ... 286
    "   "   C. F. Welden ... 288

TWELFTH PAPER: "The Divine and Human Factors in the Call to the Ministerial Office, according to the Older Lutheran Authorities, by Rev. G. Diehl, D. D. ... 292
Remarks of Rev. N. M. Price ... 309
    "   "   W. J. Morris, D. D. ... 309, 312
    "   "   J. A. Brown, D. D. ... 309, 312
    "   "   F. W. Conrad, D. D. ... 310

THIRTEENTH PAPER: "The Educational and Sacramental Ideas of the Lutheran Church," in relation to Practical Piety," by Rev. A. C. Wedekind, D. D. ...
Closing Remarks of Rev. J. A. Seiss, D. D. ... 331
Closing Resolutions ... 333
Closing Remarks of Rev. F. W. Conrad, D. D. ... 334
Adjournment ... 335

PROCEEDINGS.

The following call had for some weeks been circulated through the Church papers:

A LUTHERAN CHURCH DIET.

A Free Diet of the Lutheran Church, to discuss living subjects of general worth and importance to all Lutherans, has been arranged to be held in St. Matthew's church (Dr. Baum's), in Philadelphia, beginning at 10 A. M. on Thursday, December 27th, 1877, to be in session several days.

The chief business of this Diet will be the reading of essays on given topics by men engaged for the purpose, and the free discussion of the subject of each essay after its presentation. The essayists engaged, and with whom is the responsibility for the calling and character of this Diet, are:

1. REV. J. G. MORRIS, D. D., LL. D., of Baltimore, Md. *Subject:* "The Augsburg Confession the Source of the Thirty-nine Articles of the Church of England, and incidentally of all other Protestant Confessions."

2. REV. PROF. C. P. KRAUTH, D. D., LL. D., of Philadelphia, Pa. *Subject:* "The Relations of the Lutheran Church to Denominations around us."

3. REV. Prof. J. A. BROWN, D. D., of Gettysburg, Pa. *Subject:* "The Four General Bodies of the Lutheran Church in the United States; wherein they agree, and wherein they might harmoniously co-operate."

4. REV. PROF. H. E. JACOBS, D. D., of Gettysburg, Pa. *Subject:* "The History and Progress of the Lutheran Church in the United States."

5. REV. PROF. M. VALENTINE, D. D., of Gettysburg, Pa. *Subject:* "Education in the Lutheran Church in the United States."

6. REV. PROF. S. A. REPASS, D. D, of Salem, Va. *Subject:* "The Conservatism of the Lutheran Church in the United States."

7. REV. J. A. SEISS, D. D., of Philadelphia, Pa. *Subject:* "The Misunderstandings and Misrepresentations of the Lutheran Church."

8. REV. F. W. CONRAD, D. D., of Philadelphia, Pa. *Subject:* The Characteristics of the Augsburg Confession."

9. REV. E. GREENWALD, D. D., of Lancaster, Pa. *Subject:* "False and True Spiritualism."

10. Rev. C. A. Stork, D. D., of Baltimore, Md. *Subject:* "Liturgical Forms in Worship."
11. Rev. G. F. Krotel, D. D., of New York, N. Y. *Subject:* "The Polity of the Lutheran Church as declared in the Confessions."
12. Rev. A. C. Wedekind, D. D., of New York, N. Y. *Subject:* "The Educational and Sacramental Ideas of the Lutheran Church in Relation to Practical Piety."
13. Rev. Prof. W. J. Mann, D. D., of Philadelphia, Pa. *Subject:* "Theses on the Lutheranism of the Fathers of our Church in this Country."
14. Rev. G. Diehl., D. D., of Frederick, Md. *Subject:* "The Divine and Human Factors in the Call to the Ministry, as viewed by Lutheran Theologians."

All Lutherans, clerical and lay, without respect to synodical connections, are invited to seats and membership in this Diet, with the privilege of participation in the discussions.

The Rev. Dr. Morris will preside, and the Rev. Drs. Jacobs and Baum will act as secretaries.

No essay is to exceed forty-five minutes in length, and no speech in the general discussion shall exceed ten minutes, and the essayist shall always have the right to make the closing speech on the subject presented by him.

No subjects will be discussed other than those of the essays; and no vote will be taken on any of the subjects considered.

No essay will be received which has already appeared in print, and the manuscript of each essay is to be furnished for publication; also a synopsis of each speech in the discussion.

The peculiar difficulties of the situation, and the hazardous uncertainty of calling an unorganized promiscuous convention, have induced the determination of all the arrangements in advance, as above given, and no proposed changes for this Diet will be entertained. If others should follow it, the method of procedure may be according to what is thought best after the experience in this case.

Though all these things have been, as only they could be, privately arranged, here is every reason to believe that there will be a general interest in what is thus proposed, and that our ministers and laymen will heartily second what has been done, and favor the Diet with their presence and participation.

In response to this call, a number of members of the Lutheran church, assembled in St. Matthew's Evangelical Lutheran church, corner of Broad and Mount Vernon streets, Philadelphia, Rev. W.

M. Baum, D. D., pastor, on Thursday, December 27th, 1877, at 10 o'clock A. M. Among those present during the sessions of the Diet were the following:

MINISTERS.

Rev. C. S. Albert,
" L. E. Albert, D. D.,
" J. C. Baum,
" W. M. Baum, D. D.,
" J. A. Baumann,
" J. F. Bayer,
" J. L. Becker,
" F. P. Bender,
" F. Benedict,
" H. M. Bickel,
" T. C. Billheimer,
" S. R. Boyer,
" J. A. Brown, D. D.,
" E. S. Brownmiller,
" D. L. Coleman,
" B. B. Collins,
" H. S. Cook,
" F. W. Conrad, D. D.,
" V. L. Conrad,
" C. J. Cooper,
" John Croll,
" G. Diehl, D. D.,
" J. F. Diener,
" J. R. Dimm,
" J. C. Dizinger,
" T. W. Dosh, D. D.,
" W. H. Dunbar,
" O. F. Ebert,
" W. S. Emery,
" I. N. S. Erb,
" W. P. Evans,
" R. A. Fink, D. D.,
" S. A. K. Francis,
" W. S. Freas,
" G. W. Frederick,
" W. K. Frick,
" J. H. Fritz,
" Z. H. Gable,
" D. H. Geissinger,
" H. Grahn,
" J. R. Groff,

Rev. L. Groh,
" J. B. Haskell,
" T. Heilig,
" L. M. Heilman,
" S. S. Henry,
" A. Hiller,
" C. J. Hirzel,
" E. Huber,
" F. K. Huntzinger,
" H. E. Jacobs, D. D.,
" F. A. Kaehler,
" F. C. C. Kaehler,
" C. L. Keedy, M. D.,
" D. K. Kepner,
" F. Klinefelter,
" C. Koerner,
" J. Kohler,
" C. P. Krauth, D. D., LL.D.
" J. A. Kunkelman,
" C. E. Lindberg,
" W. J. Mann, D. D.,
" H. W. McKnight,
" G. F. Miller,
" M. R. Minnich,
" J. G. Morris, D. D., LL. D.
" F. A. Muhlenberg, D. D.,
" W. H. Myers,
" George Neff,
" J. Nickum,
" S. Palmer,
" J. K. Plitt,
" N. M. Price,
" J. B. Rath,
" J. F. Reinmund, D. D.,
" J. S. Renninger,
" Prof. M. H. Richards,
" D. P. Rosenmiller,
" J. W. Rumple,
" B. Sadtler, D. D.,
" C. W. Schaeffer, D. D.,
" O. Schroeder,

Rev. A. Schulthes,
" M. Sheeleigh,
" J. A. Seiss, D. D.,
" A. Spaeth, D. D.,
" W. H. Steck,
" C. A. Stork, D. D.,
" H. B. Strohdach,
" A. Z. Thomas,
" B. W. Tomlinson,
" J. Q. Upp,

Rev. M. Valentine, D.D.,
" O. F. Waage,
" A. C. Wedekind, D. D.,
" A. J. Weddel,
" R. F. Weidner,
" C. F. Welden,
" A. M. Whetstone,
" F. Wischan,
" M. L. Young.

STUDENTS OF THEOLOGY.

J. W. Albrecht,
H. G. Artman,
W. M. Baum, Jr.,
E. Cassidy,
H. P. Clymer,
O. H. Hemsath,
J. H. Kline,
J. S. Koiner,

E. G. Lund,
F. P. Manhart,
A. B. Markley,
T. B. Roth,
M. Schaible,
C. F. Tiemann,
H. B. Wile.

LAYMEN.

Charles Baum, M. D.,
F. V. Beisel,
F. W. Bennett,
J. P. Berlin,
H. S. Bonar,
Prof. E. S. Breidenbaugh,
Martin Buchler,
F. Byerly,
E. H. Delk,
J. R. Eby,
M. E. Eyler,
E. J. Frank,
H. E. Goodman, M. D.,
S. Gerhard,
J. E. Graeff,
D. K. Grim,
J. E. Heyl,
J. K. Heyl,
Wm. E. Heyl,
L. L. Houpt,
E. M. Heilig,
N. Jacoby,
J. P. Keller, M. D.,
P. P. Keller,
W. F. Koiner,
E. F. Lott,

D. Luther, M. D.,
G. W. Martin,
J. W. Miller,
R. B. Miller,
T. J Miller,
W. J. Miller,
W. F. Muhlenberg, M. D.,
G. P. Ockershausen,
J. F. Rau,
Prof. S. P. Sadtler, Ph. D.,
F. Schaack,
W. G. Schaeffer,
P. M. Schiedt, M. D.,
E. G. Smyser,
C. A. Snyder,
W. H. Staake, Esq.,
W. E. Stahler,
L. K. Stein, M. D.,
P. C. Stockhauser,
C. P. Suesserott,
E. B. Weaver,
G. A. Weisel,
Henry Wile,
L. G. Wile,
J. N. Wunderlich,
J. B. Zimmerle.

The President, Rev. J. G. Morris, D. D., LL.D., of Baltimore, Md., opened the session with prayer.

He then made certain statements concerning the purposes contemplated in the call, as follows:

REMARKS OF DR. MORRIS AT THE OPENING OF THE DIET.

We meet to-day, brethren, under unusual and very interesting circumstances; it is not as a Synod, nor an ecclesiastical board, nor a local Conference, in all of which we have all heretofore served, but *as a free Diet* for the first time in the history of our Church in this country. We are not the delegates of any Church Association, nor are we the selected representatives of any constituency. Every Lutheran minister and layman has equal rights here, and every one is at liberty to express his sentiments upon the papers that shall be read.

It was thought that we who without presumption claim to be the mother church of Protestantism, should occasionally come together in large numbers and fraternally talk of the various distinguishing features of our Communion, not so much with the design of harmonizing unessential differences upon disputed points; not to ascertain the opinions of our learned divines on various doctrines, for those we already know; not to disturb any existing associations by attempting to merge them into one, but to demonstrate our position as a people in the great family of churches around us—to exhibit the great basis of our Lutheran faith—to make known to others the scriptural foundation on which our venerable Church rests—to bring prominently before the public our history and the men who in past times have achieved great triumphs for us in the pulpit, the professor's chair, and the author's study, and to incite our own ministers and people to the further investigation of these and allied subjects.

I have no doubt that these and other good results, theological, literary, ecclesiastical and social, will flow from the proceedings upon which we enter this day.

The difficulties of bringing this meeting into existence were many and formidable, but I am satisfied that if it had not been privately done, no Diet would have been held. If the time, the men, the place, the subjects, and other essential particulars, had been discussed in the Church papers, we never would have come to any harmonious decision. If the invitation to submit essays had been general, the number offered would have been so great as to have protracted the meeting to an inconvenient length; some of them might have been objectionable on various grounds. The necessity of a committee of inspection, which is usual in many bodies of this character, would have arisen and this work would have taken much time, and the result would have given offence. For these and other reasons, it was thought best to make the arrangements privately, although we anticipated difficulty and censure, but yet we would thus avoid protracted discussion at the opening of the meeting, the time consumed in the election of officers, the appointment of committees, and all the other time-wasting preliminaries of organizing an irresponsible assembly.

I have the best reasons for knowing that some highly esteemed and even scholarly brethren are dissatisfied with our arrangements: their friends also complain; but with all due respect let me say that we could not do otherwise—or rather we did not do otherwise. We are satisfied with what has been done, and I think that the results of this meeting will satisfy all reasonable men.

Brethren, this Diet is now declared open; you have heard the rules according to which it will be governed, and the first paper on the programme will now be read.

It will, however, first be necessary for the Diet to determine the order in which the papers shall be read.

On motion of Dr. C. W. Schaeffer, seconded by Dr. Conrad, it was resolved that the essays be read and discussed according to the published order.

The first paper was accordingly read.

THE AUGSBURG CONFESSION AND THE THIRTY-NINE ARTICLES OF THE ANGLICAN CHURCH.

BY REV. JOHN G. MORRIS, D. D., LL.D., BALTIMORE, MD.

THE Augsburg Confession is the doctrinal magna charta of all Protestantdom. Just as all free nations of the earth have drawn their principles of civil government from the English "Great Charter of Liberties," extorted from King John, in 1215, so all Protestant organizations have based their Formulas of Faith upon the greater "Bill of Rights," extorted from Charles V. in Augsburg, 1530.

An interesting and instructive analogy might be drawn between these two famous declarations of civil and religious principles.

The Augsburg Confession was the first Confession of Faith adopted after the Reformation was begun, and the substance of it, and, in many instances, its precise language, have been incorporated into every similar Declaration adopted by other Communions since that day. It is the standard of pure Protestantism, and under this banner our triumphs have been achieved.[1]

It is our purpose, in this paper, to show to what extent the Thirty-

---

[1] Its influence extends far beyond the Lutheran Church. It struck the key note to other evangelical Confessions and strengthened the cause of the Reformation everywhere. It is, to a certain extent also, the Confession of the Reformed and the so-called union churches in Germany, namely, with the explanations and modifications of the author himself, in the edition of 1540. In this qualified sense, either expressed or understood, the Augsburg Confession was frequently signed by Reformed divines and princes, even by John Calvin while ministering to the Church in Strasburg, and as delegate to the Conference in Ratisbon, 1541; by Favel and Beza, at the Conference in Worms, 1557; by the Calvinists, at Bremen, 1562; by Frederick III. (Reformed) Elector of the Palatinate, at the Convention of Princes in Nuremberg, 1561, and again at the Diet of Augsburg, 1566; by John Sigismund of Brandenburg in 1614.—*Schaff, Creeds of Christendom*, I., 235.

Nine Articles of the Church of England, and indirectly all other Protestant Confessions, are indebted to the Augsburg Confession, as well as the influence which the Lutherans of Germany had upon the English divines of those days in forming their theological basis, not only in their Declaration of Faith, but also in the completion of their Liturgy and Homilies.

The testimony shall be principally derived from eminent divines of the English Church, accompanied by that of other writers of established reputation. All these quotations are taken from the original sources.

In the year 1804, Archbishop Laurence, a distinguished dignitary of the Church of England, preached eight sermons before the University of Oxford, on "An attempt to illustrate those articles of the Church of England which the Calvinists improperly considered Calvinistical." These sermons constitute a volume of the Bampton Lectures; the new edition from which these quotations are made, is that of Oxford, 1820. The discourses are illustrated by learned and extensive notes.

The nature of the sermons may be inferred from the themes which are here given: I. The General Principles of the Reformation om its commencement to the period when our Articles were composed, shewn *to be of a Lutheran tendency.* II. The same *tendency* pointed out in the Articles themselves, as deducible from the history of their composition. III. On Original Sin, as maintained by the Scholastics, the Lutherans and our own Reformers. IV. On the tenet of the Schools repecting merit *de congruo*, and that of the Lutherans in opposition to it. V. The Article of "Free Will" and of "Works before Sanctification," explained in connection with the preceding controversy. VI. On the Scholastical doctrine of Justification, the Lutheran and that of our own Church. VII. The outline of the Predestinarian system stated, as taught in the Schools, and as Christianized by Luther and Melanchthon. VIII. The Seventeenth Article considered in conformity with the sentiments of the latter, and elucidated by our baptismal service. Brief recapitulation of the whole.

We should like to give copious extracts from this learned work, but we are compelled to be brief:

In Sermon I, p. 12, the Archbishop says:

"In this country, where the light of literature could not be concealed, nor the love of truth suppressed, Lutheranism found numerous proselytes, who were known by the appellation of 'The men of the new learning.' This was particularly the case after the rupture with the See of Rome."

Henry VIII., at that time King of England, undertook to reform the doctrine of the English Church, and the more effectually to propagate the new principles in his dominions, and to accelerate the arduous task in which he was engaged, invited the ever memorable Melanchthon to come to his assistance. That he did not solicit the co-operation of Luther on this occasion, should not, perhaps, be solely attributed to his personal dislike of the Reformer; he well knew that the Protestant Princes themselves, at the most critical period, had manifested a greater partiality for Melanchthon, and hence he urged the latter to come and help him, but he refused.[2]

Laurence proceeds to say:

"Melanchthon * * * possessed every requisite to render truth alluring and reformation respectable, and hence upon him, in preference, the Princes of Germany conferred the honor of compiling the public profession of their Faith. When Henry therefore applied for the assistance of this favorite divine, by seeking the aid of one to whom Lutheranism had been indebted for her Creed, he placed beyond suspicion the nature of that change which he meditated. * * * Some popular instructions were either published (before this) or sanctioned by royal authority, which, with the exception of a few points only, *breathed the spirit of Lutheranism*. Of this, no one at all conversant with the subject can for a moment doubt, who examines with attention the contents of what were at that time denominated *The Bishop's Book* and *The King's Book*, the two most important publications of the day."—p. 195.

---

[2] Note from Laurence. "After the commencement of our Reformation, Melanchthon was repeatedly pressed personally to assist in completing it, both in Henry's and Edward's reign. In a letter dated March, 1534, he says 'Ego jam alteris literis in Angliam vocor.' Ep. p. 717, and again October of the following year. "Ego rursus in Angliam non solum literis sed legationibus et vocor et exerceor." Ep. p. 732. Ed. Lond., 1642. The cause, however, why he did not come then, as at first he intended (for the elector of Saxony had consented to his journey, and Luther was anxious for it), he explains in another letter to Camerarius: "Anglicæ profectionis cura liberatus sum. Postquam enim tragici casus in Anglia acciderunt, magna consiliorum mutatio secuta est. Posterior regina (viz., Anne Boleyn), magis accusata quam convicta adulterii, ultimo supplicio affecta est." Epist., lib. IV, 187. In 1538 he was again solicited. During the short reign of Edward, solicitations of a similar nature appear to have been frequent." Laurence, pp. 195-99.

In speaking of a short code of doctrines, which[3] had been drawn up long before the death of Henry, the Archbishop says:

"Nor is complete originality even here to be met with: the sentiment and many of the very expressions thus borrowed, being themselves evidently derived from another source, *The Confession of Augsburg.*"

"The offices of our Church (after Edward had ascended the throne) were completely reformed (which before had been but partially attempted), *after the temperate System of Luther,* * * * nor were any alterations of importance, one point alone excepted, made at their subsequent revision. At the same period also, the first book of Homilies was composed, which, although *equally Lutheran,* * * * has remained without the slightest emendation to the present day. * * * Cranmer, who had never concealed the bias of his sentiments, now more openly and generally avowed them. He translated a *Lutheran catechism* (1547)[1] * * * dedicated it to the King and recommended it in the strongest terms. * * * The opinions of the Primate (Cranmer) were at that time *perfectly Lutheran,* and although he afterward changed them in one single point; in other respects, they remained unaltered."—p. 17.

"As little reason is there to question his ability, as his personal influence, his personal influence as his attachment to Lutheranism. This latter point seems beyond all controversy."—p. 24.

"On the whole, therefore, the principles upon which our Reformation was conducted, ought not to remain in doubt. With these the mind of him to whom we are chiefly indebted for the salutary measure, was deeply impressed, and *in conformity with them* was our Liturgy drawn up and the first book of our Homilies, all that were at that time composed."

"That *our Articles* were in general, *founded upon the same principles,* I shall in the next place endeavor to prove."

"Our Reformers, indeed, had they been so disposed, might have turned their attention to the novel establishment of Geneva, which Calvin had just succeeded in forming according to his wishes, might have imitated his singular institutions and inculcated its peculiar doctrines, but this they declined, viewing it perhaps as a faint

---

[3] This was published in 1536, under the title of "Articles Devised by the King's Highest Majesty, to establish Christian Quietness and Unity among us, and to avoid Contentious Opinions, which Articles be also approved by the Consent and Determination of the whole Clergy of this Realm." For further information, see Collier, Eccles. Hist. II. 122 fol. Burnet, Hist. Ref. I. Add, N., Fuller, C. II. XVI. B. V. 93.

[4] It was a Catechism which Justus Jonas had translated out of Dutchin to Latin, and which was taught at Nurnberg, and first published in 1533.

luminary. * * * This they might have done, but they rather chose to give reputation to their opinions and stability to their system by adopting * * * *Lutheran sentiments* and expressing themselves in *Lutheran language.*"—p. 25.

The Archbishop begins his second sermon in these words:

"On a former occasion I endeavored to prove that the established doctrines of our Church, from the commencement of the Reformation to the period when our Articles first appeared, were *chiefly Lutheran;* to point out that the original plan was ultimately adhered to, and that in the composition of our national creed, a general conformity with the same principles was scrupulously observed, will be the object of the present lecture."—p. 29.

"At the commencement of Edward's reign, it appears that Melanchthon was consulted upon this interesting subject. He was then alone at the head of the Lutherans, universally respected as the head of their much applauded Confession."—p. 36.

There was some delay in the completion of the Thirty-Nine Articles, owing to various causes, and the Archbishop continues:

"Among other reasons which may be assigned for this delay, is it not possible that one might have been the hope of obtaining the valuable assistance of Melanchthon, who was repeatedly, in Edward's as well as in Henry's reign, invited to fix his residence in this country?"—p. 39.

"If it be too much to conjecture that the delay was not imputable to the wish of submitting them to his personal inspection, and improving them by his consummate wisdom, the coincidence nevertheless of the time, during which they were postponed, with that of his much hoped for arrival here, cannot altogether escape observation."[5]

"Many of the argumentations upon points of doctrine at the same

---

[5] In addition to the quotations from Melanchthon's letters given above, we may add what he states to Camerarius, in September, 1535: "Ab Anglis bis vocatus sum, sed expecto TERTIAS LITERAS."—Epist., p. 722. And again, in April 1536: "Et sic me Angli exercent, vix ut RESPIRARE LICEAT." Id., 7, 738. This was when he was holding almost daily conference with the English ambassadors in Wittenberg.

For an account of his relations with the English, see Cardwell's Preface to the Liturgy of Edward VI., p. IV., note *b*.

It is interesting to know that he earnestly exhorted Cranmer to attempt an extension of the benefit beyond the confines of the English Church, to form a creed adapted to the Christian world at large. The Confession which he had himself drawn up, would, he conceived, prove something of this description. See his correspondence with Cranmer in Notes on Sermon II. of Archb. Laurence.

time introduced, were not only of a *Lutheran tendency*, but *couched in the very expressions of the Lutheran Creed*."

"Considering them, therefore, even in their rude outline, but more particularly in their perfect state, we discover, that, in various parts of their composition, Cranmer studiously kept in view that boast of Germany and pride of the Reformation, *The Confession of Augsburg*."

"If we, then, duly weigh the facts which have been stated, and the consequences which seem to result from them, we shall not, perhaps, be at a loss to determine from what quarter we are likely to collect the best materials for illustrating the Articles of our Church. We perceive that in the first compilation, many prominent passages were taken from the Augsburg and in the second place from the Wurtemberg Confession.[6] * * * These were the Creeds of the Lutherans."—p. 46.

"It may then, perhaps, appear as well from internal as external evidence, whence Cranmer derived the principles of our national Creed. * * * It may appear, that *from the Lutherans*, who had been his masters in theology, he had learned * * * almost everything which he deemed great and good in reformation."—p. 52.

With regard to the present Liturgy of the Church of England, the Archbishop says:

"In the year 1543, Melanchthon and Bucer drew up a Reformed Liturgy * * * for the use of the Archbishoprick of Cologne. From this work the occasional services of our own Church, where they vary from the ancient forms, *seem principally to have been derived*. It was not however, itself original, but in a great degree borrowed from a Liturgy established at Norimberg. * * * All our offices bear evident marks of having been partly taken from this work. * * * In our Baptismal service, the resemblance between the two productions is particularly striking."—p. 144.

Proctor, in his History of the Book of Common Prayer, London, 1870, p. 41, thus speaks:

"Of all the foreigners who were engaged in the work of Reformation, Melanchthon had the greatest influence both in the general reformation of the English Church, and *in the composition* of the

---

[6] This *Confessio Wurtembergica* was drawn up by Brentius, in the name of his Prince, Duke Christopher, who had resolved to send delegates to the Council of Trent. The Emperor had invited the Protestant States to send delegates, promising them full protection. Brentius prepared the Confession for that Council as Melanchthon had drawn up the *Confessio Saxonica* for the same purpose. Brentius' was approved by a commission of ten Swabian divines and by the city of Strasburg. It was also approved at Wittenberg as agreeing with Melanchthon's. *Schaff's Creeds, etc.*, I., 341.

English Book of Common Prayer, where it differed from the mediæval Service Books."

"Melanchthon was repeatedly invited into England, and it seems probable that his opinion, supported by his character and learning, had great influence on Cranmer's mind. As early as March, 1534, he had been invited more than once ; so that the attention of Henry VIII. and Cranmer had been turned towards him *before they proceeded to* any doctrinal reformation. The formularies of faith which were put forth in the reign of Henry, are supposed to have originated in his advice. On the death of Bucer (Feb. 28, 1551), the professorship of Divinity at Cambridge was offered to Melanchthon, and after many letters he was at last formally appointed (May, 1553). It is, perhaps, needless to add that he never came to England.[7]

* * * * * * *

"The first book was largely indebted to Luther, who had composed a form of service in 1533, for the use of Brandenburg and Nurnberg. This was taken by Melanchthon and Bucer as their model, when they were invited (1543), by Hermann, Prince Archbishop of Cologne, to draw up a Scriptural form of doctrine and worship for his subjects. This book contained ' Directions for the public services and administration of the Sacraments, with forms of prayer and a litany.' * * * The *Litany presents many striking affinities with the amended English Litany* of 1544. The exhortations in the Communion Service and portions of the Baptismal Services, *are mainly due to this book*, through which the influence of Luther may be traced in our Prayer Book. * * *

"They (the Thirteen Articles of 1538) not only indicate the disposition of our leading Reformers to acquiesce in the dogmatic statements which had been put forward in the Augsburg Confession, but have also a prospective bearing of still more importance, as in many ways, the groundwork of articles now in use. No one can deny that the compilers of the Forty-Two Articles in the reign of Edward VI. drew largely from the Lutheran formulary of 1530."—*Ibid.*, 61.[8]

"In the first year of the new reign (1548), he (Cranmer) had 'set forth' an English Catechism of a distinctly *Lutheran* stamp, indeed originally composed in German and translated into Latin,

---

[7] For a fuller account of the negotiation with Melanchthon to go to England, see Hardwick's Articles of Religion, 1859, p. 53, Strype, Eccles. Mem., I., 225-98.

[8] For a parallel between the Augsburg Confession and the XIII. Articles here spoken of, see Hardwick, pp. 62 seq.; and for a parallel between the Augsburg Confession and the Forty-Two Articles of 1553, see Appendix III., Hardwick; and for a parallel between the Augsburg Confession and the Thirty-Nine Articles, as finally agreed upon in 1571, see Annotated Prayer Book.

by Justus Jonas, the Elder, one of Luther's bosom friends."—*Ibid.*, 68.

"With reference more particularly to the Sacrament of Baptism, the baptismal office of our own Reformers was derived in no small measure from Luther's *Taufbüchlein*, itself the offspring and reflexion of far older manuals."—*Ibid.*, 95.

Hardwick in Articles of Religion, Cambridge, 1859, p. 13, says:

"That Confession (the Augsburg) is most intimately connected with the progress of the English Reformation; and besides the influence which it cannot fail to have exerted by its rapid circulation in our country, *it contributed directly in a large degree, to the construction of the public formularies of Faith* put forward by the Church of England. The XIII. Articles, drawn up, as we shall see, in 1538, were based almost entirely on the language of the great Germanic Confession, while a similar expression of respect is no less manifest in the Articles of Edward VI., and consequently in that series which is binding now upon the conscience of the English Clergy."

"A perception of this common basis in religious matters, aided by strong reasons of diplomacy, suggested the commencement of negotiations with the 'princes of the Augsburg Confession,' as early as the year 1535. The first English Envoy sent among them was Robert Barnes, the victim, only five years later, of his predilection for the new opinions, etc."—*Ibid.*, 53.

"But while (King) Henry was thus faltering on the subject of communion with the German League, a conference had been opened on the spot between the English delegates and a committee of Lutheran theologians. Luther himself was a party to it from the first and Melanchthon came soon afterwards (January 15, 1536). The place of meeting was at Wittenberg in the house of Pontanus (Brück), the senior chancellor of Saxony, where Fox dilated on the *Lutheran tendencies of England*, and more especially of his royal master."[9] —*Ibid.* 55.

"Afterwards Henry begged the 'Princes of the Augsburg Confession" to send to England a legation of divines (including his peculiar favorite Melanchthon) to confer on the disputed points with a committee of English theologians. * * The whole course of the discussion was apparently determined by the plan and order of the Augsburg Confession."—*Ibid.* 56-7.

---

[9] See Seckendorf Comment. de Lutheranismo, Lib. III, § xxxix., for an account of certain articles of religion which were drawn up by the mediating party in 1535 and '36. Of those, one article has reference to the Lord's Supper, and is merely an expanded version of the Augsburg Confession.

"The result of the conference with the Germans was a 'boke' (book) which is manifestly founded on the Confession of Augsburg, often followed it very closely. * * * The article on the Lord's Supper is word for word the same."—*Ibid.* 60.

Short, in History of the Church of England, London, 1869, p. 165, says:

" He (Melanchthon) appears to have been consulted in 1535 concerning the Articles which were published during the next year; and the definition of *justification* there given is probably derived from the *Loci Communes* of this author: in the whole of those articles the ideas and language of the Lutheran divines have been closely followed. Many of the Forty-Two Articles owe their origin to the same source, and even those which cannot be traced with certainty, exhibit a correspondence with the general opinion of the German divines."

"At the commencement of the Reformation in England, our reformers naturally cast their eyes on two standards of faith, on that of the Church of Rome, and that of the Lutheran churches, which had already discarded the errors of the papal court. The rule, then, which sound reason would seem to dictate is, that those points wherein the Church of England found it necessary to differ from that of Rome, it should refer to the opinions of the newly established churches and follow them as far as they were consistent with Scripture; and where that which was taught by the Lutherans appeared to be questionable, the Church of England should either borrow the expression of its opinions from some other reformed church, or construct its own articles directly from the word of God. In our articles are contained the great truths of Christianity * * there are many which are derived from the Lutheran Church. * * In our public services the greater part of the Common Prayer Book is taken from the Roman Ritual, and some portions are borrowed from the Lutheran Church, or rather drawn up in imitation of them."

"About the same time Cranmer (1548) put forth his Catechism. This work was translated from a German Catechism used in Nuremberg, through the medium of a Latin version made by Justus Jonas. —*Ibid.* 142.

" In 1535, Fox, Heath and Barnes were sent ambassadors to Smalcalde, where proposals were made to them by the Protestant Princes, that the King should approve the Confession of Augsburg." —*Ibid.* 110.

"Whatever use he (Cranmer, 1536) might have made of the Helvetic Confession in forming his own opinions, he does not appear to have introduced it into the work in which he was engaged (preparing the Forty-Two Articles), but with regard to the Augsburg Confession (1530, printed 1531, and republished with alteration

1540), there is not only a general agreement in doctrine, but in many places the very words of the one are transferred into the other."—*Ibid.* 268.[10]

"It appears that he (Archbishop Parker of Canterbury, 1559) had himself been recasting the Forty-two Articles of King Edward * * and that he added to the Articles, which had been mainly drawn from the earlier Lutheran Creeds, some new clauses obtained from the more recent confession of Wurtemberg."—*Cardwell, Synodalia, Oxford*, 1842, 2 vols., Vol. I. *p.* 35.

"These Articles, forty-two in number, the first that were constructed by the Church of England, on the principles of the reformation, were indebted to the clear theological distinctions of Melanchthon and other reformers of Germany, and derived more especially from the Augsburg Confession."—*Ibid.*, Vol., I. 1.

Bishop Bull, in his "Apology for the Harmony and its Author," bound with his "Examen Censurae," pp. 292 seq., Oxford, 1844, says in reply to Dr. Tully:

"Dr. Tully now hastens to the Augsburg Confession; where, in the first place, he finds fault with me because I called that the greatest of all the Reformed Confessions, not excepting even our own Anglican one. * * I only said the same thing that many learned men both of our own and foreign countries have said before me, and who also highly honored our Church. Now the Augsburg Confession is deservedly called the greatest, for more than one reason. In the first place (not to say anything of its most excellent and learned principal author, Philip Melanchthon), it was the first of all Confessions. Next, when it was published, it was approved of by the consent of almost all, if not of all, the Reformed Churches, Universities and Doctors. Lastly, it is still received and held in certain kingdoms and great principalities and free States. The Doctor, moreover, is offended, because I said that the heads of our Church had followed and imitated this Confession. *But what can be clearer than this?* The first article of our Confession is taken almost word for word from the first of the Augsburg. Our second is clearly copied from the third of Augsburg. Also the sixteenth in ours * * openly imitates, towards the end, the anathemas of the eleventh in the Augsburg, as our twenty-fifth does the thirteenth in the Augsburg. Again, in our homilies, how often must the attentive reader who is acquainted with Melanchthon's writings, *hear him speaking?* Add to which * * that Hooper of blessed memory * * was in the habit of copying long passages from Melanchthon's writings, almost word for word."

Bishop Bull, in his HARMONIA APOSTOLICA, Oxford, 1842, pp.

---

[10] For these Forty-Two Articles in Latin and English, and in parallel columns with the Elizabethan Articles, see Hardwick's Appendix, III., pp. 277-333.

197 seq., says, "This is the same as is meant in the Confession of Augsburg, which as it is the most noble and ancient of all the Reformed Churches, so both here and in other places, the heads of our Church *have followed it*, that whoever is ignorant of it can scarcely conceive the true meaning of our articles."

Bp. Whittingham, of Maryland, in the charge to his clergy, 1849, says, "that with the Augsburg Confession their (the Thirty-Nine Articles) connection is of a nature the most intimate and direct, substantiable by superabundant evidence, both internal and circumstantial. In more than one respect, the Augsburg Confession is the source of the Thirty-Nine Articles of the Church of England and America—their prototype in form, their model in doctrine, and the very foundation of many of their expressions; while others are drawn from its derivative expositions and repetitions."

It is not inappropriate to introduce the testimony of another distinguished witness, not of the Church of England :

"The Thirty-Nine Articles were established as the law of the land under Queen Elizabeth, in 1571. * * * They are based on German Confessions of faith. Very probably the thirteen which were found among Cranmer's papers were the result of Conferences between German and English theologians, begun in Wittenberg, 1533, and continued in London in 1538, who aimed at a union of both churches. These thirteen closely follow the order of the first seventeen Articles of the Augsburg Confession, and are copied nearly word for word."—*Herzog's Encyclop.*, Vol. I., 325, which see also for the differences between the whole Thirty-Nine Articles and the Augsburg Confession.

Schaff, in Creeds of Christendom, I. 623, says:

"The Edwardine Articles were based in part, as already observed, upon a previous draft of Thirteen Articles, which was the joint product of German and English divines, and based upon the doctrinal Articles of the Augsburg Confession. Some passages were transferred verbatim from the Lutheran document to the Thirteen Articles, and from these to the Forty-Two (1553), and were retained in the Elizabethan revision (1563 and 1571). This will appear from the following comparison. The corresponding words are printed in Italics."

After giving the comparison in parallel columns, Schaff thus concludes :

"Besides these passages, there is a close resemblance in thought, though not in language, in the statements of the doctrine of original sin and of the possibility of falling after justification. Several of the Edwardine Articles * * * were suggested by Article Seventeen of the Augsburg Confession, which is directed against the Anabaptists."

And finally, one extract from one of our own writers:

"As to the Twenty-Five Articles, which embody the acknowledged doctrines of the Methodist Societies, they are in language and substance so nearly identical with the Thirty-Nine Articles of the Church of England, that they must be traced through them to the same source They are only remoter issues from the same Lutheran fountain."

"It is, therefore, with justice that the Lutheran Church takes to herself the high appellation of *The Mother of Protestants.*"—*Seiss, Eccles. Luth.*, p. 124.

Thus, the Lutheran Origin of the Thirty-Nine Articles has been fully illustrated. Many more extracts from the writings of great divines of the Church of England, might have been given, but they only reiterate and confirm what the earlier writers have said, and, therefore, it is deemed superfluous to insert them.

The second paper was then read.

THE RELATIONS OF THE LUTHERAN CHURCH TO THE DENOMINATIONS AROUND US.

An Essay by Charles P. Krauth, D. D., LL. D., Norton Professor of Systematic Theology and Ecclesiastical Polity in the Evangelical Lutheran Theological Seminary, at Philadelphia.

I. THE DENOMINATIONS AROUND US.

"The relations of the Lutheran Church to the denominations around us," very naturally lead us to ask, who, and what, and why, are the denominations around us?

The term Denominations.

A denomination, as we use the term, is, in the sphere of Religion, a class or collection of individuals, called by the same name; a body of persons who have separated, or are separate from others, in virtue of their holding in common some special doctrine, or set of doctrines, or government, or usage, or discipline. The word, though it is in this sense the resort, if not the outgrowth of an evasive courtesy, is preferable to the terms sect, or schism—which are its nearest historical equivalents—because in itself it simply marks a fact, without expressing or insinuating an unfavorable judgment. It is preferable in discussion to the word "Church," for it does not involve a judgment. In a word, it is a colorless objective term expressing the thing we mean, without committing us to an opinion of it.

Who and What are the Denominations around us?

The denominations around us are real and distinct organizations, with distinct names, creeds, constitutions, books of worship, terms of admission to the ministry, terms and tests of membership, and a discipline; with a distinct religious literature, publishing houses, theological schools and missions. As organizations they are as really distinct as states, or nations, or associations. The intense partisanship which builds up walls, and the flabby unionism which pretends to disregard them, seem at first in hopeless dis-harmony—but they really are part of one idea. When men are to be kept in, Denominationalism magnifies its walls; when men are to be let in, it makes them very low.—or has abundant openings in them.

The denominations around us cover nearly every leading form of Christianity and of its distortions, and a number of its smallest bodies, parasites, and parasites of parasites. About thirty years ago Rev. E. N. Kirk[1] said "In the Western Reserve," "that New England of the West," "there are forty-one sects; all professing to believe the Bible." If our land were searched through all its borders, the number of denominations would be seen to be simply appalling—some in vigorous life, some rising, some dying out, some dead and dusty but not swept out of sight, some fossilized into a sort of stony existence, others like soap-bubbles expanding in glittering swiftness toward their bursting.

Classification: Historical.

When we ask, What they are? and Whence they came? Why they are around us? we shall find that the history of their origin is largely the explanation of it. With respect to their purely historical basis, their genesis and rise as particular churches, the great bodies and tendencies into which Christendom is divided may be thus arranged:

I. The *Roman Catholic* Church takes her name from her identification with herself of the Catholic Church proper, as the Church of the Redeemed, out of which there is no salvation. She makes the Church Catholic an organization which centres in the See of Rome, with an infallible Pope at its head, and rests on the theory that Peter was Primate of the Apostles; that at the end of his life he was Bishop of Rome, and that the primacy and official infallibility which belonged to him as an apostle, were transferred to his successors as bishops.

II. The *Greek Orthodox* Church marks in its name Greek, the separation from the Roman in the divided empire, and adds "Orthodox" to assert its claim to the possession of the pure faith. It is strongly anti-papal without being Protestant.

III. The *Evangelical* Church, popularly called the *Lutheran* Church, whose centre is the Gospel; Gospel Grace against Legalism; Gospel Sufficiency over against Traditionalism, the Abuse of Reason and Fanaticism; and Gospel Unity in Faith and Sacraments over

---

[1] Sermon in behalf of Am. H. Miss. Soc., May, 1848.

against the separatism of sect, and the spurious Unionism of compromise and of ignored truth.

IV. The *Calvinistic-Reformed* Church of the Continent, considered in its unity. It embraces especially the German, Dutch and French Churches, and is represented in our land mainly by the descendants of immigrants of its original nationalities.

V. The *Eclectic-Protestant* or *Anglican* Church, the Church of England, her sisters in Scotland and Ireland, her daughter the Protestant Episcopal Church, and now her grand-daughter the Reformed Episcopal Church.

VI. The great conflicting bodies which grew out of *governmental* divergences from the Established Church of England and Scotland, or from each other. The *Presbyterians* and *Independents* arose first from the assertion of the divine right of Church government opposed to the *Prelatical*, and then divided from each other, on the assertion on the one side that this government of divine right is the *Presbyterian*, on the other that it is *Independent* and *Congregational*. Presbyterianism overcame Episcopacy, and till 1797 was scarcely troubled with Independency in Scotland; but Independency proved the mightier movement in England. It vanquished Presbyterianism in their earlier battles; it sent forth its colonists of flint and steel to New England; it stamped itself through them and their descendants on the institutions and thinking of our New World. It evolved the Yankee race, and produced a brain which claimed to be a universal solvent. When Socinianism swallowed up English Presbyterianism, Independency in the Congregational and Baptist Churches gave shelter to the few who still held the old faith. But in the mystery of history, New England's Independency has repeated the sorrowful experience of Old England's Presbyterianism—perhaps because that patent universal cerebral solvent, in which it trusts, has sometimes had pearls dropped into it, which are better undissolved.

VII. The divergent bodies which added to the Independent view of Church government, peculiar views of the mode and subject of Baptism—the *Baptists* of various Schools, Particular or Calvinistic, General or Arminian. The *Mennonites* hold the Baptist view of the subjects of Baptism, but reject immersion as its necessary mode.

VIII. Under the general spirit and modes of Pietism; contemplating association for religious ends within the Established Church; dividing from the beginning on the Calvinistic doctrines; under the conflicting leadership of Whitefield and Wesley, there came forth in the Church of England a divergence in spirit, ripening into a division in fact, marked by the desire of larger freedom in doctrine and worship, more positive emphasis of the evangelical doctrines, and especially of the subjective elements of the plan of salvation, larger play for the emotions and the expression of them, more complete adaptation to the supposed wants of the masses and their peculiarities, and stricter discipline in a compact organization. This divergence has matured into *Methodism*.

IX. Not large, but for many reasons memorable, is the body known variously as Herrnhuthers, Brothers of the Unity, Bohemian and Moravian Brethren. The fragments of the Bohemian and Moravian Brethren, left after many a storm of war and persecution, sought refuge from new dangers, 1720, and found it under the fostering care of Count Zinzendorf. Their earnest piety, their domestic virtues, blessed of God, gathered around their new home, the village of Herrnhuth. Preserving intact in their homes their ancient, simple and peculiar modes and careful domestic discipline, they became communicants in the neighboring Evangelical Lutheran Church at Bertholsdorf. This drew to them others, not Bohemians or Moravians, but who, regarding them as brethren in the Lutheran faith, joined them and conformed to their peculiar discipline, as calculated to promote holy and happy living. The growth became so great that Herrnhuth needed a pastor of its own, and by the influence of Zinzendorf, Steinhofer, a clergyman of the Lutheran Church, was called 1733. In their original form the Herrnhuthers were nominally an Evangelical Lutheran congregation, in which, in conformity with the liberty which the Lutheran Church maintains, they claimed to preserve the ancient discipline of the Brethren in Unity. So Zinzendorf and the Herrnhuthers themselves define it.[2]

Out of this simple beginning Count Zinzendorf developed a system of marked peculiarity in faith and discipline. The Moravians of our day are distinguished by indeterminateness on the points of doctrine which divide the Church, careful organization, and system, discipline milder than the old, yet still strict, a quiet home-life, simplicity of manners, heroic devotion to missions; and have made the most effectual answer to the earlier charges against them, by confessing what was wrong and removing it.

X. *Arminianism* has not, as such, embodied itself with any force

[2] Büdingsche Sammlung, I., 48, 115.

into a distinct denomination, but it has shown its power as a tendency which has influenced or disturbed all denominations. It is the doctrinal system of the Jesuits as against the Jansenists. It was originally characteristic of the High Church party, beginning with the time of Laud (one of the charges against whom, in the trial which led to his beheading, was his Arminianism); but it is now the general position of High, Low and Broad alike, with few exceptions It is the system of the Methodist Episcopal Church, of some of the Baptist communions, and of the Cumberland Presbyterians. It has been winning point after point in the very heart of nominal Calvinism. From its early, cautious, negative tendency, in which it was no more than a gentle protest against the five extravagances of Calvinism, it ran out, first in the passionate development, which was aided by proscription and persecution, and afterwards, by its essential tendencies, into Socinianism, or became a bridge by which Calvinism made a transition into the same system.

XI. *The Friends* arose partly in reaction against the formalism of the Church of England and the polemical spirit of Puritanism, and partly in the general spirit of religious enthusiasm which marked the period of the great civil war. They are now divided into the Orthodox Friends, the Hicksites, and the Primitive Friends. The worldly thrift, the persistency of their witness against the evils of war and slavery, and their humanity, have made the Friends an important social element.

Denominational Names.

To express the characteristic diversity in a name, where diversity has been so great and complicated, has been no inconsiderable tax of ingenuity. Some of the denominations take their name from a single doctrine, as Advent, Unitarian, Universalist. Some reach new names by disavowing all particular names, as Bible Christians, Church of Christ, Church of God; some take their names from their theories or modes of Church government, as Congregational, Episcopal, Presbyterian. In some cases the names of leaders have been fixed on churches or systems, as Arminian, Calvinists, Mennonnites, Wesleyans. Some bear historical nicknames, as Methodists, Quakers. Some derive their name in whole or part from their original nationality or language. The term *Reformed* plays a large part in denominational terminology. We have Baptist Reformed; the Reformed Church in America, or Dutch Reformed; the Reformed

Church in the United States, or German Reformed; the Reformed Episcopal; the Reformed Presbyterian (original); the Reformed Presbyterian (General Synod); the Reformed Presbyterian (Synod). We see coupled in some of these titles, Reformation in the fifth potentiation.

In this single city of Philadelphia, this city of brotherly love, we have around us nearly all the leading forms of Protestantism, Heresy and Sectarianism. The mere display of names is indeed in some respects illusive; first, because, except as the revelation of a dangerous tendency, many of the sects are insignificant—the offspring of ignorance and fanaticism, and destined to speedy extinction. Secondly, because, taking the great denominations, great in numbers or clearly defined in principle, the points of diversity are at their root few. It is the varied combinations which make so great a number of sects. The Rule of Faith and how to interpret it, the eternal decrees of God, the person of Christ, Justification, the internal nature of Word and Sacraments, the Polity of the Church, external ceremonies, are the grand points of diversity.

And yet the names associated with peculiarities and classes form an important basis of classification. So far as a direct divine warrant for any peculiar name is concerned, they are all alike; for though the name be a Biblical one, it has no divine warrant as the exclusive property of a denomination. There can be no divine warrant for applying a divine name except to a divine thing—and that a denomination as such, is not. "Believers," "Disciples of Christ," "Brethren," "Friends," mark true Christians as individuals in all denominations. "The Church," the "Church of God," without a plural, is the Church Catholic and invisible. The name Christian is of human origin, and is applied to the individual disciples, not to the Church even as a whole, still less to particular churches. All the particular names, with their specific application, have risen in history, and are defensible only as the history which became the occasion of their necessity is defensible. The most offensive and intensely sectarian of all names are those which are in Scripture, and mark the whole Christian communion as such, but are diverted to be the trade-mark of any denomination.

A name is a claim—and a false name is a stereotyped lie. Hence the responsibility of assuming or tolerating a name is in itself very great. A name is in itself a creed; a man is bound to what the name really means which he bears, and no amount of private disavowal neutralizes the obligations and responsibility of it. While a man calls himself Roman Catholic, Methodist or Calvinist, he binds himself to be Roman Catholic, Methodist or Calvinist, and we are bound to treat him as such. If he privately repudiates the claim of his Church name, so much the worse for his intelligence and sincerity.

The Right to Exist.

And this leads us to ask as preliminary to our just relations to them, on what grounds of *principle* do the denominations around us *vindicate their right to exist?* To some of the sects this question would come like a thunderbolt. They have never raised it. They never knew that such a question could be raised. In the Sectarian Declaration of Independence, among the certain inalienable rights are sectarian life, sectarian liberty, and sectarian pursuit of happiness. They may deny a man's right to wear a coat or a hat not fashioned after the sacred pattern shown them in the mount of their private hallucination, but as to a man's right to join himself to any sect he thinks good, or to make another sect if the existing sects do not suit him, of that they never doubted. In the Popery of Sect, "Stat pro ratione voluntas"—their best reason is, they wish it so.

Yet this question is a great question. It is *the* question. The denomination which has not raised it is a self-convicted sect. The denomination which cannot return such an answer to it as at least shows sincere conviction that it has such reasons, should be shunned by all Christians who would not have the guilt of other men's sins.

We draw a line then at once between those denominations which either *give no reason* for their rightful existence, or a reason so transparently false as to defy credulity; and those on the other hand which *have reasons*—reasons of such plausibility as to satisfy us that thoughtful men may sincerely hold them.

There is also an obvious line to be drawn between those communions which went *forth from Rome*, the primal forms of Protestantism; and those which have arisen by division and subdivision *within* Protestantism,—between the genera of Protestantism and the species of those genera—between those with whom Rome made schism, and those which have made schism in the Protestant body.

We must also look with very different eyes on *those bodies* whose historical record and present acts are in accordance with the official principles on which they rest their right to exist ; and those which desert the principles which gave them name, creeds and position—*those bodies* which exist on one principle and act on another, which lengthen out their lives by abandoning what they once considered sacred, ignoring their history, concealing their confessed doctrines, or evading the necessary consequences of them, and who make their name and their very existence a fraud,—and whose intensest hatred is inflicted on those who remind them of their history, and of the doctrines which gave them their original being.

II. HISTORY OF THE ORIGINATION OF THE QUESTION IN DISCUSSION. RISE OF DIVISIONS: DENOMINATIONALISM AND UNIONISM.

It may help to shed light upon the question we are to discuss, to look at the way in which it has risen. What are the historical sources of the laxity which has become a characteristic of our time, and especially of our country, and with this the sources of the Unionism which has attempted to cover over the laxity and glorify it? The common roots of both s'retch far and wide.

So tremendous a movement as the Reformation was inevitably attended by various imperfections and distortions. The need of some sort of reform was universally admitted. Rome then admitted it, and now admits it. But the ultra-conservatism which was represented in the reformatory part of the Romish Church which would not break with it, proposed little more than a superficial correction of some evils, while their real causes remained undisturbed. Antipodal to this there was a radicalism which proposed to sweep away everything existent, and to make a new start from its own interpretation of the letter of the Bible, ignoring the centuries of the Church's history. There was fanaticism which proposed in new revelations to find what it imagined the old revelation had failed to furnish. The real heart of the Reformation was with that part of the movement which was conservative toward the good, radical toward the evil ; which, tenacious of the letter, was guided by it to the spirit; which recognized the Church as God's work, through the Word ; which over against Rome maintained the sole authority of the Word ; over against Fanaticism, the sufficiency of the Word; over against Radicalism, the witness of the Church, whose pure text was to be reached by sifting the various readings of the ages. There came also into the history of the Reformation, as there comes into every history, ignorant assumption, envy, ambition, love of novelty, and all the human passions which hover around the great battle-fields of the world, the host of camp-followers, the clouds of vultures. The test of every cause is its ability to endure its friends. The little finger of Carlstadt and Munzer was thicker than Tetzel and the Pope's loins.

Nothing so endangers the great principle of the right of private judgment, as a misunderstanding of what the principle is, and a false application of it. The *right* to search the Scriptures is not to be confounded with the *evidence* that the Scriptures have been searched. The *judicial* responsibility of the conscience to God alone is not to be confounded with that responsibility which every man must assume in the recognition of another man's views as truth; a responsibility to which every man must submit his own views who wishes to make them a basis of recognition and fellowship.' The right of private judgment is not a right to force fellowship in the results of *our* private judgment on those whose private judgment is assured that we have abused ours. It is not their right to force themselves on us. That was a private judgment of Peter's which was met by " Get thee behind me, Satan." The right of private judgment in the exercise of which a man becomes a Romanist is not the right to be accepted as a Protestant. There is no principle in nature or revelation which justifies the conscientiously wrong, in demanding assent or silence from the conscientiously correct. The right of private judgment is not the right of public recognition.

The disturbing and radical element in the Reformation prepared the way for the later laxity and the Unionism which attended it. The tendency which was represented in Carlstadt and Œcolampadius, and most energetically and consistently in Zwingli, gave an early impulse in this direction. This it did, not simply in setting forth the great error which originated the divisions in the Protestant Reformation, but by the levity with which it regarded the whole matter of division. A division which meant the rending of the Reformation, its confusion before its enemies, and the periling of its existence, was regarded as a something which must be held at every cost, and yet, whose guilt could be condoned by the shedding of a few tears, the offer of a hand.

Luther and Zwingli at Marburg.

At Marburg the whole question was epitomized, and Luther there passed through a sorer struggle, a mightier temptation, and showed himself more matchless as a hero than at Worms—for what is harder than to reject the advances of seeming love, which pleads for our acknowledgment on the ground of devotion to a common cause. Luther saved the Reformation by withholding the hand, whose grasp would have meant the recognition of fundamental error—either as in unity with faith, or as too little a thing to be weighed. Not only Luther's personal qualities, but his religious and reformatory principles, were precisely the same as revealed against Rome and against the Zwinglian tendencies. There is no consistency in blaming him in his relation to the latter, while we praise him for his attitude to the former. It would have been a surrender of the vital principle by which the Reformation itself stands or falls—the authority and clearness of the Word. Concession at the point at which Zwingli demanded it would not have stopped there. Other concessions to other errors would have been demanded, with equal justice, on the same grounds. The political element was no small one in this early desire for Unionism, and the complexion it would have given would have brought a Capel, at which not Zwingli but the Reformation itself would have fallen. We know well that there are good people so blinded to the real character of the scene at Marburg that they regard Zwingli's course as the very embodiment of Christian love, and Luther, they think of, as hurried away by the zealotry of partisanship. When Zwingli declared that he desired fellowship with no men so much as with the Wittenbergers, he pressed on them the hand of fraternity, he wept because they declined taking it. What a loving, large spirit is that! men exclaim; and how poor before it seems the narrowness of Luther and of Melanchthon, of whom the editor of Zwingli's works has said that "at that time he was almost harsher than Luther himself."[3] But the men of Wittenberg had not forgotten how Zwingli, in 1524, had endorsed the book which Carlstadt had directed against Luther under the title : "Of the execrable abuse of the Eucharist." They had not forgotten that, in 1525, Zwingli had assailed Luther in his "Commentary of true and false Religion," had pronounced Luther's language on the Eucharist as "monstrous," and had said in the most sweeping way that "neither were those to be listened to who though they saw that the opinion cited" (Luther's) " was not

---

[3] H. Zwingli's Werke : (Schuler u. Schulthess) Vol. II. iii. 55.

only coarse, but impious and frivolous, yet said that we eat Christ's true body, but spiritually." The Wittenbergers had not forgotten that he had called those who held the doctrine of the true presence "Carnivori," "a stupid set of men," and had said that the doctrine was "impious, foolish, inhuman and worthy of anthropophagites." And these were the amenities of Zwingli at a period when Luther had not written a solitary word against him. The Wittenbergers had not forgotten that in that same year the book of Zwingli had been followed up by another, in which he characterizes the holders of Luther's view as "cannibals." They had not forgotten that in 1527 Zwingli had distinctly declared that his own view involved the fundamentals of faith, and had condemned Bucer for saying that "either view might be held without throwing faith overboard." On this Zwingli says: "I do not approve of his view. To believe that consciences are established by eating flesh, *is* conjoined with throwing faith overboard (*cum fidei jactura*).[4] The Wittenbergers had not forgotten that in 1527 Zwingli had written a book against Luther, had dedicated it to the Elector of Saxony, and charged Luther to his own Elector with "error and great audacity," which he claims to have "exposed." All this the Wittenbergers could not forget, but all this they could have forgiven had it been sorrowed over and withdrawn; but all this remained unretracted, unexplained, unregretted. Zwingli himself being judge, there was not the fraternity of a common faith. The conflicting modes of interpretation involved in fact the whole revelation of God. What Zwingli still held of the old faith would have gone down before his rationalistic method, just as surely as what he already rejected. All went down before it in aftertime. Luther uttered the warning, but Zwingli would not believe it. His course was the beginning of that effusive sentiment of compromise, which from the rill of 1529 has gathered to the torrent of 1877, and before which we are expected to allow, without a struggle, all fixed principle to be swept away.

How fleeting the better mind of Zwingli was, is shown by the fact that on the margin of a copy of the Articles of Agreement at Marburg, he wrote annotations, which prove how hollow, superficial and untrustworthy the whole thing was on his part.

The violence of Zwingli had been the more unpardonable because he had originally held the same view of the Lord's Supper as

---

[4] Exegesis ad Lutherum.

Luther, and must have known that it did not involve what he charges upon it. Even in 1526 he wrote to Billican and others who held Luther's doctrine: "You affirm that Christ's true body is eaten, but in a certain ineffable manner." Zwingli, indeed, confesses in so many words that he had rejected the literal and historical interpretation of the words of the Lord's Supper, before he was able to assign even to his own mind a reason for it. He tells us that after he had made up his conviction without a reason, a dream suggested a reason. It was indeed a reason demonstratively irrelevant—an interpretation which his co-workers, Carlstadt and Œcolampadius, both rejected, and at which a fair scholar of any school would now laugh—but it was enough to begin the great schism whose miseries live and spread to this hour. The mode which unsettles the doctrine of the true presence, unsettles every distinctive Evangelical doctrine—the method which explains it away, explains everything away. To give it up is in principle to give up everything. The division began at the doctrine of the Eucharist; the union must begin at the point of division. The bone must be knit where it was broken, or the arm of the Church will continue to be distorted and enfeebled.

In a few months after the scenes at Marburg, without a vocation from God or man, Zwingli prepared a Confession, part of whose object was to condemn the views of our Church, and to mark his own separation from it. He attempted to thrust upon the Diet at Augsburg his rationalistic speculations, whose tendency was to throw contempt upon our Confession, to weaken and endanger our cause, to peril the liberty and lives of our confessors, and to hazard the cause of the entire Reformation. It was an uncalled-for parading of division in the presence of a ruthless enemy. In his Confession, he classes the Lutherans with the Papists, and speaks of them as "those who are looking back to the flesh-pots of Egypt." He characterizes our doctrine as an "error in conflict with God's Word," and says that "he will make this as clear as the sun to the emperor, and will attack the opponents with arguments like battering-rams." This is dated July 3d, 1530. Contrast it with the brief and gentle words, which on June 25th, had been presented in the Tenth Article of the Augsburg Confession: "Therefore, the opposite doctrine is rejected," "and they disapprove of those who teach in a contrary way."

History of Interdenominational Fellowship.

The system of denominationalism had hardly fairly been inaugurated by the writings and acts of Carlstadt and Zwingli, before the inconsistencies, miseries and disasters it involves began to manifest themselves.

By the system of denominationalism, we mean the system which theoretically or practically rests on the supposition that two or more Christian bodies can, without imputation either of fundamental error or schism on either part, have conflicting names, creeds, altars, pulpits, discipline — that they can occupy and struggle for a common territory, and yet keep the unity of the Spirit in the bond of peace—can have doctrines and sacraments so diverse as to necessitate the formation of distinct communions, and yet be in the unity of full Christian fraternity.

Bucer aided the general tendency by his ambiguity, insisting that the differences were not real; abandoning Zwinglianism, yet insisting that it differed from Lutheranism only in terms; abandoned by Zwinglianism, yet trying still to render it tractable. *Calvin* at times pursued the same general line of movement toward the Lutherans. The Calvinists avoided an absolute condemnation of Lutheranism, largely but not exclusively for reasons of policy. They constantly took the ground that they were right, and that the Lutherans were wrong, but not so wrong as to prevent unity. But where Calvinism had no interest in being mild toward Lutheranism, it spake out with a severity indicative of its real feeling. *Castellio*, as the forerunner of Arminianism, favored a general laxity, but did not find Calvin or his friends disposed to indulge him in it. But the real consistent movement to a broad principle of comprehension began with the *Socinians*. In this respect, as in others, the matured *Arminianism* of the left wing, on the continent, showed a Socinianizing tendency. The *Friends* helped to break down the authority of the written word, and the sense of the importance of creeds. The *Brownists*, and later *Independents*, in England and in New England, were helpers to the same end, as soon as the rigidity of party ardor passed away. The *unhistorical* bodies generally have contributed to this tendency, among whom have been specially active the *Methodists*.

Literature.

There is a great body of irenical Unionistic literature. Every great division of Western Christendom has furnished some distinguished names in this department. Among nominal Roman Catholics are prominent the names of Erasmus, Wicel, Cassander, and Hontheim. In the Reformed Church we find the names of Duraeus, Francis Junius, the younger Turretin. The Arminians have been thus specially distinguished in their whole spirit. Grotius was most eminent among them in this, as in so many other departments.

In the Lutheran Church *Calixtus* and his entire school defended Syncretistic views, not intercommunion indeed, or exchange of pulpits, but general fraternity. *Pfaff*, and the irenical school of the Eighteenth Century, followed in the same general line of thinking.

The Unionistic Controversy of recent times in Germany, looking to the blending of the Lutheran and German Reformed Churches, has drawn forth an immense number of works on both sides.

Among the books which in this country have had an extraordinary influence in leading to the practice of Unionistic communion, the ablest and most influential has been the Plea of Dr. John M. Mason, for what, by a very bold begging of the question, he was pleased to call "Holy Communion on Catholic Principles." In August, 1810, the Associate Reformed Church in the city of New York, then recently formed under the ministry of Dr. Mason, was led to hold its assemblies in "the house belonging to the church under the pastoral care of Dr. John B. Romeyn, of the General Assembly of the Presbyterian Church in North America." As the hours of service were different, the first effect of this arrangement was a partial amalgamation in the exercises of public worship; the next an esteem of each other as "united in the same precious faith;" and finally, after a very short time, invitations on both sides to join in the Lord's Supper. The bulk of the members of both churches, as well as some belonging to correlate churches, communed together. The Communion thus established has been perpetuated, and has extended itself to ministers and private Christians of other churches. "Such an event," says Dr. Mason, "it is believed, had never before occurred in the United States." It was in part a reaction against the unscriptural form of close communion which existed between the Calvinistic Churches. The Associate Reformed Church was founded in the union of two branches of Secession in Scotland, and from the Reformed Presbytery. The posture of matters testified to five divisions, all Calvinistic—all

Presbyterian—but not only separate and exclusive, but hostile communions. It was a shameful confession of separatistic tendencies, but a mere communion, with the cause of their separation, or want of cause, unconfessed, helped matters very little.

The movement of Dr. Mason, however, was the expression of feelings widespread, strong, and growing. From the first quarter of the Nineteenth Century there has been a general breaking down of old landmarks in this country. Popular and influential forms of embodying Union sentiment have become more and more common. We have Sunday-School and Tract Unions, Union Revivals, Union Prayer Meetings, the Evangelical Alliance, Young Men's Christian Associations, all involving compromise on the principles of individualism, and all tending to laxity and indifferentism.

The world has been coming into the Church, with its easy-going policy. There has been a large influx of unworthy professors, a relaxation of discipline, a spirit of social complaisance taking the place of principle. Under all these influences the Church has so lost her vitality that men of the world have begun not only to notice it, but to see something of its real causes. They tell us plainly that one of the greatest factors of the decline in church morals, has been the decline in fidelity to church doctrine. Real morality must have its root in real faith. If the doctrine of a Church be good, fidelity to it makes the doctrine a mightier force; if the doctrine be bad, personal inconsistency makes it worse. A consistent Protestant is better for his consistency, for it is the accord of a good life with a good faith. A consistent Romanist is better for his consistency, for the inconsistent Romanist is simply adding the lie of his life to the error of his judgment. The struggle of Indifferentism at first was against making the doctrines in which "the Evangelical denominations" differ, a test. But the struggle at this hour is against making any doctrines a test. Denominationalism with spread sails filling in the gale of Unionism, and without pilot or helmsman, is bearing full upon the rock of absolute individualism. When that rock is fairly struck, the vessel will go to the bottom.

III. THE RELATION OF THE LUTHERAN CHURCH, DE FACTO AND DE JURE, DEFINED.

The question of the relation of the Lutheran Church *in fact*, to the denominations, must be a question involving what is in fact *called* the Lutheran Church, whether it be rightly so called or not. The question of fact covers what exists in fact in the Lutheran Church, whether that existence keeps itself in harmony with right principle or not. It involves the *de facto* relations of what is *de facto* called the Lutheran Church. This is the preliminary part of the total question.

When, however, we come to the real question—the heart of the whole question—the question of *right* relation, we consider the relation *de jure*, of what is called the Lutheran Church *de jure*, and with which relation the Lutheran Church *de facto* ought to coincide throughout.

1. *The Relation de facto.*

To the question, what are in fact the relations of the nominally Lutheran Church to the denominations around us, the answer must be that they are of the most multifarious and conflicting character.

There are indeed a few principles so generally accepted that we may consider them as covering as far as they go, a ground of practical harmony. All our Lutheran Churches now would reject from their altars those who avow the errors which directly tend to the destruction of individual salvation—the damnable heresies in which men deny the Lord who bought them. There was a time when in parts of our Church, men suspected of the taint of Socinian and Universalist views were not subjected to discipline—days of uncontrolled Latitudinarianism, Rationalism, Syncretism, and Indifferentism. No conflict of views agitated the surface of the stagnant waters then. Those were the happy days, undisturbed by discussion, for which some now sigh as a golden age—not that they would have error, but that they would have truth without a battle. But perfect peace and perfect purity never can go together on earth: "I came not to bring peace, but a sword." Peace with God, peace with our own consciences—these we may have; but peace with Satan, peace with heresy, peace with persistent ignorance, error, and unreasonableness, we can never have—and these will rise as long as man is man.

Our Church is very much of a mind furthermore in relation to those parts of Christendom which, though they accept the General Creeds, are yet involved in very dangerous errors, as for example the Roman Catholic and the Greek Churches, and certain extravagant "Churchmen" who are ashamed of Protestantism and of whom

Protestantism is ashamed. We desire no official relation to them, but if we did we could not have it. Rome and the Greek Church refuse communion with each other and with the "Churchmen," and refuse it with us.

But while those who are *confessedly* heretics and fundamental errorists are excluded from our pulpits and are theoretically excluded from our altars, there are usages in parts of our Church which weaken our discipline, throw down the bar, and facilitate the approach to our altars even of the worst heretics and errorists, or of the most ignorant and deluded.

History of Interdenominational Communion in the Lutheran Church in America.

The history of this authorization of untested communion in our Church in America is very instructive.

In the Agenda of the Evangelical Lutheran United Congregations in North America, 1786, the first published in this land; with the venerable names of the three Kurtzes, of Bager, Helmuth, Schmidt, Kunze, Heinrich Mühlenberg, Streit, Göring, and other worthies, with our old prince and patriarch, Heinrich Melchior Mühlenberg, Doctor of Theology and Senior of the Ministerium, at their head— the directions guarding the altar are very explicit. The Communion is to be announced from the pulpit at least eight, or if possible fourteen days before the administration, with a statement of the time when the people (die Leute) purposing to commune are to notify the pastor, and have their names recorded. The minister shall keep a register of communicants. In case the preacher discovers, by the notification of those designing to commune, that any one is living in enmity or in open scandal, and the pastor cannot himself adjust the difficulty, he shall call together the church council and determine who is guilty, that he may be called to account. On the day preceeding the communion, all the communicants who have given this notification come together in the church. The practice is approved of reading from the pulpit, at this service, the names of those who have thus come together to confession. After the reading of the names, a verse is sung, and the minister, going before the altar, records the names of those who for cogent (erheblichen) reasons have not been able previously to notify him of their desire to commune. Then follow the questions of the preparatory service. Should there yet be some who, early on the Sunday or festival, notify the pastor of their desire to commune—persons who have been unable for weighty (wichtigen) causes to come to the confession—the pastor has confession for them before divine service, and announces to them the absolution.

This defines the relation of our Church in America to the question of intercommunion with a clearness to which comment could add nothing; nor was there anything in the original usage of our fathers in this country fairly answerable to what is now practiced under the name of exchange of pulpits.

In 1795 the first authorized Liturgy of our Church in the English language was set forth by Dr. Kunze, Senior of the Lutheran Clergy in the State of New York. It professes to be, and is translated from the German of the liturgical part of the Agenda of 1786.

In 1797 appeared what called itself the Liturgy of the English Lutheran Church of New York, edited by George Strebeck, at the request of his congregation, and without any pretence of authority.

The edition of the Liturgy of 1806 is Kunze's, with modifications by Ralph Williston, showing the tendency which ended in taking him into the Episcopal Church.

The first Liturgy in our church in America which gave authority to an unguarded invitation to the Lord's Supper, is that published by order of the Synod of New York, in 1814. At that time a negative avoidance of the fundamental doctrines of Christianity prevailed in that body; and men suspected of doubt, if not actual disbelief of the doctrine of the Trinity, the Deity of Christ, the eternity of future punishments, were not only not subjected to discipline, but were leading men in it. In the Liturgy of 1814 the minister uses the words: "In the name of Christ, our common and only Master, I say to all who own Him as their Saviour, and resolve to be His faithful subjects: ye are welcome to this feast of love." The Formula, left to the interpretation of those who heard it, would justify to all denominations, even the most heterodox, or indeed to those who are not members of the Church at all, an approach to our altar.

In 1818 appeared the German Liturgy of the Synod of Pennsylvania, in some respects, but alas! not in others, a second edition of the Agenda of 1786. For the form of confession and preparation for the Lord's Supper, the same rubrics are in it as far as the end of the 2d part of the 4th paragraph. The reading from the pulpit of the names of those who desire to commune is no longer mentioned. The fifth paragraph now reads: "Should there be some who early on the Sunday or festival notify their desire to commune, who for weighty reasons have not been able to come to the confession, the preacher speaks heartily with them in private, and they may yet be admitted to the communion." There comes then a second formula, but under the same rubrics. For the Lord's Supper there are three formulas. The first has no invitation. The second has the invitation nearly word for word, which we have given from the New York liturgy of 1814. All of them have the Rationalistic, Unionistic form of distribution, and the noble service of 1786 is not even given as one of the optional forms. The same is true of the German Liturgy published in the name of the Synods of Pennsylvania, New York and Ohio, 1842.

The New York Formula of 1814 is given in the Liturgy published by order of the Synod of South Carolina, edited by Dr. Hazelius, 1841. In the General Synod's Liturgy the invitation is made yet broader: "In the name of Jesus Christ, I say to all who sincerely love Him, ye are welcome to this feast of love." In the Liturgy recommended and published by order of the General Synod, 1847, the service for the Lord's Supper has four formulas. The first is without a general invitation. In the second the minister, in inviting the communicants to the altar, says: "This invitation is cordially extended to all who are members in good standing of other Christian denominations. In the name of Jesus Christ, I say to all who sincerely love Him, ye are welcome to this feast of love." In the third formula the minister is authorized to use these words: "In the name of Jesus Christ, our common Lord, I say to all who have embraced Him as their Saviour and are resolved by His grace to live as becomes His true followers, ye are welcome to this feast of love." In the Liturgy published as part of the Book of Worship by the Evangelical Lutheran General Synod in North America, in the rubric of the Order of Confession, p. 79, it is said: "Those who intend to commune may report their names to the pastor after the notice has been given, and all who have failed to do this should be *required* to do it at the time of holding the preparatory service, that the pastor and council may know if any member neglects the Holy Communion. The names of the communicants should be recorded in the church book. Immediately after the names have been taken down, the elders of the church shall examine the list, and if any suspended or expelled members shall have handed in their names, they shall be directed not to approach the sacred board until restored to their standing in the church."

At the Supper, the minister giving the invitation says: "This invitation is cordially extended not only to all visiting disciples of our own communion, but also to all who are members in good standing of the Christian Church. In the name of Jesus Christ, I say to all who truly love Him, ye are welcome to this feast of love. We are all one in Christ." In the rubric of the Confession, and in this of the Supper, the irreconcilable systems and practices clash together. The first is Lutheran, the second is not.

Inferences.

A study of these historical facts shows :

1. The original position of our Church in America was one of entire unity in theory and practice as regards intercommunion. It knows of none but Lutheran communicants at Lutheran altars, of none having the privileges of our Church without being subjected to its discipline.

2. The changes and departure from early usage took place when the patriarchs were gone, and was the result of a response on the part of Rationalism and Unionism within our Church, to Rationalism and Unionism outside of it.

3. The General Invitations of a later period are of such a character as to destroy all the force and significance of the preparatory service. Those who hear the invitation being constituted judges in their own cases, members of heterodox churches, members of no church, expelled or suspended members of our own Church and of other churches, could come to the altar upon them. The general invitations mean chaos and contempt of the ordinance of the Lord.

II. *The Relations of the Lutheran Church de jure.*

The consideration of the history and state of our relations *de facto*, has prepared us for the yet weightier question, What is the relation *de jure* of the Lutheran Church, genuinely such, to the denominations around us ? To this question we answer:

FIRST : The relations are such as involve and are in harmony with the principles on which the Lutheran Church vindicates her right to exist. She claims a right to exist because she is the Church in which *faith* takes its true place, as the central bond to the central and supreme object, Jesus Christ—Christus Solus, Fides Sola. She is the Church of Faith, as knowledge, assent and trust, divinely given, wrought by the Holy Ghost through the Word and Sacraments, and justifying us as it lays hold of the merits of the all sufficient Saviour. She restored to the Church and taught to the nations that faith is a conviction which binds the conscience unreservedly, and is not to be confounded with opinion.

She claims a right to exist because she is a *Biblical* Church. Judging as she does of faith, our Church must emphasize the *Rule of Faith*, as the organ by which faith is generated. The Work of the Spirit, which is faith, and holiness through faith, will consummate itself by an organ adapted to its end. A sure faith must have a sure rule, a clear faith a clear rule. A faith to bind us must have a rule to bind it. If the faith is to be sufficient for shaping mind, heart and will, the rule must be sufficient to shape the faith. That is not a divine faith which is not shaped by a divine rule, and that is not a divine rule which does not produce a divine faith. If we are responsible for our faith to God, the rule by which he shapes it will be such as to demand and justify the responsibility. Hence our Church knows of no Rule of Faith from which we may depart, on a mere agreement to differ; none which may yield to self-reliant reason; none which may give way to fanatical revelations or fanatical interpretations; none which a man may put aside passively on the ground that certainty cannot be reached, or is not worth the trouble it will give to reach it. She rests on the Word as clear, harmonious, self-interpreting, binding.

Our Church claims the right to exist because of her *confessional* position. She clearly confesses the whole truth of God. In the acceptance of the whole Word of God, this Confession, where the sense of that word is undisputed, is *implicit*. But wherever the sense of that Word is denied, obscured, perverted or ignored, her Confession is *expressed* and set forth in the Theses and Antitheses of her Symbols. Having a clear faith, resting on a clear rule, our Church cannot but emphasize a clear, unmistakable Confession of Faith—her witness to the true sense of God's Word, claiming derivative authority as the expression of that sense. Resting the obligation of the Confession on that ground, and her children being those who recognize the validity of that ground, she can do nothing, allow nothing, in conflict with this conviction. The Confession must be the test of her pulpits, the guardian of her altars, or, she, on her own showing, forsakes the Word, abandons the faith, is disloyal to God. He who rejects her Confession of Faith rejects her Rule of Faith in its right teaching. The Confession of Unbelief makes the Rule of Faith a Rule of Unbelief.

She claims a *historical* right to exist. Her history proves her divine origin and necessity; and as our Church has been needed in the past, so is she needed in the present. She is needed not only for her motherhood to her own children, but for the great wants of Christendom and of the world. She is needed as a witness to that doctrine which is conceded in terms by the whole Protestant world, but which is invaded primarily or by necessary inference by every system which is at war with ours—the doctrine of Justification by Faith. Inadequate views of the person and work of Christ; false views of election and reprobation; of the means of grace, the Word and Sacraments; the mode and subjects of Baptism; the nature of the validity and efficacy of the ministry,—all are in conflict, covertly it may be, but really, with the true doctrine of Justification by Faith. Romanism and Ritualism directly assail it; Rationalism destroys it; Fanaticism, sometimes with an affectation of zealotry for it, confounds justification by faith with justification by sensation, and leads the penitent to rest, not on the old, eternal promise, but on a new personal revelation. No Church holds the doctrine of Justification by Faith in that consistent integrity and harmonious relation within itself and with all other doctrines, in which it is held and confessed in the Lutheran Church.

With the principles on which she rests her claim to be of right a church, all the *acts* of our Church for which she is fairly responsible have accorded. Her *pulpits* and *altars* have been meant for those only who have borne the tests which she imposes, as necessary to separate those who give credible evidence of fidelity to the obligations of her pulpits and altars, from those who have never been subjected to these tests. Her name, her existence, her creeds, her Agenda, her standard divines of all schools, her whole history, up to this hour of anti-unionistic struggle against state-force in Europe and sect-craft in America, are witnesses to her position of fidelity. She can have no fellowship of pulpit and altar where there is no attested fellowship of faith; the attestation of felloshwip of faith is by public confession. She cannot accept the teachers of the denominations as her teachers, nor acknowledge their members at her altars, as her children, or as in the full fraternity of an incorrupt faith.

The Common Judgment of Christendom.

SECONDLY: The relations of the Lutheran Church to the "evangelical denominations" around us are in accord with the *common judgment* of Christendom until the time of the decline of Faith and the rise of Unionism. They are relations justified by the official principles and official acts especially of *the evangelical denominations* themselves. We narrow this point to the "evangelical denominations;" for whatever may be the exceptional extreme of looseness, the only open question to the larger part of our Church in regard to pulpit and altar fellowship is limited to those denominations around us which are somewhat vaguely styled "evangelical."

The term is so vague that we can perhaps only make it distinctive by enumerating the principal bodies or parts of bodies embraced in it. It usually covers the Reformed, German and Dutch; the Presbyterians of all the divisions; the Baptists; the Methodists; the Congregationalists; the Episcopalians (the Puseyistic portion excepted); the Moravians. There is a herd beside of small sects—small in every sense—who cover themselves with it, and who seem to think that the Evangelical element, like a homeopathic remedy, is potentiated by division. Their

> "wound is great because it is so small,
> And would be greater were it none at all."

What ought to be the principles controlling the relations of the Lutheran Church to these denominations, the denominations themselves, in their official character and expression, being the judges? We say "their official character and expression," by which we mean their Confessions, and the authorized exposition of them, and their Constitutions and Discipline, interpreted by their acts when they were yet confessedly faithful to their principles. For the official judgment of these denominations is not to be gathered from the lawless, careless, irresponsible usage of individuals, or even of a general usage which has crept in. Were there no other reason, we should have too much self-respect, and too much regard for law to avail ourselves of unauthorized invitations to take the pulpits or approach the altars which are opened to us by irresponsible men, who in doing so violate their ordination vows, and treat with contempt the principles and order of the Church they pretend to serve. No minister of ours has a right to open his pulpit or altar without being able distinctly to show how he acquired that right—who gave it to him—and to prove that those who gave it to him had the right to give it; and he has no right to give it except on the principle on which he got it. So have we no right to accept the invitation to pulpit or altar of others unless we know that they have the right to offer it.

In point of moral consistency, not one of these denominations has the right to invite us as Lutherans to its pulpits and altars. They have names which in their historical definition mean something which implies that we are so far wrong that they are obliged to form or maintain communions distinct from ours. They have Confessions which they have no right to have, unless they believe before God that they contain the principles which alone can determine what must be taught as the very truth of God in the pulpit, and which if it is the very truth of God must not be rejected at the table. They all have modes of testing without which their own members cannot be admitted to their pulpits, and which they cannot consistently remit in our case. They all have modes of testing and admitting their own members to communion, and they have no right to admit us without these tests, or if they should so admit us, they should so admit their own.

And in point of fact, a number of these denominations do consistently exclude us and others. No *Episcopalian* admits us to pulpit or altar without defying the Canons and the Book of Common Prayer; a number of the smaller *Presbyterian* bodies exclude us and all but their own ministers and members from pulpit and altar; the *Baptists* sometimes inconsistently admit us and others to their pulpits, but the great body of them consistently with their convictions exclude us and others from their altars. Whatever may be the laxity of practice which has grown up, all the historical Churches of Christendom coincide in their real principles, which regulate the relation of pulpit and altar, with the very strongest and extremest held in the theory, or carried out in the practice of the most consistent part of the Lutheran Church. These coincident principles are:

1. That pure doctrine and pure sacraments are essential marks of the Church.

2. That a Church has no right to a being on its own showing except as it claims these marks. A Church which does not know that it has these marks does not know that it is a pure Church. A Church which does not believe that it has these marks has no right to believe that it is a pure Church.

3. That Confessions are mainly designed as modes of stating what are the features of doctrine and sacraments which the Churches which set them forth believe to be essential to the manifestation and maintenance of purity.

4. That Churches are to be judged by and treated in accordance with their Confessions and the official interpretation of them.

5. That communions opposed to the Confession of a pure Church are so far opposed to the truth itself, and so far not in fellowship with the pure Church itself.

6. That subjection to the tests and discipline of a Church are essential to the right to enjoy its privileges.

7. That avowed or implied rejection of the Confession, is in fact a rejection of the Church which accepts it, and should bar access to its pulpits and altars.

IV. THE RELATION OF THE LUTHERAN CHURCH TO THE DENOMINATIONS AROUND US VINDICATED.

Objections to the Lutheran Position.

We now propose to meet the most plausible objections which have been urged against the position of our Church. This we shall do in the form of *negative* definitions of our relation. In so doing we would say:

FIRST: That it is *not* a relation which refuses to make *discrimination*. It does indeed put all on a common level so far as untested admission to pulpit and altar is concerned. So do all associations, with their distinctive official rights and privileges. So does the State with hers. *Any* man who is not a citizen cannot vote, or be elected to an office. *Any* foreigner who is not naturalized is debarred from the distinctive rights of citizenship. *Any* one under legal age is denied access to the polls. And yet how untrue it would be to say that there is no discrimination on the part of our government toward those not under it—none of feeling, none of desire or hope of closer relationship, of friendship and of affinity—that she does not discriminate between the English and German, on the one side, the

Chinese and the Hottentot on the other. With some nations she cultivates close amity, others she treats with caution, others she holds at a distance. So does our Church maintain distinct and different relations to the various denominations around us. She discriminates with reference to their grades of error and their grades of truth—the degrees of responsibility for schism connected with their origin and principles. She distinguishes between Churches and individuals who are friendly, appreciative, just, and kind toward us, and those who are coarse, ignorant and unjust. These discriminations are marked in our Confessions, which attest our sympathy with all truth, and with all men so far as they hold it—they are marked by our personal regard, by our recognition in our literature, and books of worship, and by all kindly tokens, which involve no compromise of principle. We sympathize with the remnants of Evangelical life in the Roman Catholic Church over against its corruptions; with genuine Protestantism, as against Popery; with historical conservatism, sobriety, culture and religious principle, in whatever denomination, over against radicalism, fanaticism, coarseness, and impulsive sensationalism—wherever they may be—and we cast our weight as a Church against all the evil and for all the good around us. Our practice simply subjects to one and the same test those born in our Church and those not born in it.

Fundamentals.

SECOND: The relations of our Church to the denominations around us, involve no rejection or ignoring of the just distinction between *fundamental* and *non-fundamental*. Our quarrels with error are not on questions touching Tobit's dog, or as to the capacity of a legion of angels to dwell in the eye of a cambric needle or hover on its point. The doctrinal terms of communion in our Church involve fundamentals only—doctrines which directly or by necessary consequence involve the integrity of that *distinctive* truth which Revelation is given to teach, and which the Church is to defend and extend, the impairing of which begins with destroying her well-being and ends in the loss of her life. What is *fundamental* truth? The practical answer to this question in the only shape in which it comes up here is, Truth which is rightly made a term of teaching and of communion by embodiment in the Confessional standards, and the permanent official acts of the Church. Either the denominations regard their Confessions as statements of fundamental truth *in this* sense, or they do not. If they do, then we deal with them as, for ourselves, asserting that the Articles of our Standards are fundamental in this sense, and that they hold that theirs are fundamental in the same way. If they do not, then they make what they confess to be unnecessary, non-fundamental things, terms of teaching and communion; they are self-convicted of schism, and they render official church-fellowship with them, on our part, impossible.

If they say, these may be necessary terms of *permanent* teaching and *permanent* communion, but not of occasional teaching and communion, they either assert, or their practice assumes, that what is wrong in principle as a constant thing, is right in principle as an occasional thing, which is as flagrantly illogical as to say that it is right to violate the moral law occasionally though it is wrong to do it constantly; *or* they must say that it is not a question of principle but of expediency, into which the occasional may enter. In this case they acknowledge that their confessions and their denominational life with them are based not on immutable verities but on expediency, and again they proclaim themselves sects and make it impossible for us to have church-fellowship with them.

There may be, and there are, denominations which, without violence to their faith, may admit that our Church holds *fundamental* truth, and is involved in no *fundamental* error, in regard to whom we are constrained to say that they do not confess all *fundamental* truth, and that they are involved in *fundamental* error. From their definition of a doctrine, the error—*our* error, as they allege—may not be *fundamental;* while from our definition of the doctrine, the error—*their* error—may be fundamental; for a fundamental error must be arrayed against a fundamental truth. There can no more be fundamental error without a fundamental truth, than a man can have heart disease in his little finger, though disease in a non-fundamental may result from or be a proof of disease in the fundamental, or spread from it and affect the fundamental. The question, In what respects the doctrine of the Lord's Supper is fundamental, can not be settled without reference to the question, What is the Lord's Supper? The determination involves a definition. On the *theory* that the Lord's Supper represents something, but conveys nothing, is a symbol of grace, but not one of its means—that whatever there is in it, it has in common with a number of other things—granting this theory, it is clear that the importance of the Lord's Supper is relatively little, and that error in regard to it is comparatively innocuous. A truth or an error merely involving a figure of speech, a symbol, a single species of a genus, is not speculatively, nor practically, like a truth or error, involving a literal verity, a solemn reality, a something unique in its nature, design and blessings. A correct estimate or a mistake of the weight and value of an ounce of copper known to be such, is not like a right or wrong estimate about the weight and value of an ounce of gold. But it is a great mistake to think that a piece of copper is a piece of gold, or a piece of gold a piece of copper, or to confound skillful paste with pearls, or pearls with paste. When a dispute arises as to whether certain metal be copper or gold, certain jewels paste or pearls, he who is sure that the thing in dispute is copper or paste, cares comparatively little about the decision—it is *non-fundamental* to him. To him who is sure it is gold or pearl, the question is fundamental. It is no sacrifice to the one to risk his ignoble metal and counterfeit—but to the other to risk pure gold and a priceless pearl, is something from which he shrinks. A Zwinglian may admit that a Lutheran is not in fundamental error—a Lutheran cannot admit it in regard to a Zwinglian. To claim that what is but bread and wine really, is Christ's body and blood, may be a great absurdity—but it is the result of too absolute a trust in His word, it is the superstition of faith; but to say that what He really tells us is His body and blood, is but bread and wine, implies lack of trust in His word—it is the superstition of unbelief. But the astonishing thing is that those who reproach us for treating the doctrine of the Lord's Supper as *fundamental*, do themselves treat it in the same way. They treat it as *fundamental* by making it a part of their Confession, and in every one of the aspects in which our Confession considers it. It is in the XXXIX Articles, the Westminster Confession, and in every other great Protestant Confession, carefully stated, and guarded not only against Rome, but guarded against our Church. That is an official admission and claim that the doctrine is clearly revealed, that they hold it in its purity, that we are wrong in it, and that a clear confession on the very points in which they are right and we are wrong is needful. Their own Confessions witness against them when they say that the Lutheran Church should not make her doctrine of the Lord's Supper a term of teaching and communion.

They make their own doctrine such a term, and yet they have far less reason to do so than we. They have a metaphor to literalize;

we accept a verity deep as the incarnation itself, a verity involving the incarnation and involved in it.

It has pleased them sometimes to represent the whole matter as a dispute about mere phrases. We are agreed, they say, about the thing—but the contest is kept up about words. If this be so, and as we believe that our words are necessary to guard the thing, why will they not consent to our words? To us it is no logomachy. If it be so to them, why do they not give up their "mere phrases?" And where did those, who attempt to make us odious for insisting on our faith in regard to the Lord's Supper, ever engage to be silent in regard to their own? The history of the controversy from the beginning shows how eager and persistent the Zwinglians and Calvinists were in urging their own doctrine and assailing ours. The plea for liberality to be shown on our part meant freedom for themselves to hold and teach error, without wholesome moral correction from us. It means all through, We will rob you of your faith if we can, and if we cannot, we will insist that you shall at least think it of little account.

But while our relations discriminate between *fundamental* and *non-fundamental*, they are not meant to lower the dignity and value of any truth. We exalt *fundamentals* over *non-fundamentals*, but we lift both as truth over all error. The Church is not to treat with indifference any false teaching.

Infallibility.

THIRD: The relations of our Church to the denominations around us rest on no claim to *infallibility*. *Infallibility* is incapability of failing, and belongs to nothing human as such. The *infallibility* of the Church is the *infallibility* of the Church catholic or invisible; that is, this Church will always exist, and its very existence implies that it is infallibly secure from soul-destroying error,[5]—there cannot be a total lapse of the entire body of true believers from those essentials of faith without which the soul of man cannot be savingly knit to the Redeemer. Not only is this so in fact, but it is so of divine necessity. "One holy Christian Church *must* be and abide for all time."[6] So much of the Church invisible as is within the Lutheran Church is so far infallible. But this is equally true of every part of

---

[5] Gerhard Loci., Loc. xxiii. Cap. ix.
[6] Augsb. Confess., Art. vii.

the Church visible, and does not prove that there will always be such members within a communion bearing the name Lutheran, or in any of the communions bearing the names under which at present the Christian Church is classified. No particular Church is incapable of erring, of apostasy, decline and destruction. Many particular Churches have erred and perished, or have erred and still exist. "As the Churches of Hierusalem, Alexandria and Antioch, have erred, so also the Church of Rome hath erred, not only in their living and manner of cere'ronies, but also in matters of faith."[7]

The Lutheran Church, therefore, does not claim infallibility. She has not overthrown one Rome to set up another. She simply claims that in fact she has not erred in the Articles of Faith, and this freedom from error she ascribes, not to herself in her human powers, but alone to the grace of God operating in His own appointed ways in accordance with His own immutable promises.

The Church of Rome says: The Catholic Church is *infallible;* the Church of Rome is the Catholic Church; the Church of Rome is *infallible.* We say the entire Catholic Church, as entire, alone is infallible, and that simply in respect of all the fundamentals of personal salvation. The Lutheran Church contains but a part of the Catholic Church, therefore she is not infallible. But our Church says also: *Any* part of the Church which seeks the truth in complete accordance with God's commands and promises will be kept from failing. The Lutheran Church has so sought the truth; therefore she has been kept from failing.

It would be indeed a lamentable thing if the question of the *claim* of one thing, could be identified and confounded with the question of the *fact* of another thing. If to assert that in fact there has been no failure, is to assert in claim that there is infallibility, then it holds good of every individual, of every communion, and of the totality of communions. No man can claim not to have failed, for no man can claim infallibility. No man or Church can claim to have escaped failure in a single doctrine, for no man or Church is infallible in a single doctrine. No Christian communion can maintain that its system as a whole or in any one part is free from error, for no particular Church is infallible, either in its total doctrine or in a single doctrine. Nor are all particular Christian Churches together infallible, even in the doctrine they hold in common or in any one

---

[7] XXXIX Articles of Church of England. Art. xix.

article. You may multiply or divide the zero of fallibility any number of times, and it never makes infallibility. We end where we began. No Church on earth, by this line of reasoning, nor all Churches on earth together, can claim to have reached unmixed truth in whole or in part, for they are each and all fallible.

It is a principle of law that no man shall be arrested on a general warrant, or condemned on a general charge. A man is neither seized nor convicted on the general charge of being a thief. His warrant and conviction must distinctly state what he has stolen, and he must have been convicted on many particular charges before he is even watched as a professional thief. No man has a right to treat our Church as the law would not permit him to treat a suspected thief. No man has a right to bring against our Church the general charge that she claims infallibility, without specifying when and where and how she claims it. The charge is wholly untrue. It is made general because an attempt to make it particular would at once reveal the falsehood. She does not claim infallibility. She distinctly repudiates it.

But neither has any man the right to convict her on the general charge that she makes a groundless claim not to have failed. He is bound to specify in what she has failed. Put your finger on the doctrine in which you pretend she has failed, and prove that she has done it, or grant her claim not to have failed.

It is another sound principle of law that when testimony is conformed to the proper demands of evidence, that where the witness cannot be shown to have deviated in any respect from the truth, no one has the right to attempt to set aside that specific testimony on the general ground that all men are liable to mistake. It must be shown in what he has made a mistake, or his evidence stands. In a court the power of testimony does not depend upon the assumption that it can be infallible, but on the evidence that in fact it can be so guarded as not to fail.

Now to take up the particular points. We meet here as true Catholic Christians, so far as assent to the general creeds is concerned. It will not be necessary, therefore, to show that in reasserting the great doctrines of the General Creeds, our Church has not erred. We are here as Protestants. It will not therefore be necessary to argue that in what she asserts and denies over against distinctive Romanism, our Church has not erred. We are here as

Lutherans in claim. Is it consistent with that name that we should think that our Church has erred in whole or in part over against any or all of the non-Lutheran Protestant systems? We have supposed that their existence separate from us rested on the claim that they had not erred, where we have erred; and that on the other hand a Lutheran was one who held that we have not erred, where they have erred. They say that we have failed, and they have not. We say they have failed and we have not. They hold us responsible for our failures, as we hold them responsible for their own. But the whole attitude of all the Churches is really the same to the main question here. It is that they who rightly approach the Word of God, need not fail and will not fail; that is, that in the nature of the case it is as really possible to avoid failure on the points of confessional difference as on the points of confessional agreement. The man who calls himself a Lutheran as a means of testifying his conviction that Lutheranism is wrong, is like a man who assumes the title of a Christian that all men may thereby know that he is a Jew.

Nevertheless, there have been men on both sides the sea, who within our Church, accepting its privileges, the honor of its name, perhaps eating its bread, have met the challenge to specification. Some on the broad ground of Rationalism have said, The Lutheran Church has failed in the very fundamentals of religion—the doctrine of God, of Sin, of Salvation, and of the Saviour. She ought to have been Socinian and Universalist. There is no line possible if we accept individualism as the test. If a man can be a Lutheran who thinks our Church has failed, and whose guide to that in which she has failed is that he thinks so, where can you stop? If we admit that it can be done with *one* article, who shall settle which one? If with more than one, how many? If with some, why not with all? If with one set this year, why not with another set next year? And this is no logical imagining. This is the exact ground actually taken by the consistent men of the position of which we now speak. There is no firm ground between strict confessionalism, and no confessionalism. All between is hopeless inconsistency.

We think that on every point on which our Church's faith has been challenged, it can be triumphantly sustained. But that is not the point here. Let us suppose the objector to say, "The Lutheran Church has failed on the person of Christ, on Baptism, and the Lord's Supper." He can only know she is wrong on these points by knowing himself what is right—what is the right doctrine, where hers is wrong. He says, in effect, "The Lutheran Church is not infallible, but I am"—or more modestly, "The Lutheran Church has failed, but I have not. The Lutheran Church is wrong, but I can set her right." The whole thing means, "She fails when she don't agree with me, and she is infallibly right when she does." It is the transparent self-conceit of individualism.

It is very preposterous to say that our Church may without claiming infallibility justly claim not to have failed in ninety-nine points, and yet that to claim that she is right on the hundredth point *is* to claim infallibility. Especially is this the case if the hundredth point is reached by the same processes of interpretation by which the ninety-nine have been reached. If we may summarily dismiss the assertion of a doctrine of our Church, because our Church is not infallible, we can just as summarily dismiss the rejection of it by another Church, because that Church is not infallible. Infallibility is just as much required for unchallenged rejection as for unchallenged acceptance. He who can infallibly know every part of the wrong of every question, can infallibly know the right of it—for truth and error are eternal antitheses—correlates, the knowledge of which is one.

"Methods" of Romanism.

This whole style of dispensing with particular proof is exactly in the line and spirit of the so-called "Methods" of the Romish Polemics. One method was to reduce the whole question between Rome and Protestantism to the point of antiquity and novelty; another was the method of challenging Protestants to proofs from the direct words of Scripture without inference; another was the method involved in the question, Where was your Church before Luther? another method was to assume that an inspired Rule was useless without an inspired interpreter; another was the method of prescription and possession; another was the method of urging the visible Church as the Catholic Church; another was the method of safety—we Romanists deny that salvation is possible with you, you admit that it is possible with us; there was also the method of authority, and the method of non-fundamental difference between Rome and Protestantism. These methods proposed to do away with all particular investigation, all proof from facts, by establishing or assuming some one theoretic, general principle. These methods with all their variety, had the common feature that they proposed to argue without reason, and to reason without argument, and can be reduced to the common foundation that Rome was to be made judge in her own case.

The One Method.

Now over against all these methods, genuine Protestantism has but one method—the method of examination—honest, thorough investigation. "Search" and "Try" are divine injunctions. But it is a Romish method to the core, in defiance of the fundamental principle of Protestantism, to get rid of the claim which a Church makes of purity in every one of her doctrines, not by particular proof that some of her doctrines are false, but by a general appeal to fallibility. Fallibility is not failure. To show a general possibility of it in the nature of the case, is very different from showing an actual result. Fallibility implies that we may fail or may not fail. Possibility involves that a result may be or its contrary may be. To settle which has actually been reached requires particular evidence. Our Church therefore proposes—not like Rome, by a claim to infallibility, but by a particular proof in each case—to show that she has not failed. The only way to confute her, if she can be confuted, is to take up the alleged mistake and prove it to be such.

"Agnosticism."

Our Church does indeed rest her relations to the denominations around us on her conviction that her system is in all its parts divine, derived from the Word of God and in accordance with it. And there are those who object to this position, not that they charge any specific error on our Church—they waive even the consideration of that question—but that in general they assume that we are not prepared to treat any system as throughout divine. A system, they say, may be divine, but we cannot know that it is. We see in part, we know in part. It is not probable that any one denomination has all the truth on the mooted questions. We think we are right. Others think they are right, and they are as much entitled to assert the possession of truth for themselves as we are for ourselves. The Church is still seeking: the Church of the unknown future may perhaps see things in their true light.

This is bringing into theology what is a pet theory of the philosophy of our day under the title "Agnosticism"—which presses our ignorance until it makes of it a sort of omniscience of negation. There are no such vices in the world as the affectations of virtue. Sanctimony apes sanctity, prudery modesty, masked egotism humility—and on the basis of universal ignorance a man offers himself as a universal sage, and systematizes ignorance in many volumes.

It is true that the Church on earth is imperfect, and that in her best life, and because of it, she ever grows. But she must have a complete life to have a constant growth. An acorn is not an oak, but the vital force in the acorn is that which makes the oak and abides in it. The question here is, Has the Church reached such a clear, binding faith on the great vital questions, not only of individual salvation but of her own highest efficiency and well-being, as justifies her in making them a term of communion and of public teaching? The question is not whether she can reach more truth, or apply more widely the truth she has, but whether what she now holds is truth, and whether seeking more truth by the same methods she can be assured of finding it.

The Old Testament has been teaching for thousands of years; the New Testament has taught for two thousand years; and yet it is pretended by those who profess to hold the clearness and sufficiency of Holy Scripture, that no part of the Church of Christ, not even that part which they declare they hold in highest esteem, has reached a witness which can commend itself to human trust, or can tell whether it has failed or not. Then there is not a man on earth who has any choice except as between systems either of certain or of possible error. He cannot build up unmixed truth anywhere. He cannot build up truth without building up error. He is sowing seed, and may be sowing tares. He is trying to pluck up weeds, and may be pulling up the grain. He cannot do the Lord's work without doing part of the devil's work. If the divine truth has no self-asserting power, sufficient to dispel doubt, how shall we reach any sure ground? Shall we say that all nominally Christian systems are alike in value, or that if they differ in this no one can find it out? This on its face seems self-confuting, but if we had to confute it, we could only do so by showing that God's Word is clear on the points on which Churches differ. If we do not believe that we are scriptural over against Rome, we have no right to be separate from Rome. If the Churches divided from us do not believe that they are scriptural, they have no right to be divided from us; and if we have no assured conviction that we have the truth, we have no right to exist. This Agnosticism is at heart unbelief, or despair, or indolence, or evasion of cogent argument.

Romanizing Tendency.

Of all Romanizing tendencies the most absolute is that which puts the dishonor on God's Word, and on the fundamental principles of the Reformation, implied in this view. It may be safely asserted that ecclesiastical bodies will not claim less for themselves than they are entitled to, and when it shall be said that no part of the churches of which the Reformation was the cause or occasion, even pretends to have an assurance of the whole faith it confesses, then will men regard Protestantism as self-convicted, and if they do not swing off to infidelity, will say: Rome at least claims to have the truth, and if truth is to be found on earth, it is more likely to be found with those who claim to have it, than with those who admit they have it not. To sum up, we say Rome is fallible, the Denominations are fallible, and the Lutheran Church is fallible: but the Romish Church has failed in Articles of Faith, so have the Denominations; the Lutheran Church has not.

Donatism.

FOURTH: Our Church in her relations to the denominations around us occupies *no Donatistic* attitude. "They condemn the Donatists," says the Augsburg Confession and Apology, "and others like them, who denied that it is lawful to use the ministry of evil men in the Church, and hold that the ministry of the evil is useless and inefficient," "and that men sin who receive the sacraments in the Church from unworthy, ungodly ministers." "Christ hath admonished us in his discourses of the Church, that we are not, because we are offended at the private faults either of priests or people, to excite schisms or separation as the Donatists wickedly did." All this means that personal excellencies do not make official acts, nor do personal defects mar their validity. God's pure Word at the lips of a bad man remains God's Word; error at the lips of a good man remains error still. The Word bears the power, the man does not. Pure gold in a polluted hand is pure gold still, and the brassy counterfeit, however clean and fair the hand which brings it, is brass still. In the proper sense of the word Donatism, to apply it to Lutheranism is not only unfounded but ridiculous.

Exclusiveness.

That the Lutheran Church has no narrow segregative spirit like that of the Donatists, has no *false exclusiveness*, will be manifest to any one who knows her history, and her principles. We say a false exclusiveness, for there is a true exclusiveness which pertains to the nature of all truth, and most of all to Christianity, because it is the supreme truth. Because it is divine it is exclusive of all that is not divine. Those who separate themselves from us in our truth compel us to be separate from them in their error.

"Exclusiveness," says D'Aubigne, "is a character of Lutheranism...This exclusiveness is necessary to unity. It must enter into the construction of the admirable machine prepared by the hand of the great Artificer three centuries ago. Exclusiveness is essential to the Church. Who was more exclusive than he who said, 'No one cometh to the Father *but by me;*' and again, '*Without me,* ye can do nothing.' The Church ought to have a holy jealousy for the eternal truth of God; for *latitudinarianism* is its death. The history of all ages has demonstrated this fact, and nothing could demonstrate it more clearly than the history of our own. This exclusiveness was what was confided to the charge of Martin Luther... Luther believed that the corporeal presence was God's truth, and he went out of himself for that truth. Thou didst well, O great Luther!...God gives us, what thou didst not understand, to treat with mildness those who differ from us in opinion. But God grant at the same time, as with thee, that the rights of the truth inspire us, and the zeal of God's house eat us up." And this is D'Aubigne's concession to the exclusiveness which he is attacking.

The animus of Donatism, whether in its specific error or in its general narrowness of spirit, is not in the Lutheran Church, but in the fanatical sects, who confound the visible with the invisible, and by a coercive and legalistic discipline attempt and pretend to have a ministry and communion of none but saints. The pretences of a more rigid discipline have originated many of the sects, which, swelling at their first ardor till they burst the bulb, are found now on the ground frozen and fixed below zero.

There is no body of Christians on earth more remote from all the pretences of Donatism, in its letter or its spirit, than the Lutheran Church. There is none which is so large and liberal in all things, which are really in the sphere of the liberty of the Church. Contrast her largeness of view in things indifferent with the pitiful littleness of ultra Puritanism on the one side, of Romish and Puseyistic Ritualism on the other. Mark her scriptural candor in regard to special forms of Church government as one example of a spirit illustrated in manifold forms. Our Church is inflexible in nothing but in the pure Word and pure Sacraments, and in what they involve.

"Close Communion."

FIFTH: The relations of our Church to the denominations around us are not those of a *communion which is close*, in any sense in which God's Word enjoins that the communion shall be open. A Christian communion must in some sense be a close communion to be Christian at all—close from heresy, avowed and organized error; close from refusal to receive the gospel with a teachable spirit; close from those who reject the scriptural discipline and control of the Church. The first communion was close communion. None were admitted to it but tested disciples—open confessors of Christ. No leaders or members of hostile or contesting organizations were there. Judas was there, but Judas was a professor of discipleship; his profession was credible, his unworthiness unknown, except to the Searcher of hearts. It may be that our all-knowing Saviour would, in the very admission of Judas, teach us that we are to guide ourselves in discipline by what we know, and not by what we assume or conjecture the omniscient knows, whether of good or evil, in men.

In the Apostolic Church all confessed rejectors of the Apostolic doctrine—all heretics, schismatists and fomenters of faction, or those who were joined with them, were cut off from the communion of the Church. Heresy in the New Testament is whatever destroys the unity of the Church, and therefore by pre-eminence, false doctrine, which is its greatest divider. No Church received or retained communicants who were not subject to its discipline. As Apostolic pulpits were for Apostolic doctrine alone, so were Apostolic altars for those alone who were disciples of Apostolic doctrine, and subject to Apostolic discipline.

"Close Communion" in the Ancient Church.

The ancient Church of post-Apostolic times rigorously confined its pulpits and altars to those who were attested and approved as in the unity of the faith. "In the primitive Church," says Lord Chancellor

King, in his classical work, "the Unity of the Church Universal consisted in an Harmonious Assent to the Essential Articles of Religion, or in an Unanimous Agreement in the Fundamentals of Faith and Doctrine. The corruption of that doctrine was a breach of that unity, and whosoever so broke it, are said to divide and separate the unity of the Church, or which is all one, to be schismaticks. If we consider the word Church as denoting a collection of many particular churches, its unity may (be said to) have consisted in a brotherly correspondence with and affection toward each other, which they demonstrated by all outward expressions of Love and Concord, only receiving to Communion the members of each other."[8] The concession that two conflicting Christian churches can, with co-ordinate right and without the violation of fraternity, occupy the same locality, was simply impossible to the early Christian mind. The separation of admission to privilege and of subjection to discipline would have been looked upon with horror. The discipline was strict—and excommunication from one particular Church was confirmed all the world over. The inestimable right to communion in one Church involved a right to communion in all, on proper testing and authentication. The cutting off from a communion in one was a cutting off from all. No Christian traveling was admitted to communion in any Church in which he might be sojourning, unless he had written official evidence of his being in full communion with the Church at home. There could be no "interdenominational" communion, for there were no denominations. The ancient Church knew of nothing between the Church on the one side, and sect, schism, heresy on the other.[9] None were admitted to the Lord's Supper but those in full communion, and after the doors of the Church were carefully shut and watched, the deacon made a proclamation, describing the classes of persons who were not suffered to remain as communicants. These were the unbaptized, the catechumens, the ordinary hearers, unbelievers, and last of all, those of another faith, the heterodox, either reputed heretics or false teachers, separatists or those under discipline.

Christian Love.

SIXTH: The relations of the Lutheran Church to the denominations around it are *not* in conflict with true Christian *love*. On the

---

[8] Primitive Church, ch. ix.

[9] Baumgarten, Christlich. Alterthümer (Bertram). Halle, 1768, 506-513.

contrary they are in the highest harmony with it. She feels compelled indeed to contend for the truth, but it is in love. The wounds she gives are the faithful wounds of a friend. That is better than the deceitful kisses of an enemy. "Am I therefore become your enemy" says St. Paul, "because I tell you the truth?" "Have no fellowship with the unfruitful works of darkness, but rather reprove them." All error, heresy, schism, separatism, belong to the works of darkness Sectarianism is a work of darkness, though particular members of sects may be children of God.[10]

"Policy."

SEVENTH: The proper relations of the Lutheran Church to the denominations around us are not really *impolitic*, are not in conflict with her duty of self-preservation and of self-extension. Of a fleshly policy which courts worldly success by deviation from principle, I need not speak, because, a Christian man, I address Christian men. The presentation of an argument for such policy would be impossible to me, intolerable to you. Let such policy go. Whether it be the policy of the Devil or of Cæsar, and whether Cæsar be a single tyrant, or a mob of tyrants, let us stand with Christ against both Devil and Cæsar. There was but one apostle who pursued a policy by which he made earthly gain of his relation to Christ. Let us not stand with him.

In this aspect the case is too plain. Even the presentation of an argument against such policy would be worse than useless. But the policy consistent with true wisdom, and pure motive, high ends, and lofty means, and indeed the embodiment of them, is not in conflict with that attitude of our Church which, we have tried to show, consistency demands. When the Lutheran Church acts in the spirit of the current denominationalism she abandons her own spirit. She is a house divided against itself. Some even then will stand firm, and with the choosing of new gods on the part of others there will be war in the gates.

No seeming success could compensate our Church for the forsaking of the principles which gave her being, for the loss of internal peace, for the destruction of her proper dignity, for the lack of self-respect which would follow it. The Lutheran Church can never have real moral dignity, real self-respect, a real claim on the reverence and loyalty of her children, while she allows the fear of the de-

---

[10] See Theses on the Galesburg Declaration.

nominations around her, or the desire of their approval, in any respect to shape her principles or control her actions. It is a fatal thing to ask, not, What is right? What is consistent?—but, What will be thought of us? How will the sectarian and secular papers talk about us? How will our neighbors of the different communions regard this or that course? Better to die than to prolong a miserable life by such compromise of all that gives life its value. This dangerous tendency has been fostered by some parts of our Church accepting pecuniary aid from denominational sources. They have been taking bribes, and selling a sort of control to those whose charity they accepted. Then comes naturally the next Scene in the Farce—the benefactors are implored not to impute to the mild, liberal part of our Church (which accepts sectarian alms) what is really the spirit only of a few bigots unworthy of the name of Lutheran. We have among us a sort of charity which not only does not begin at home, but never gets there. It is soaring and gasping for the Unity of Lutherans with all the rest of the world, but not with each other. It can forgive all the sects for assailing the truth, but has no mercy for the Lutherans who defend it.

When there is official fellowship between those who hold the higher and positive position, and those who hold a lower and negative one, the communion is always to the benefit of the lower at the expense of the higher. For however the holders of the higher view may protest as to their personal convictions, the act of communion is regarded as a concession that the convictions, if held at all, are not held as articles of faith, but only as opinions. If a Socinian and a Trinitarian commune, each avowing his own opinion as not changed, nor involved, which cause is hurt and which benefited? It looks equal; but Socinianism, whose interest is laxity, is advantaged, Trinitarianism is wounded. It gives fresh life to error, it stabs truth to the heart.

Contact imparts disease, but does not impart health. We catch small-pox by contact with one who has it, but we do not catch recovery from one who is free from it. The process which tends to the pollution of the unpolluted will not tend to the purification of the evil. "If one bear *holy* flesh in the skirt of his garment, and with his skirt do touch bread or pottage, or wine or oil, or any meat, shall *it* be holy? And the priests answered and said, *No*. Then said Haggai, If one that is unclean by a dead body, *touch* any of them, shall it be *unclean?* And the priests answered, *It shall be unclean."*

When the transfer is made easy between *wealthy* denominations and poor ones, many go out of the poor church into the rich one, few from the rich to the poor. The Lord chooses the poor of this world; but many of his nominal disciples seem to think they can —so far at least—improve on their Master's example.

When the transfer is made easy between churches of great *social pretension* and those of humbler claims in the world of fashion, the people who are feeling after social recognition go into the fashionable church, the people of the fashionable church stay where they are.

When churches which have the *nationality,* language, tradition, modes of feeling and of acting, of a country, are separated by low walls from churches of other nationalities, largely using another tongue, having another culture, the churches of the country absorb those that are foreign. To introduce the language of the country into the foreign churches reaches but a part of the difficulty, and brings in another. For back of the language, to those to whom it is native, are the whole history, and life, and literature it embodies; while the foreign church must use the lip of one land for a soul and heart which are of another. Our Church may speak English. It is well. But if she stops with that, her new tongue will decoy her into a new life. All living tongues have living hearts back of them and carry us out into the current of their own life. Our church is not to become the handmaiden of the language, instead of making it her own handmaiden. It will in that case not be the old Church getting a new language, but the new language transforming her into a new Church—not the Church mastering the English, but the English mastering the Church. Even in their mistakes on the point of language, our fathers in America were not the absolute incapables it is now the fashion to consider them. It was the English life of the land, rather than the English tongue, which swept away thousands of our Church's children.

When churches whose principles involve lax doctrinal obligations come in contact with those whose principles involve strict doctrinal obligations, but whose practice is at war with their principles, the lax with the lax practice overcome the churches which have strict theory conjoined with lax practice. For such churches are burdened with the odium of their strict theory without its advantages, and get the weakness of laxity without sharing its popularity. Men who aim at combining in a third view the strong points of conflicting systems, generally get the weakness of principle from the wrong, and the unpopularity of practice from the right. They think they can sit on the two stools—in fact they fall between them.

But when a church has right principles and is steadfast to them, no matter what denominations are arrayed against it, it will have true success. It will be dear to God, precious to those who love Him, a safe guide of sinners to the Saviour, and will build up saints on their most holy faith. It will be a conservator of sound doctrine, of right government, of healthy discipline. It may not be fashionable, rich, or popular, but it will be a blessing to the world and a nursery for heaven.

Adjourned.

SECOND SESSION.

DECEMBER 27th, 2:30 P. M.

Prayer by President Sadtler, D. D., of Muhlenberg College.

The Diet proceeded to the discussion of Dr. Krauth's paper.

Rev. D. P. Rosenmiller (General Synod) said that the relation of the Lutheran Church to other denominations who hold the fundamental doctrines of the Gospel, should be one of kindness and charity. They are the different branches of the same family of the living God. The name Lutheran, applied to our Church, was an accident, resulting partly from its enemies. The original name was Evangelical; for it was no new organization, but the Church separated from the errors of the Papacy. Even the Augsburg Confession came into existence accidentally. Had there been no indictment brought by the Papal Court, against the friends of evangelical religion, there would have been no occasion for the Confession. In that case, the Bible would have been our only Confession. For the main point with Luther was to give the Church the Word of God as her guide; and hence all who hold it sincerely, without gross heterodoxy, should receive charity from us.

REMARKS OF REV. C. W. SCHAEFFER, D. D. (*General Council.*)

The relations of Lutherans to the members of the denominations around, as far as these relations are personal or social, ought to be kindly, and controlled by Christian principles. But when these relations enter into the sphere of the Church, and influence the Confession of Christian doctrine, then the first and highest aim of Lutherans should be to maintain the pure doctrine of the Word, as expressed in the Confessions.

The doctrine of the Sacraments comes up so often that I would if I could, avoid it now. But it affords such a good illustration of my meaning that I venture to introduce it.

The doctrine of the denominations around us is to the effect, that the chief element, the distinguishing characteristic of the Lord's Supper, is a mere human act, a devout exercise on the part of communicants, in which they bring to the table a grateful remembrance of Christ, and by eating and drinking show forth His death. If this, which of course is true, were the whole truth, then the Lutheran Church ought to, and without doubt, would, most heartily and devoutly, unite in the Holy Supper, with all evangelical denominations, with all who love the Lord; since in respect to a grateful remembrance of Christ and a devout showing forth of His death, there can be no difference between those who believe in Him and love Him.

But the Lutheran Church receives from the divine Word, and repeats in her Confessions, a very different doctrine, to the effect, that the Lord's Supper is first of all a divine act, that the Lord Himself is the chief actor, that its distinguishing characteristic consists of what the Lord gives us, and we only receive; that what He gives us is, as He Himself says, His body and His blood for the forgiveness of our sins, and that what He thus gives us in the bread and wine, is not given and cannot be received in any other place or time or way, than at the Supper of the Lord.

Now this is denied by the denominations around us. Some state their denial in one form, some in another. Yet though differing among themselves, they all agree in a decided and positive denial of the doctrine of the Lutheran Church.

Supposing then that the Lutheran Church is bound to maintain not human opinions, but what it accepts as the doctrine of the divine Word, how can Lutherans unite, in celebrating the Lord's Supper, with denominations that ignore and deny what the divine Word declares is the distinguishing feature and controlling element of the Supper itself? Such an act would be an acknowledgment, on their part, that the nature and the doctrine of the Holy Supper is a matter of no consequence, and that we reach the full measure of it when we observe it as a mere mnemonic act of our own. In declining such communion, Lutherans do not deny or question the evangelical character of denominations around them; they seek only to testify their fidelity to the doctrine of the Word.

These low views of the denominations, tend strongly, and quite naturally, to reduce the Holy Supper from its rightful prominence in the Church's life, down to the common level of ordinary devotional exercises. I find in a theological work of a distinguished divine, of illustrious name, occupying an honorable position in a prominent Seminary of the Presbyterian Church, the following conclusion arrived at:—"It follows that in the same sense in which it is done at the Lord's Supper, believers do receive and feed upon the body and the blood of Christ, at other times without the use of the sacrament, and in the use of other means of grace, as prayer, meditation on the Word, etc., etc." With such views, of course, the Lutheran Church can have no sympathy or fellowship.

REMARKS OF REV. F. W. CONRAD D. D. (*General Synod.*)

We shrink from engaging in this discussion in ten minutes, when six hours would be inadequate to do justice to it. We do not expect ever to be "educated up" to the positions taken in the paper just read. The degree of unanimity of sentiment which it requires, is practically unattainable. The multiform character of revelation, and the diverse influences under which Christians have been reared and lived, renders absolute agreement on all points impossible. To each believer, the Bible is given, and he is directed to search it—to every disciple of Christ, the Holy Spirit is promised, and he is permitted to pray for His enlightening influences. Through these and other agencies and instrumentalities, Christians form their religious opinions. But while true believers may and do thus come to an agreement on fundamental doctrines, they will, in all probability, differ on non-essential points. This occurs in spite of their sincerity, in consequence of the deterioration of the human reason. Their religious mistakes must not, therefore, be regarded as willful errors, neither should they, on this account, be classed with heretics and excluded from Church fellowship.

Martin Luther maintained the supreme authority of the Scriptures, and claimed the right of private judgment in interpreting them. He, accordingly, exercised the liberty conferred by Christ on every believer, and formed his religious opinions in independence of popes and councils. His coadjutors exercised the same right, and formed their own religious opinions. On all essential points they agreed; on many non-essential ones they differed; and yet they extended the hand of fellowship to each other.

In the exercise of the same rights and the enjoyment of the same liberty, we, Lutherans in America, have formed our ecclesiastical opinions. On all undisputed fundamental doctrines we agree; on manifestly non-fundamental ones we differ. Let us not, on account of our differences, withhold, but on account of our agreements, extend fellowship to each other.

Various denominations have arisen, in the providence of God, in different ages and lands. They constitute the pure parts of the one holy catholic Church. They are entitled to the prerogatives of true churches of Christ, because they adopt the Œcumenical creeds, and they do not become heretics, unworthy of pulpit and altar fellowship, because their particular creeds differ in some points from ours. While, therefore, we can accept the positions taken by Dr. Krauth on Fellowship as a rule, we cannot accept his exclusive interpretation of it. We, on the contrary, hold that it is right and proper to grant pulpit and altar fellowship to the ministers and members of orthodox Protestant churches, in exceptional cases, as a matter, not of right, but of privilege, and maintain that the extension of such fellowship is sustained by Christ's instructions, by apostolic example, by the practice of the primitive Church, and by the general judgment of the Christian world.

REMARKS OF REV. J. A. BROWN, D. D. (*General Synod.*)

I would not say anything on the paper read, did I not fear that my silence might be misconstrued into an endorsement of all that it contains. Whilst there is much with which I might agree, it contains assumptions and looks to conclusions to which I can by no means yield my assent. By the very terms employed—though not in the subject as originally published—"*the denominations around us,*" omitting "*other,*" it is assumed that the Lutheran Church has claims as a Church of Jesus Christ, which cannot be accorded to these denominations. To set up such a claim, it seems to me, is to ignore God's providential dealings with His Church, and also to refuse to recognize the manifest tokens of His presence and favor. Might not God choose to reform the Church and restore the pure Gospel and ordinances, without necessarily employing the same human instruments, or giving to the work precisely the same form in every respect? As He chose Luther and his co-laborers in Germany, may He not have chosen other instruments in England, Scotland and elsewhere? and what right have we to sit in judgment on His and their work? Have we a right to say that other denominations (I use the word "other") are not part of the true Church of Jesus Christ, and to be treated by us as such?

It is not, and will not be, denied that in these other denominations, there are thousands and tens of thousands of humble, devoted believers. It is not, and will not be, denied that these denominations have furnished a full share of distinguished scholars and theologians, of self-denying pastors and missionaries, and of zealous and devoted laborers in every department of Christian activity. They, sometimes put us to shame by their enlightened liberality and zeal in the cause of our divine Redeemer. In this country especially they have taken the lead and outstripped us, in the work of preaching the Gospel to the millions at home and abroad.

Now I cannot see by what right, or on what ground we can refuse the fullest recognition to these denominations that are so manifestly owned of God, and whose labors are crowned with so much favor. If these Churches are true Evangelical Churches, and their members are true members of the body of Christ, who are we that we should undertake to legislate and prescribe the terms on which we will recognize those whom the Master owns, or set up arbitrary conditions of relationship among the Churches of Jesus Christ?

There is something utterly incongruous and unscriptural in a true disciple of Christ, an acknowledged subject of Christ's kingdom, with the genuine *"marks of the Lord Jesus,"* being denied his rights and privileges in that kingdom. In the Apostolic Church a Christian was a Christian, and a subject of Christ's kingdom was recognized wherever he went among his fellow Christians. Even citizenship in the Roman empire carried with it all the rights and immunities of citizenship, wherever the Roman empire extended its domain or asserted its authority. The simple utterance, "I am a Roman citizen," was enough to claim protection in the most sacred rights. Wherever the tread of the Roman legion was heard, or the banner bearing the Roman eagle floated, there were secured the rights of Roman citizens. The kingdom of Christ is more widely extended, and offers to its subjects privileges superior to those of imperial Rome. This kingdom is marked by no geographical boundaries; it is confined to no country or clime or race; in it "there is neither Jew nor Greek, there is neither bond nor free, there is neither male nor female : for ye are all one in Christ Jesus." Can it be that subjects of this kingdom, whose dominion is from sea to sea, and from the river to the ends of the earth, have a more restricted exercise of their rights than the subjects of the smallest and most petty earthly power? Must a Lutheran Christian be acknowledged only among Lutherans, and Reformed only among Reformed, and so this universal kingdom of Christ be dwarfed or divided until only those are recognized who belong to our own particular party or section? Shall we as Lutherans set up the absurd claim of being the peculiar chosen people, and treat the [other] denominations around us as aliens?

I am not concerned just now with the question of responsibility for the divisions in the Christian Church. They exist as a matter of fact. They have existed for centuries. The great Head of the Church has not refused to acknowledge these different Churches or to bestow upon them His benediction. True, He has prayed that all might be one. And so has He prayed and taught us to pray,—"*Thy kingdom come.*" Shall we refuse full recognition to other denominations because not in all respects one with us, or deny His kingdom because it does not yet come in full power and glory?

It seems to me unfortunate that the discussion on this subject has taken so one-sided a turn, and that it has been mainly the discussion of "*pulpit and altar fellowship.*" Indeed, it is narrowed down very much to the question of altar fellowship, or allowing others to commune with Lutherans, or Lutherans extending the Sacrament of the Lord's Supper to those of other denominations. This is not the time nor the place for a full discussion of this subject. Individual congregations or denominations may adopt such regulations not inconsistent with the letter or spirit of the New Testament, as they may deem best calculated to secure the purity and promote the welfare of the Church. But they should be very careful not to exercise a right, with which their Lord has never invested them. The Apostle Peter has set us a good example in this respect, and announced a principle which may aid in settling a point which seems to sorely vex some. Averse as he was to recognizing any except Jews as properly belonging to the Church, when he saw what the Lord was doing, he said: "*Can any man forbid water, that these should not be baptized, which have received the Holy Ghost as well as we?*" If the Holy Ghost is bestowed on others as well as on us, if they give proof of the presence and grace of the Spirit, as well as we, who can forbid to them the use of the Sacraments? There is no authority in God's Word for this wide separation between what God has joined together in this Church—the Sacraments of Baptism and the Lord's Supper—and throwing the one so widely open, that almost any baptism is recognized, Romish or Protestant, clerical or lay, and then hedging about the table of the Lord so that none but a Lutheran may approach a Lutheran altar. Against this spirit of exclusivism, we ask, in the language of Peter, "*Can any man forbid water?*"—or can any man forbid the administration of the Sacraments to those who "*have received the Holy Ghost as well as we?*"

Against the exclusivism of this paper, as well as against the sectarianism of this age, we must express our most decided objection.

The discussion was participated in also by Revs. L. E Albert, D D., F. Klinefelter and S. R. Boyer. Their remarks have not been furnished for publication. The discussion was closed as follows:

REMARKS OF REV. C. P. KRAUTH, D. D. LL. D. (*General Council.*)

In the theme accepted by me, as stated to me—and properly stated—the Lutheran Church is not coördinated as one denomination with others. Her moral right to live turns upon the proof that she is a Church with the New Testament essentials—doctrine pure in every part, and right sacraments. Those who cut her off from them, or cut themselves off from her fellowship, and erect their hostile denominations, either reject the truths she holds, and in rejecting truth are heretics or errorists, or if they concede that our Church holds the divine system, are schismatics in continuing in voluntary sundering from her.

If you once say sectarianism is venal, sects are good because there are good people in sects, where will you stop? What lovely people there are in the Church of Rome; what characters of exquisite beauty, to all human observation, there are among Socinians; what pathos of sweetness strikes us at times, even amid Paganism! The great world has men and women who put to shame false, or careless, or conventional, Christians. Is slavery to be compromised with because some of the best of men have held slaves? Could we as patriots officially recognize, because of their private excellencies, citizens of a government at war with ours? We recognize as cordially as any man, the personal virtues and achievements of Christians everywhere; but if they feel bound in conscience to confess adversely to our Confession, to keep up denominations to build up that Confession, to withhold themselves from permanent communion with us; and to guard their pulpits against the constant preaching of the whole New Testament doctrine,—which is the doctrine of our Church—then do they bind us, on their own showing, to confine our pulpit to those who constantly preach what we are sure is the whole truth, and our altars to those who are the disciples, imperfect it may be, but willing, of that truth. We have common terms for all, and if we relinquish a system of tests and safeguards for others, we must relinquish them for ourselves.

This style of reasoning defies the universal judgment of historical Christendom, which with unbroken unanimity maintains that unity in confessed doctrine is an essential element of Church unity. For this we are asked to substitute a unity of good people, or people we conjecture to be good, without reference to their faith. It is the compendious method of the poet—

"He can't be wrong, whose life is in the right."

Throughout the argument we are meeting, there runs the fallacy of confounding the Church as invisible, with the Church as visible. Who form the Church invisible it is for Him, who alone sees the invisible, infallibly to judge. In the Church visible, we must have not wavering and individual surmises, but carefully considered and uniform principles of test and discipline, resting on what we can see and know. External profession of the pure faith, made credible by the acts of men, is the only test to which we can bring the claim of internal possession of it. The eloquent description of the Roman Empire has no applicability to the visible Church militant, either as it is in fact, or in the divine description of its state on earth. In the mouth of a Romanist, it would have consistency: in the mouth of a Protestant it has none. The Roman Kingdom was a kingdom which imposed the cross; the Kingdom of Christ is a kingdom which bears the cross, and will bear it till her King comes again. Yet even a Romanist would hardly fall into the confusion of the dead and the living, the nominal and the real, which gives plausibility to the illustration. The utterance, "I am a Roman citizen," made indeed a *claim* to Roman rights; but the rights were not conceded till the claim was tested by modes of uniform principle. Roman privilege were bound up with subjection to Roman law, fealty to Roman rules, and fidelity to Roman duty. What we are discussing is the privileges of *Lutheran* pulpits and of *Lutheran* altars. If it is sectarian to have these we should abandon them; but if it is sectarian to have others, the others should be abandoned. The Saviour and His Apostles, and the early Church, knew of but one communion. All outside of that was sect or schism. Christendom should be one communion with one faith, and one confession—its faith the faith of the Gospel—its confession the unmixed witness of that faith. This is the faith we believe our Church has. This is the faith she embodies in her Confession. This position allows of no compromise. If it is false we must abandon it, and let our Church go. If it is true we must stand by it, and all who wish fellowship with us, must come to it. This is no egotism of Church vanity; it is consistency with principle.

It is no fault of ours that others have thrown forth sectarian banners. We did not go out from them. They have gone away from us, or have followed those who abandoned us. Dr. Brown claims for them the right to forsake us, to repudiate our distinctive faith, and yet to have untested all the privileges of our own faithful children. He proposes to accept their claim as their proof—yet if their claim to be right is valid, ours cannot be. Contradictions cannot both be right.

It is surprising, too, that he fails to see that in all the points here involved there is no parallel whatever between baptism and the Lord's Supper, to say nothing of the pulpit. The adult seeker of baptism from us is not a member of another communion. The child who seeks it through the parents is not of another church-household. Does any one pretend that the tests of fitness for baptism are throughout identical with those of fitness for the Supper; or will any one say that consistency requires that we grant that every one whose baptism we acknowledge as valid, is thereby shown to be entitled to come to our communion?

When a protest is made at the close against sectarianism, the whole line of previous thought seems to imply that what is meant is not the sectarianism which makes sects, magnifies their virtues, veils their mischiefs, ignores their crimes, and treats the divisions they create as if they were not destructive of unity. It rather seems as if the sectarianism which the speaker had in view is the fidelity to principle which resists sects, and the sect-spirit, most of all when they come in the pretences of a spurious unionism, and shuts upon them the pulpit and altar. In such a construction of sectarianism the relations of our Lutheran communion to the denominations around us would be, not the relations of a Church to sects, but of a sect to Churches.

The following paper was then read:

"THE FOUR GENERAL BODIES OF THE LUTHERAN CHURCH IN THE UNITED STATES: WHEREIN THEY AGREE, AND WHEREIN THEY MIGHT HARMONIOUSLY CO-OPERATE."

REV. J. A. BROWN, D. D.,

Professor of Doctrinal Theology in the Theological Seminary of the General Synod, Gettysburg, Pa.

The "*four Bodies*" referred to are "*The General Synod of the Evangelical Lutheran Church in the United States;*" "*The General Synod of the Evangelical Lutheran Church in North America;*" "*The General Council of the Evangelical Lutheran Church in North America;*" and "*The Synodical Conference of North America.*"

THESE are separate and distinct bodies of Lutherans at present, some of them once united and still holding much in common, yet differing so far as to maintain each its own organization and individual existence. Their separations are in part the result of local and temporary circumstances, and in part of deeper lying causes. Each one has a history of its own, and each is now aiming to work out its own mission. Between some of them there may be a greater affinity than between others, yet among them all are family likenesses and strong points of sympathy and resemblance. Some of them may possibly be so little acquainted with each other, and others so unhappily alienated, as not to care to trace the resemblance or to acknowledge the relationship, but the truth will reveal itself, and even their speech bewrayeth them. All these Lutherans talk Lutheran, and sometimes indulge in what seems to outsiders a little like boasting over the great Lutheran Church, to which they claim to belong, and of which they are quite willing to be considered a part.

The subject for our discussion is one concerning which there will very naturally be great diversity of sentiment; and no treatment of it or conclusions reached, will likely prove satisfactory to all or probably to even a majority of those present. The very fact of the existence of four such bodies, implies differences of some kind, and the question, "*Wherein they agree,*" implies points in which they disagree; and so the other question: "*Wherein they might harmoniously co-operate,*" implies difficulties in the way, or some things in which they are not able thus to co-operate. That such has been and still continues the case, all very well know. We do not at present harmoniously co-operate.

But we are not now to search after the points of difference, or to see how much ground we can find for our separations. Our differences have, no doubt, been magnified enough, so as to make our separation wider than need be—even wider than between us and those who do not bear the same family name. We are now to look after some of the points of agreement, and, I suppose, to see whether, after all our bickerings and separations, we do not all belong to the same "household of faith," and whether we might not live together in unity and peace, and "*stand fast in one spirit, with one mind, striving together for the faith of the Gospel.*"

Agreement between individuals and Churches in religious matters is relative and not absolute; and it may be well to bear this in mind during this discussion. As God has made no two faces absolutely the same, nor any two souls absolutely alike, though all in His image and likeness, so no two Churches are absolutely alike, and no two members of any one of these four bodies are in perfect accord in thought, sentiment, feeling, purpose and action. It is not necessary nor desirable that it should be so. There may be absolute uniformity or sameness in dead particles of matter, but genuine life is infinitely diversified. All that can be expected or desired is substantial agreement, or such an agreement as will secure harmony of views, feeling and co-operation—according to the divine Word, "*Keeping the unity of the Spirit in the bonds of peace.*" When the apostle exhorts the Corinthians to "*be perfectly joined together in the same mind and in the same judgment,*" he does not mean, as the words in the original do not, that they must all believe, and think and feel precisely alike—which would be practically impossible—but that there should be no such differences as would cause divisions and strife among them. It was a party spirit that he warned them against. If any are disposed to look for absolute agreement between all or any two of these bodies, as a condition of co-operation, they will look for what they will not find within any one of them, and for what they will search in vain anywhere in the Church on earth. Each of these four bodies, if candid, will admit that it is not free from very considerable diversity of views on various points, even of doctrine, and that some of the meetings of these bodies are not the most harmonious, nor the co-operation the most cordial. We are simply stating what every one knows, and it is one of the commonplaces of Church history, that ecclesiastical bodies are not always distinguished for harmony of views and action. They are chasing a phantom, who expect to find this ideal of unity and agreement here on earth, which belongs only to a state of perfection in heaven.

Using the term "agree" in its popular and also in its Scriptural sense, we may find many points *"wherein these four bodies agree,"* some of them of more significance than others, but none of them entirely destitute of meaning and force. To a disinterested observer we have no doubt that these points are such as to make our disagreements appear strange, if not worse than strange.

I. POINTS WHEREIN THEY AGREE.

In calling your attention to some of the points, "wherein they agree," we begin with:

1. *A common name*—LUTHERAN. There is something in a name, little as we are disposed to make of it. A name is used to express some quality or property of an object. We recognize and distinguish other Churches to some extent by their names. Presbyterian, Episcopal, Methodist, Baptist, express severally distinct denominations, and types of our Protestant Christianity. The name Lutheran serves the same general purpose. At first, the name was not a matter of preference or voluntary choice, but applied as a term of reproach; yet, like the name Christian, having been applied by enemies it was accepted, and no part of the Lutheran Church would now hastily abandon its use. We are not, as some imagine, followers of Martin Luther, but we are not unwilling to bear the name of that chosen instrument of God to restore to His Church doctrines which we hold dearer than all human names. We are Evangelical Lutherans, because we accept the Gospel which Luther rescued from Romish perversions and abuses. There have been and still are other discriminating and qualifying appellations along with Lutheran, some of them at times used to express invidious distinctions. Thus we have had German Lutheran, Swedish Lutheran, English Lutheran,

American Lutheran, Missouri Lutheran, and divers other kinds, but all bearing the generic name, Lutheran.

As no one of these four bodies is inclined to abandon the name, so no one intends to allow any other a monopoly of its use or honors. Some, indeed, may regard themselves as more Lutheran than others, and better entitled to wear the ancestral name, but this is a matter open to discussion. Some may be less Lutheran than Luther was, and others may be more Lutheran than the reformer himself. The divergencies in this respect may indeed be considerable, and may vary with the same body at different times. There may be as much difference in the same body at different periods in its existence, as between two of these bodies at the same time, but still they do not surrender the title. In a family one son may be more like the father than another, but this does not deprive either of the right to wear the family name. And it not unfrequently happens that the likeness reappears most striking in a succeeding generation, where it had been least apparent in a former one. So it has happened again and again with Churches, which have still held on to the old family name. These bodies all mean to be known and recognized as Lutheran.

The absurdity of any one of these bodies attempting to set up an exclusive right to the use of the name Lutheran is manifest from the fact, that no two of them would agree as to who should have the right to wear it. It must be admitted that if not Lutherans, then we are nothing at all: for none of us are Baptists, or Methodists, or Presbyterians, or Episcopalians, much less Romanists, or Rationalists—and surely we are somebody. If not Lutherans, it is time we should know what we are, and that the world should know. We are called Lutherans. We *are* Lutherans—all Lutherans, bearing the name, and entitled to bear it. If any are disposed to dispute this point, or challenge the right of any one of these bodies to the Lutheran name, it may be added, that so far as the highest civil authorities can determine the point, they have decided that we shall be acknowledged and held in law as Lutherans, and entitled to the rights and privileges of Lutherans.

2. *A common origin or descent.* There is something in blood as well as in a name. Religion and Churches have been largely affected in their character by nationality or race. It is true that God " made of one blood all nations of men for to dwell on all the face

of the earth;" but it is also true that He has made use of them in different ways and for different purposes in accomplishing His own most holy will. This principle showed itself in the times of the Apostles, between the Jewish and Gentile portions of the Church; and soon afterwards between the Eastern and Western Churches. Each had its special origin and mission.

At the time of the Reformation some nationalities took more kindly to one form of Protestantism, and some to another. Luther himself was a German, not only by birth, but in soul and spirit, in heart and life, and his magnetic influence is felt among Germans and their descendants to the present day. And this extended itself to those peoples or nationalities most intimately connected by blood and language with the Germans. On the other hand, Scotland, Ireland, and England did not take so kindly to Lutheranism as did the Germans and some other nationalities. They accepted what is generally known as the Reformed faith, and they continue in that faith. These different phases of Protestantism have perpetuated themselves through these several nationalities from the Reformation to our own times. The prophet asks: "*Hath a nation changed their gods?*" It is no small or easy thing for a people to change its religion, even where the change is only from one type of Protestantism to another. History records but few examples of a people or nation changing one form or type of a religion for another, even when these were closely allied, unless under some powerful movement, or by special divine interposition.

Some may indeed hold that Lutheranism is Christianity, pure and unmixed, that any departure from it is a departure from true religion, and that it is adapted to all nations, ages and climes. They may hold that all other forms of Protestantism are less pure, and that we should refuse to recognize other denominations as entitled to a like claim with ourselves to be parts of the true Church of Jesus Christ. It may be argued that as genuine Christianity, Lutheranism is bound to triumph everywhere. But still the stubborn fact remains, that our progress has been chiefly among the descendants of those who originally accepted the Lutheran form of the Reformation, and that we are making slow progress among those who from the beginning have accepted and practiced a somewhat different form of Protestantism. If it indeed be true that Lutheranism is Christianity and Christianity Lutheranism, then there is a poor showing for

Christianity throughout a considerable part of the Protestant world, including the larger part of our own professed Christian population, with nearly all our large cities and centres of Christian activity. It must be confessed that our chief progress thus far has been among those who claim a Lutheran ancestry; and, whilst neither our labors nor our success should be limited to these, they have on us peculiar claims, and we have in them a fruitful field of labor. It might almost be said to require some mixture of German blood to make full-blooded Lutherans.

These four bodies can claim a common origin or ancestry. Some of them may be a little further removed from their original tongue and characteristics than others, but all have something to say of the *vaterland* and the *mutter-sprache*. It is in the memory of those now living, when those portions of the Church at present most English in speech and customs, knew scarcely anything but German; and in all of these bodies the great mass of the membership is either from the home of Lutheranism in the old world, or from their descendants in the new. In their veins there flows the same blood, and they have not only a common name, but are brethren according to the flesh. Alas, that difference of language or shades of belief, or diversities of any kind should have to any degree alienated those who are kindred of one family.

3. *The acceptance of the Augsburg Confession.* This Confession is the oldest of modern Confessions. It is older than the decrees of the Council of Trent, or the Tridentine Catechism—the Confession of the Catholic Church. It is older than the Orthodox Confession of the Greek Church. It justly claims a greater antiquity than any other Confession of any of the separate parts of Christendom. It moreover furnishes the basis of most of the other Confessions set forth by other Protestant denominations. It is indeed a grand old Confession, and any attempt to eulogize it would be as presumptuous as it would be unnecessary.

The reception and profession of this Confession has for more than three hundred years been the acknowledged passport of genuine Lutheranism. Wherever the Lutheran Church has confessed her faith, in any quarter of the globe, she has done it by means of the Augsburg Confession. To this Confession, because of its evangelical character, no less than because of its historical renown, the Church clings as one of her chiefest glories.

In its reception and profession all these bodies are agreed. There may be and there is some difference in the terms in which this Confession is subscribed. Different forms of subscription have existed from the very beginning of Lutheranism. They have been common in the old world as well as in the new. No particular form of subscription has been established as essential to genuine Lutheranism. Whilst some have hesitated to adopt a form of subscription that binds to every jot and tittle of the Confession, others have not hesitated to go beyond the Confession, and bind to what is not required by its letter or spirit. It is easy to make charges of un-Lutheran and hyper-Lutheran ways, but in such a controversy it is not so easy to convince each other of error.

If the question were asked of any one of these bodies : *What is your Confession of Faith?* the answer would be—the Augsburg Confession. If the additional question were asked—Nothing more, nothing less than this? there would doubtless be explanations to be offered, and some differences of sentiment discovered, just as there would be in regard to the Apostles' Creed. But the fact still remains, that all agree in receiving and professing this venerable Confession. Moreover each body would doubtless be ready to defend its mode of receiving the Confession as the most consistent and most truly Lutheran. All that we deem important just now, and this we do deem important in this discussion is, that all agree in the one point of making the Augsburg Confession their Confession of Faith.

Time will not allow us to consider particular doctrines, but one or two have always been held by the Lutheran Church as so fundamental to evangelical religion, and so broadly distinguishing the Lutheran from the Roman Catholic and from all Romanizing tendencies, that they may be briefly noticed.

(1) *The doctrine of Justification by Faith.* It may be imagined that this doctrine is so common to all Protestant Churches, that it is folly to mention it as characterizing these bodies of Lutherans. But we claim that no other denomination has made it so prominent in its doctrinal system, and none have adhered to it with such uncompromising strictness. Other denominations have magnified some denominational peculiarity, so that they are chiefly known by such marks, but the Lutheran Church has kept central and most vital in her system this great doctrine of the Reformation.

And this is true, we believe, to-day of all these bodies of Lutherans. It provokes a smile to hear the question from some other denominations—as it has been heard—"*Do these Lutherans really believe in the doctrine of justification by faith?*" It might as well be asked, had Martin Luther really the courage to fight the pope and the devil? Only ignorance could prompt either of these questions.

Amid all the diversities in forms and ceremonies of Church polity and ecclesiastical regulations, there is agreement among us in holding fast to the doctrine on which the Reformation hinged, the doctrine transcending all others in importance to the salvation of souls and the purity of the Church—the doctrine for which the Reformers hazarded everything—salvation by faith in Jesus Christ alone. It would betray an ignorance or prejudice provoking in others, but inexcusable in Lutherans, to question that any one of these bodies does maintain this common article of the Lutheran faith.

(2) *The priesthood of believers, and yet the divinely instituted office of the ministry.* No righteousness before God but that of Christ, and no other priesthood than His, are twin doctrines. On the latter of these the Reformers insisted no less than on the former. The denial of these constituted the grand error of the papacy. So long as the doctrine of human merit and a human priesthood stands, there is a foundation for all the corruptions and abominations of the Romish Church. Remove these and the system must fall.

But this leaves full room for the office of the Christian ministry—an office divinely instituted—to preach the Word and administer the Sacraments. This office is not the mere creature of the general body of believers, created or changed or abolished at its pleasure, but exists by divine appointment, and is a necessary part of the divine economy for the establishment, perpetuity and extension of the Church of Christ on earth.

In this general doctrine all Lutherans agree. There has been no little controversy in the Church on the subject of the ministry, and not a little diversity in practices that to the superficial observer might seem to indicate the widest difference of views. In some places and in some congregations there has been an amount of form and ceremony, a degree of ritualistic observances, that would satisfy the highest of high Churchmen, even of the Anglican or Romish order; whilst in others there has been a Puritanic plainness even to baldness, that might gratify the lovers of " meeting-houses." But amid this diversity of outward forms and ceremonies, from the lowest to the highest style of Church order, there has been a substantial agreement in rejecting every Romish idea of the ministry as a priesthood, and holding fast to the New Testament idea of the Christian ministry. No Church has been more free from Romanizing tendencies, or furnished fewer recruits to the Church of Rome than the Evangelical Lutheran Church. In this it may be safely said that all these bodies agree. They are all Lutheran, and they are all Evangelical Lutheran.

4. *The religious training of the young by means of catechetical instruction, and the ratification of their covenant relation with the Church by confirmation.* Luther's Catechism and Luther's practice of catechetical instruction are still prominent features of Lutheranism. There have been times in the history of the Church, in the old world as well as in the new, when this system of religious training was well nigh abandoned. New methods have been tried, and not by one part of the Church alone. There have been times when the ancient practice of confirmation was a "new measure" in the Lutheran Church, and that in the early home of Lutheranism. Neither Rationalism nor Radicalism is answerable for all the strange fire that has been kindred on Lutheran altars.

But there is a growing conviction in favor of the good old ways, not to the exclusion, however, of the wisdom to be gathered from observation and experience under the teaching of the divine Word and the guidance of the Holy Spirit. The old is not to be cherished simply because it is old, nor the new to be rejected simply because it is new.

In all of these bodies, so far as we know, there is agreement in the importance and value of catechetical instruction, and of a careful indoctrination of the young and the old in the great truths of our most holy faith. Some may be more zealous and faithful in this duty than others, but all agree in the general practice.

On this part of our subject, we only add:

5. *The Lutheran love of liberty and agreement in diversity.* If there were nothing else "wherein they agree," they surely agree in this—that the largest liberty is claimed and practiced, and that great diversity prevails among the Churches in all of these bodies. As a rule no two churches, even in the same place, have precisely the same service. They all have manuals of worship, and to a certain extent the churches conform to the recommendations of their respect-

ive bodies; but they also have an invincible love of liberty, so characteristic of Lutherans and Germans, and refuse to be fettered by ecclesiastical regulations.

For this good Lutheran authority might be cited. At the very outset the Reformers declared that in order " to the true unity of the Church, it is not necessary that human traditions, rites or ceremonies instituted by men, should be everywhere alike," and even the Form of Concord, prepared in the interests of the strictest Lutheranism, teaches that "no Church should condemn another because one observes more or less than the other of those outward ceremonies which God has not commanded."

If in anything Lutherans have always and everywhere manifested their adherence to the teaching of the Symbolical Books, it has been in this particular. On opposite sides of the same street, and in the same city or town, they are found using different forms of service, and worshiping in the beauty of almost infinite diversity. This is true, we are informed, in Europe, as we all know it to be in this country. It may be regarded as characteristic of Lutheranism.

In this these four bodies agree. They differ among themselves as well as from each other, but they agree in this endless diversity. In the matter of wearing the gown, the use of a liturgy, the extent of liturgical services, the variations in the services on different occasions, the administration of ordinances—the use of the wafer or bread, etc., etc., almost every congregation is a law unto itself. And no one can well condemn another, seeing they all claim the same law of liberty. It may be well for us all to remember the words of the apostle: "*Happy is he that condemneth not himself in that thing which he alloweth.*"

We have now briefly noticed a few of the points wherein these four bodies agree. Others might be mentioned, and these dwelt upon at greater length, but a due regard to the time allowed and to the patience of our hearers, forbids a more extended discussion. Besides, it is quite sufficient to indicate, without enlargement, such points of agreement as may serve to furnish a comprehensive and intelligent judgment on the subject.

If I have passed by the points of difference, or made no account of them, it will be understood that it is just because this is no part of the task assigned me, and I leave to others this duty. There may possibly be opportunities enough during the meetings of this

Diet to show wherein we differ, and to make manifest some points of disagreement. It would be altogether gratuitous for me to anticipate what others will have, if they choose, a better right to say and show.

II. "WHEREIN THEY MIGHT HARMONIOUSLY CO-OPERATE."

It is not likely that those who arranged the programme for this Diet, and in their selections assigned me this subject for discussion, had any special reference to our comfort, but it is a matter of some relief as well as satisfaction, that it has been put in the very form it is. Had the wording been, "Wherein *can* they harmoniously co-operate," judging from past experience and present aspects, the answer would be, in nothing save possibly in holding such a free Diet, in which no one is responsible for anybody but himself, and that responsibility understood to be of a somewhat general character. Even the holding of a Diet has been ridiculed by some as visionary, and opposed by others as likely to result in all manner of evils to the Lutheran Church, and the serious detriment of those who participate in it. Perhaps few have been without grave suspicions as to the result.

We must be frank enough to say that with these different organizations existing as they are, with all the machinery necessary to their separate and distinct work, we do not see how they *can* harmoniously co-operate, if this means uniting energies and efforts in joint labors. If it means, as we suppose it does, something more than amicable relations, and non-interference with each other's interests, then co-ooperation seems to us difficult if not impossible, without the surrender of principles which some or all of these bodies profess to hold of vital importance, and to which in some degree they owe their separate existence. But we are not asked to consider "Wherein they *can* harmoniously co-operate," but "wherein they might." What we *can* do in certain circumstances, and what we *might* do with these circumstances largely at our control, are very different questions.

Nor are we required or expected to turn prophet, and forecast the future, telling how in the good time to come all divisions will be healed, all differences forgotten, and we present the picture of a perfectly united and harmonious Church. This may be left to those whose "bright visions" extend to the dim future, and who can see farther and clearer than common mortals. Such a time we may not only hope will come, but we might all fervently pray, Even so, let it come quickly.

But we are now to consider "*wherein these four bodies might harmoniously co-operate.*" This leads us to look at the reasonable probabilities of the case. Not what they *can* do, just now and as they are; nor what they some day may or will do, but what they *might* do. This implies a change or modification of their policy and action in some respects, and implies that this is a thing of possible accomplishment. It does not, however, imply the abandonment of these several distinct organizations. Indeed, the very contrary is implied in the question, for it is how these bodies as separate bodies might thus co-operate. But it does imply the abandonment, to some extent at least, of separate and rival interests, and that these interests should be pursued in common and harmoniously by all these bodies. It does imply, we think, a mutual recognition of each other as Lutheran bodies, and a willingness to labor together in the service of a common Lord and Master. It would seem like sheer folly to talk of harmonious co-operation, and yet hesitate to recognize each other's character and labors as true and genuine Lutherans.

And such a recognition might take place. The stern logic of events will probably sooner or later compel it. Churches as well as individuals are sometimes constrained to yield to enlightened public sentiment and the ongoings of Divine Providence. The deepest prejudices and the bitterest animosities have melted away under the softening influences of time, and the subduing power of the Spirit of God. Paul and Barnabas once separated, and after a "sharp contention," but we have good reason to believe that they became reconciled, and harmoniously co-operated in the cause of their Redeemer. Such things have often occurred in the history of the Church, and may occur again. What thus often occurs in the Church *might* take place even in the Lutheran Church, and among these four bodies. They might be led to see that it was their duty and interest to cease contending with one another, and in one spirit, with one mind, strive together for the faith of the Gospel!

Viewing this subject, then, in this light, as to what they *might* do in the direction indicated, instead of saying, "in nothing," we would rather incline to say they might co-operate in everything. We see nothing "wherein" they might not co-operate—nothing of a general character and pertaining to the general welfare of the Church. They might co-operate in the preaching of the Gospel, in the building of churches and the support of the ministry, in the work of Home and Foreign Missions, in Publication, in the establishment and support of Literary and Theological Institutions, in a word, in all the great work of the Church.

Impracticable, utterly impracticable, perhaps it will be said, is such an idea. "*Can two walk together except they be agreed?*" Have we not heard this repeated a thousand times, and have we not found it to be true? Well, it may be impracticable. It may be that Lutherans are not yet cured of their folly, and cannot or will not co-operate. But remember, we are not considering what *can* be done with all our impracticabilities, but what *might* be done, if we were willing and disposed to do it.

Perhaps it is expected that I should specify the particular departments of labor, in which they might co operate—name the general interests, or mark out the common ground, where they might meet, forgetting differences, and unite in the common cause. It is no doubt imagined by some that it would be much easier to co-operate in some things than in others, and that a beginning thus made would gradually result in a more general co-operation. But I do not see where to draw this line. Some, perhaps many, would say, in the work of Foreign Missions at least. There, it may be said, if nowhere else, we should forget our differences in laboring for the salvation of the heathen. This may be on the principle that the field of labor is so distant that the angle of vision cast by our differences vanishes before it reaches the place; or possibly because our efforts in behalf of Foreign Missions have been so lamentably small, that it is not deemed worth while to contend with one another. But if we might co-operate in the work of Foreign Missions, why not in that of Home Missions, of Education, of Church Extension, and of all general Church work? Substantially the same difficulties meet us at every point, and what we *might* do in one we might about as well do in all.

We do not mean, however, that there could not be a practical co-operation in some things without a co-operation in all. For instance, we might agree to co-operate in the work of *Missions*, without abandoning our separate educational or publication interests; or the very reverse, we might agree to co-operate in establishing a great *Lutheran University*, after the fashion of some in the old world, where different denominations even are represented, and yet maintain our separate interests in Missions and other objects. If we must co-operate only in part, and religiously cherish a horror of too much unionism even among Lutherans, then the particular part must be a matter of individual preference or voluntary choice.

That such reasonable co-operation *might* take place, if the parties so desired, or that such a thing is not utterly impracticable, a few considerations will be offered to show.

The differences existing between these four bodies are not really greater than those which have existed in other churches, or between denominations, where such co-operation was practically maintained. In the Episcopal Church there exists to-day as wide a diversity in faith and feeling as prevails among these four bodies of Lutherans, and yet there is co-operation, if not always so harmonious, yet quite earnest and efficient. Except when they elect a bishop, or some other matter where party spirit displays itself, they merge their differences in the common cause. High and low Churchmen, ritualists and anti-ritualists, all recognize each other as belonging to the same Church, and work together. Forty years ago the differences in doctrine and spirit and practice in the Presbyterian Church were deemed so material that a division took place, and two bodies were formed as distinct and antagonistic as any two of our Lutheran bodies. Accompanying this division were the severest criminations and recriminations, with litigations in court, and angry discussions in print. The cries of heresy were frequent and loud. Rival institutions of different characters were established by both parties, and for a period of thirty years a vigorous warfare carried on. Some nine or ten years ago a treaty of peace and concord was established, the two bodies became one again, and now there is not only co-operation, but organic union. And yet everybody knows that the same diversity of views and feelings prevails now as did during the thirty years of division and separation.

These bodies have not deemed absolute agreement necessary to united and harmonious co-operation. Cases might be cited of denominations, bearing different names and with different confessions, co-operating in most important Church work, as that of education and missions. Lutherans themselves have united with other denominations in the erection of churches, support of schools, and various interests belonging to the Church.

To this there will be raised the cry of *unionistic* Lutheranism. Be it so. It is not quite certain that a *unionistic* spirit is any worse than a *separatistic* one, or that needless divisions are any more pleasing to God or men than doubtful unions. The Lutheran Church may be in quite as much danger of sinning in the direction of exclusivism and separatism, as in the direction of too great a love for union. But we only cite the facts to show what has been done, and what might be done.

It is repeated again and again by Protestants of almost every name, that the Roman Catholic Church is as much divided, or has existing within her as many divisions and as great diversities as are found in the Protestant Church. These diversities are on leading points of doctrine, and produce strong antagonisms, resulting sometimes in violent controversies and bitter denunciations; yet they co-operate earnestly, and, so far as their chief ends are concerned, harmoniously. In this respect, the wonderful organization and effective co-operation of that Church commands the admiration, and at times the serious apprehension, of states and empires, as well as that of the rest of the Christian world. Their union and co-operation in spite of all diversities and differences, make that Church a mighty power in the world. Can Lutherans learn nothing from examples such as these, and without imitating the errors of Rome, might not we at least learn the value of united co-operation?

It may perhaps be still more in point to observe that diversities similar to those now existing in and between these four bodies have existed in the Lutheran Church from the very beginning, and without destroying her unity or forbidding co-operation. This may possibly be called in question, but our appeal is to the testimony of history. The two leading tendencies were exhibited in Luther and Melanchthon; and have continued to show themselves in every successive period from that day until the present. Not now to speak of other and even wider diversities which have prevailed within the old historic Lutheran Church, these two diversities have always existed, and have not always compelled division or rendered co-operation impracticable. There have always been unyielding, uncompromising spirits, who have sought to make such diversities a ground of controversy and separation, as they did between Luther and Melanchthon, but not always with success. Luther clung to Melanchthon and Melanchthon to Luther, in spite of their diversities, and in spite of the efforts of those who sought to sow the seeds of discord and division.

It has indeed been the boast of Lutherans that there are no Lutheran sects, that her system of doctrine and forms of worship are so catholic and liberal, that all truly Evangelical Christians may find a home in her inclosure; and that a wide diversity of views and tastes may not only be tolerated, but exist of right, according to her free and liberal spirit. If this boast has any true foundation, then it is utterly inconsistent with the spirit of Lutheranism to be exclusive or intolerant, or to refuse co-operation where it is practicable.

Let it not be forgotten that the Lutheran Church has nourished a Melanchthon as well as a Luther, an Arndt, a Calixtus, a Spener, a Francke, and a Muhlenberg, as well as a Flacius, a Calovius, and others of that school. It is doubtful if any one of these divisions would care to disown men of whom the whole Christian world may be justly proud. But if there is room in this grand old Church for a Luther and a Melanchthon, a Calovius and a Calixtus, what hinders the co-operation of these four bodies of Lutherans? Are there any greater diversities among them than have existed in the past, when there was co-operation? Spener was charged with holding and teaching more deadly errors than are charged against all these bodies combined, and yet all now claim him. History records strange reversals of ecclesiastical judgments. Let us beware lest our judgments should be reversed in the years to come, if we decide against co-operation and in favor of continued opposition.

I will not anticipate objections. If any are ambitious to see the divisions in the Lutheran Church perpetuated, to see her strength frittered away in feeble and unpromising efforts, to see one part of the Church arrayed against another, whilst the hosts of darkness present a united front against our advance; if they are satisfied to live and die, having achieved the glory of keeping alive controversies which centuries of debate and strife have done little or nothing to settle, let them make their own choice. I envy them not their following nor their glory. I shall be glad, if in this Diet I have said one word that may have any, the very least, weight on the side of union and co-operation among all Lutherans here and elsewhere throughout the world—a union that would be orthodox enough and catholic enough, Lutheran enough and liberal enough, to embrace not only a Luther and a Melanchthon, but all those who have the same spirit with those illustrious reformers, and who are willing *"to keep the unity of the Spirit in the bonds of peace."*

REMARKS OF REV. D. P. ROSENMILLER. (*General Synod.*)

The four ecclesiastical bodies of our Church agree in adopting the Bible as a supreme authority in Christian doctrine, and also in the acceptance of the Augsburg Confession as a declaration of the fundamental truths of the Bible. But there are some who go beyond this, and enter upon ground not laid down in the Augsburg Confession. By laying aside all confessional writings except the Augsburg Confession, they could become a unit in faith, at the same time according to others the liberty which they claim for themselves. They could then co-operate in the education of ministers, with feelings of kindness toward each other, and renewed interest in Home and Foreign Missions would exemplify the unity of the Church.

REMARKS OF REV. W. J. MANN, D. D. (*General Council.*)

It is understood that silence here must not be misunderstood, otherwise I would feel completely vanquished. It is certain that the Augsburg Confession alone would not have made the Lutheran Church. Luther's Small Catechism has done much more for her practical life. Bro. Rosenmiller uses the Augsburg Confession as a cloak for unionistic indifferentism. The language of the Augsburg Confession is so short and concise, that it is often unfairly used for whatever perversions may be desired. It must, of course, be interpreted in the sense in which the authors of the Confession themselves understood it. Anything else is a falsification. What the precise understanding of the Augsburg Confession is, is a point concerning which there can be no doubt. Luther's Catechism preceded the Augsburg Confession. In the sense of the Catechism the Confession is to be understood; otherwise Luther would contradict himself even in public documents. It is doing a great wrong toward him and the Lutheran reformers to place such a sense upon their words, as for instance in the doctrine of the Holy Supper, as they on every given occasion most strenuously rejected, and regarded as heretical. To use the Augsburg Confession as a bond of union for those who seriously differ in their interpretation of it, is consequently totally out of place.

REMARKS BY PROF. V. L. CONRAD. (*General Synod.*)

I do not wish to occupy the time of the Diet, but as others appear to hesitate, I have a word to say in reply to the remarks of Dr. Mann. He remarked that the doctrine of the Lord's Supper is one of the great distinctive and fundamental doctrines of the Lutheran Church, and after explaining its relations, closed by asking, "How can there be co-operation without agreement on this important and fundamental doctrine?"

To this I reply: If the *manner* of our Saviour's presence in the Eucharist be made the great central, distinctive and fundamental doctrine of the Lutheran Church, instead of justification by faith, the supreme authority of the Word of God, the universal priesthood of believers, and other doctrines presented by Dr. Brown in his essay just read; and if precise uniformity of view respecting the *manner* of that presence be made a necessary condition of co-operation among Lutherans and Christians, then, of course, no such co-operation is practicable or possible, because diversities of view on that aspect of doctrine, and on others of equal importance, exist in the Lutheran Church, and have existed from the beginning.

The *doctrine* of our Lord's presence in the Holy Supper is declared in the Augsburg Confession, and is accepted. But the *manner* of His presence, as set forth in the Form of Concord, is not declared in the Confession, it is not in Christ's words of the institution, and should not, therefore, be made confessional. If the explanation in the Form of Concord be made a test to determine who are Christians and Lutherans, then Christ himself was not a Christian, and Melanchthon, who wrote the Augsburg Confession, was not a Lutheran.

REMARKS OF REV. W. J. MANN, D. D. (*General Council.*)

No Lutheran has ever denied the salvation of any one who believed penitently that Christ had died for His sins, and that His blood is the atoning sacrifice for us. But this is not the question before the Church in her opposition to others. The most important question to her is: *What is the truth?* She is set to teach the truth, the whole truth, and therefore to watch over it. She has no right to say that this or that truth is of no account. The time may come when even those apparently far-off points may be of the highest practical value. The attack against any part of the fortification is an attack against the whole fortress. We have to guard them all, and to answer for them all. The responsibility of the Church is not identical with the possibility of the appropriation of salvation by the individual soul. It is, however, a great mistake to suppose that any point of doctrine has no fundamental bearing. As to the Lord's Supper, it is as clear as daylight that the teachings of the Roman Church have a decidedly Manichean and Docetic tinge, while the Reformed view is undeniably materialistic, rationalistic and Ebionistic, and that such views, if applied to the *person of the God-man* himself, will most certainly, when consistently carried out, destroy the idea of incarnation. Luther knew why he laid all the stress upon the "very God" and the "very man" in the person of Christ. If the finite and the infinite, man and God, cannot truly be united, then the person Jesus Christ was not the God-man. But if they were united by that personal union, called incarnation, then they can never be severed, as we would then have to fall back upon a theophany, or even the personation of a stage-actor. But since they cannot be severed, as Christ gives to us Himself, the Lord's Supper can give us no less than divinity *and* humanity, consequently also His flesh and blood. He gives *to* the Church, what He gave *for* the Church. Considering the subject under these aspects, we are very far from thinking that the question about the Lord's Supper is a mere theological or scholastic squabble. There is much more behind it than most people suppose.

REMARKS OF PROF. V. L. CONRAD. (*General Synod.*)

I accept the *man* Christ Jesus as Jehovah God, because that is clearly revealed in the Scriptures, and is also in the Augsburg Confession. But the *manner* in which he is present in the elements of the Holy Supper, is not clearly revealed in the Scriptures, and is not in the Confession. It is a matter of inference or deduction. It is supernatural, mystical, mysterious—difficult to define, explain or understand. Indeed, it is acknowledged to be inexplicable, and should not therefore be held as properly confessional, but free. Nor should it be magnified beyond measure into a fundamental doctrine upon which to dogmatize and separate Lutheran Christians, and prevent them from co-operating in the work which Christ has given them to do.

REMARKS OF REV. F. W. CONRAD, D. D. (*General Synod.*)

The able papes before us discusses a subject of great practical interest. It presents the points on which the four general Lutheran bodies in this country agree and *might* co-operate. The fact of their separate existence recalls the times and the circumstances under which they became separated. The General Synod South was organized in consequence of, and during the continuance of the late civil war. The admission of the Franckean Synod at York, and the decision of Dr. Sprecher at Fort Wayne, became the occasion of the organization of the General Council. Prior to 1860, the General Synod South, and prior to 1864, the General Council, not only co-operated, but were organically united with the General Synod North.

The General Synod South is the foster-child of the General Synod North, and in their confessional standpoints and ecclesiastical principles and practices these two bodies are still identical. We can, therefore, discover no valid reason why they should not be able to co-operate. If the division between the General Synod North and the General Council had occurred ten years earlier, it might have been regarded as a product of the ecclesiastical tendencies of the age; but taking into consideration the time and circumstances under which it occurred, it seems to us, when contemplated from our standpoint, to have been unnecessary, and should have been avoided. While, under the overrulings of Providence, incidental benefits may have resulted from their organization and efforts as separate bodies, the direct and inevitable evils resulting therefrom, in our judgment, overbalance them.

The question introduced by the topic of the paper, is not whether these bodies could at this time unite, but whether they *might* not co-operate with each other in the prosecution of the work of evangelization at home and of missions abroad? While their differences still prevent union, should not their agreements, which are more numerous and far more important, secure their co-operation? Born of Lutheran parentage and tracing my ecclesiastical lineage to the Old Trappe Church, ministered to by Muhlenberg, I have consecrated myself to the service of the Lutheran Church. To see her divisions healed, her scattered forces united, and her mighty energies concentrated in the prosecution of her great mission in this western world—this has been the ecclesiastical idol of my life. Interpreted by the sacerdotal prayer of Christ, that all His followers may be one, this must be "a consummation devoutly to be wished;" and stimulated by the hope of its realization, let us all continue to labor and pray.

REMARKS OF REV. A. C. WEDEKIND, D. D. (*General Synod.*)

I see no particular difficulty in the way, why these general bodies might not co-operate in the various enterprises of the Church. It surely cannot be supposed that absolute oneness is required, on all the details of a theological system, for such co-operation. If that be the law, then there is scarcely a family in Christendom, where co-operation in its own affairs can be secured. I venture to say, sir, that there is as much general *doctrinal* and *cultus* assimilation, between three of these four general bodies, at least, as there is between the various parts of each. I have just attended a special meeting of a very large and influential Synod, *not* in connection with the General Synod, which was to settle some difficulties; and the diversities of views which obtain among these brethren, are certainly not less by any means than those which are supposed to exist among these general bodies. The discussions, adjourned from their rival papers to this extra session of Synod, for two long days, elicited a diversity of sentiment declared on all hands to be most vital, that was to me astonishing. If it was not exactly like Ephraim envying Judah, and Judah vexing Ephraim, it came very near to it. Yet with all these *vital* differences, these brethren have hitherto co-operated and are still co-operating.

Nor is the case very much different in the good old Synod which is the mother of us all. It needs only a glance at their periodicals and their official transactions to see the differences that prevail there. As far as we are now informed, these differences are irreconcilable. And it would certainly take a bold prophet to predict that these diversities would come to a speedy and harmonious oneness. If an armistice has been concluded, it is doubtless on the general principle of agreeing to disagree. And yet all these brethren co-operate in the great enterprises before them. These diversities do not interfere with their Christian activities. Their educational and mission operations, and their institutions of learning and piety, are alike dear to them all, receiving their hearty and united sympathies and aid. And yet I hesitate not in saying, and take all the responsibility of the statement, that the differences of most of these general bodies are not a whit greater than these smaller family differences.

Why then should it seem an unreasonable thing to suppose that such co-operation could be had among them? It surely does not demand, as already stated, a oneness of sentiment in all the *minutiæ* of religious views. No sane man will demand that. Well, then, sir, it is absolutely certain, that these general bodies will never be of one mind on every little detail, any more than these sub-bodies. What then? Let them remain in eternal antagonism? No, sir! If they cannot be of one mind, let them be, like the first Christians, of *one heart and one soul!* Let charity ascend the throne, and trample *prejudice*—that devil's wasp—into the mire. Let but simple honesty be done to all, and Luther's explanation of the eighth commandment be carried out, and I have no fears of the consequences. That matchless allegorist, John Bunyan, says in his Holy War, that Mr. Prejudice fell and broke his leg; and then adds: "I wish he had broken his neck." From my innermost soul I say, *Amen*, to that devout wish!

REMARKS OF REV. R. A. FINK, D. D. (*General Synod*.)

I have listened to the discussions in this Diet with deep interest from the beginning, and it seems to me that the chief cause of division in the Church, and difficulty in the way of general co-operation in matters of general interest, grow out of one thing; that is, the manner of explaining or attempting to explain the mode or manner of Christ's presence in the Lord's Supper. That He is present we all agree; but as to the *how*, we differ. I think the surest way to bring about union and general co-operation in the Church would be to cease requiring a uniform explanation of the manner of the Lord's presence. In my acquaintance with Lutherans and Lutheran ministers, I know of very few, if any, who if asked, "Do you believe that the Lord is really present in the Holy Supper?' would not unhesitatingly say, "Yes, I believe." "I believe Chrst meant what He said when He declared, 'This is my body,' etc.—i's a mystery—I can't explain it." For myself, I adopt unhesitatingly the very words of the Augsburg Confession, as I do the word of the institution itself. I call it a sacramental presence.

Several voices: In the bread?

Dr. Fink: Yes, in the bread.

The difficulty, I repeat, arises from an attempt to expain the manner, and the *modus operandi* of imparting the promised blessing. This is the fruitful source of difference amongst us. Let us, then, not require any manner of explanation of the myster of the Lord's presence in the Eucharist, as we require none of the mystery of the Trinity in the formula of Holy Baptism. This difficulty out of the way, and the whole Church, it seems to me, could easily be brought together, and could most harmoniously co-operate in the great work of the spread of the gospel; other differences would soon vanish.

REMARKS OF REV. W. S. EMERY (*General Council.*)

I can well see why Dr. Brown refused to be stopped at the rap of your gavel when his time had expired. The closing sentences of his paper were the finest, the most beautiful and touching, in his entire essay.

The paper was prepared with considerable care and research; but unfortunately, it repeatedly used the phrase, "the four general bodies in our Church all agree *substantially*." This term "substantially" was used throughout the entire essay, without one word of definition. The undefined use of this prominent and equivocal word constitutes the great weakness of the essay.

This is especially noticeable, as it comes historically on the heels of the formulary so much used for thirty years in the reception of the Augsburg Confession. I refer to that formulary which reads:

"We believe that the fundamental doctrines of God's Word are taught in a manner substantially correct in the Augsburg Confession," which was formerly used as a means of evading the force of any article in the noble Confession, that any one chose to reject.

If Dr. Brown, however, mean literally what he says, with an unexceptionable definition in its historical connection, then this historical substantial agreement must be received in the spirit, the life, the theology, the entire doctrinal agreement, in the very words of our noble Confession. The candid and clear belief of our great Confession, and an upright confession of its doctrines everywhere, would form a glorious bond of all Lutherans, in all languages and all lands.

REMARKS OF REV. J. A. BROWN, D. D. (*General Synod.*)

I am not at all ambitious to occupy the time which belongs to me in closing this discussion. There is little that I desire to add. If I have failed to make myself understood in the forty-five minutes allowed me to read, it is not likely that I will improve the matter by ten minutes' extemporaneous speaking.

So little exception has been taken to the essay that it might be inferred that we are all in favor of "harmoniously co operating." If this be so, it should be the cause of devout gratitude. About the only exception formally taken, has been to the use of the word "substantially," or that these bodies "agree substantially," without defining the term. As the word itself is a defining term, it seems ridiculous to ask that it again be defined, for this would be to start on a process that has no end. We think most persons understand the meaning of the word *substantially;* and the fling at one of these four bodies in which the term is said to have been covertly used, is neither timely nor wise. That body is not here on trial, and if it were, it would not be wanting for cheerful and willing defenders. It would perhaps be wiser and better for any who are anxious for work of this kind to look well to their own defences.

Should any, as a matter of taste, prefer any other term to express the same general idea, I certainly have no objections.

For myself, I have no such difficulties as some are exercised with, about either substantial agreement, or harmonious co-operation. The platform on which I stand is broad enough, and I will venture to add firm enough, to receive all genuine Lutherans. I stand where I have stood for nearly a third of a century, and where I hope to continue standing as long as I am permitted to remain in the Church on earth. In this position I find no difficulty, on my part, in co-operating with Lutherans of different tendencies, providing only that they recognize me as I recognize them. On this broad catholic Lutheran basis I could fellowship and co-operate with those who believe a great deal more than I do. I should not quarrel with any for receiving all the Symbolical Books, and believing every word contained in them. But I ask the liberty of not making their capacity to receive and believe the rule for me, if I am not able to believe quite so much. I will respect their faith if they respect mine, and I will respect their Lutheranism if they respect mine. With this mutual respect for each other, we can agree to co-operate, and co-operate as Lutherans. But just here is the difficulty. Some are not willing to grant any such liberty, or to recognize any such differences in the Lutheran Church. Whilst I would be willing to acknowledge their Lutheranism, though preferring my own, they are not willing to acknowledge mine. And if any think that this is a concession of their superior claims, I have only to say, so much the worse for them that they are thus unwilling. We are as well satisfied with our Lutheranism as they can be with theirs. Co-operation on our part is invited on terms alike scriptural and honorable to all, and if any will not, they are left to God and their own consciences.

I can but reiterate the points "wherein we agree," and express the conviction that they are quite sufficient for harmonious co-operation. Other denominations around us have differences greater than ours, and yet co-operate. Similar differences exist in each one of these four bodies, and yet they severally co-operate. I can see no good reason why Lutherans might not do the same. We are now a spectacle and a wonder to many round about us, who do not understand our differences, and the time may come when we will be a greater wonder to ourselves than we now are to others. But I have said all that I care at present to say, and will close with the expression of my most ardent wishes for unity of spirit, harmony and co-operation throughout the whole Lutheran Church.

Adjourned.

THIRD SESSION.

DECEMBER 27th, 7:30 P. M.

After prayer by Rev. J. F. Reinmund, D. D., of Lebanon, Pa., the fourth paper was read.

THE HISTORY AND PROGRESS OF THE LUTHERAN CHURCH IN THE UNITED STATES.

BY REV. H. E. JACOBS, D. D.

Franklin Professor in Pennsylvania College, Gettysburg, Pa.

ALTHOUGH the foundations of the Lutheran Church in America are only now beginning to be really laid, yet the efforts of the present cannot be fully understood without a consideration of the lessons that our past history, as a Church on this continent, has taught us.

It is a fortunate circumstance, that we possess such full contemporary records of many of the earliest struggles of Lutheranism in America;[1] and that in later years, a number of our brethren have been so diligent in presenting to our English speaking people the story of the labors of their fathers, and in accumulating material for the future historian of our Church.[2] It is our purpose to

---

[1] (*a*) History of New Sweden, by Israel Acrelius, formerly Provost of the Swedish churches on the Delaware, Stockholm, 1759. Translated by W. M. Reynolds, D. D., Philadelphia, 1874.

(*b*) Nachrichten von den vereinigten Deutschen Ev. Luth. Gemein. in America, absonderlich in Pennsylvanien. Halle, 1758-87.

(*c*) The Urlsperger Reports from the Lutheran Salzburger pastors in Georgia.

[2] History of the American Lutheran Church, by E. L. Hazelius, D. D., Zanesville, O., 1846. The American Lutheran Church, by S. S. Schmucker, D. D., Philadelphia, 1852. The Salzburgers and their Descendants, by Rev. P. A. Strobel, Baltimore, 1855. Early History of the Lutheran Church in America, by C. W. Schaeffer, D. D., Philadelphia, 1857. Memoir of the Life and Times of Henry Melchior Muhlenberg, by M. L. Stoever, LL.D., Philadelphia, 1856. History of the German Settlements and of the Lutheran Church in North and South Carolina, by G. D. Bernheim, D. D. To these we may add the Reminiscences of Lutheran Ministers, by Dr. Stoever, in the

condense into the limits allowed us, the leading facts scattered through these various sources.

The Lutheran Church in America is probably over two hundred and fifty years old. The precise year of earliest origin, is involved somewhat in doubt; yet we may consider it at least probable, that fifteen years before the Baptists, sixty-five before the Presbyterians, and one hundred and forty before the Methodists had made a beginning, and only a year or two after the landing of the Puritans on Plymouth Rock, there were faithful confessors of the Lutheran Church already on these shores; and that the land which, in 1523, gave our faith its first martyrs, gave it almost a century later its first witnesses in this western world, in fulfillment of Luther's prediction that the voices of those two youths who were burned in the Netherlands, would yet be heard proclaiming the testimony of Jesus to many nations.[3] Worthy successors of their martyred countrymen, were the Dutch Lutherans of New Amsterdam. Few in number, among their countrymen of the Reformed faith, no persuasion could induce them to enter into the communion of the Churches that subscribed to the decrees of the Synod of Dort, and persecution proved as unavailing as persuasion.[4] They were forced to meet in private houses; they were fined; £100 was the penalty

---

Evangelical Review, and his contributions to Sprague's Annals of the American Lutheran Pulpit, and McClintock and Strong's Cyclopædia, and several articles by Dr. W. M. Reynolds, in the *Evangelical Review* (Swedish Churches on the Delaware, 1 : 161; Lutheran Church in Netherlands and New York, 6: 303; German Emigration to North America, 13 : 1; Scandinavians in the N. W., 3 : 399, etc.). The *Evangelisches Magazin* of Dr. Helmuth, the *Lutheran Intelligencer* of Dr. D. F. Schaeffer, and the *Lutheran Magazine* of Dr. G. A. Lintner, contain considerable historical material. We have been greatly aided in the preparation of this paper by the use of the Library of the Historical Society of the Lutheran Church, in the Theological Seminary at Gettysburg, which contains an almost complete set of the Minutes of Lutheran Synods in America, and much other rare and valuable material.

[3] We find Lutherans mentioned in the earliest classification of the inhabitants of the New Netherlands, according to their faith. See report of the Jesuit Father Jogue (1643), Documentary History of New York, IV. p. 19. Hence the inference that there were Lutherans in the colony from the beginning in 1622.

The same paper notices the presence in New Amsterdam also of Roman Catholics, English Puritans and Anabaptists, called Mnists.

[4] For details, see Brodhead's History of New York, I. 582, 617, 634, 642.

for preaching the Gospel; £25 for attending a Lutheran service; they were imprisoned; their "conventicles" were broken up. Even the year after the West India Company had rebuked this intolerance of Gov. Peter Stuyvesant, Rev. John E. Goetwater, sent as a Lutheran pastor by the consistory of Amsterdam, was saved from immediate banishment upon reaching New Amsterdam, only by his ill health, which procured a stay of procedure for four months. In the published archives of the State of New York,[5] there is an interesting letter from Megapolensis and Drisius, Reformed pastors, dated August 5th, 1657, recounting "the injuries that threaten this community by the encroachments of the heretical spirits," in which the following occurs: "It came to pass that a Lutheran preacher, named Joannes Ernestus Goetwater, arrived in the ship, the Mill, to the great joy of the Lutherans, and especial discontent and disappointment of the congregation of this place; yea, of the whole land, even of the English. * * We already have the snake in our bosom." * * In conclusion, these earnest champions of the Reformed faith, beg that "a stop be put to the work, which they seem to intend to push forward with a hard Lutheran pate, in despite and opposition of the regents." Our Dutch brethren do not seem to have been unwilling to attend the Reformed service, and to show proper respect to the religious convictions of their countrymen; but the controversy centered especially upon the administration of Baptism, in which the effort was made to extort from them the promise to train up their children in the doctrines of the Synod of Dort. The conquest of the colony by the English, in 1664, gave the Lutherans religious liberty; but nine years before this deliverance, the same power that oppressed the Dutch Lutherans, when it prevailed in New Sweden, had banished two of the three Swedish Lutheran pastors. The third was allowed to remain, because other troubles diverted the attention of the government, and "we had no Reformed preacher to establish there, or who understood their language."[6] A recent writer has brought to light the history of a colony of Dutch Lutherans on James' Island, S. C., as

---

[5] Documentary History of New York, 3: 103.

[6] *Ev. Review*, 1: 176, from O'Callaghan's History of the New Netherlands, 2: 289, 290, translation of letter of Dominie Megapolensis, by Rev. Dr. De Witt.

early as 1674, and the proscription which they suffered from the Church of England.[7]

Meanwhile, the Lutheran Church had gained another foothold in this country. Almost on the very territory on which this diet is to-day assembled, the colony of New Sweden was planted, two hundred and forty years ago. The first Lutheran Church edifice on this continent was erected within the walls of Fort Christina, now Wilmington, Del., probably in 1638; and the first Lutheran minister was the Rev. Reorus Torkillus, who after eight years' service here, died in 1643.[8] Campanius, the second pastor, was the first Protestant missionary to the North American Indians, being several years earlier in this work than the distinguished John Eliot. He translated Luther's catechism into the Delaware language, and to his influence and that of his successors, belongs much of the credit for the success of the Indian policy of William Penn;[9] as the Indians with whom Penn had to do were those among whom these Swedish pastors had lived and labored. The first Lutheran Church in Pennsylvania was built in Delaware county, in 1646.[10] Not long after, the present limits of this city were entered. An old block-house at Wicacoa served for awhile as a house of worship, and on its site, in 1700, Gloria Dei Church was dedicated.[11] Altogether, there were at least six of these churches, ministered to for over a century and three-quarters, by a succession of thirty-five pastors, most of them men of strong faith and eminent devotion, the last of whom died in 1831.[12] They were presided over by Provosts, of whom the most prominent were the historian Acrelius and Von Wrangel. Some of their ministers preached in English, German and Dutch, besides Swedish. Thus we find Rudman serving the Dutch Lutheran Church at Albany[13] in the beginning of the eighteenth century, Dylander organizing into congregations the Germans of Lancaster and Germantown, and Von Wrangel preaching for the churches at Lancaster and York.[14] Three of their pastors in 1703, administered, in Gloria Dei Church, the first rite of Lu-

---

[7] Bernheim's History, 56.   [8] Acrelius, 85.

[9] Acrelius, 85, 366. Schaeffer's Early History, 21. Dr. Reynolds in *Ev Review*, I: 173. A copy of this catechism is in the library of the Lutheran Historical Society at Gettysburg.

[10] Acrelius, 43.   [11] Acrelius, 203.   [12] Acrelius, 313, 344, 349.
[13] Acrelius, 213.   [14] *Ev. Review*, I: 142.

theran ordination in America, the clergyman ordained being the Rev. Justus Falkner,[15] serving congregations in Montgomery county, and afterward pastor of the Dutch Lutheran Church in New York. In 1743, the year after the arrival of the patriarch Muhlenberg, a union between the Germans and Swedes was proposed; but was frustrated chiefly by the efforts of Nyberg, whose affiliations with the Moravians rendered him especially hostile to Muhlenberg, as the latter had just rescued the German Church in Philadelphia from Zinzendorf,[16] and whose erratic career subsequently occasioned the church at Lancaster so much trouble,[17] and resulted in his deposition by the Swedish Archbishop.[18] At the organization of the Ministerium of Pennsylvania in this city, in 1748, two of their pastors were present and took a prominent part in all the proceedings,[19] and at succeeding meetings of the Ministerium, recorded in the Halle Reports, the Swedish pastors were always represented, Provost Von Wrangel in his day being no less active on the floor of Synod than Dr. Muhlenberg himself. But unfortunately as the churches became anglicized,[20] neither the Swedish nor German ministers could supply them with sufficient English preaching, and English Lutheran ministers were not to be found. The Protestant Episcopal Church, in its weakness, had been nursed by the Swedish Lutheran pastors. When unable to worship in a house of their own, the Lutherans had permitted the Episcopalians to hold service regularly in their church; and Lutheran ministers who had command of the English language, had repeatedly served them for considerable periods, both in the pulpit, and in pastoral ministration.[21] Occasionally an Episcopal minister would also fill a Swedish Lutheran pulpit, and they would even assist in the consecration of the churches of each other.[22] The result, therefore, was almost inevitable, that, in their perplexity,

---

[15] Acrelius, 214. [16] Acrelius, 245,

[17] Hall. Nach., 67, 69, 230, 232, 673, 1354. [18] Acrelius, 336.

[19] Especially in the ordination of Rev. William Kurtz, Hall. Nach., 284.

[20] Divine service in English became necessary in the Swedish Churches as early as 1750. See Acrelius, 305, 342. The manner in which it was introduced, more fully given, p. 360.

[21] Acrelius, 219, 220, 361. This service not only was rendered without compensation, but often, as Acrelius states, without any return to the Lutheran pastors of expenses incurred in this extra service.

[22] Acrelius, 361, 220.

they would turn to the Episcopal Church for help, and that they would be sure to find it. Episcopal ministers first became the assistants of the Lutheran pastors. The charters were first altered, so as to allow the services of either Lutheran or Episcopal pastors;[23] and the Lutheran name at length disappeared altogether.[24]

The German emigration to American began about 1680,[25] although we find no record of a German Lutheran Church or pastor until the next century. 1703 is the date of Falkner's ordination, and his early labors in Montgomery county.[26] 1708 notes the emigration of the Palatinate pastor Kocherthal,[27] and his little colony, to the west bank of the Hudson, where on the present site of Newburgh, fifty acres were given each colonist, and a glebe of five hundred acres donated "for the maintenance of a Lutheran minister and his successors forever," but which unfortunately at last fell into the hands of the Episcopalians. In 1710, other Lutheran Palatinates settled in the neighborhood of Newbern, North Carolina.[28] About the same time, another band, after a voyage of almost incredible hardship, reached New York, and with many sufferings, making their way through the wilderness, purchased land from the Indians, and formed the settlements at Schoharie.[29] Others found a home on both sides of the Hudson, a hundred miles north of New York,[30] and together with the Dutch Lutheran element previously settled, formed the basis for the twenty-two congregations, now in Columbia, Dutchess and Ulster counties.[31] Others remained in New York, and added to the strength of the Dutch congregation;[32] while still others

---

[23] *Ev. Review*, 1: 194. Hazelius' History, p. 23.

[24] As late as 1873, the Church at Upper Merion, Montgomery co., still remained independent of the Episcopal Church, although ministered to by Episcopal rectors. Reynolds' Acrelius, 350.

[25] Hall. Nach., 665.   [26] Supra.

[27] The history of this colony is given with considerable fullness in the Documentary History of New York, 3: 540-607. See especially the protest of Rev. Knoll against the transfer of the glebe to the English Church, p. 583.

[28] Fullest account in Bernheim, p. 67 *seq*. See also *Ev. Review*, 13: 19.

[29] For many cotemporary documents, see Doc. Hist. of N. Y., Vol. 3; also article of *Ev. Review*, above quoted; Schaeffer 72 *seq*.; Hazelius, 26.

[30] Hall. Nach., 74.   *Ev. Review*, 13: 27.   [31] U. S. Census for 1870.

[32] *Ev. Review*, 13: 24.   *Quart. Review*, 7: 272.

settled in Pennsylvania along the Swatara and Tulpehocken.³³ The Dutch congregations in New York and Loonenburgh were diligent in caring for their German brethren; but in Pennsylvania, notwithstanding the ministrations of the Swedish pastors, the spiritual destitution among the Germans was appalling, and the people were at the mercy of impostors. The deputation sent to Europe in 1733 by the churches of Philadelphia, New Hanover and Providence, present in the Halle Reports a sad picture of the condition of our Church at that time "in a land full of sects and heresy, without ministers and teachers, schools, churches and books."³⁴ The result of this mission was the identification, with our succeeding history, of the names of Muhlenberg, Brunnholtz, Handschuh, Kurtz, Schaum, Schultze, Heintzleman, Helmuth, Schmidt and others, who were sent from Halle during the period from 1742 to 1769. We cannot dwell upon the almost superhuman labors of Muhlenberg and his associates, in contending with impostors, organizing churches, founding schools, preaching the Gospel from house to house as well as in churches, and diligently supplying the long-neglected wants of their countrymen.

Meanwhile, in 1734, the Salzburgers, refugees from Romish persecution, with their two ministers, Bolzius and Gronau, had settled at Ebenezer, Ga.;³⁵ and before the middle of the eighteenth century, a church had been established as far north as Maine,³⁶ and important centres had been formed in Maryland, Virginia, and the Carolinas.

At the beginning of the nineteenth century, the prospect presented to an observer would have been as follows: The Ministerium of Pennsylvania with its semi-centennial³⁷ already past, and

---

[33] Hall. Nach., 976. Schaeffer, 76.   [34] Hall. Nach., 4.

[35] Prof. Walker, late Superintendent of the U. S. census, has fallen into the same error as Bancroft, in his paper in the volume, "The First Century of the Republic," p. 232, by referring to the Salzburgers as Moravians. Strobel, Bernheim, Hazelius, Schaeffer, Muhlenberg's Journal in *Ev. Review*, 1: 390, 534; 2: 113; 3: 115, 418, 582; 4: 172, and Dr. Stoever's memoirs of Bolzius, and J. E. and C. F. Bergman, *Ev. Review*, 9: 1, 13; 6: 553, give interesting details.

[36] For the history of this congregation, see article of Dr. Pohlman, in *Ev. Review*, 20: 440.

[37] The date of organization was August 14th, 1748. Hall. Nach., 284.

the last of its founders[38] deceased for four years, embraced also Maryland and Virginia, and reported 53 ministers, 300 congregations, and a population of 50,000 families.[39] The Ministerium of New York, organized fifteen years before with fourteen ministers,[40] had decreased to eight.[41] At least six ministers were serving congregations in the Carolinas,[42] gathered three years afterwards into the North Carolina Synod. Altogether, after the efforts of one hundred and seventy-five years, we numbered less than 70 pastors, where we now have 2900.[43] Zion's, the mother church in this city, of which Dr. Helmuth and Rev. Schmidt were the joint pastors, was strong, as may be inferred from the fact that in a year in which the mortality was not exceptional, 187 deaths are reported in the congregation.[44] It supported four parochial schools, with Dr. C. F. Endress, then a young man of twenty-five, as superintendent, attended by 250 pupils.[45] Dr. Helmuth[46] was also Professor in the University of Pennsylvania, in which he had succeeded his predecessor in the pastoral office, Dr. Kunze. Dr. F. D. Schaeffer was at Germantown; C. F. Wildbahn, after a pastorate of eighteen years, was still performing occasional ministerial acts at Reading; Dr. Henry Ernst Muhlenberg was at Lancaster; Jacob Goering at York; Henry Mueller at Harrisburg; John Grob was organizing the church at Gettysburg; Dr. J. G. Schmucker was at Hagerstown; Dr. Geo. Lochman, at Lebanon; Dr. F. W. Geissenhainer, sr., in Montgomery county; Dr. J. D. Kurtz, in Baltimore; Christian Streit, at Winchester, and J. G. Butler, missionary of the Ministerium of Pennsylvania, in West Virginia and Tennessee. In the New York Ministerium, Dr. Kunze was pastor in New York, and Professor in Columbia College, while his

---

[34] The founders of the Ministerium were Dr. H. M. Muhlenberg, † 1787, the Swedish Provost Sandin, who died the same month that the Ministerium was organized, Handschuh, † 1764, Brunnholtz, † 1758, Schaum, † 1778, J. N. Kurtz, † 1794, Hartwig, † 1796. Naesman, the second Swedish pastor, returned to Sweden a few years afterward, and the date of his death is uncertain.

[39] Hazard's Register of Pennsylvania, 4: 372.

[40] Hazelius, 109.   [41] Hazard, as above.   [42] Do.

[43] Lutheran Almanac for 1878, 2905; Lutherische Kalender, 2914.

[44] Hazard's Register, 4: 373.   [45] Hazard, do.; *Ev. Review*, 6: 23.

[46] For the most of these data, see Stoever's Reminiscences, in *Evangelical Review*, and Sprague's Annals of the American Lutheran Pulpit.

English assistant Strebeck was organizing a congregation, which afterwards went over bodily to the Episcopal Church, not however until their pastor had preceded them several years.[47] Farther south C. A. G. Stork and Paul Henkel were laboring as yet harmoniously in North Carolina, both in that very year astonished and confused by some of the earlier revival movements of this country.[48] The venerable John N. Martin, for a quarter of a century pastor of the church at Charleston, S. C., had died only five years before; and the churches at Ebenezer and Savannah were still served by the elder Bergman. Dr. Kunze was acknowledged as among the first Oriental scholars in America,[49] J. F. Schmidt, of Philadelphia, was an accomplished astronomer, while Muhlenberg, of Lancaster, and Melsheimer, of Hanover, by their cultivation of special branches of Natural History, still hold an eminent place among naturalists. One of our ministers had been a Major-General in the Revolutionary army, and another, his brother, the first speaker of the National House of Representatives. Franklin College at Lancaster, under the joint control of Lutheran and Reformed, with Dr. H. E. Muhlenberg as its first President, had been established thirteen years before.[50] The University of Pennsylvania and Dickinson College both contained among their trustees representative men of our Church.[51] Dr. Helmuth and Rev. Schmidt had for fifteen years already been conducting a private theological seminary in Philadelphia, in which such men as J. G. Lochman, Endress, J. G. Schmucker, J. Miller, Baker, Butler, Goering, Baetes and others, were prepared for the ministry.[52] Two years after this, viz., in 1802, the labors of Dr. Lochman, sr., in the same direction, began.[53] The introduction of English preaching was already agitating the congregations. Dr. Kunze, at an early period, had insisted on its necessity. At successive elections from 1803-6 in the German church in this city, the opponents of English preaching prevailed by only a small majority. In the election of 1806, 1400 votes were polled, and as the result, a colony withdrew and founded St. John's, the first exclusively English Lutheran church in Pennsylvania. In 1814, the

---

[47] *Quarterly Review*, 7: 278.   [48] Bernheim, 350.
[49] See the opinions of Dr. Samuel Miller, of Princeton, and J. W. Francis, M. D., of New York, in Sprague's Annals, 55.
[50] *Ev. Review*, 10: 534.   [51] *Ev. Review*, 10: 288, 290.
[52] *Ev. Review*, 10: 555; 6: 5.   [53] *Ev. Review*, 6: 21.

desire for English preaching again became strong in the German congregation, and led in the course of time to the founding of the second English church, St. Matthew's, whose guests we are to-day.[54] These were not isolated occurrences, but symptoms of a movement that was manifesting itself throughout the entire country. So strong was it, that in 1805 the Ministerium of Pennsylvania felt the necessity of passing the enactment that it must remain a German speaking body,[55] and, in 1814, Drs. J. D. Kurtz and G. Lochman, in the name of the same Ministerium, published an address[56] devoted mostly to the necessity of maintaining German schools and German divine service. We can fully sympathize with the regret of these worthy men, that with the loss of the German language, the religious instruction of the young was neglected, German diligence and frugality abandoned, and the precious hymns, and prayers, and books of devotion forgotten; yet that even adherence to the German would not necessarily preserve a congregation in the faith of our Church, was demonstrated by the sad history of the congregation of the venerable Dr. Kurtz himself. The anglicizing of the people was inevitable; and the call made upon the Church then, as now, was to so control this process that it would involve only a change of language, and not, at the same time, of faith. The New York Ministerium, owing perhaps to the presence of the Dutch element,[56a] the earlier German settlement, and the diminishing of the tide of German emigration to that State, was comparatively soon anglicized. As early

---

[54] Hazard's Register, 4 : 372.

[55] The resolutions are as follows: " 1. The present Lutheran Ministerium in Pennsylvania and adjacent States must remain a German-speaking Ministerium, and no proposition can be entertained which would render necessary any other language than the German, in Synodical meetings and business transactions. 2. English-speaking Lutherans, who cannot understand the German service, may organize themselves into congregations of their own. 3. In case such English Lutheran congregations be established, the German Lutheran Ministerium will regard their members as brethren, and is willing to recognize their delegates, and also, after an examination, their ministers as members of Synod, provided they submit to its constitution, and attend the meeting of Synod." Passed at Germantown, June 12, 1805, and published in the " Ministerial Ordnung" of 1813, p. 19.

[56] Address to "all the Germans of the United States, and especially the German inhabitants of Virginia."

[56a] *Ev. Review*, 6 : 327.

as 1815, it was almost entirely English; although, unfortunately, wanting in a clear confession of our faith, and hence unfit for the foundation of the work of our Church in the English language.

Nor were the churches of that period deficient in missionary activity. In 1806, the Ministerium of Pennsylvania appointed three missionaries. One died. A second set out from New Market, Va., traveled southwest three hundred miles to the Great Kanawha; thence northwest sixty-six miles to Chillicothe; thence southwest forty miles to Brush Creek; thence seventy miles to Lebanon; thence north thirty miles to Montgomery Co., O. The report states: "Our tongue cannot describe the triumphs won by his presence, or depict the impression made on many hearts." The third traveled thirteen hundred miles in one hundred and twenty-two days, and preached sixty-seven times. A similar report was made to Synod two years later.

Our first regular theological school, Hartwick Seminary, New York, was established in 1816,[57] with Rev. Dr. Hazelius as the first professor of theology. In 1818, against the advice of the mother Synod, the Synod of Ohio was formed by the missionaries of the Ministerium of Pennsylvania, living west of the Alleghanies, and nine years afterwards numbered 25 ministers and 95 congregations.[58] In 1820, the Synod of Maryland and Virginia was organized, and the rupture occurred in the North Carolina Synod, that resulted in the formation of the Tennessee Synod.[59] The same year witnessed the convention held at Hagerstown, by the delegates of the Ministeriums of Pennsylvania and New York, and the Synods of North Carolina, and Maryland and Virginia, to form the General Synod.[60] At the first convention of that body, held the succeeding year, the New York Ministerium failed to appear. In 1823 the Ministerium of Pennsylvania withdrew,[61] and as a consequence,

---

[57] The classical school at Hartwick was opened December 15th, 1815. Its charter as a theological seminary is dated August 10th, 1816. Hartwick Memorial Volume, pp. 37, 38.

[58] Hazelius, 155.

[59] Bernheim, 440; Hazelius, 148; *Luth. Intelligencer, passim.*

[60] See the "Proposed Plan for a General Union of the Evangelical Lutheran Church in the United States of America," adopted by the Ministerium of Pennsylvania at Baltimore, in 1819. *Ev. Review*, 12 : 590.

[61] The withdrawal of the Ministerium of Pennsylvania was not because of

the churches west of the Susquehanna left the Ministerium in 1825, and, under the title of the West Pennsylvania Synod, remained in the General Synod.[62] One year before this, the South Carolina Synod was organized. At the end of the first quarter of the present century, our church had grown to 164 ministers, 475 congregations, and 45,000 communicants. Of the congregations reported, no less than 100 were without pastors.[62a]

Three theological seminaries soon came into existence, and contributed largely to our further development, viz., in 1826, that of the General Synod at Gettysburg, and in 1830, that of the Ohio Synod at Columbus, and of the South Carolina Synod, first at Newberry, then at Lexington, then again at Newberry, and now transferred to the General Synod of North America, and located at Salem, Va.

The influence of a Lutheran press also began to make itself felt. As early as 1811, the Ministerium of Pennsylvania started a synodical organ—in German—under the editorship of Dr. Helmuth and Rev. Schmidt, which ran its course in about three years. The *Lutheran Intelligencer*, edited by Dr. D. F. Schaeffer, at Frederick, Md., from 1826-31; the *Lutheran Magazine*, edited by Dr. Lintner, and published for three years at Schoharie, N. Y.; the *Lutheran Observer*, founded in 1831, and whose first editor is the president of this Diet; the *Lutheran Preacher*, published by Dr. Eichelberger, at Winchester, Va., in 1833-4; the *Lutheran Standard*, founded in 1842, whose first editor, Dr. Greenwald, we had hoped to find with us to-day; the *Missionary* of Dr. Passavant, founded in 1848; the *Evangelical Lutheran*, the *Olive Branch*, the *Home*

---

dissatisfaction with the new organization, but because of the unreasonable fear prevalent in many of its congregations of an increase of ecclesiastical power. See the comparatively recent reference in "The Synod of Pennsylvania, and the late Convention at Ft. Wayne, Ind., 1866," p. 12; and the resolution on p. 16, Minutes of 1823: "Resolved, That the above resolutions shall remain in force, until such time in the future as the congregations themselves shall see their mistake of our true intention, and shall call for a reconsideration of these resolutions."

[62] See manuscript record of the preliminary conference between Drs. J. G. and S. S. Schmucker and Rev. J. Herbst, in Library of Historical Society.

[62a] See Address to the congregations of the West Pennsylvania Synod by Revs. Dr. J. G. Schmucker, J. G. Graeber and J. Herbst, 25, p. 2.

Journal, the *Lutheran*, the *Lutheran and Missionary*, the *Lutheran Watchman*, the *Lutheran Visitor*, *Our Church Paper*, the *Church Messenger*, the *Evangelical Review*, the *Quarterly Review*, not to mention any but English papers,[63] or even to make their list exhaustive, all have performed an important part in the development of the interests of the Church. With all the defects that have marred many of their issues, the Church owes to-day a great debt of gratitude to its press. At present, every tendency within the Church that would assert its claims, feels the need of an organ, and for every advance the Church has made, the press has heralded the way. The utterances of our Church press carry more weight with them than even the resolutions of Synods, which are easily passed, and unless vigorously supported by the press, as a rule are soon forgotten.

We cannot enter into the details of the last fifty years. There are venerable men in this Diet, who have been prominently identified with the movements of our Church in that period, to whom we must look for a full record of the struggles through which we have gathered the strength of to-day. A few facts, however, must be noticed. Such are the increase in strength of the General Synod, by the return, under certain clearly defined conditions,[63a] of the

---

[63] The principal German periodicals have been *Das Evangelische Magazin* of Helmuth and Schmidt, mentioned above; *Das Evangelische Magazin* of Rev. Herbst and Drs. S. S. Schmucker and E. L. Hazelius, Gettysburg, 1829-33; the *Hirtenstimme* and *Kirchenbote* of Rev. C. Weyl, Baltimore, of which the latter was afterwards edited at Gettysburg and Selinsgrove by Rev. Anstadt; the *Lutherische Kirchenzeitung*, edited by Rev. F. Schmidt at Easton, Pa., for several years after 1838; the *Jugenfreund;* the *Lutherische Zeitschrift*, and *Theo-Monatshefte* of Pastor S. K. Brobst; the *Lutherische Herold*, published in New York; the *Lutherische Kirchenzeitung*, published at Columbus, Ohio; the *Lehre und Wehre*, *Lutheraner*, *Magazin für Ev. Luth. Homiletik*, of the Missouri Synod; the *Kirchenblatt* and *Kirchliche Zeitschrift*, of the Iowa Synod; the *Informatorium* and *Wachende Kirche*, of the two sections of the Buffalo Synod; the *Gemeindeblatt*, of the Wisconsin Synod; the *Kirchenblatt*, of the Canada Synod; the *Kirchenfreund*, of the General Synod, etc.

We enter upon 1878 with 60 periodicals, exclusive of Almanacs, viz., 27 German, 17 English, 4 Swedish, 12 Norwegian and Danish. In 1854, only 11 in all languages are reported.

[63a] Minutes of New York Ministerium for 1836, p. 19; of Min. of Pa., 1853, p. 18.

Ministerium of New York in 1837, and of Pennsylvania in 1853, and the admission of numerous other Synods, a few of which were very small and soon became extinct, or were merged into others. These Synods were the Hartwick, admitted in 1831, the South Carolina in 1835, the Virginia in 1839, the Synod of the West in 1841, the English, of Ohio,[61] the Alleghany, the Southwest Virginia, and East Pennsylvania in 1843, the Miami in 1845, the Illinois, Southwest and Wittenberg in 1848, the Olive Branch in 1850, the Pittsburgh, Texas and North Illinois in 1853, the Kentucky, English District of Ohio and Central Pennsylvania in 1855, the North Indiana, South Illinois and English Iowa in 1857, Melanchthon in 1859, New Jersey in 1862, Minnesota and Franckean in 1864, Susquehanna, New York, Central Illinois and (second) Pittsburgh[65] in 1868, Kansas in 1869, Nebraska, Ansgari and German Maryland in 1875, Wartburg and Augsburg in 1877. The civil war caused a division in the General Synod, resulting in the withdrawal of the Synods of North Carolina, South Carolina, Virginia and Southwest Virginia. A second division was occasioned by the admission of the Franckean

---

[61] The student of the history of our Synods is liable to be confused among the English Synods of Ohio. The original English Synod of Ohio was a district of the Joint Synod. In 1840 it split, one division remaining in the Joint Synod, and the other leaving it, and both claiming the name of English Synod of Ohio. In 1857, the body which left the Joint Synod, and united with the General Synod, changed its name to Eastern Synod of Ohio. The other body in time left the Joint Synod, and following the Ministerium of Pennsylvania, united with the General Synod in 1855, left it in 1866, aided in the organization of the General Council, and was finally merged, in 1872, into the English District Synod of Ohio (No. 2) and Pittsburgh Synod. The English District Synod of Ohio (No. 2) was formed after the separation of its predecessor from Joint Synod, participated in the organization of the General Council, and in turn also left the Joint Synod. The English District Synod of Ohio (No. 3) was formed after the separation of No. 2 from the Joint Synod, and still maintains its connection, as one of the district Synods of that body.

[65] At its Twenty-fourth Convention at Rochester, Pa., in 1866, the Pittsburgh Synod, by a vote of 50 to 23, left the General Synod, and at the next meeting by a vote of 63 to 21, adopted the "Fundamental Principles of Faith and Church Polity" of the General Council. The most of the minority, viz., ten ministers and seven laymen, withdrew, claiming the name and corporate rights of the entire body, on the ground of an alleged violation of the constitution by the majority. The action of the General Synod in 1868 approved this claim, by recognizing the minority as though no resolution of withdrawal had ever been passed.

Synod in 1864, which led the delegates of the Ministerium of Pennsylvania to withdraw, in view of the fact that the Franckean Synod had not as yet received the Augsburg Confession as its confession of faith.[66] Two years afterwards, the exclusion of the delegates of the same Synod from the organization of the meeting at Ft. Wayne, resulted in the withdrawal of the Ministerium of New York, and the Synods of Pittsburgh, English Ohio, Minnesota and Texas, and the disbanding of the old Synod of Illinois. In the fall of 1860, when the General Synod had reached its greatest numerical strength, it numbered 864 out of 1313 ministers, and 164,000 out of 245,000 communicants, *i. e.*, two-thirds of the Lutheran Church in this country. In the fall of 1868, it had left 572 out of 1792 ministers, and 86,000 out of 350,000 communicants, or one-fourth of the entire Church. Its comparative strength according to the latest statistics in the almanac, published for its churches, is 812 out of 2905 ministers, and 116,000 out of 605,000 communicants.

---

[66] The resolution of admission was: "Resolved, That the Franckean Synod is received into connection with this Synod, with the understanding that said Synod, at its next meeting, declare, in on official manner, its adoption of the doctrinal articles of the Augsburg Confession, as a substantially correct exhibition of the fundamental doctrines of the Word of God." Minutes of General Synod, 1864. p. 18. The report of the President of the Franckean Synod in 1865, makes the following explanation: "For a quarter of a century, we maintained a separate existence, but at last concluded to form a connection with it (the General Synod), as it might serve a good purpose to unite all the district synods in grand council, and as there was nothing in the constitution to burden our consciences. Our admission, however, was opposed by a party, mainly on the ground that we had not formally adopted the "Augsburg Confession;" and, as a compromise, we were required to adopt its *doctrinal articles as a substantially correct exhibition of the fundamental doctrines of the Word of God*. Thus qualified we could consistently adopt it. Now, however, we are asked to do much more; viz., to amend the constitution by inserting in it an unqualified recognition or endorsement of the entire Augsburg Confession, and bind it as a creed upon our Synods, and our consciences. Are we, my brethren, prepared to do this, to do violence to our honest convictions, and become the reproach of Protestant Christianity? I hope not!" Minutes for 1865, p. 8. The revised doctrinal basis of the General Synod, received, accordingly, only one vote, p. 39.

In justice to many who voted for the admission of the Franckean Synod, it should yet be added, that they regarded the adoption of the constitution of the General Synod, by that body, a virtual adoption of the Augsburg Confession. Minutes of General Synod for 1864, p. 42.

The General Synod of North America, organized during the war in the Southern States, has embraced the Synods of North Carolina, South Carolina, Virginia, Southwest Virginia, Georgia, Mississippi and Holston. The Synod of North Carolina withdrew in 1871, and the Holston Synod in 1872. At the period of its greatest strength, it numbered 121 ministers, and 16,000 communicants; and is now reduced to 98 ministers, and 13,000 communicants.

The General Council was organized by a convention at Reading, Pa, in 1866. At its first meeting at Fort Wayne in 1867, the Ministeriums of Pennsylvania and New York, the English Synod of Ohio, the Pittsburgh, the Wisconsin, the English District of Ohio, the Michigan, the Augustana, the Minnesota, the Canada and the Illinois Synods, united as full members; while the German Iowa and the Joint Synod of Ohio accepted the invitation to be represented by delegates, with the right of debate, but not of vote. At the succeeding meeting in Pittsburgh, the Synod of Texas was received; at Chicago in 1869, the withdrawal of the Synod of Wisconsin was announced; at Rochester, in 1871, the withdrawal of the Synods of Minnesota and Illinois, was also announced; in 1872, the Indiana Synod was admitted, and in 1874, the Holston Synod of Tennessee. The Joint Synod of Ohio ceased all connection with the Council after the first meeting. The German Synod of Iowa has been represented in every convention except one, while the Norwegian-Danish Augustana, since 1871, has maintained the same relation to the General Council as the Iowa Synod. At its first meeting, exclusive of synods in an anomalous relation, it numbered 515 ministers and 136,000 communicants. The last official report,[67] rejecting also the anomalous synods, gives 593 ministers and 175,000 communicants; or, adding these two Synods, 743 ministers and 197,000 communicants.

The Synodical Conference was organized in 1872, and includes at present the Synods of Missouri, Ohio, Wisconsin, Illinois, and Minnesota, the Norwegian Synod, and the English Conference of Missouri, numbering altogether 1076 ministers, and about as many communicants as in the General Synod and General Council combined, and nearly twice as many as in the General Synod in the time of its greatest numerical strength. The synods unconnected with

---

[67] Minutes of the General Council, 1877.

general organizations scarcely amount in communicants to one twelfth of our entire number.

Between 1825 and '35, our strength was more than doubled; between 1835 and '53, it was again doubled; between 1853 and '68, it was doubled the third time; and, from present indications, before 1880 it will have been doubled for the fourth time. According to this, we are doubling our strength on an average every fourteen years, the ratio of increase in number of ministers not equaling, however, the increase of membership.[68]

---

[68] The following data, gleaned from various trustworthy sources, give a general idea of our strength by Synods, previous to the publication of our Almanacs:

1825	Min.	Cong.	Com.
Ministerium of Pennsylvania	58	212	26,882
" " New York	23	40	2,258
Synod of North Carolina	7	27	1,147
" " Ohio	24	96	6,676
" " Maryland and Virginia	30	48	5,137
" " South Carolina	10	19	1,025
" " Tennessee	11	?	?
	163	442	43,125

1834	Min.	Cong.	Com.
Ministerium of Pennsylvania	60	191	22,403
" " New York	24	37	2,404
Synod of North Carolina	12	24	1,621
" " Ohio, Eastern District	21	60	8,168
" " " Western "	27	83	4,019
" " Maryland	17	48	4,756
" " Tennessee	13	38	?
" " South Carolina	11	27	1,752
" " West Pennsylvania	34	132	9,872
" " Virginia	8	24	1,976
Hartwick Synod	16	37	4,000
	243	703	60,971

In 1833, the *Lutheran Preacher* (p. 80) estimated the Lutheran population in the United States as 750,000; while the N. Y. Ministerium (Minutes for 1833, p. 25) claimed a population in that State of 50,000.

An estimate by decades in *Ev. Review*, 7,298, supplemented by the statistics for 1863 and '73, gives:

	Min.	Cong.	Com.
1823	175	900	38,036
1833	337	1,017	59,358
1843	430	1,371	147,000
1853	900	1,750	200,000
1863	1,431	2,677	285,217
1873	2,309	4,115	485,085

The increase in the first period of ten years, finds its explanation in the better organization of the churches, the increased supply of ministers, the establishment of literary centres, the increasing power of the press, and the growing activity, both in the General Synod and out of it, in home missionary work. But before many years, unless a new factor enter into the account, the ratio of this increase would necessarily be greatly diminished by the exhaustion of the fields for new work, and the limitation of the growth of the churches to the natural growth of their population. This new element we find in what we may regard the fourth basis for Lutheran Church development in America. The Dutch on the Hudson form the first, the Swedes on the Delaware the second, the Germans of the eighteenth century the third, and the Germans and the Scandinavians of the nineteenth century the fourth basis. Nine-tenths of the two General Synods, less than one-half of the General Council, and about one-fourth of the members of Synods not included in any general organization, are the descendants of emigrants of the last century; while nineteen-twentieths of the Synodical Conference, three-fourths of the independent Synods, one-tenth of the General Synod, and more than one-half the General Council, are either foreign-born or the descendants of those who have come hither since 1825. How vast the work that has been thus thrown upon our Church in America, and how small a fraction of the whole, we who represent the anglicized portion of the Church, are becoming, may be learned, when we find that the official reports of emigration enumerate, between 1820 and 1837, over 231,000 Swedish and Norwegian, and 34,000 Danish immigrants, all of whom, with a few exceptions, are Lutheran, and 2,764,000 German immigrants, among whom we are largely represented; and that in the year 1873

We make no attempt to reconcile the discrepancies between the tables. It is gratifying, however, to notice how closely the number of congregations reported by the census for 1870 accords with the almanacs.

The two almanacs for 1878, that have attempted to compute the strength of the entire Church, report as follows:

	Min.	Cong.	Com.
Lutherische Kalender (Brobst's)	2,914	5,136	655,529
Lutheran Almanac (Kurtz)	2,905	5,004	605,340

The higher figures are the more trustworthy; yet both almanacs in their estimates are manifestly too low, as the synodical parochial reports for 1877 show many omissions.

alone there were 34,000 Scandinavians and 133,000 Germans landed on[69] our shores. Hence, is it wonderful that our increase *per annum* equals now the entire strength of our Church in this country fifty years ago? With a proportionate increase of a ministry fitted for pioneer work among those vast masses—hundreds of thousands of whom are our brethren in the faith—with the harmonious co-operation of the entire Church, and suitable provision to control the inevitable anglicizing of the foreign Lutheran population, so that their loss may be only one of language and nationality, but not of faith, ought not the rate of our Church's increase to be still greater? Are we not perhaps losing annually a number equal to the aggregate of the losses for the first two centuries that we so much deplore?

As fair an estimate as we can make from our personal knowledge of the field, upon the basis of the statistics gathered last year,[70] gives 117,000 Scandinavians, ministered to by 349 pastors; 312,000 foreign Germans, ministered to by 1315 pastors, and about 210,000 Americans and Pennsylvania Germans, ministered to by 1042 pastors. Surely we can no longer be reckoned, as we were twenty-five years ago by Dr. Baird, in his "Religion in America," among the smaller Presbyterian bodies.[71]

This development upon the fourth basis has thus far been largely influenced by the Synod of Missouri. This Synod had its origin in a colony of Saxon Lutherans, who, with their six pastors emigrated to Perry Co., Mo., in 1839, as the result, we are told in a narrative of a Missouri pastor, of a correspondence that their leader had in 1830, with Dr. Benjamin Kurtz, of Baltimore.[72] Thus the mission of Dr. Kurtz to Germany, to procure funds for the Gettysburg Theological Seminary, became indirectly the means of introducing into this country a powerful movement in favor of the strictest confessional Lutheranism. Scarcely had they reached this country, when they found their leader a deceiver. Thrown upon their own resources, the six pastors with great faith at once applied themselves,

---

[69] Annual American Cyclopædia for 1873. Another fact bearing upon the future development of our Church, is that the last census showed that nearly all the Scandinavians had settled west of Lake Michigan, and two-thirds of the Germans west of Buffalo, New York.

[70] Church Almanac for 1877.

[71] Baird's "Religion in America," p. 516.

[72] Köstering's Auswanderung der sächsischen Lutheraner, p. 10.

not only to the care of their people, but also to the work of educating candidates for the ministry to labor among the scattered Germans. Soon they were joined by others, especially by a number of ministers who had left the Synod of Ohio, on account of its alleged doctrinal laxity, and in 1847 the combined body held their first synodical meeting with twenty-seven pastors. Much aid was derived for some years from the distinguished Löhe, of Neuendettelsau, in Bavaria. Now they number over six hundred pastors, and support two theological seminaries, with over a hundred students, to say nothing of the other Synods, in which their influence amounts almost to a practical control. We should notice also in passing, as bodies of especial importance belonging to this fourth basis of development, the large Norwegian Synod, founded in the Northwest in 1859, with its 142 pastors and flourishing college at Decorah, Iowa; and the Swedish Augustana Synod, nearly as old and almost on the same territory, with its 120 pastors and flourishing institutions at Rock Island, Ill., in which, provident of the future, it supports two English professors.

Such are some of the general features of the external history and progress of our Church in the United States. Neither should its inner history be over-looked.

1. *Doctrinal Position.* The Dutch Lutherans of New York in various documents, pledge themselves, sometimes to the Unaltered Augsburg Confession,[73] and sometimes to the Symbolical Books of our Lutheran Church.[74] The instructions to the Governor of New Sweden in 1642, charged him to see to it, "that divine service be zealously performed according to the Unaltered Augsburg Confession."[75] The Halle Records repeatedly indicate that the foundation of the Ministerium of Pennsylvania was laid upon the Word of God, as confessed in the Augsburg Confession and the other Symbolical Books.[76] But near the close of the eighteenth century, no other confession but the Augustana was made binding, and at last even this requirement was sometimes omitted, as we find in the constitution of the New York Ministerium of 1816;[77] where it is laid down as a fundamental rule of the Synod, "that the person ordained shall not be required to make any other engagement than this, that he will faithfully teach, as well as perform all other minis-

---

[73] *Ev. Review*, 6: 313. [74] *Ev. Review*, 13: 366 [75] Acrelius, 39.
[76] *Ev. Review*, 3: 420; 5: 208. Hall. Nach., 285; 1287.   [77] P. 20.

terial duties, and regulate his walk and conversation, according to the Gospel of our Lord and Saviour Jesus Christ, as contained in Holy Scripture." Dr. S. S. Schmucker pertinently asks on the margin of the copy of this constitution, now in the Historical Library at Gettysburg: But "what is 'faithfully teaching' the Gospel of our Lord Jesus Christ?" It is generally acknowledged that especially in the New York Ministerium of that period very serious errors were prevalent. As an example of manifest indifference to the interests of our Church, we need only refer to the resolution by that body in 1797: "That on account of an intimate relation subsisting between the English Episcopalian and Lutheran churches, the identity of their doctrine and the near approach of their church discipline, this consistory will never acknowledge a newly erected Lutheran Church, in places where the members may partake of the services of the said English Episcopal Church."[78] Three years before, the ministers of our Church in North Carolina had ordained Rev. R. J. Miller, as "an Episcopal minister," and charged him in his ordination certificate "to obey the rules, ordinances and customs of the Christian society, called the Protestant Episcopal Church in America,"[79] and then, with this understanding, permitted him to labor in Lutheran congregations for twenty-seven years. In 1821, the North Carolina Synod entered into an agreement with the Protestant Episcopal Church of the same State, whereby each body sent deputations to the conventions of the other, with the privilege not only of a voice, but also of a vote.[80] The reaction was natural, by which the members of the Tennessee Synod a few years later not only placed themselves upon a decidedly confessional basis, but went so far as to incorporate a provision in

---

[78] *Ev. Review,* 7: 533; 11: 183. Yet in the minutes for 1824, we find lay-reading commended as a means of keeping together Lutherans, where they were without a pastor, and of " resisting the encroachments of other churches," p. 31.

[79] Bernheim, 339.

[80] Bernheim 450, *sq.* During this period the Episcopal Church was often popularly called the " English Lutheran." See *Eine Zuschrift von der Corporation Deutschen Lutherischen Gemeine in Philadelphia,*" Germantown, 1805, p. 9: " The expression German Evangelical Lutheran Doctrine is unusual to us; and if any one should have used it, it perhaps was done in antithesis to the English Episcopal doctrine, which is called by many from ignorance Lutheran, and English Lutheran."

their constitution that: "No subject whatever, which may be comprehended under these Articles, shall be decided either according to a majority or a minority of votes; but only according to the Holy Scriptures, and the Augsburg Confession of faith;"[81] and to send for consecutive years to the Ministerium of Pennsylvania formidable documents, challenging its Lutheranism, which the latter passed by in silence.[82] The great question that agitated our Church in this country for many years of the present century, was in substance: "Shall we retain our historical connection with the Lutheran Church of our fathers, or shall we surrender the distinctive doctrines for which they contended, and as a religious society become simply a member of the Reformed family of Churches by which we are surrounded?" This was the question that lay beneath nearly all our controversies. We were in danger of being carried away by the strongest currents prevalent for the time in the denominations around us. The doctrinal controversies concerning Original Sin and the Holy Sacraments, and the practical controversies concerning the necessity and obligation of confessions of faith, concerning a recension of the Augsburg Confession, concerning Old and New

---

[81] Minutes, 1827; p. 23.

[82] The questions addressed to the Ministerium of Pennsylvania in 1823 were:
1. Do you believe that Holy Baptism, as it is administered with natural water, in the name of the Father, Son and Holy Ghost, worketh forgiveness of sins, delivers from death and the devil, and gives everlasting salvation?
2. Do you believe that the true body and blood of Christ is present in the Holy Supper, under the form of bread and wine, and is there communicated and received? Do you believe also that the unbelieving guests of this meal eat and drink also the body and blood of Christ, under the form of bread and wine? We ask not whether the unbelieving thereby receive the forgiveness of sins, but whether in this sacrament they receive also the body and blood of Jesus?
3. Do you believe that Jesus Christ should be worshiped as true God and man in one person?
4. Is it right that the Evangelical Lutheran Church should seek to unite in any religious form of government with those who deny the doctrine of the Augsburg Confession and Luther's Catechism? or is it right that Lutherans should go with such to the Holy Supper?
5. Is your Synod hereafter to be governed by a majority of votes?
6. Do you still intend to present the excuse that "Jesus Christ, the Supreme Head of His Church, has prescribed no specific directory for its government and discipline," as is said in the constitution of the General Synod? Min., p. 13.

Measures, concerning orders of service in divine worship, can be traced to external influences; and our Church was in danger of perishing on this continent from a lack of self-assertion, and a forgetfulness of her mission from the very beginning as a teacher to all nations and all Churches, of the very purest form of the Gospel. There were, of course, other elements that entered into these movements. The intense subjectivism of Pietism prepared the way here as in Europe for dangers from Rationalism. The desolation wrought in the mother country only touched our shores with its remotest and feeblest waves; yet these were sufficient to cause an undervaluing by otherwise excellent men, of those strongholds of the Christian faith, the distinctive doctrines of our Church. Then, on the other hand, it must be confessed that the partisan zeal, bitter spirit, and imprudent counsels of some who in the period of greatest indifference protested against the prevailing laxity, were adapted to repel rather than attract earnest men. Our ministers (and we would give due honor to those venerable men, so abundant in labors and sacrifices,) were so overwhelmed in their work, that they had little time for special studies. The cotemporary literature that came from Germany, was infected with the poison abounding there. With the anglicizing of the people, the congregations were left without a Lutheran literature. Earnest and devout members of our congregations were naturally led to procure and read the devotional and practical works of other Churches, to the neglect of the rich ascetic literature in which our Church abounds. John Arndt, Scriver, Gerhard, Heinrich Mueller, Herberger, were replaced by Baxter, Doddridge, Bunyan, Wesley, Edwards. Many candidates for the ministry were instructed in the schools of other Churches, and, even though on their guard, unconsciously drew in the spirit of these Churches, acquiring with much that was truly precious, much also that obscured the strength and simplicity of the Evangelical faith. The English churches had the start of our Lutheran peasantry in education and general intelligence, and, by a higher social position, presented attractions for those not well grounded in the faith; while intermarriage also contributed its element to the confusion; sometimes to our gain, more frequently to our loss. Non-Lutheran Sunday-schools, and the repetition in Lutheran schools by unwary teachers of what they had drawn from authorities prejudiced against our Church and its doctrines, also had their influence against us.

The only wonder is that the result was not worse; and that there was anything of Lutheranism left among us. Yet the devotional works of our Church were still read in many a quiet corner; the German hymns were not altogether forgotten, and, even when no longer heard in public service, brought comfort and joy to many an aged servant of Christ; Luther's Catechism was still taught in the Church, and even when neglected in the Sunday-school, or supplanted[82a] by imagined improvements, was handed down for generations from the memory of pious parents, and more than anything else except the Holy Word itself preserved and nourished our vitality during that season of trial. Many a devout but uneducated layman, many a plain but thoughtful mother, was thus shaping in the family the future theological course of a new generation in the ministry.

The Lutheran Church in the United States has certainly made great progress within the last twenty-five years in fuller acquaintance, higher appreciation and heartier acceptance of the theology of the Reformation—a progress manifested not simply in the doctrinal tests of our general organizations,[83] our synods, our seminaries,

---

[82a] Resolution of N. C. Synod in 1825: "As the complaint is universal, that so many different English catechisms are circulating under the name of Lutheran, and which are partly abridged or not well translated, it was unanimously *Resolved*, That none of our ministers can receive any catechism, thereby to instruct children, which in the articles of faith or doctrinals departs from Dr. Luther's Small Catechism; because we are bound by the constitution of the General Synod of our Church, to make no change in the doctrine of the Church." Minutes, p. 11.

"In consequence of the long delay of the committee appointed by the last session of the General Synod, to have an *exact* translation of Dr. Martin Luther's Catechism printed," etc. Minutes of N. C. Synod for 1826, p. 6.

See some excellent remarks by Dr. Hazelius on the spiritual desolation resulting from neglect of catechisation, in Minutes of N. Y. Ministerium, 1830, p. 26.

[83] CONFESSIONAL BASES OF THE PRINCIPAL LUTHERAN BODIES IN AMERICA.
I. *The General Synod.*

"We receive and hold, with the Evangelical Lutheran Church of our fathers, the Word of God, as contained in the canonical Scriptures of the Old and New Testaments, as the only infallible rule of faith and practice, and the Augsburg Confession, as a correct exhibition of the fundamental doctrines of the Divine Word, and of the faith our Church founded upon that Word."

II. *The General Synod in North America (South).*

"We receive and hold that the Old and New Testaments are the Word of

but in the change that can be readily discerned in the entire habit of many of the Churches which we have classified as belonging to the third basis of Lutheran development in America. A leaven is working, slowly it may be, yet none the less surely, which encourages the hope that in the not very remote future we may be able to apply ourselves with greater harmony to the great work before us in this country. Our greatest danger lies in our impatience, that the processes in operation do not advance with sufficient rapidity. Where, however, is the openly proclaimed Rationalism and Socinianism of the first part of this century? Where is the body claiming to be

God, and the only infallible rule of faith and practice. We likewise hold that the Apostles' Creed, the Nicene Creed, and the Augsburg Confession, contain the fundamental doctrines of the sacred Scriptures; and we receive and adopt them as the exponents of our faith."

III. *The General Council.*

"We accept and acknowledge the doctrines of the Unaltered Augsburg Confession in its original sense, as throughout in conformity with the pure truth of which God's Word is the only rule. We accept its statements of truth, as in perfect accordance with the canonical Scriptures. We reject the errors it condemns, and we believe that all which it commits to the liberty of the Church, of right belongs to that liberty."

"In thus formally accepting and acknowledging the Unaltered Augsburg Confession, we declare our conviction that the other Confessions of the Evangelical Lutheran Church, inasmuch as they set forth none other than its system of doctrine, and articles of faith, are of necessity pure and Scriptural. Preeminent among such accordant, pure and Scriptural statements of doctrine, by their intrinsic excellence, by the great and necessary ends for which they were prepared, by their historical position, and the general judgment of the Church, are these: the Apology of the Augsburg Confession, the Smalcald Articles, the Catechisms of Luther, and the Formula of Concord, all of which are with the Unaltered Augsburg Confession, in the perfect harmony of one and the same Scriptural faith."

IV. *The Synodical Conference.*

"The Synodical Conference acknowledges the canonical Scriptures of the Old and New Testament, as God's Word, and the Confession of the Evangelical Lutheran Church of 1580 called 'the Concordia,' as its own."

V. *The North Carolina and Tennessee Synods.*

"We believe that the Unaltered Augsburg Confession is, in all its parts, in harmony with the Word of God, and is a correct exhibition of doctrine."

"We believe that the Apology, the Catechisms of Luther, the Smalcald Articles, and the Formula of Concord, are a faithful development and defence of the Word of God, as set forth in the Augsburg Confession."

Lutheran that any longer ventures to reject the Augsburg Confession, or even to adopt a mutilated recension of the same? What, too, has been the fate of books which a quarter of a century ago were considered standard among English-speaking Lutherans, that avowedly rejected, and attempted to refute parts of our Confession? And where does the strength of Synods, whose acceptance of the Lutheran faith is said to be least decided, lie? What congregations manifest the steadiest growth and the greatest permanent activity but those among them administered most in the spirit of our Confession? A few hours' study of the parochial reports will furnish the answer. It is true that success, measured by earthly standards, will never be the lot of a pure Church; yet manifest tokens of the divine presence with us should not be overlooked.

2. *Church Government.* The foundation for the general form of the constitutions of congregations, that has been in use in most of the churches of the General Council and the two General Synods, was laid by the fathers of the Ministerium of Pennsylvania. The constitution of the German church in Philadelphia[84] provided for a church council, elected by the congregations, consisting of trustees, elders and deacons. Under this provision, Muhlenberg and Handschuh were both elected trustees, and thus made members of the church council. The constitution prepared by Muhlenberg, in 1757, for the Church in Georgia, differs in this particular, as it prescribes that the church council shall consist of "the oldest minister as president, and the regular elected deacons."[85]

3. *Worship.* Owing to the wide extent of territory embraced in the charges of our earlier pastors, but few of their congregations enjoyed Divine service every Lord's day. The Swedish pastors often had a double service in the morning, the first consisting of a hymn or the Te Deum, a sermon on some parts of the catechism, a prayer and concluding hymn, followed by an explanation of the sermon, and examination upon it by the teacher. Then came the principal service, called "High Mass," in which the order of the Church in the mother country was observed.[86] The German Lutherans of Pennsylvania of the last century, at an early period, prepared a liturgy on the basis of that of the Savoy congregation in London.[87] In 1747, Muhlenberg prescribed to Rev. Schaum an

---

[84] H. N., 964. [85] *Ev. Review*, 3: 126. [86] Acrelius, 218.

[87] "We took the printed Kirchen-Agenda of the Evangelical German con-

order which he was to observe invariably in public service,[88] viz.:
1. Confession. 2. Gloria in Excelsis. 3. A Scriptural Prayer. 4. Reading of the Epistle. 5. A familiar hymn. 6. Reading of the Gospel, followed by the Creed. 7. Singing of a hymn, during which the minister ascends the pulpit. 8. Sermon. 9. Reading of a liturgical prayer. 10. Catechisation of the children. The Order of Service in the Church in Georgia in 1757,[89] differs in its details, but comprises an opening prayer that is read, the use of the Gospel and Epistle for the day, the reading of a general prayer or the use of the Litany after the sermon, always ending with the Lord's Prayer. The Liturgy of the Ministerium of Pennsylvania of 1786,[90]

---

gregation at Savoy in London, as the foundation, because we had no other at hand." II. N., 676.

[88] *Ev. Review*, 7 : 544.

[89] *Ev. Review*, 3 : 423 : "The order of the public worship of God on Sundays and festivals, shall be observed and conducted in the two principal churches, as follows : (1) In the morning at the usual time, the minister commences with a prayer out of the London Liturgy, or a suitable prayer out of J. Arndt's Paradies Gärtlein; (2) the schoolmaster reads a portion of the Holy Bible, following in order the prayer; (3) a hymn is given out by the minister from the Halle Hymn Book ; (4) the minister reads either the appointed Gospel or Epistle ; (5) another hymn is announced ; (6) the minister prays extemporaneously, and closes with the Lord's Prayer ; (7) he reads either the Gospel or Epistle, or text from which he intends to preach ; (8) the sermon follows, concluded with prayer ; (9) the minister reads the general prayer in the London Liturgy, or the Litany in the Hymn-book, and closes with the Lord's Prayer; (10) Publications are made ending with an Apostolic wish ; the congregation sings, and is dismissed with the Benediction of the Lord.

[90] The order in the Liturgy of 1786 is as follows : 1. A suitable hymn. 2. The minister goes before the altar, and makes the exhortation to confession, and the confessional prayer, ending with the Kyrie. 3. He pronounces the votum : "The Lord be with you," to which the congregation reply, "And with thy Spirit." 4. He prays again, either extemporaneously or one of the Morning prayers in the Hymn-Book. 5. Reading of the Epistle. 6. The principal hymn, during which he ascends the pulpit. 7. The sermon, which may be preceded by the Lord's Prayer and the Gospel for the day. 8. He prays either the prescribed General prayer or the Litany, and must not vary from this rule without necessity. The prayer closes with extemporaneous intercessions for the sick, if desired, and Lord's Prayer. 9. Necessary notices then are given. 10. He pronounces the benediction, "The peace of God which passeth all understanding, keep your hearts and minds through Christ Jesus unto everlasting life. Amen." 11. Several stanzas are then sung, during which alms may be col-

the English Hymn Books of the churches in New York at the close of the last century,[91] and the record of Dr. Geo. Lochman in his little volume on the Lutheran Church,[92] all present similar forms.

lected for the poor. 12. The minister comes again before the altar, and again pronounces the votum, which is responded to by the congregation. 13. He prays an extemporaneous prayer, or the short form given in the Liturgy. 14. Singing of "the Lord preserve our coming in and going out," or of a stanza of a hymn, at the discretion of the minister. Pp. 1–12.

[91] The following is the order in the "Collection of Evangelical Hymns, made from different authors, and collections for the English Lutheran Church in New York. By George Strebeck, New York: 1797."

1. Singing. 2. Exhortation to Confession. 3. Confessional Prayer, closing with the Kyrie. 4. "The Lord be with you," responded to by the congregation: "And with thy Spirit." 5. An extemporaneous or read prayer, at the discretion of the minister. 6. The Gospel and Epistle for the day. 7. Singing. 8. Sermon. 9. The invariable use either of a prescribed general prayer or the Litany, closing with the Lord's Prayer. 10. Announcing of the hymn, and the sentence: "The peace of God which passeth all understanding," etc. 11. The minister descends from the pulpit, and pronounces again: "The Lord be with you," responded to again by the congregation, makes a short prayer, either according to a given form, or extemporaneously, and concludes with the patriarchal benediction.

That prescribed in the "Hymn and Prayer Book for the use of such Lutheran Churches as use the English Language, collected by John C. Kunze, D. D., senior of the Lutheran clergy in the State of New York, New York: 1795," is almost identical with the order given by Mr. Strebeck. A copy of both volumes is in the Library of Pennsylvania College, and of the Lutheran Historical Society.

[92] "Public worship is at present regulated and conducted in the following order: The beginning is made by a few passages of Scripture, or by a short ejaculation, and by singing a hymn. Prayers are then read, consisting of confession of sins, praise and thanksgiving, petition and intercession; or the minister may pray *ex tempore*. A portion of Scripture is read, which may be either the Gospel or Epistle for the day, or any other portion suited to the occasion, and relating to the subject on which the sermon is preached. Another hymn is sung. Then the sermon is preached, which should not take up more than three-quarters of an hour. Before sermon, a short prayer *may* be offered up, but after sermon, it is considered necessary to pray. Another hymn is sung, during which or before which the alms are collected. The congregation is dismissed with the benediction. In some congregations, a doxology is sung after the benediction." "History, Doctrine, and Discipline of the Evangelical Lutheran Church," by George Lochman, A. M., Harrisburg, 1818, p. 151.

In all parts of the Church, the Church year was diligently observed."[93] Its omission in some of our English churches has been a deviation of a comparatively modern period. The sermons of the earlier ministers were generally prepared by the writing out of a very full and well arranged scheme, which was thoroughly committed. Several manuscript volumes of such schemes by Dr. Kunze, are in the library of Pennsylvania College. Dr. Helmuth writes of his colleague, Schmidt, that whereas his Mss. contained dispositions on nearly all the texts in the Bible, yet that he left only two sermons that were written in full.[94] However inconsistent with the rules the practice may have been, yet the *Kirchen-Ordnung* of 1763 forbids the filling of the pulpit in the pastor's stead, " by any preacher or student who has not been examined and regularly called and ordained, according to our Evangelical Church Constitution."[95] The value they placed upon the Sacrament of Holy Baptism is manifest from the care which our fathers took to have their children baptized at the earliest age.[96]

We have thus briefly traced a few of the features of our inner history. The great problem before us now is to properly avail ourselves of this history in laying broad and deep the foundation for the promising future that is opening for our Church. The individualism which most of us have inherited from our German ancestors, must be

---

[93] Acrelius and Hall. Nach., *passion*. See orders of service given above. The following from the constitution of the Church in Georgia is worthy of note: " As has been customary from the beginning, the three grand festivals, Christmas, Easter and Pentecost shall be celebrated two days ; also shall be celebrated New Year's day, Epiphany, the anniversary of our fathers' arrival between the 9th and 11th of March ; Maundy Thursday (when the doctrine of the Lord's Supper shall be especially explained for edification), and Good Friday, every year. From *Esto Mihi* until Easter, in the afternoon service, the history of the sufferings of our Lord and Saviour shall be propounded and explained, catechetically and paragraphically, either from an Evangelist or from a Harmony approved by our venerable fathers." *Ev. Review* 3: 424. All the older Church records show that they followed invariably the Church year.

[94] *Evangelisches Magazin*, Vol. 2 (1813), p 7. [95] Hall. Nach., 963.

[96] The earliest records of our churches in Adams county, served in the last century by Pastor Bager, give abundant testimony on this point. Here is one memorandum we have made : Out of 61 children baptized in the Benders' congregation, the age of 8 is not given, 23 were baptized under the age of one month, 23 between one and two months; the oldest baptized was between seven and eight months, while one was baptized when two days old, a second when

subordinated to the welfare of the whole. The progress of our one Lutheran Church must be esteemed of more importance than that of any particular branch. Development on the third and fourth bases is to be rendered harmonious; not by the dominancy of either party, but by the careful study, and the humble submission of both to the unerring Word of God. German love of liberty, conscientiousness, cordiality, respect for antiquity, delight in research, steadfast courage and undaunted perseverance; Swedish seriousness, devoutness and subjection to law; Norwegian vigor and purity; Danish caution, thoughtfulness and love of peace; Icelandic simplicity, generosity and earnestness in religion; Finnish affection and tenderness, are to unite with American enterprise, energy and love of the practical, on the vast plane for development amidst varied elements almost in perpetual motion, opened for our Church on this continent. We have much to learn from one another. We lament our divisions, and all declare them to be wrong. Yet each of our general bodies has, perhaps, a special office in the present emergency to train the Church of the future for its high mission; and, on the one hand, to guard against Rationalism and Infidelity, and, on the other, to transmit the influences of our Lutheran faith to other communions. For as we believe that our Church teaches the gospel in its purest form, so also we hope and pray not only that all who bear our name, but also all Christian people in this land, may confess it as such.

We are yet in a formative state. Our Church feels bewildered amidst its new surroundings, and confused by many of the entirely new issues that she encounters, and modes of adaptation necessary in this western world. She has learned some lessons by bitter experience; she is learning others by new trials. The age of experiments is gradually yielding to that of sober and mature manhood; and beneath all, there is the vigor and enthusiasm and perpetual youth of a strength derived from the possession of the truth, that must triumph finally over all obstacles, and result, after many struggles and apparent defeats, in a Church united upon the foundation of the Apostles and Prophets, Jesus Christ Himself being the chief corner-stone.

---

four days old, a third when eight, and three when nine days old. The records at Arndstown, and those at Christ's church, Littlestown, during the pastorate of Wildbahn (1763), show that the practice there was the same.

REMARKS OF REV. F. W. CONRAD, D. D. (*General Synod.*)

Dr F. W. Conrad said: In referring to the history of the General Council, the author of the instructive paper just read stated, that the Franckean Synod had been received by the General Synod without having adopted the Augsburg Confession. This statement, according to my recollection, I regard as, strictly speaking, incorrect. The facts of the case are these:

Dr. B. Kurtz, President of the General Synod, was requested by letter to inform the members of the Franckean Synod what they must do in order to be admitted into the General Synod. He replied, that nothing more was necessary than to adopt the Constitution of the General Synod, and appoint the requisite number of delegates. The constitution of the General Synod was accordingly adopted by the Franckean Synod, and delegates appointed to the General Synod.

The Constitution of the General Synod provided that any "regularly constituted Lutheran Synod, holding the fundamental doctrines of the Bible, as taught by our Church," might be received into connection with it. These doctrines are set forth, according to unanimous consent, in the Augsburg Confession. Now, although the Franckean Synod had not directly adopted the Augsburg Confession, they had indirectly and really adopted it by adopting the Constitution of the General Synod, and thereby declared that they held "the fundamental doctrines of the Bible as taught by our Church," in the Augsburg Confession. This was tantamount to its adoption by a formal resolution, and imposed the same confessional obligation. It pledged the synod to teach "the doctrines of our Church," as taught in the Augsburg Confession. The delegates of the Franckean Synod, accordingly, declared in writing that their Synod clearly understood that, in adopting the Constitution, it adopted the doctrinal basis of the General Synod, as expressed in its formula for subscribing the Augsburg Confession contained in its Formula of Government and Discipline. But, as the General Synod imposed upon the Franckean Synod, as a condition of full reception, the formal adoption of the Augsburg Confession, according to its Formula; and as it did not receive its delegates at Fort Wayne until after being certified that the imposed condition had been complied with, its reception at York was only conditional, and the Franckean Synod was not fully admitted into the General Synod until it had formally adopted the Augsburg Confession.

The construction and confessional force which we have given to the adoption of its Constitution has been exemplified by the official acts of the General Synod. Neither the New York Ministerium, nor the Pittsburgh Synod, nor the Ministerium of Pennsylvania, had by express resolution adopted the Augsburg Confession, prior to their applications for admission into the General Synod. But they had all adopted the Constitution of the General Synod, by which they declared that they held " the fundamental doctrines of the Bible as taught by our Church." This the General Synod construed as involving a real, although indirect, adoption of the Augsburg Confession, and constituted each one of them, as well as the Franckean Synod, "regularly constituted Lutheran Synods," in the sense of the Constitution.

In the heat of the discussion the fact was overlooked that, as "no man can serve two masters," neither can a Synod be governed and characterized by two different confessions. As soon, therefore, as the Franckean Synod adopted the Constitution of the General Synod, it subjected itself to the Augsburg Confession, and became Lutheran. And by necessary consequence, it could no longer be held subject to its former confession, and ceased to be an isolated, separatistic body.

It may not be amiss to recall and improve another occurrence at York. God is said to have the hearts of all men in His hand, and that He can turn them as He doth the rivers of water. He accordingly governs the Church, through the sincere convictions and conscientious judgment of its ministers and members. When, therefore, an important ecclesiastical question has been thoroughly discussed and a decision reached by an almost or quite unanimous vote, that judgment ought to be regarded as determining the question for the time being under existing circumstances. To disturb a decision thus attained immediately afterwards, without additional light and the most urgent necessity, must be hazardous, and its reversal often proves to have been ill-advised, unfortunate, and not unfrequently wrong.

Such a case occurred at York. Differences of opinion prevailed in regard to the character and continued force of the Articles of Faith of the Franckean Synod, as well as its adoption of the Augsburg Confession. The subject was discussed during an entire day and an almost unanimous decision reached at its close. This decision was reconsidered the next morning, and after a long and an exciting debate, reversed. A protest signed by members of ten Synods was presented, an answer followed, the delegates of the Pennsylvania Synod withdrew, the General Synod was rent in twain and the Lutheran Church again divided! While, therefore, I maintain that the Franckean Synod had met the constitutional requirements of the General Synod, and cannot justify the grounds upon which the delegates of the Pennsylvania Synod withdrew from it, I am nevertheless compelled, in the light of the facts of this case, and all the consequences resulting therefrom, to regard the reversal of that decision as one belonging to the class of injudicious decisions just described. Some "things are lawful, but not" always "expedient." But He who can make even the wrath of man to praise Him, can and will overrule all things for the good of His Church.

REMARKS OF REV. PROF. J. A. BROWN, D. D. (*General Synod.*)

There will be but one opinion, I suppose, in regard to the value of the paper which has been read. It presents a very clear narrative of some of the most important events in our history, and is just what many will desire to possess. I will venture to make a few additional statements on the point raised by Dr. Conrad's speech. The General Synod was not hasty in its action. After long discussion, the General Synod declined to receive the Franckean Synod on the ground of its not having adopted the Augsburg Confession. Subsequent to this action the delegation presented a paper, stating that in adopting the Formula of the General Synod, they understood they were adopting the Augsburg Confession as their confession of faith, and pledging themselves to comply with the requirement of the General Synod in this respect. The question of their reception was reconsidered, and they were received, but only provisionally; that unless satisfactory evidence was furnished of their acceptance of the Augsburg Confession, they would not be considered in the General Synod. And accordingly at the next meeting, at Fort Wayne, these delegates were not received until after the organization, and the evidence furnished that they had fully complied with the conditions of their reception. The action of the General Synod was very cautious and conservative.

This recalls another case which deserves to be mentioned. The Melanchthon Synod made application for admission into the General Synod under circumstances very similar to those of the Franckean Synod, and met with similar opposition. It was maintained that the Melanchthon Synod had not adopted the Augsburg Confession, or fairly complied with the conditions of admission. Its whole history was regarded as irregular and not very Lutheran. The opposition was very decided and persistent. Yet the General Synod received the Melanchthon Synod, without imposing conditions, but with a very humble request that it would conform its position to the requirements of the General Synod. There were no withdrawals of delegates, nor divisions in the body. I hope I will not be deemed discourteous, when I remind the Diet that my friend, Dr. Krauth, was the champion at that time of the Melanchthon Synod, and of its admission into the General Synod. Unless my memory is at fault, he drew up the resolutions for the admission of the Melanchthon Synod, using such gentle terms, and withstood the opposition. Times have changed.

Now I do not see on what grounds so much ado is made by some over the reception of the Franckean Synod, while the reception of the Melanchthon Synod is justified. It seems to me that the action of the General Synod was more cautious and more conservative at York than at Pittsburgh. I think the action of the General Synod at York can be consistently defended, and that that body is not responsible for the consequences.

REMARKS OF REV. PROF. C. P. KRAUTH, D. D., LL. D.
(General Council.)

Dr. Krauth spoke in terms of strong commendation of the paper read by Prof. Jacobs. It shows great thoroughness of research, especially in directions where the difficulty of obtaining facts can only be estimated by one who has had occasion to attempt the same sort of work. It is clear, well arranged, presenting facts in just proportion, and with the most absolute fairness. The production of this paper alone would have repaid for the calling of this Diet.

As the Franckean Synod had been brought into the discussion, he would take the opportunity of correcting a misapprehension in regard to the position of his venerated father on that question. His father was quoted as one who held the ruling at Ft. Wayne to be correct, and there his testimony was supposed to end. It was true he did so regard it, and looked upon the Pennsylvania Ministerium as having put itself out of the General Synod by the withdrawal of its delegates at York. But he constantly added, with no reserve as of a thing spoken confidentially, as all who heard him speak of it can testify, that "the admission of the Franckean Synod was an outrage, fully justifying the Ministerium of Pennsylvania in withdrawing; and that the only matter of regret was that having withdrawn for so righteous a cause, it should have endeavored to return."

The action at the close of the first day was of the gentlest and most conciliatory kind. It completely harmonized the General Synod. The Franckean Synod itself was not dissatisfied—so reasonable and moderate was the action. The influences which disturbed the settled question were at work outside of the hours of meeting, and were partisan and mischievous. The Franckean Synod had not undergone any very radical change from the time when the General Synod had passed a resolution condemning its fanatical and disorderly practices. The whole debate showed that it was completely un-Lutheran, and that there had been no intelligent conformity with the requirements of the Constitution. After its reception at York, many of the best men in the General Synod, some of whom are still among its most honored names, united in protest against the admission.

In reply to Dr. Brown, Dr. Krauth said that he had not been the champion of the Melanchthon Synod; on the contrary, he had strongly opposed, on principle, its admission. But when the facts showed that the precedents established in the admission of a number of other Synods, and the retention of various bodies which openly threw away the Augsburg Confession for the Definite Platform, had made it gross inconsistency and virtual self-destruction for the General Synod to reject the Melanchthon Synod, he had offered as the best thing the case allowed, that to the reception of the Melanchthon Synod should be attached a request that it should take action which would remove the causes of offence. This was all, in fact, the General Synod had left itself the power of doing. It was the thorough-going opposition which he had felt and shown to the admission of the Melanchthon Synod, which made him the proper person to offer this resolution. But there were very many respects in which the character of the Melanchthon Synod, and of its plea for admission, was free from that which made the Franckean Synod so totally unfit to be a member of any Lutheran Body.

As to the implication of change, he had never waited to have his real change of views brought as a charge. He was the first to make that change known by frank acknowledgment. There is no peril greater to a man's love of truth than a false pride of mechanical consistency. But his seeming inconsistencies were the long growth of ripening consistency. They were not the result of want of a fixed principle—the shifting from principle to principle—but the outgrowth of one great set of principles, maturing and bringing into more perfect harmony the conviction and the act—such as (to compare the very little with the very great) Luther himself passed through. From the hour that by God's grace, through many a sore struggle and conflict, he had begun to approach the firm ground, up to the present, he had moved in one line. His present convictions were connected by unbroken succession with those earliest ones. The law of growth is the law of life. The inconsistencies of the earnest seeker of truth are like the inconsistencies of the oak with its acorn. There are changes, but it is the one life which has conditioned them all.

Dr. Conrad had spoken of the testimony as to alleged errors in the Augsburg Confession—the Testimony adopted by the General Synod at York—as identical with the one which had been prepared by Dr. Krauth, and adopted in the Pittsburgh Synod. But not only did the history of the two documents involve a difference in their meaning, where they coincided in words, but the language itself was in some respects materially changed. The two documents were related somewhat as the Invariata and the Variata, but with the changes made by other hands, against the will of the author. He disavowed, therefore, the Testimony of the General Synod as properly his.

Dr. Conrad's acknowledgment of the great mistake made in disturbing the original disposition of the Franckean Synod case, was worthy of his candor, and could not fail to do good.

REMARKS OF REV. D. P. ROSENMILLER. (*General Synod.*)

For many years in the Constitution of the Synod of Pennsylvania, only the Augsburg Confession was mentioned. It has, in fact, been only about twelve years since it was altered, and the other symbolical books adopted in such a shape that the Augsburg Confession dare not speak in any other sense than they speak. In the Liturgy adopted by the Synod in early days, the word Lutheran did not occur in the services for Ordination, Adult Baptism and Confirmation. These first documents were drawn up by the patriarch of our Church, and he evidently had the impression that the German Reformed and Lutheran would merge into one Evangelical Church. I have examined the Church Constitutions, drawn up by him, in which he gives the right to ministers, during the week, by day or night, to hold meetings for edification and prayer.

In this connection I would endeavor to throw some light on a document which had some connection with the unfortunate separation which took place at Fort Wayne. After the delegates of the Pennsylvania Synod, two years previously at York, Pa., had protested against the reception of the Franckean Synod, and reported to their own Synod, a committee of seven was appointed to report on their action. The report of that committee was, that the action of the delegates should be approved and sustained. But the chairman [Rev. Rosenmiller.—ED.] explained before the Synod that this report did not decide that the action of the delegates was correct. But, as they acted according to their honest convictions, although their judgment may have been wrong, yet their action should be approved and sustained. And this approval was not considered as a separation from the General Synod, on the part of the Synod of Pennsylvania.

The fifth paper was then read:

EDUCATION IN THE LUTHERAN CHURCH IN THE UNITED STATES.

BY REV. M. VALENTINE, D. D., PRESIDENT OF PENNSYLVANIA COLLEGE, GETTYSBURG, PA.

IN calling attention to Education in the Lutheran Church in the United States, I am permitted to feel that the subject is one of intrinsic importance and wide bearings. It does not, indeed, express anything belonging to the Church's divine foundation, but it concerns her great work. Without the importance that attaches to discussions settling the dogmas of the faith, it must, however, carry the interest that ever belongs to the chief means by which the mission of Christianity and the work of the Church are to be accomplished. The relation of *means*, it must be remembered, gives even to doctrine its high importance. Christianity, even as a whole, in all its grand truths and divine powers, is not for itself, but a means looking to the salvation of men and the redemption of the earth. Education looks to the same end for which God has given the sacred doctrines. It expresses one of the modes through which the power of salvation goes into effect and pushes on toward its goal. How directly, as if by normal action, this power moves to the accomplishment of its mission through the agency of education, is apparent from the rise of Christian schools among the first manifestations of the Church's life and activity. As if the earliest preaching of the gospel was the marshaling of the fit agencies for the grand work of conquest and progress, these schools quickly sprang up and stood in the front lines of the holy service. We see them at Alexandria, Antioch, Edessa, Nisibis, and elsewhere. They held forth the word of life, uplifted high the standard of the cross, and became conspicuous summits of the Church's power and defence in those early centuries.

There can be no doubt that the life of the Church of Christ has been meant to enter into and ally with its own blessed ends all normal human powers and movements. Christianity is not a thing to be, or capable of being, held as a thing by itself, apart from the offices and activities of life. It comes as a force to enter every other force that legitimately belongs to the constitution of the world, and to sanctify and claim all for God and righteousness. It may not usually, indeed, undertake the functions of other constitutions, but it is to permeate all with its supernatural truth and life, and make each department, in its own sphere, bear its proper part in the aggregate redemption of the earth. Education, however, is a function that falls so immediately in the line of the Church's work, expresses so directly what is part of her essential office, that it may not only be pervaded by her sanctifying influence, like, for instance, the separate civil power, but be possessed and used as her rightful agency. The Church is instrumentally the light of the world. Her great office is to teach—to teach all nations. She holds the highest knowledge. This highest knowledge includes and appropriates all the rest, and so Christianity normally flows through learning into its best efficiency and appropriate victories.

The Church can never admit that Christianity and science are antagonisms. She knows how utterly false is the impression, sometimes sought to be made, that these are in irreconcilable conflict, and religion is *per se* unscientific and science must be irreligious. She understands well that they are the readings of God's two great revelations, and if both are read correctly all the various colored facts blend and shine in the pure white light of God's full truth. Without doubt Creation is an expression of God's thought, as Redemption is of His love; and there can be conflict only by wresting the Bible or Nature and putting false speech into its lips. And as Redemption, foreseen and provided for before all worlds, expresses the final cause, the ultimate end of all the framework and movement of the world, Nature stands necessarily as a subordinate factor in this aggregate movement, and can be rightly understood only in the light of the great fact of Redemption. This world's structure and history yield to us their true meanings only when viewed in the interpretative illumination of the cross of Christ and the eschatology of the New Testament. The Church, therefore, holds the true key to the solution of Nature. Christianity has thus the highest commission to lead the way through the fields of science. A sublime ordination to the work is given in the qualification to do it. To atheistic evolutionism, which denies all design, adaptation, and end in Nature, or to infidelity, which fails to see that end in the new earth of redemption, Nature is of course an insoluble mystery, and science fragmentary, disjointed, incoherent. The Church is the best teacher of the truth in these broad domains of culture. The children of light, with the torch of God's truth flashing every way and lighting up the world, are to lead men, especially the young, into the divine thoughts that lie fixed, like compactly written hieroglyphics, in all the phenomena of the earth. Thus will come the right correlation between science and religion—revelation assisting and guiding reason to the highest and best conception of nature, and then, in turn, receiving the light of all scientific discovery thrown back on it, for still profounder and more perfect understanding of its own meaning. Science then—the term being used in the broadest sense, for all known truth in the higher ranges of learning—is a true handmaid of religion and falls rightly into the service of the Church of redemption. As among the mightiest agencies that bear on human welfare, mold civilizations and guide enterprise and progress, this is ever to be held by the Church, as pre-eminently her own, to be pervaded by her own light and power for conducting the world's movement to the consummation to which Providence is holding the helm.

In coming to these shores the Church seized a point of grandest power and success, in undertaking to give the country its higher academic and collegiate education. In her various branches, she began the planting of schools and colleges, that the education of the young for all the higher spheres of life and influence might be conducted under Christian auspices. So our land has been made a land of Christian education. Of the nine colleges established before the revolution, eight were begun under Church auspices. Of the three hundred and forty-two colleges now reported in our national statistics of education, two hundred and eight six are in such general Christian relation.[1] The good thus accomplished, in Christianizing all the subordinate ranges of education, in shaping leading and regulative thought for the whole land, in elevating our common morality and securing a generally favorable attitude toward the Gospel, is simply incalculable. What the condition of our land or the state of the Church would be without this, or with the order reversed, imagination may only faintly picture. If the higher education had been left by the Church

---

[1] Art. Colleges, Kiddle and Schem's Cyclopedia of Education.

to merely secular control, with purely secular principles and secular ends—if skepticism and unbelief had been left in possession of the philosophy, science and culture of the schools, making, as they are wont, these great powers seem to contradict Christianity and discredit the verities of faith—if such godless higher education had then unchristianized our common-school education, as it would have done, for the millions of the masses—what floods of irreligion and sin would be sweeping over the land, endangering every holy thing in which we to-day rejoice!

Education in the Lutheran Church in the United States must be viewed as on the background of these general principles and facts It is to be looked upon, at least so far as college education is concerned, as the part that belongs to us in this great work. What that part should be, and how it may be best accomplished, are the questions that concern us in this discussion.

I. The proper position and range of work for our Church in education should be held, it seems to me, as imperatively fixed for us, by a number of considerations.

First. The fact that the Lutheran Church arose in living connection with the agencies of higher learning. The restoration of Biblical Christianity took place among the fruits of study and the power of universities God made Luther climb up through all ranges to the summits of learning, before putting into his hand and deep in his soul, the commission to reform the Church. He seated him in a university chair. He gave him co-laborers in similar position. Providence wheeled these institutions into front line. From the lecture-desks of Wittenberg the Church of the Reformation did much of the grandest work of that grand century. She took organic form with this instrument of power in her hands.

Secondly. The Lutheran Church has always been an educating Church, standing, with its great institutions and learned men, in the very first rank of Christian scholarship and culture. Through all her history she has been distinguished for her renowned universities and her erudite scholars. She has been the patron of learning, using its power for the defense and victory of the Gospel.

She owes it, thus, to her historical characteristics to take no inferior or unworthy relation to the higher education in this country. At present, we speak only of academic or collegiate education. And we assert that, with no denomination of Christians in our land would indifference to education or an inferior standard in it be in greater degree a contradiction and denial of itself than with the Lutheran Church. We feel, too, that we have a clear warrant to impose on ourselves the obligation of a full share in Christianizing the higher culture of the country, in the claim we make for our Church, that she is in an eminent degree the Church of the pure doctrine of the Gospel. If we believe that her confessional position and consequent Church life represent the best and truest onflow of genuine Christianity, we must believe that we have a commission, with a clear divine signature, to bring to the greatest degree possible the power of this education under the shaping influence of our Church.

It is not to be forgotten that there is, at the present time, the pressure of an increased obligation on *all* the Christian Churches of our land, to strengthen their educational work. As a result, on the one hand, of the attitude of the Roman Catholic Church toward common schools; and on the other, of the efforts of skepticism and unbelief, a strong tendency has set in toward a secularization of the whole educational system of our land. The idea of State universities, wholly dissevered from ecclesiastical influence, is strongly urged by many educators, backed by a large part of both the secular and rationalistic press; and the air is full of petty flings at what are called denominational or sectarian colleges. There is a constant clamor, too, on the part of every faction of anti-Christian scientism, for a separation of scientific inquiry from an alleged hindering influence on free inquiry in these colleges. It is one of the great, far-reaching questions of our day, whether the Church is, in the interest of true science and of righteousness, to retain control of the higher education which it has given to our land. If the State is, through secular universities, to have charge of this education, fostered by taxation—a taxation urged by some even upon the property devoted to the work by the benevolence of the Churches—then we will have the principle pressed, as it is in relation to the common schools, that State impartiality as to religions must exclude the Bible and Christianity from being recognized as proper forces in this education. Of course, the classics of the old paganisms would remain in the curriculum. Vedic literature would cover the religions of the East. But the Text-Book of Christianity would come under ban of this fine secularism, which the Christian people of this land would be called on to support through their taxes. So the higher education would be un-Christianized in this Gospel-created land. As the final struggle with this anti-Christian and anti-Church tendency comes on, it is needful that the Church not only hold that fast which she has, that no man take her crown, but strengthen her work, that her institutions shall be in the future, as they have been in the past, the most commanding, the ruling centre of learning in the land. And the Lutheran Church, if she wishes to be true to her historic character, or to her claim of representing the best type of revived or Protestant Christianity, cannot be content simply to let this work be done by others, or to take anything short of the fullest share that the Head of the Church has made possible to her.

Thirdly. The proper training of young men for our ministry—such a culture as will prepare them for their true position and efficiency—requires a high standard for our educational work. It would be an insult to any intelligent body of men to raise before them, at this date, the question of an educated ministry. It needs no word. But the question may well be raised whether our Church appreciates what grade of institutions she should furnish to supply the education now needed. The colleges and theological schools that can rightly serve the Church's true strength and victory are such as shall be able to set forth the young ministry abreast with the most advanced results in science, philosophy and theological inquiry. This is necessary to prevent them from becoming entangled in the misleading plausibilities and errors of the times, and to fit them to maintain the supremacy of God's truth in its incessant conflicts. Even aside from this ministerial education, our Church's prosperity is dependent, more than most persons think, on an elevated standard of collegiate education. Other things being equal, it is almost self-evident, the Church that educates the most and best and controls the best institutions will outrank others, and do most for the cause of Christ.

If these principles be true, it is easy to see what position our Church should occupy on the subject we are considering. What, now, are some of the chief facts that mark the educational work in our Church, and some of the features open to criticism, and needing revision?

Our Church was slow in beginning this work. Were we to count from the Swedish Lutheran settlement on the Delaware in 1637, a century and a half of her history in this country elapsed before any successful movement to take part in the higher education was made. But though there had been scattering immigration of Lutherans from that date onward, our Church can hardly be regarded as having been organized here before the coming of the Germans, at different dates from 1710 to 1742. We may justly count a half century of our Church's history here as passed when Franklin College, at Lancaster, the institution to which I refer, was founded in 1787. And this institution was only one-third part under Lutheran auspices, and failed to be permanent. The prevalence of the German language in our Church was in the way of any early success in establishing a college that should rise to commanding position. German institutions could have only a limited prosperity; and any other our Church was not prepared to found, until the Lutheran population became largely Anglicized. And when Pennsylvania College, our oldest college, was organized in 1832, it lacked only a few years of being two centuries after colleges under other auspices had begun in their work and laid the foundations of a wide prosperity. As Hartwick Seminary, established in 1815, though highly useful, belongs to the category of academic and theological institutes, our college education, apart from our share in the institution above named, has a history of only forty-five years. During this period the progress has been wonderfully rapid, testifying that whatever may be the wisdom that guides the work, it is urged forward by worthy and earnest interest. The latest statistics give us, besides twenty-two academic institutes, a list of eighteen colleges or institutions claiming to be such, under the auspices of our Church, located within a compass reaching from New York around by the Carolinas, Texas, Iowa and Wisconsin, representing four different languages, and as many types of Lutheranism. In these there are, as nearly as can be ascertained, 2,036 students under 127 professors. Nine of the colleges may be counted as English, with 72 professors and 988 students. Five are German, with 34 professors and about 687 students. Two are Swedish with 13 professors and 171 students. Two are Norwegian, with about 200 pupils under 8 professors.

These facts, its seems to me, cannot but justify several criticisms:

The first is that there has been a very unwise multiplication of institutions of this class. To whatever causes it may have been due, whether to the apparent necessities of language, the territorial convenience of location, the divisive action of theological partisanship, or the obstinate leading of ambitious individualism, the result is apparent, that the power of our Church in this branch of work, has been terribly sacrificed in this multitudinous planting of colleges. In this respect the college work in general, under *all* the Christian denominations, and other bodies that have established them, has been misguided and greatly damaged. Weakness rather than strength has come to it in this way. If it be claimed that this multiplication, by planting colleges in close proximity in every section, bringing educational facilities to the doors of the people everywhere, draws out and educates more of the young than could otherwise be reached, it is evident, however, that the widening of the range has been purchased at the expense of its proper elevation. In its depression of the average grade the aggregate loss has been greater than the gain by numbers on the lower level. This principle more than holds as to the work in our own Church. The division of the pecuniary resources, and of the patronage, among so many institutions, prevents any of them from rising unto their true efficiency, prominence, and service to the Church. I assume that all the means, contributed from local, partisan, or personal considerations, *should* have been given under a wiser and better adjusted system. The nine hundred and eighty-eight students reported as in the nine English colleges could surely all be instructed in *four*. If the endowment and patronage that now only keep these nine in straitened and hampered work, with professors loaded down with excessive labors and little pay, and some of the institutions almost *in articulo mortis*, were accumulated in four, the educational products would unquestionably be above the present grade of many of them, and our college work would stand out in more attractive prominence than now. Our institutions could be rightly built up, and developed into commanding position for the honor and power of our Church. It seems to me to require a microscopic eye to see, for instance, the wisdom of trying to carry on three colleges under our Church in three adjoining States of the South. Were the efforts thrown into one, it could be lifted into triumphant success and broad usefulness. This would be far better than the present divided enterprise, in which the struggle of some for existence is hindering the true efficiency of all. In our Middle States, neither the strength of the Church nor the compass of territory calls for more than the first *one* of our colleges.

Two English colleges, at most, are sufficient to represent our Church and do its work in the West—one in the nearer and the other in the remoter West. Plainly it would be gain both as to vigor of educational work and the harmony of the Church, if we had but a single Swedish college combining the funds and patronage of the present two. The same is evidently true as to the Norwegian education. Is there any just reason, indeed, why Swedish and Norwegian might not be united in the same institution, or better still, form departments in one of the English institutions? As to the German colleges, four of them being in the West, it is hard to believe that the division of the efforts is not depriving the work of its true ease and efficient strength.

The correctness of this opinion is not disproved by the admitted fact, that this rapid multiplication of our colleges has been inevitable from the divided condition of the Church. It does not better the matter that this weakness comes from another weakness, that this crippling of our work arises from our bad antagonisms, that the evil is simply the symptom of a deeper evil. It does not make this system wise, that it is the fruit and revelation of the folly that wastes our Church's life in alienations and strifes. It is no recommendation of it, that it has been shaped by one of the worst facts that mar the beauty and cut the sinews of our Lutheran strength.

All the real advantage, by drawing out the young through numerous colleges easily accessible, supposed by some to justify this multiplication, can be better attained through high-grade, efficient academies in every community. These can be made almost as numerous as our pastoral charges, and can furnish, along with a preparation for college, the early inspiration to the advanced course. It is just this system of numerous local schools, that can best quicken our churches into more general education, and send the proper numbers on to fill our college halls and give our higher education its true encouragement and success.

But a second thing—the facts furnished by our statistics of colleges, suggest that there is prevalent among us, as a background of much of the evil I am criticising, a mistaken notion as to the true sphere and relations of the college. A careful examination of the list of eighteen cannot fail to reveal the fact that many of them stand for types of theological thought, or have been made to accept the rivalship of a neighboring new-born college because of being unwilling to be contracted into some such narrowness. It is plain that colleges have been looked on much in the light of simple instruments for success in theological warfare. They have been sought chiefly as outposts to some special "school of prophets." Now, if I have rightly conceived the function and relation of the college, as the college under auspices of the Lutheran Church should stand in the great American system of Christian higher education, it is to occupy a much wider and more catholic position. The college is not simply a small Church-school. It is not a theological seminary. It is not simply a feeder to any one, nor to all. It is for that broader work which shall give the higher education, in its best and fullest wealth of science, philosophy, and literature, under Christian auspices, for *all* the callings of life. The college *is*, indeed, to educate for the theological seminary. It is a feature of perhaps more worth than any other, that it trains the young of the Church for the great service into which they pass through our theological schools. And just because it is needed for this great service, as well as for other, the college must be conceded a higher and wider office. The young for the ministry in our day should enter the theological course with a discipline and culture in the broad range of scientific and philosophical thought, such as can be given only in institutions with a curriculum arranged after this full conception of collegiate education. It is true the pulpit is not to preach science or philosophy. Its power to save men is not even through the philosophy of the gospel—but the gospel itself. But the pulpit, in this age of skeptical scientism and misleading speculation, will lose its proper hold on public confidence, if it is without masterful knowledge in these pretentious departments of inquiry. It must never be said that the ministry is behind the age on the broad ground of general and thorough education. The Church's colleges, to give this education, dare not be of inferior grade, or enclose their students' course within a range that stretches over only the ecclesiastical segment of the horizon of knowledge. The training must be broad and efficient. Upon the foundation of such an education, a theological course can build up, in the Church's everlasting truth, true sons of Issachar, with understanding of the times and knowledge of what Israel ought to do.

If it is thus indeed, as it seems to be, a mistake to hold our colleges to serve simply as porches to particular schools of prophets;

if the true idea into which they should be molded is that of seats of highest Christian culture, affording the proper broad and thorough preparation for the various professional courses, for public life or business, the question is legitimately raised: What degree of organic connection and control ought the Church to hold in and over the colleges she builds up? How, without making them sectarian, or reducing them to the littleness of party schools, can they be made secure to the service and control of the Church, and safe from liability of perversion to secularism or infidelity? The case of Harvard University, passing from control of the communion that dedicated it *"Christo et Ecclesiæ,"* to a management which has used it largely to discredit the faith it was built to promote, is known to all. Dickinson College, in this State, has passed from under Presbyterian auspices to Methodist Episcopal control. Meant for this Christian service under our Church, the surest possible safeguards ought to be employed for the permanence of our colleges in this status. Important as it is to avoid confounding the office of the college with that of the theological seminary, and to maintain its proper Christian, or at least denominational catholicity, it is also of the highest moment to have it so guarded, that it cannot swing loose to any unchurchly perversion, or be wrested from the control of the Christian communion that founded it. No settled principle on this point has been adopted among us, and the Church's practice has been irregular and conflicting. The relation between the college and Church is varied through all grades of control, from the extremes of practical *synodical ownership and management* to a separateness in which there is no *organic* Church-relation whatever. If in some cases the partisan ecclesiastical grip has been so tight as to disallow the free life and growth essential for the right development of a Christian college, in its true ideal of wide and comprehensive education, and has illustrated, in the sphere of education, the wisdom of a method that is employed in forming Chinese feet, some have so free a relation as, perhaps, to make additional guarantees for the Church's permanent and best control of them desirable. The relation which the Church should claim for itself, in order to assert, without transcending, the proper degree of control in its colleges and hold sufficient guarantees for the future, is a subject that needs careful revision and settlement among us.

It is an interesting fact, and strikingly illustrative of the connection between educational work and Church prosperity, that this period of the rapid enlargement of this work has been the period of our Church's most rapid development and progress. Since 1845, when the educational work through Hartwick Seminary, the Theological Seminary and the College at Gettysburg, and other institutions, was beginning to produce its fuller results in the increase of the ministry and the quickening of the educational impulse which afterward founded so many other colleges and seminaries, the growth of the Church has been greatly accelerated, advancing from 843 to 5,905 congregations, and from 90,629 communicant members to the present 605,340. It may, indeed, be justly claimed that the enlargement of our educational enterprise is, in great degree, the *effect* of our Church's growth; but probably, in larger measure, it has been a cause and agency for that growth. As education has been fostered—and it is a gratifying fact to be recorded, that some of our colleges, despite the unwise multiplication of them, have done a noble work and risen to honorable distinction among the best institutions of their States—this education has given preparation to the ministry, without which, so enlarged in numbers, this progress of our Church would have been impossible. At any rate, it is a fact to be remembered that the two things go together, and that the period of our Church-growth has been joined with the period of our educational activity.

II. In *theological education* we reach a department of our educational work which is determined by different aims, and must be judged of by different standards. As a rule, I conceive, this begins properly only after the collegiate course, or its equivalent, has laid the proper cultural basis for it. The deviations from this rule ought to be more strictly exceptional than they have been among us, for the sake of both the theological course itself and the student and the Church. This brings up at once a fact that calls for a new departure. Whatever reasons may, in the past, have justified a large application of the principle of exceptions to the rule in question, the character of the times into which we have come, require, and the resources of the Church now admit, a more stringent enforcement of the higher standard for entrance into our theological schools. Honorable as has been the general culture of our ministry, surely comparing favorably with that of the ministry of Churches around us, and blessed with divine power as have been the labors of many who have entered the service with only an inferior education, we have plainly reached a point at which we may, and should, make an advance movement and approach nearer to the high standard which, I think, has always been the prospective ideal of the Church.[2]

The true aim of theological education is more peculiar than is generally thought. It is not only to be contrasted with collegiate training, furnishing general intellectual culture under Christian auspices, by being a professional course for the acquisition of some full-orbed system of divinity; but it means, largely, the deep cultivation of piety, and the kindling of soul into the earnestness of a full consecration to the appointed work. The ministry is not simply a profession—rather, is not a profession, or craft, at all—but a great divine service. And so, our theological schools are not like schools of law or medicine, which give the knowledge of some professional art or activity as a means of support or honorable distinction; but they are meant, while holding the student above such simply professional conception of the office to which he is looking, to fill his mind, through the Holy Spirit's blessing on the instruction, with the living truth of the gospel and an inspiration to self-sacrificing usefulness. It is a place where, pre-eminently, he is to be endued with power from on high, before going forth to the holy work. He is to be kindled into glowing fervor by the truth he receives there in its theological completeness, as the necessary preparation for kindling the souls of others with the truth and power of salvation.

Our theological institutions have been founded, I believe, in this true conception of their work. The limit of time for this paper forbids any attempt to trace, historically, the earlier methods of training our pastors, and the facts connected with the establishment of our theological seminaries. The facts are full of interest, but we can note them only as they apppear in the results now reached.

---

[2] At the first meeting of the General Synod, 1821, five years before the establishment of the Theological Seminary at Gettysburg, it was resolved: "That it be recommended to the several Synods, to admit, for the present, no young man to the study of theology, before he has obtained a diploma, or some similar testimonial, from a public institution, wherein the usual branches of science are taught; or before he has been examined in such branches, and found sufficiently qualified, by a committee appointed for the purpose."

The earliest founded of our theological schools was Hartwick Seminary, for which provision was made by the will of Rev. John C. Hartwig in 1796, but which went into operation only in 1815. In 1826 the Theological Seminary of the General Synod was established at Gettysburg. Since that time, enterprise in this direction has been exceedingly active; and leaving out of count several abortive and dead efforts, fifteen others have been added to the list. In these seventeen seminaries or theological departments, there are, as nearly as the statistics show, forty-one professors, and four hundred and ninety-seven students. Five of them, with eleven professors and eighty-two students, are connected with the General Synod North; two with three professors and thirteen students with the General Synod South. Two, with eight professors and sixty-two students, are connected with the General Council[3]; and four in which eleven professors teach one hundred and ninety-five students, with the Synodical Conference. The rest are connected with independent Synods.

Abundant testimony to the great value and efficiency of these institutions is furnished in the large number of well instructed and earnest ministers they are annually giving to the work of the Church. The enlarged and comprehensive curriculum of three years, adopted by a number of them, and insisted on with increased rigor, is auspicious for still augmented efficiency of service. The division of labor also, through an increase of our theological faculties, is adding strength to these seminaries. However, it seems to me plain here, as with our colleges, that there has been an unwise multiplication of these institutions. Blessed as has been the service rendered to the Church by our theological education, greater and better things had been and still are possible to us under a policy less divisive of effort and more concentrative of our resources. It is not my business here to point out particular cases in which this divisive and weakening action has taken place, or to arraign the propriety of the existence and work of any special institution. I wish to be distinctly understood as not undertaking to do this. But it is permitted me to deal with the general principle or policy pursued, and this policy, whatever

---

[3] Wartburg Seminary, at Mendota, Ill., in connection with the Synod of Iowa, and the Practical Theological Seminary at Marshal, Wis., under the Norwegian-Danish Augustana Synod, are not included here, because these Synods are not in full connection with the General Council.

may have been the causes that led to it, may, it seems to me, be justly arraigned as misguided, on several grounds.

It is violative, for instance, of a wise and true principle of *economy*, both as to men and means. This multiplication of seminaries greatly increases the amount of endowment, or direct contributions, necessary to meet their expenses and support the professors—if indeed they are supported. It consumes the time and energies of more men in professorial labor than would be called for under a system of wise combination of work. It is an unwise demand on the resources of the Church. Further, it prevents the best breadth and thoroughness of our theological education, in necessarily keeping the teaching force in each institution smaller, and their labor larger, than they should be. But the greatest evil of all appears in the doctrinal disharmony and misunderstandings which they keep up and intensify in the Church. The seventeen schools we have represent and foster at least half a dozen types of what is claimed to be Lutheran Theology; and varieties of these are shaded out, some places, into minuter diversities. Even within the schools connected with the same general Lutheran organization, divergences occur. The carrying on of our theological education in so many institutions which are led, by their rivalries and jealousies, to magnify their typical differences and overlook the points of their agreement, emphasizing all the divisive peculiarities on which partisanship feeds and grows, training, it may be, and inspiring skilled polemics rather than earnest servants of Christ and His truth, and sending them forth prepared to misconceive and misinterpret, but not to trust and love one another—this is something, it seems to me, that requires us to put a clear seal of condemnation upon this policy. It may be that, with the various nationalities in our Church, and otherwise divided as we have unfortunately been—though not more than some other denominations—the course pursued was unavoidable. If so, it becomes a revelation of a sadly abnormal condition of our Church life and consciousness, and only shows what a severely condemnatory judgment we should put on the distractions and divisions, into which a noble love of the truth has led us, through unwise methods of defending it. It may be that the error is now incapable of correction. The work of the past cannot, perhaps, be undone. But a wise economy, and the harmony and strength of the Church, require that it be pursued no further. It may be, that the law of the survival of the fittest, will have to bring the only possible solution of the difficulties created by what has been already done; but, possibly, wise counsels and Christian love may yet bring into unity some of our divided theological educational work. Much better would it be if we could combine this work into, at most, one-half the number of our present centres of theological training, with the enlarged funds, faculties, and libraries, such united effort would make possible.

I am reluctantly compelled to omit any discussion of the education of the *daughters* of the Church, and of the close connection of this education with the Church's best growth and prosperity. Our history is not without honorable records of worthy, earnest and self-sacrificing effort in this direction. We have had, and have now, men and institutions laboring in this way, with honor and advantage to the Church, if not with pecuniary success to themselves; the fruits of whose services it would be a grateful task to recall. It is enough to point to such schools as Lutherville Seminary, Hagerstown Seminary, Staunton Female Seminary, Marion Female College, etc. The results of effort in this direction, though not all that have been desired, are abundantly worth all the sacrifice made. It needs only be added, that thorough culture in the daughters, wives and mothers of a Christian communion, touches so directly and with such decisive power upon its whole social standing, intelligent religious activity, efficient service, and general influence, that it justly claims increased attention and more earnest encouragement among us.

REMARKS OF REV. C. A. STORK, D. D. (*General Synod.*)

I am glad the paper just read touched on one point in the interest of the Higher Education, viz.: The need of more and more efficient academic or preparatory schools scattered broadcast throughout the land. But I wish to dwell on that point more fully. It ought to be brought out.

It is obvious I think to all who are interested in the question of the Higher Education, and who have studied the subject at all, that the drift of the age is away from scholarship. Our statistical tables show that relatively fewer of our young men pursue a full collegiate course than in the beginning of the century. Absolutely, of course, there are more that are college-bred; but relatively there are fewer. The scholar is not as great as he used to be. The influence and admiration and power that he commands are not the same. The reason for this I think is very obvious; it is to be found in the spirit of the age. We know what the age is; what its drift is; it is almost wholly in the direction of material interests. Investigation is turned to the searching out of material problems, and the activities of the age, its hopes and enthusiasm, are to the furtherance of material prosperity. So our young men grow up in an atmosphere, and launch out into a current that are all for material interests. The promises of life are not as they once were, in large measure for the scholar, the thinker; they are for the active man, the speculator, the organizer of capital, the man strong to manage trade. All this sets the current of young ambition and aspiration away from the university, the quiet life of meditation, and slow study.

What is the corrective for this? Not, I think, at this time, more colleges or better colleges; not a grander and richer university. Those, whatever they may be, are remote from the life of the day; they are secluded from the rush and tide that catches the young man and whirls him away. What is needed now, it seems to us, is a system of academies which, bringing the allurements of learning, of the studious atmosphere, to the homes of the young, shall give them a taste for letters, for thought, and direct their attention to the world of better and higher things that exists for them.

And to do this is the work of the Church. She has always been the fosterer of the Higher Education. She planted our colleges and universities. Now she must see to opening rills that shall feed them. The State cannot do it; the State never will do it. Now in the Providence of God, it seems as if that office of nurse of letters which she once filled, and men have thought she could fill no longer, is once more offered her.

If in all our country towns we could, under the fostering care of our Synods and Conferences, establish academies and higher schools, we should be doing the greatest work for the interests of the Higher Education.

Let me say, too, that we as a Church have especial need of some agency that will bring a higher education to our laity. There is a greater gulf in this matter of education, between the body of our people and the clergy than exists in most of the great denominations. Our ministers are as well educated as those of any conspicuous Christian body; but with the laity it is otherwise. This makes a gap between the pulpit and the pews. Some may like to see that difference; it may flatter their pride to feel that they are more cultured than any of their flock. I am not one of those. I could wish that the people might have knowledge. I rejoice to see men and women in my congregation, my peers in culture and knowledge. It would be good for us all, and good for the Church's work, if the minister felt that there were before him those who knew more about many points of a generous culture than he did.

And to the academy preparing the way to the college and the university—to the academy founded throughout our country districts and fostered by the Church—do I think we must look for help in this matter.

The hour of adjournment having arrived, further discussion was postponed until the next morning at 9 o'clock.

Dr. Seiss stated that a press of duties had prevented Rev. Dr. Repass, of Virginia, both from attending the Diet and from preparing his paper. There would, therefore, be a vacancy in the programme for to-morrow morning. It was unfortunate that the laity had been overlooked in selecting essayists for the Diet. There was, however, a layman present, a member of the family of the great Reformer, who had prepared a paper on the Linguistic Relations of the Lutheran Church in this country. He moved that the vacant place be assigned Dr. Diller Luther, of Reading, Pa.

Adopted.

FOURTH SESSION.

DECEMBER 28TH, 9 A. M.

Prayer by Rev. W. K. Frick, of Philadelphia. The discussion of Dr. Valentine's paper was resumed.

REMARKS OF REV. J. F. REINMUND, D. D. (*General Synod.*)

The Common Schools sustain an important relation to the higher education, which can and should be utilized for the prosperity and success of colleges. These public schools ought to have the encouragement and influence of the ministry for their proper direction and efficiency. They offer excellent opportunities for ministers of the Gospel to get into contact with the minds of the young, to turn their attention to collegiate education, and to encourage them to secure it. His own experience had satisfied him that much could be done in this way. The public and high schools have made it difficult to sustain efficient academies; and in the present relations of education in our country, the most available way, perhaps, of promoting the higher Christian education in our Church, is for the ministry to use the opportunities open to them to encourage and influence education through these schools.

REMARKS OF REV. A. SPAETH, D. D. (*General Council.*)

I would not like to underrate the importance of theological and collegiate education in the Lutheran Church of this country, but I am convinced that in order to do justice to our duty on the field of education, we must begin to lay the foundations deeper in the religious instruction of the home circle and the congregational school. No other Church possesses a treasure equal to our own "Catechism," written for this very purpose, that the head of the family should teach it to his household, and that the pastors and teachers should use it to instruct the young. The year 1845 has been mentioned as marking the beginning of an increased activity and success on the field of education within our Church. I have no doubt that this date is correctly given. But if I am not very much mistaken, the real cause of this remarkable increase since that time, is the fact, that from that time on, the German Lutherans in the West, especially our Missouri brethren, who have been the chief instrument to save the great West for the Lutheran Church, commenced their work. They not only preached the Gospel in the pulpit, but gathered the lambs into the folds of the parochial schools, the pastor himself serving as the teacher in the parish school, if no other suitable man could be found. This is the duty we owe to our Church, to the faith of our fathers. It is all the more our duty as we stand comparatively isolated between Romanism on the one side and the Protestantism of the Reformed type on the other side.

[NOTE FROM DR. VALENTINE.]

Owing to an unintentional oversight of the Chair, the opportunity of closing the discussion on this paper was not given to the author. It was his purpose to add a few words on several points referred to in the discussion. First, that the subject of the earlier education of the children, justly held to be so important, had not been touched on in the paper, because it formed the topic of another paper for the Diet. Secondly, that the Public School was available for the purposes of our Church Education only in exceptional cases; and that classical instruction, to fit students for college, was probably in excess of what rightly belonged to the Public School system.

The sixth paper was then read.

THE INTERESTS OF THE LUTHERAN CHURCH IN AMERICA AS AFFECTED BY DIVERSITIES OF LANGUAGE.

BY DILLER LUTHER, M. D., READING, PA.

I PROPOSE some thoughts and reflections on the subject of the interests of the Lutheran Church in America, as affected by diversities of Language. It is my intention to content myself with a mere outline, believing that such general observations as all will admit to be correct, will of themselves be sufficiently suggestive of the proper conclusions, without any argument to establish them.

The Protestant Reformation had its origin on German soil. It was in Germany, where the seeds of religious liberty were first planted and took root; it was there, where the rights of conscience were boldly and fearlessly advocated and maintained. The struggle to recover the pure doctrines of God's Holy Word, for so many years hidden under the corruptions of the Roman Hierarchy, was commenced and successfully conducted there. They were held and defended, in defiance of papal bulls, of arbitrary edicts by the civil powers, and amid such persecution and cruelties as have scarcely had a parallel in history. No sacrifice was deemed too great, to protect them against the opposition and destruction, with which they were constantly threatened. Country, home, property and life itself, would be surrendered if occasion demanded. History may be searched in vain, from the earliest period down to the present time, for an example of a more inflexible adherence to truth and principle, than was exhibited in this great contest.

The struggle to maintain the Protestant doctrines was soon followed by religious wars. The massacre of St. Bartholomew took place in France in 1572. In 1598 was published the Edict of Nantes, granting equal rights to Protestants. In 1685 this Edict was revoked, and Protestants were again persecuted in France. Children at the age of seven years, by apostatizing, were declared independent of their parents; military executions were employed to enforce uniformity of worship; Protestant marriages were declared illegal, and their offspring illegitimate. Hereupon 15,000 persons fled to Hamburg and Amsterdam in Holland; and in the five years following, no less than 1,000,000 fled to Holland, England and America —for William Penn, in 1682, had already colonized Pennsylvania.

The tide of German emigration set rapidly towards our shores. Settlements upon the Hudson river in New York were first made, but preferring the liberal spirit of the Penn government, the emigrants directed their steps towards the fertile valleys of our Commonwealth. The lands in many sections of the Colony were soon occupied. With their practical knowledge as farmers and proverbial habits of industry, the soil was made to yield abundant crops. They built comfortable homes, enclosed their farms and erected the necessary farm buildings; neighborhoods and villages rapidly grew up— the mill, the store and mechanics' shops soon followed, and gave evidences of prosperity. Then came the school and the church. A lot sufficiently large for the church, the school and the parsonage, was selected in an eligible location. With the aid and means of all, each one ready and willing to contribute to the work, the walls of the stately edifice were rapidly reared; the spire pointing heavenward, was added to give it grace and dignity; with the altar, organ, and pews, all arranged in the approved style of that day, the whole in a short time was made ready for occupation. The school and parsonage soon followed. Church after church was thus erected in the valleys of which the Germans had become inhabitants, some of which may be seen to this day.

At the early period of which we are now speaking, the services of the Lutheran Churches were conducted in the German language only; the settlements being entirely German, there was no necessity for any other. Indeed, in many of the original charters, the exclusive use of that language was made obligatory, which in many instances continues to be literally observed to this day. For a time— it may be said for a long time—these churches prospered; they became strong in numbers and in influence. The early ministers being generally foreigners, received their theological training in the schools of Europe, and were pious and learned. A necessary part of the general system then in use, was to train the young inside, instead of outside the Church as now pursued—a departure of modern times which is by no means universally admitted to be wise. The parsonage, with a sufficient number of acres surrounding it to produce the needed supplies, completed the Church arrangement.

I now pass to another period in the history of the early Lutheran churches in this country. As neighborhoods became more densely settled and the population more mixed, the English language became a barrier to the continued prosperity of the German churches. The educational institutions, the business of Legislative bodies, of Courts, and of ordinary trade, were conducted in the national language. English churches were established and became prosperous. The inclination to follow the popular current on the part of the young could not be restrained. The fathers were content with the Church as they had established it; they remonstrated and endeavored to resist, but could not prevent a continued outgoing into the English Churches. An effective remedy could have been found in the introduction of the English language into the Lutheran churches, but that was neither countenanced nor sanctioned. The consequences which followed are known to all. Failing to provide for the young, the churches declined and in very many instances with all the membership passed out of existence.

The policy of our ancestors in this respect, has been variously criticised. From one standpoint, it is unsparingly denounced and condemned. From another, it is defended and admired. The tenacity with which they adhered to the exclusive use of one language, is commended by some, as significant of a deep-seated love for the Church, for which such sacrifices had been endured. By others, it is regarded as nothing more nor less than Teutonic perversity, an obstinate blindness and unwillingness to conform to new relations, by which great interests may be protected and saved, simply because the means to be used do not accord with long-cherished prejudices and mistaken tastes.

But the conduct of our fathers, if not altogether wise, was at least reasonable and natural. For the Lutheran Church, as then organized and conducted, they had suffered much. They had forsaken country and home, to enjoy it in a foreign land free from molestation from any one. It was a German Church, German in its origin, in its traditions and broad liberal spirit. The desire naturally would be to transplant it to this country, precisely as it existed at the home they had left, not only in language but in all other particulars. The Church must be German here, because it was German there. For the doctrine of change to conform to new conditions, the true German has little respect, especially in matters pertaining to the Christian Church. To require him to agree to a change of language in the Church, was tantamount to a surrender of all he held dear. It was like a transfer not only of title, but of possession, in an estate which he considered peculiarly his own.

That the policy pursued by our ancestors, with reference to the question we have been considering, though influenced by the views and feelings just presented, was a mistaken one, is obvious from the deplorable consequences which followed. It was as wrong in theory, as it was injurious in practice. The attempt to confine it to one tongue and one nationality, was an insult to its great founders and entirely at variance with the broad spirit upon which it was established. The basis upon which it was reared, was sufficiently broad and comprehensive for the whole Protestant Church. Such was not the spirit of Muhlenberg. He taught in three languages. It was not the spirit of Kunze at New York, who wept at seeing the outflow from his own church into those of other denominations. It was not the spirit of their co-laborers at other central points, for they saw the inevitable consequences which must occur from the failure to provide for the young in our own churches.

When we consider the injury which has been inflicted upon the Church by the course pursued, we cannot refrain from congratulating ourselves that the conflict on the question of language, has in a great measure ceased. It would be an anomaly at the present day, for ministers to insist that English-speaking families should learn the German language, in order to avoid the necessity of introducing English services into the Church. How generally this course was pursued, especially in the larger cities and towns, to their great injury and in some instances to their ruin, is well known. For years under the ministers who had charge of our churches, and who were capable of speaking in one language only, the policy was one of unyielding opposition to the use of the English language, the sad consequences of which may be seen in every city and town in our State.

The question must now be briefly considered, whether the Church is fully relieved of the injury caused by the conflict of languages. It is undoubtedly true that the opposition to the use of the English language in the Lutheran churches, has in a great measure ceased. English Lutheran churches have greatly multiplied and grown strong; German churches have also greatly increased and prospered. But why this continued jealousy and hostility? Why this never ending and bitter controversy with which our weekly and monthly publications are so filled? Why these numerous divisions, these rival institututions and agencies, to carry on the work of the Church? You may cry peace, peace, but there is no peace; the corroding ulcer, though cicatrized, is not healed. It still remains to fret and worry. The disease is not cured, but masked; it continues, but in a different form. For upwards of one hundred years, has the Church in this country bled and suffered from it; for all that long time, has it been agitated, distracted and divided.

And now I approach a point where I would tread cautiously. Is it indeed true that no adequate remedy can be found for the relief of the Church from these festering sores? Are we never to see the dawn of that day, when the different branches of the firstborn of the Reformation will be at peace with each other? when they will unite and co-operate in the important work committed to them? Are the elements, of which the different divisions are composed, so discordant and incongruous as to render any efforts to harmonize them entirely futile?

It cannot be denied that the results of past efforts in this direction do not warrant any very sanguine hopes of success in the future. And yet we need not despair. The experience of the past merely shows, if it shows anything, that the methods chosen were not adapted to secure the desired object. Peace and harmony are not to be obtained by Synodical resolutions. Nor are the members composing ecclesiastical bodies, to be forever kept separate by a parliamentary ruling, though it be influenced by a regard for the rights of a party. The trouble is deep seated, and requires for its treatment remedies of a radical character—palliatives have been tried without effect—nothing short of the knife of the surgeon will remove the corroding canker. And what, it will now be asked, is that remedy? I answer, it is simple, it is radical, and in a larger measure than can possibly be realized from any other, will be effective. It is separation. It is based upon the experience of the past, which teaches the lesson unmistakably, that the interests of the Lutheran Church in this country, cannot be successfully secured on the union principle. It has been tried in churches and failed; in our educational institutions and various church agencies and enterprises, it has met with no better success; but has always resulted in the withdrawal of one or the other party, and the organization of separate establishments. In separation, then, to a certain extent and in a definite way, is to be found the peace which we seek. Separate churches, separate Synods and separate agencies and educational institutions, but one in the essential doctrines in the Church, one in the forms of worship and one in general aim and purpose. To a large extent this separation has already been established, and the only reason why the trouble is not entirely eradicated, is that both the German and the English parties continue to be members of the same organizations. The conflict exists in these bodies themselves, from whence it is transmitted to the body of the Church, and if traced to the cause which produces it, will be found to arise from the same disturbing element—the difference of language and of the views and usages peculiar to each. The idea, then, is that the work of the Church should be pursued separately—not in a spirit of antagonism, but in harmony—the German and the English branches each pursuing the same great end, and in that sphere of usefulness for which its means best adapt it. The opposite course has been repeatedly tried and always failed, and from the force of circumstances will fail, in whatever form it may be proposed.

To a certain extent unity is practicable, and great benefits to the Church would result from it if established. There may be unity in essentials. All can accept the Augsburg Confession as it is given to us. It is broad and liberal, and is the corner-stone upon which all other Protestant Church creeds were built. We can accept it as Presbyterians accept the Westminster Confession of Faith; as the Protestant Episcopal Church accepts the Thirty-nine Articles. Not a plank need be disturbed, with a view to a more definite platform; nor need its liberal spirit be marred by the interpolation of additional points or rules—rules which no one can understand or explain, and which, seemingly at least, are at variance with its spirit, if not with the spirit of Christianity itself. One in doctrine and forms of worship, with friendly correspondence, but separate in the respects named,—when that comes to pass, then will we have peace and a larger unity than any we have yet enjoyed. In separation of such a character there is growth and expansion; in an enforced union, or one established by the resolutions of Synods, there is restriction, conflict, dissension. With such a policy, Lutherans may be kept in

Lutheran churches, and, instead of building up those of other denominations, will build up their own.

I say, then, in essentials, unity; in non-essentials, liberty—not the liberty which tolerates and excuses compromises of established ssytems of belief—not the liberty which leaves to individual taste, correct, crude, or eccentric, as may happen, the forms of worship to be observed. In sacred things let us have uniformity, rather; one prescribed form to be observed by all, and in all things charity,—not the charity which sanctions erroneous interpretations of fundamental truths, and permits irregularity in religious observances—but that charity which refuses to denounce and condemn the different phases of personal piety as developed in different individuals.

In behalf, then, of the great body of the laity of the Church, I invoke peace. Let us be careful that the chasm which divides us does not grow wider and deeper, but, rather, that the day may soon come when we can clasp hands across it, and be one in fundamentals, one in forms, one in aim and purpose. Then will all the branches grow and expand. Then will the Lutheran Church increase in numbers, in power and influence.

REMARKS OF REV. L. E. ALBERT, D. D. (*General Synod.*)

He was compelled to differ with Dr. Luther in the plan proposed for solving the problem of language. The German and the English elements were necessary to each other; and even although there was occasional friction, yet there were advantages in their union that more than compensated for the disadvantages and embarrassments that sometimes gave trouble. He was compelled to testify, that of the members whom he received into his congregation from other churches, those from the German churches were almost always the most faithful. They had been carefully trained in the doctrines of the Church, they were ardently attached to it, and were to be found in their places long after many from other quarters, who had at first promised well, had disappeared. On no account would he favor any separation on the basis of language. The closest intimacy and best understanding between the representatives of the two languages should be cultivated.

REMARKS OF REV. J. K. PLITT. (*General Council.*)

I have listened with much interest to the essay of Dr. Luther. It is unusual to have the pleasure of hearing *laymen* in productions so carefully prepared. But whilst the Doctor has given a graphic description of certain evils afflicting our Church, he presents a rather startling remedy, and seems to be self-contradictory. *Separation* of the languages in congregations, institutions, etc., is what he proposes, and yet, at the same time, he would have unity in doctrine, uniformity in worship, and oneness of aim and purpose. But if we can have the latter, why the former? Diversity in doctrine is the chief thing that causes separation. Let us be united in the faith —for that is the great point on which a true unity hinges—and we will have no need of separation. Other matters will soon right themselves—our divisions will soon be healed.

REMARKS OF REV. J. B. RATH. (*General Council.*)

I am sorry that I am unable to agree with the essayist in the main point of his paper, separation, as the remedy for our troubles between the German and the English. The evils which he represents as growing out of the contact of the two languages, do indeed exist to a considerable degree, and no one deplores them more heartily than myself. But the remedy he suggests for their removal, appears to my mind worse than the evils themselves. He recommends the radical remedy of separation—separation of congregations, of Synods and of theological institutions, on the basis of language. Instead of this measure being a cure of the troubles complained of, I fear it would prove itself the mischievous cause of rendering them worse. Whatever success as a Church we have had, at least in Pennsylvania, is owing largely to the joint use of the two languages in our congregations, Synods and Seminaries. The history of the English churches in Lancaster, Lebanon, Reading, Easton, Bethlehem and other towns in eastern Pennsylvania, is a standing witness to this fact. These congregations nearly all took their origin in

German congregations that introduced the English language into their services, and maintained the same for years side by side with the German, until the English elements were sufficiently strong to separate from the parent congregations, and to establish themselves as entirely English churches. Had, however, the policy of separation prevailed, the policy of not allowing both languages to be used jointly in the same congregations, some of these prosperous English churches to which we have alluded, would have no existence to-day. We do not deny that some of our German congregations opposed English services in their churches too long, but this fact simply shows that they held on to the idea of separation—German separate from English—too long. Where this suicidal measure was never adopted, or abandoned very early, there the two languages were used conjointly without any unpleasant friction and with good results. The true remedy, therefore, it seems to us, is not separation, but closer, more harmonious union and co-operation. The beauty and excellency of the united employment of the two languages, are also illustrated in our Synods and theological Seminaries. If you wish to represent to your mind the condition of things, as they would naturally be as the result of the mistaken policy of radical separation, imagine in this city of Philadelphia, instead of our one theological seminary with its harmonious co-working of both languages, the existence of two seminaries arrayed against each other on the score of language. Or imagine the dividing line of language arbitrarily drawn between Synods occupying the same geographical territory, and that a territory, on which Providence has brought both languages into the same localities, into the same congregations, and even into the same families—how, under such circumstances, would it be possible to avoid still greater rivalries, oppositions and contentions than those we are now troubled with? German and English brethren should not thus be separated, when Providence has indicated that they should both dwell in concord in the same house, in the same congregation, in the same Synod. To this union of languages is also applicable the Master's injunction: "What, therefore, God hath joined together, let not man put asunder." If here and there be prejudice and conflict between brethren, simply because one speaks a different language from the other, let not such a state of things be endorsed and encouraged by separation of persons and interests, but let it be remedied by dwelling together, and praying that the grace of God may take from our hearts such childish antagonisms. For verily the alienation or opposition of Christians, on no other ground than that of using different languages, is no more respectable before men or justifiable before God, than that which bases itself upon the cut of a coat, the presence of a button, or the breadth of the brim of a hat.

May the Lord grant us grace to overcome any and all such insignificant obstacles in the way of harmony and peace.

REMARKS OF REV. J. KOHLER. (*General Council.*)

The brother who has just spoken, is probably not so well informed as some others, in regard to the introduction of the English language in the churches to which he has referred. There was opposition on the part of the Germans. Instead of being helpful to its introduction, they generally opposed it. In Reading particularly, was there great opposition, and it was only after some members of Trinity Church went out and organized an English congregation, that steps were taken to have English services in that church. Almost everywhere was the introduction of the English language resisted. Had the English language been timely used, and our people properly provided and cared for, our Church in this land would now be larger than any two of the largest denominations together.

But it is more particularly in regard to that part of the essay which refers to uniformity, that I wish to speak. It is here, that there is a great want in our Church—even in regard to the German and English. I think it would be a great advantage if there were more similarity in the services. If the Germans, coming into our English churches, noticed the same service as in their own, they would be more readily drawn to the English churches. If you go into our German churches in this city, and then into many of our English churches, you will see little or no similarity. In the German churches, the pastor wears a gown, uses a liturgical service, and everything wears a churchly appearance; but in most of our English churches it is quite different. I have known members of German churches to remark this. There should be uniformity, so that when our German people come into an English church, they will see everything as in their own, and then they will more likely unite with it. As it is, they find little difference between most of our English churches and those of the denominations.

There should be uniformity in all our churches, so that our people, English and German, going into a Lutheran church anywhere, would at once know that they were in a Lutheran church, and could feel at home. Such a uniformity would do much towards drawing the different parts of the Church together, and keeping them together.

In the essay of yesterday afternoon, there was reference made to the Presbyterian and Episcopal Churches; though there are doctrinal differences among them, they are yet united. But these Churches maintained uniformity. In the Episcopal Church, there are probably greater doctrinal differences than in ours, yet Episcopalians keep together and co-operate with each other. They are held together by their order of service, which is the same everywhere. Go into any of their churches, and there is the same clerical dress, the same order of service—the same hymns and prayer-book—and so it should be among us.

I am aware that this is not the main thing, and that doctrine is of more importance. But this outward uniformity is also a matter of great importance—our laity attach importance to it—and they complain because there is such a lack of uniformity. I have considerable acquaintance with our churches in eastern and central

Pennsylvania; and everywhere, and from persons on both sides of the house, I have repeatedly heard complaints about our want of uniformity. Whatever the order be, let there be but one, they say. And in my humble judgment, it would do much towards bringing all parts of our Church closer together, if we could have the same external order—the same order of service, the same hymn-book, the same clerical dress, and the same polity; and let it be our aim to bring about such a uniformity.

President Sadtler (General Council,) remarked that it would undoubtedly give the Diet great pleasure to hear from the representatives of the German churches, Drs. Mann and Spaeth, on this subject.

REMARKS OF REV. W. J. MANN, D. D. (*General Council.*)

It is practically impossible to draw a line of demarkation between the English and the German; it is impossible in family life, in social intercourse, and everywhere. This condition of the Lutheran Church in this country, is a simple fact, but as such a very stubborn thing. It only requires of the two parties, thus brought into contact, some degree of good will and common sense, and things will soon set themselves right. The German, being placed in an entirely new order of things, in Church, State, and society, has to learn a good deal and is benefited by it. The Americans also have to learn from the Germans. There is not a pastor's library, from Maine to California, in which you cannot find translations of German theological works; and the influence of German literature, for good or for evil, is felt all over the world. Consequently, Lutheran theological students, especially, can do nothing better than to do their best in studying German, and thus make themselves infinitely more useful.

REMARKS OF REV. A. SPAETH, D. D. (*General Council.*)

I am heartily with those who oppose the separation or division of the Church on the basis of language alone. I am so warmly attached to the old Synod of Pennsylvania, because it is, as Dr. Krotel calls it, the paradise for those who understand both languages. I have never opposed, nor will I ever oppose, the tranfer of a member of my German Lutheran congregation to an English "Lutheran" church, simply on account of the language. But if the hope is expressed, that the members of our German Lutheran churches would feel themselves more at home in the English churches, if they would there find the gown, the altar, the baptismal font, and other features of a churchly character, I wish to correct such an idea. Wherever there is a truly Lutheran feeling amongst our people, these outward things will not in themselves satisfy them as the signs of the true Church of their fathers. Our people will have to look for other evidences. They will have to regard the *doctrine* taught in the congregation, with which they intend to connect themselves; they will have to examine the books of worship, the "Catechism," etc. And though the gown should be used in this church of St. Matthew's, and though our old German tunes should be sung, which are so dear to my heart, still I could not and would not recommend this congregation to any member of my church, as long as he would find here another catechism, than the pure, unaltered Catechism of Dr. Martin Luther. Let us first be one, truly one in the *faith*, and the difference of language will not be able to separate us!

After a few remarks by Rev. H. S. Cook, the discussion was closed by Dr. Luther as follows:

REMARKS OF DILLER LUTHER, M. D. (*General Synod.*)

The injury caused by the conflict of languages to Lutheran Churches, particularly in the earlier period, is so well known that I am surprised any one should deny it. If the clerical brother from Bethlehem, will but inquire into the history of those churches in past years, he will find that their decline is owing to that single cause, and that in almost every locality, the congregations of other denominations are composed very largely of persons received from Lutheran families.

It has been stated also that little or no difficulty occurs from this cause at this time, that interchanges are made from time to time between English and German congregations, and that these transfers are made in a spirit of the utmost good will. This is just what we desire to see, but will my friend Dr. Albert inform us to what extent this kind of fraternal amiability is practiced in his community? I can understand that when a member finds he has made a mistake, and is not in the Church to suit him, that he will be handed over to another; but I have yet to see the minister or church that will part with one-half or two-thirds of the membership, without manifesting very decided displeasure.

But this does not touch the point in the argument. That these transfers should be made and are desirable, is just what we plead for, because as we now have both German and English churches at almost every place, they are perfectly practicable. Formerly this was not the case. And even yet, in many instances, it is not practiced, but sternly discountenanced. What I complain of, is, that the German portion of the Church has never adopted a policy favorable to building up English Lutheran churches, and that, therefore, it is to the interest of both parties to pursue their work separately. Both parties have become too strong to be controlled or trammeled. So long as immigration continues, we will have a German and English party —a German and English policy. For it must be remembered that our Church in this country, is exceptional, in that it is composed of people of two different tongues. Hence our trouble. The attempt to conduct religious work together in the churches, was a mistake and a failure from the very beginning.

When my learned friend, Dr. Mann, states that he would consider it a hardship, to be deprived of the pleasure of social intercourse with his children, because of their being instructed in several modern languages, I can understand perfectly that these accomplishments will not in any degree disturb the domestic harmony. But this does not convey a proper idea of the difficulty. When persons of two or three different nationalities, with their families—German, French, and if you choose, Irish—undertake to keep house together, will the doctor favor us with his opinion, whether a very exalted degree of social happiness, is to be expected in a household thus made up? And yet the kindest and most friendly relations may be maintained between them by living separately. And so it is with churches and congregations, where discrepancies such as have been referred to exist—the greatest harmony, unity and co-operation are to be found, not in intimate association, but in the separate pursuit of the work of the Church. Separation in the way pointed out, does not mean antagonism. It is the way to peace, and the method best calculated to ensure the largest growth and prosperity, for both branches of the Church.

The seventh paper was then read.

MISUNDERSTANDINGS AND MISREPRESENTATIONS OF THE LUTHERAN CHURCH.

BY REV. JOS. A. SEISS, D. D., PHILADELPHIA, PA.

IT seems to be the fate of Lutherans, even from the beginning, to be under necessity to contend with an infinite variety of misunderstandings and misrepresentations.

Before the great Diet of Augsburg was held, Luther tells us, a certain doctor was sent from France to Wittenberg, who publicly declared that the French monarch was fully persuaded there was no church, no magistrate, no wedlock, among Lutherans, but that all lived promiscuously, each according to his inclination, as mere brutes.

Alphonsus, chaplain of one of the high dignitaries of Spain, after hearing the Augsburg Confession read to the Emperor, said to Melanchthon, "Dear Philip, in Spain we hear quite other things of you; for there the people are taught to believe that you are men who deny the Holy Trinity, speak in a blasphemous manner of Christ and His holy mother, pervert the Sacraments, hold the Lord's Supper to be no more than any other sign, disregard authorities, live in open unchastity, and give place to other dreadful sins and lusts."

The presentation of that immortal document, which is the common confessional bond and note of all proper Lutherans, served to sweep away effectually all such slanders, where people have been at the pains and honesty to inform themselves. But still, even after the lapse of three centuries and a half, filled with the noblest, clearest, and most widely-sounded testimonies of the modern ages, the abuses of the public mind, in some quarters, are hardly less outrageous, if some who claim to be instructors are to be believed. Yea, surely, if to have all manner of evil said against us falsely is a blessedness, then are Lutherans a highly blessed people.

Often from within, as well as from without, the presentations have sometimes been awry. Even in the wording of the theme assigned me, there is a phrase—one in the most common use, and for which it is hard to find a substitute equally convenient, yet liable to give an erroneous impression, and conveying an idea which some accept and argue from without perhaps proper foundation for so doing. We talk and write familiarly about " *The Lutheran Church.*" We know what we mean by it, and in some measure the terms express what we mean. But, taken in the same sense in which we speak of the Roman Catholic Church, the Greek Church, or the Church of England, the phrase is not quite correct. In that sense there is no such thing as *The Lutheran Church.* There are Lutherans by the million; there are particular ecclesiastical establishments, in different countries, which accept and confess the Lutheran formulas of doctrine; there are Lutheran Churches, Synods, and general consociations; and, for convenience, we may call the totality of these, *The Lutheran Church.* But in so far as corporate oneness, organic unity, interdependence of one part on another, or uniformity of government and administration, are implied, the language is inapplicable and misleading.

Taking it as part of our fundamental confession, that it is not necessary that human traditions, rites, or ceremonies, instituted by men, should be everywhere alike, the Lutheran Churches, from the beginning, exhibited very great differences and variety in their liturgies, their forms of government, and their methods of doing. In some countries, the old Episcopal order has been retained, as in Sweden; in others, a new semi-Episcopal arrangement was instituted; in a few places an independent congregationalism held; and no one general court for the whole has at any time existed. Like the primitive Churches, the Lutherans never have had any governmental concorporation with each other. They have no one outward head or centre. They do not acknowledge themselves amenable to any one earthly ecclesiastical authority. And whilst we can very properly speak of Lutheran confessions—of Lutheran Churches—provincial and individual—of Lutheran consistories, synods and consociations, and may readily trace a common family likeness between them, more or less answering to their family name—when we come to speak of the whole as *The Lutheran Church*, we cannot do so in truth in any such sense as would imply a common jurisdiction, organic connection, unity of external order, or any corporation or establishment to command, bind, or speak with authority. Whether it be our infirmity or our glory, such is the fact, and there is no way of altering it.

Many of the books in popular circulation describe *Lutherans* as "the disciples and followers of Martin Luther," "the followers of the doctrine of Martin Luther," "the followers of Luther," "those Christians who follow the opinions of Martin Luther." In a subordinate and imperfect sense, this language may be tolerated. It recalls an incidental historical fact, which it partially expresses, but connects with it a suggestion which is entirely unjust. Our accepted name would seem to warrant it; but it quite ignores the restricted and only sense in which that name *is* accepted. Though we be called *Lutherans*, it is not that we build on Luther, or accept him as our prophet, or fashion our belief or religion to anything attaching to his person, or to any supposed authority on his part to propound a new faith, or to make a new Church. We do, indeed, recognize in Luther a noble instrument of God's providence, in recalling the Church and the world from the destroying errors and aberrations which had crept into Christendom, and in directing attention again to the old foundations of the one only Gospel of salvation. Notwithstanding the adverse judgments of such scholars as Palivicini, Hallam, Hamilton, Pusey, and others of lesser note, we gratefully acknowledge him as a highly gifted servant of Jesus Christ, the sincerity of whose heart, the purity of whose aims, the strength of whose character, the clearness and vigor of whose faith, and the value of whose evangelic labors render him one of the most deserving of men, and one of the chief treasures of Christendom since the days of the Apostles. Still, it is not Luther we follow, but the Word of Almighty God, delivered by Apostles and Prophets, which he so clearly perceived, and did so much to restore to mankind. He brought forth the old Bible, released it from its bonds, and re-enunciated it as the divine and only rule of faith and life. So we also receive and hold that sacred Book of books, albeit, not for Luther's sake, but for the sake of that God who therein speaks to men, and demands this of all who would be His children. To the one only way of salvation through faith in the only Mediator, the God-man, Christ Jesus, he was marvelously led; and the same he re-asserted from the sacred oracles of the written Word over against the falsities with which the Papal system had encumbered and obscured it. This one only way of salvation we embrace, and hold forth to a perishing world as man's only hope—not, indeed, for Luther's sake, or because Luther taught it, but because it is the veritable truth of Jehovah, and the heart and sum of all the teachings of Divine Revelation. For such agreement with Luther, enemies have attached to us his name; and for such agreement we care not to disown it, lest we should be found disowning or compromising the truth of God. But Luther is not our Lord and Master, as Mahomet to the Mahometans, or the Pope of Rome to the poor misbelievers who accept his *dicta* as infallible. In any sense, therefore, involving authority in Luther to teach or command us, except as God's own written Word teaches, we are not his disciples or followers.

In a recent work on *The Creeds of Christendom*, quoted by one of the essayists who has preceded me, among other ungracious things said of the Lutherans, the stale charge of *man-worship* is again insinuated against us. "The towering greatness of Luther" is there put forward as the particular fly in the ointment of our sanctity. We may be excused for remanding it to its source as a particular falsehood. Whether the enunciator of the truth be a saint or sinner, great or small, that truth we must acknowledge. Mere persons, or the worth and credit of men, are nothing to the obligations of truth. For this reason we would be bound to acknowledge Luther as a witness, were he a score of times greater or less than he was. Gold is gold, whether on the finger of the king, or on the neck of a harlot; and the truth is the truth, equally divine and binding, whoever speaks it. We are bound to confess it, fully and without stint, even with a Martin Luther, though his "towering greatness" be "a misfortune," and "a constant temptation to hero-worship." But we are not quite ready to admit that God, in ordering His Providence concerning His Church, made a grand mistake in not availing Himself of the wisdom of certain Reformed theologians.

Of late years, a class of writers and ecclesiastical operators has arisen, who have discovered that, somehow, the great Reformation, though necessary, was a great mistake. They have come to the conclusion that it was an unfortunate dislocation in the Church of Christ. Accepting, in general, the principles which governed it, and, in some instances, subscribing to a very Lutheranizing creed, they yet have most serious fault to find with Luther, with the outcome of the Evangelical cause in general, and with its representation by Lutheranism in particular. They admit that some break was unavoidable, but speak of the fracture as badly managed—"a leg badly set, which needs to be broken again to be set right." In the ideal held forth by these people, Lutherans are necessarily schismatics, and full of vital defects. We do not rightly conceive of the Church. We have not been careful enough to retain the episcopate, and do not lay sufficient stress upon orders. We are too radical in our denial of the priestly mediatorship of the clergy, and the self-operating power of episcopally administered sacraments. Our doctrine of justification by faith only, is too antinomian, unsafe for souls, and detrimental to practical godliness. And, in one way or another, they have a particular quarrel with Luther and the Lutherans.

This sort of twaddle has its "head centre" among the Tractarians and High Churchmen of England, who are echoed by a somewhat corresponding class in this country. Scores of the greatest lights in the English establishment, for 300 years, were accustomed to speak of the Lutheran Churches of the Continent, as "*the Church of England's dearest sisters abroad.*" One of the greatest champions and defenders of the English establishments, "the judicious Hooker," put it in his greatest book, "*I dare not deny the salvation of the Lutheran Churches, which have been the chiefest instruments of ours.*" In the times of the formation of the Church of England, the Lutheran theologians were looked to as the preëminent representatives of renewed and proper Christianity, and were besought and welcomed to take the highest places which that establishment had to give. In our day, the Lutheran Prince Albert, of Germany, and the Lutheran Princess Alexandria, of Scandinavia, are as fully acknowledged by the English Church as its own noble Queen Victoria, and that Queen's daughters are transferred to the churches of the Continent without thought or ceremony of a change of religion. And these new doctors themselves have, as their only public creed to this day, those Articles of Religion which have been shown to be so largely derived from the Lutheran Formulas, and use and honor a Book of Common Prayer, whose main contents have come through Lutheran hands, and bear a Lutheran mold. And yet, when they come to speak of Luther and the Lutherans, they exclaim in holy horror at the defects and heresies they find. With them Protestantism is a failure, and indefensible without radical changes. It must be reconstructed. The whole Reformation must be done over. The past 350 years must be ignored, and a new departure taken. Just what the new thing is to be, they are not yet able to tell. That is the problem yet to be worked out. Whether or not we are to have a pope, to serve as a centre of the new unity, is an open question; only the schism of the 16th century must somehow be healed. Concerning the infallible supremacy, purgatory, and the worship of the Virgin Mary, a little "understanding" is necessary, but that can be afterwards adjusted. The existing Formulas must be revised and denuded of their positiveness. The doctrine of justification by faith must be set aside, at least from the central position which the Lutherans assign it. Ministerial orders and sacerdotalism must be restored, and duly legitimated. The confessional, and the whole round of a gaudy ceremonial, minus, perhaps, a few abuses, must be brought back. Brotherhoods and sisterhoods, with special vows and commissions, must be encouraged and re-established. Good works and special sanctities must have more stress laid upon them. And so the suggestions run on. But the real spirit is easily divined. It carries its mark on its forehead. *It means Romanism*—return to the old abominations of Egypt and Babylon, whither scores on scores of these new Reformers have already betaken themselves, as the only outcome of this proposed resetting of the limb so badly managed by the old doctors. The multitudinousness of the perverts to Rome by this road, ought, of itself, to open the eyes of all thinking people to the folly and ruin of listening to such quacks as would fain repair the bungled surgery under which the most virtuous and enlightened of the earth, for three and a half centuries, have lived and prospered.

As to the tumid assaults of these people on the great Reformer, Archdeacon Hare has made noble answer, in his triumphant *Vindication of Luther*. He has shown to their shame, how little they knew of him whom they so harshly judge, how little they cared to know of him, and with what malignant prejudice they have rehashed and exaggerated the false and oft-refuted charges of the Romish controversialists. Bossuet's *Variations* and Moehler's *Symbolik* have furnished about the only armor they have brought to bear in the case. And from the base insinuations and garbled quotations thence derived, these new lights have ventured assertions which even the Romish partisans, in all their hatred, did not dare to make.

That a great and incurable breach did occur between the Lutherans and Rome during the 16th century, history amply attests. But that it was a guilty schism from the true Catholic Church, the sin of which lies at our door, is an unmodified falsehood, as all the facts conclusively prove. Palmer, in his *Treatise on the Church*, without at all touching the real depths of the matter, quite exculpates our fathers from every shade and degree of separatism or schism. Had he put the whole case, the showing to his purpose would have been completely overwhelming.

From the days of the Apostles to the time of Luther, there was not a creed of the true Catholic Church which the Lutherans did not fully accept and retain; not a heresy or perversion of the truth condemned and rejected by the true Catholic Church, which the Lutherans did not likewise condemn and reject; not a book of the sacred Canon, not a law for interpreting the Scriptures, not a principle with reference to their authority and use, not a legitimate tribunal for the final settlement of controversies about the faith, accepted and approved by the true Catholic Church, which the Lutherans did not also accept, approve, and propose to abide by. In the greatest of their Confessions, solemnly laid before the Diet of the empire in the name of them all, the assertion is made, and reiterated again and again, as holding throughout the twenty-eight articles, and in all the sum of doctrine held and taught among Lutherans, that " there is nothing which is discrepant with the Scriptures, or with the Church Catholic, or even with the Roman Church, so far as that Church is known from the writings of the fathers." And in all the controversies then or thereafter, no one has ever been able to show that it was not the exact truth. It therefore follows, that, in all matters of faith and doctrine, which are everywhere and always the chief and constitutive things of the Church, the Lutherans were neither heretics nor schismatics.

And as to external fellowship, there never was, among any people, a more earnest and persistent endeavor to maintain connection with the order which then obtained, than that which the Lutherans exhibited. When the Reformation begun, Luther had not the slightest idea of separating from the Church. Nay, from first to last, he never ceased to appeal to its authority, and to pledge himself to the most humble obedience whensoever its legitimate decision should be duly ascertained. He even wrote the pope, in terms so submissive that they now look more like the words of a craven, than those of a defiant revolutionist. Everywhere, and on all occasions, he held himself as ready to recant as he had been to assert, provided only, that it should first be fairly shown that he held or taught "contrary to the Scriptures, the councils, and the fathers." He was willing to accept any German bishop as his judge, and to abide by the decision. He ever protested that he never meant to attack or injure the authority of the Roman Church, to cause disturbances about small matters, or to refuse obedience in anything which should lawfully be required of him. And even when condemned and excommunicated by the pope, he still expressed submissive acknowledgment of the authority of the Church, and earnestly sought to maintain his fellowship with it, by a legitimate appeal to a general council. This was the attitude at the Diet of Spires, at the Diet of Augsburg, and on all occasions while the great controversy raged. In the name of all Lutherans, the Augsburg Confession proposed and agreed that the whole Romish jurisdiction might stand and would be humbly obeyed, provided certain usages and traditions contrary to the Word of God were not enforced. Conference after conference did the Lutherans seek and attend with a view to adjust the trouble, and always with a spirit at antipodes with the spirit of sect and schism. They were willing to do everything, and bear anything, provided only that they should be left in peace and quietness to hold, preach and practice according to their profound convictions of the teachings of the Scriptures and of the true Catholic Church.

But this proviso did not suit the proud conceit and usurped dominion of the papacy. And because, in right obedience and loyalty to God and conscience, our fathers could not consent to let go the Word of God, and would not debauch themselves any more with the worship of saints and relics of dead men, nor trust in any mediator but Jesus, nor allow human works, payments or goodnesses as entering into the procuring cause of forgiveness of sins, Rome excommunicated them, by cities, nations and millions, thrust them away from her fellowship, and delivered them over to her intensest anathemas forever.

Thus came about the tremendous dislocation; but by no fault of the Reformers. Rome forced the issue, and made the decision, and with her must rest the blame that belongs to the result. The one only alternative was, either to let the eternal and saving truth of God be stifled and smothered under the incrustations of damning falsehood and superstition, allowing the race of man to drift on to perdition without the light God in mercy gave for our salvation, or *the Churches called Lutheran had to come into independent being*. And with this as the one distinct question in the case, is there a true man living to doubt which was the side of right? As the authority of God is above popes—as man's obligation to truth is above all other claims—as the worth of a pure Gospel is above all man-made regulations and outward order—as self sacrifice for the truth's sake is above sacrifice of the truth for self's sake,—so great, and so complete, is the justification of the existence of our Churches, as over against Rome; the Tractarians to the contrary notwithstanding.

As remarked in several of the essays already presented, it is our lot to live in days, and in a land, of sects and denominations, in which altar is set up against altar, society against society, and meeting and ministry against meeting and ministry, begetting the utmost confusion and perplexity to simple and honest inquirers, and shamefully distracting and weakening the whole Protestant cause. The evil of this state of things is deeply felt and largely deplored. It is seen to be a fruitful cause of indifferentism, and a self-justifying nothingarianism, enervating and obliterating the Church, strengthening the hands of infidelity, and trampling under foot the truth as it is in Jesus. Again and again, the evil thing has been multiplied by attempts to cure it, and the anti-sectarians have shown themselves the greatest makers and fosterers of sects. Even the unionism and undenominationalism with which many good-meaning people would salve it over, tend only to encourage it, and to make it appear innocent. That there is great wrong in it, most agree; but the sin of it is continually being lodged at the wrong place, and those most adverse to it, and the most consistently arrayed against it, are generally loaded with the blame for it.

In this babel of beliefs, unbeliefs and non-beliefs, the Lutherans are frequently put down as *one of the sects*, on the common basis of all the rest, only a little more sectarian, because not generally so pliant with regard to the thousand goodishnesses got up for all sects and Churches alike to take hold of and sustain. And just here there is another grand mistake and misrepresentation, which needs to be pointedly brought out. This splitting up of Christendom into fragments and separatistic fractions, we do most heartily lament and deplore as an unspeakable evil; but we distinctly and unqualifiedly disclaim all responsibility for it. The breach with Rome we accept, and go before the world, before angels, and before God, for our justification in that business. Everything was done that could be done, but Rome would not in any sense or degree tolerate us without a surrender of the evangelical faith of God's Word. For the old and everlasting truth we were made a separate communion, not by our secession, but by Rome's unwarranted and persistent excommunication. We were thrust out by a monstrous usurpation, and there was no other help for the Gospel or for us.

But which of all the antagonizing sects or parties around us can plead such an apology for their separate being? The Lutheran Churches existed, in great and mighty strength, before them. The Lutheran communion was born, baptized, confirmed, and had reached its sublime majority, before any of these bodies had their present form or being. Ere they were, we had already so fully grasped the proper evangelic truth and life, and recovered and defined such a doctrinal and liturgical basis and foundation for the conservation of the pure Church and wholesome Christian growth and sanctification, that it must for ever remain an embarrassing puzzle to all subsequent separatists and denominations to give just and Christian answer why they exist, and continue to maintain their separatism. In this country, something must indeed be allowed for the differences of nationality, and the home education of the different classes of colonists here thrown together. It also may be hard to find out a practical cure for what all seem to lament. But, when it comes to the kernel and right of the thing, so far as these separate communions have any true, settled and saving Christian faith, or any just title to be called true Churches of Jesus Christ, it is simply and only because they have accepted the teachings, copied the Confessions, and built upon the foundations, which the Lutherans before them had dug out of the papal congest, and made their own. There is no Episcopalianism, no Presbyterianism, no Congregationalism, no Methodism, and no other kind of ism, so far as unmistakably grounded on the Scriptures of God, or reconcilable with the orthodox historic faith of the Church of Christ, which really needed for itself, or needs now, any other communion, or establishment, than the one original Protestant Church, which we represent, and from which they all, directly, or indirectly, derived the essential substance of all the Christian doctrine and faith they have. Some of them are built on particular forms of government, some on particular human methods, some on particular rites and ceremonies, or modes of administering divine ordinances, and some on mere accidents; but none of these things enter properly into the being and legitimacy of the Church. They have ever varied with times, countries and circumstances, without affecting the divine foundations of faith and salvation. Some of them are more desirable and edifying than others; but they are not therefore just grounds on which to erect separate and antagonizing communions. Because they are not essential, therefore some argue the right to exercise their own pleasure in the matter, and so would justify sectarianism. But the true bearing is exactly in the contrary direction. Because these things do not enter into the essential being of the Church, therefore, to emphasize them in such way as to make them the corner-stones of separate and antagonizing communions, is to pervert the Gospel, and to build the Church of God on what is variable, indifferent, accidental, provisional and human, instead of on the divine verities which are everywhere and always the same. That which determines the character, legitimacy, and proper Christianity of a Church, is its true, clear, rotund, balanced and unmistakable confession of the doctrines of salvation through the incarnate Son of God, as set forth in the Scriptures, and contained and verifiable in the testimony of the true Catholic Church from the beginning. Where this already is and lives, whatever other diversities exist, or particular preferences are unmet, *there* is the true Church of Christ, in its just and sufficient integrity; so that he who dissents and separates from it, to set up an opposing communion, thereby makes himself guilty of sectarianism and schism. And with whatever pretexts he may seek to cloak and embellish his doings, he will ever try in vain to make out a justification for himself from these Scriptures.

We do not say, and far be it from me to say, that saving doctrines of Christ are nowhere held and taught but in the Lutheran Churches so called. We know to the contrary, and are happy to acknowledge the fact, to honor the truth wherever we find it, and to treat as Christians all who prove themselves such. Such at least is my case. But it is our right to say, on the clear evidences of holy Scripture and historic verity, that the true and only saving doctrines of Jesus Christ are embraced, held and taught by the Lutheran Churches and Confessions, fully, purely, and without stint or distortion; and were thus held and taught before the multitudinous parties and sects about us had a being. Nay, this also may be added in all confidence, that if salvation cannot be securely found and obtained in the Churches called *Lutheran*, there is no such thing as salvation. What true God is there whom our Churches do not confess and worship; or false god, which they do not reject and despise? What true Scripture of God is there which they do not receive and teach, or false scripture which they do not cast from them and condemn? What true Christ is there who is not the centre of their Creed, hope and trust; or Anti-christ against whom they do not warn and admonish with all fidelity? What means of grace have been ordained of God which they do not use and insist on having used; or what substitutes or superadditions devised by man, which they do not censure and oppose? What divine promises or terms of salvation are there, which they do not put before men for their spiritual comfort; or false hopes against which they do not caution? What genuine Gospel is there which they do not confess and preach, or true ministry of God which they do not acknowledge, or other thing entering into the substance of Christianity which they do not accept and defend? And in all the reforms and improvements by which men have thought to get up something better, more Scriptural, more effective, where, in all the length and breadth of this earth, can be found a more thoroughly tried and reliable guide and helper to the full truth of God, a sanctified life, and eternal salvation, than the system of faith and life confessed and upheld by the Lutherans? And as this communion of believers existed, and had spread itself out among the nations, before any of our modern sects and parties were, we scorn to be rated as one of them, and before God most solemnly disclaim all share in the unholy business of which they are the cherished memorials. If men will accept and honor them as right, legitimate and Christian, and thus lend themselves, influence and means, to perpetuate the distractions which so weaken and disgrace the cause of evangelic Christianity, we cannot say them nay; but *on them* be the burden of answering for it to their Maker and Judge; for we have no part nor lot in the matter.

With reference to the more particular doctrines of our Lutheran Confessions, there are also many misunderstandings and misrepresentations abroad, which ought of right to be touched. Indeed, there seems to be an incurable obtuseness in some people to comprehend what Lutherans hold and teach, though there is not another communion in the world which has so fully, exhaustively, and on all points, set forth its doctrines, as the Lutheran.

On the great and all-important subject of the Person of Christ, people persist in misrepresenting us, and often to the great damage of their own clearness of faith, and consistent apprehension of salvation.

The same is true with regard to our doctrines concerning the means of grace, particularly of the sacraments of Baptism and the Lord's Supper. People wish to get away as far as possible from everything which they think smacks of Romanism, and by their unguarded assumptions disable themselves, so that they cannot see the difference between our pure scriptural teachings and the monstrous perversions and abominations of the Council of Trent. With our blessed Lord, we teach the necessity of being "*born of water and of the Spirit;*" with the inspired Paul, we do not hesitate to speak of the application of salvation "*by the washing* (or bath) *of regeneration, and renewing of the Holy Ghost;*" and, with all the teachings of the New Testament, we constantly refer to Baptism as a great spiritual treasure; and lo! we are charged with the superstition of attaching a magic charm to a mere outward ceremony! When we speak of the Word as an earthly vehicle or medium in and through which the Saviour communicates Himself and His salvation, there is no difficulty in understanding us; but when we say the same thing of the corresponding "visible Word"—of the Lord's Supper—people exclaim in horror, "*Transubstantiation*"—"*Consubstantiation*," —or some other abomination, which our Confessions distinctly reject and condemn, and all our theologians repudiate. The old lie of the sacramentarian controversialists, so often refuted and exposed, which charges the monstrosity of consubstantiation upon our invulnerable doctrine of the Holy Eucharist, we had hoped was effectually buried, never to appear again in any author worthy of respect; but, alas, I find it resurrected, and again put forth, in the recent volumes on *The Creeds of Christendom*, to the great discredit of their author, who certainly ought to know better, if he does not.

And even among professed Lutherans themselves, from one cause or another, the presentations of our position and spirit have not always been as consistent and just as they should have been. Everything with which man has to do, however sacred or good, will show the traces of his weaknesses. And so has it been here. There have been, and there still are, particular schools and tendencies, bearing the Lutheran name, which have proven about as sectarian as the sects, some in the way of alleged devotion to the faith, and some in the way of laxity with regard to it. Like the Church universal, in the earlier times, our Churches have had their more favorable and their less favorable ages, sections and departments. And what has been in the past, is still largely represented in the present. There are those who unfortunately lose sight of the fact, that Lutheranism commenced with *a Melanchthon* as well as a Luther; while others are equally oblivious to the fact that it embraced *a Luther*, as well as a Melanchthon. Within it, and of it, there has been a Helmstaedt and a Halle, as well as a Wittenberg and a Leipsic; but, at the same time, a Wittenberg and a Leipsic, as well as a Helmstaedt and a Halle.

What I take to be the true soul and spirit of our Churches is not what appears in any one of these tendencies, past or present, as over against the other, or without the other; but the one interpenetrated, permeated and modified by the other, each in each, in one living, golden mean of all, the best illustration of which is perhaps to be found in the illustrious intermediate school of Jena. Professed Lutherans misrepresent their Confession, largely negative it, and compromise their cause, by sympathizing too freely with Calixtus, Horneius, Dreir and Latermann; but they do no better for themselves, or for the Church, when they propose to swear every body by the *Consensus Repetitus*, or give place to the spirit which felt itself constrained to bring two hundred and sixty-three charges of heretical error against the pure and heavenly-minded Spener.

But I cannot now enter further on these matters. Perhaps, in the judgment of some, I have not myself succeeded in making the right presentations. But what I have written I have written, and must abide by the results.

With these observations I submit the subject to those who are to follow me.

REMARKS OF REV. C. W. SCHAEFFER, D. D. (*General Council.*)

Dr. Seiss has said that the Lutheran Church cannnot be charged either with heresy or with schism; and furthermore, as I think I understood, that there is no evangelical doctrine accepted by the Church of Christ which the Lutheran Church does not confess, and no error in doctrine rejected by the Church which the Lutheran Church does not condemn. This being admitted, and I believe it, what value ought we to attach to the Confessions of the Lutheran Church? how should we understand and represent them?

Not long ago I read an article in print, that ended somewhat in this manner, "We believe in a perfect Bible, in a perfect forgiveness of sin, in a perfect Saviour; but we have no idea that such a thing, as a perfect creed exists." But are not the facts such that we ought to recognize Divine guidance in the preparation of our Confessions, and discountenance insinuations against their reliability as Confessions?

What was the character of the Reformation itself? Was it a Divine work, or merely or chiefly human? No doubt we will all be prompt in recognizing, even in the midst of all its human instrumentalities, the presence, the controlling influence of Divine wisdom and power and grace, in the beginning and promoting of that great work of the Church.

Now when the time came for the Church to do an act of the very highest importance for itself and for the glory of its Head and of His truth, that is, to declare its answer to the revelation of the Gospel, and to confess its faith in the Divine word, ought we not rather to believe that the same Divine guidance which had been granted to it hitherto, would be specially near and positive and active in the execution of such a work? The promises of the aid and teachings of the Holy Ghost, according to the Word, are still in force, and they are on record for all time. Does not the proper understanding and truthful representation of the Lutheran Church, then, require of us a recognition of this element in the preparation of her Confessions? Does it not forbid us to place those Confessions on the low level of ordinary human productions, which, whatever may be their ability, are always strongly marked by human ignorance and infirmity?

We ought rather to maintain, that the Confessions, as Confessions and as far as they go, are perfect, true, unerring testimonies of the Divine word, and may be safely relied upon.

REMARKS OF REV. J. A. BROWN, D. D. (*General Synod.*)

It is possible that Dr. Schaeffer has done me the honor of referring to something that I have said and printed. At least I have used language of a somewhat similar character. If I am mistaken, both he and this Diet will pardon me for presuming that I may be the person referred to. I did say in print, not long ago, "*We believe in an infallible Bible, an infallible Saviour, but an infallible Creed, and an infallible Church, we do not believe in, whether the pretence is set up in the General Council or by Rome;*" and by this declaration I am ready to stand, here in this Diet, and everywhere. I take no backward step from this position, as it is fundamental to Protestantism, as well as to genuine Lutheranism. There is but one perfect book, but one infallible record of Divine truth,—the inspired Word of God. This is infallible just because it is inspired, and "holy men of God spake as they were moved by the Holy Ghost." This absolute infallibility is true only of the Scriptures as contained in the originals. We do not affirm it of any translation, ancient or modern, however excellent. These translations are more or less imperfect, and are subject to change and improvement from time to time, and must be compared with the infallible originals to determine their merit. They may answer for all practical purposes, but it would be absurd to set up a claim of infallibility for any version, as Rome has done for the Vulgate. The final appeal must be to the original inspired Word. If this be true of any and every translation of the Bible, how much more so in regard to any production of mere men?

It is of the utmost importance that we understand and maintain the truth in this respect. Creeds or Confessions are merely human productions, and everything human is imperfect and fallible. There is no infallibility in Popes, or Councils, or the makers of Creeds. Every Creed, from the Apostles' down, has been subjected to revisings and alterations. The Augsburg Confession underwent changes and improvements until nearly the last hour before its presentation to the Emperor at Augsburg; and almost immediately afterwards, Melanchthon continued his work of altering and trying to amend. At present, among the various editions, no one can tell what was the true original Augsburg Confession. We have editions in Latin and German varying considerably, and we can only approximate to the original Augsburg Confession. Which is the perfect, infallible one? The case of different editions of the original Scriptures furnishes no parallel, for there we know where to look for infallibility.

We are willing and ready, according to our humble ability, to advocate and defend the Augsburg Confession, over against other modern confessions, as the very best and most Scriptural of them all. We admire its truly Catholic and Evangelical character. As a Confession, and for the legitimate purposes of a Confession, we may be justly proud of it as our own. But when there is set up for it a claim, which we believe to be unwarrantable, and inconsistent with the very character of a Confession of Faith, then we feel bound to utter our protest. When real or virtual infallibility is claimed for this or any other human production as a Confession of Faith, to which we are to be absolutely bound, as we are to the Word of God, as the Rule of our faith, we must proclaim our dissent. On this point we would not be misunderstood, and we are glad to believe and know that we are standing on firm Lutheran ground.[1]

---

[1] Müller, in the "*Historical Introduction*" to his edition of the Symbolical Books, says, "The Church, then, does not wish to ascribe to her Symbols immutable authority; she admits that some one might discover a defect in them; she finds in them merely a temporary expression of her faith; she reserves to herself

But we would like to ask Dr. Seiss a plain question. It is very ungracious, and imposes an unpleasant task, to say a word to mar the effect of the very forcible and eloquent address to which we have just listened To most of it we could say yea and amen. We believe that as a defence of the great Reformation against the accusations of Rome and certain Anglicans, it was triumphant. The Lutheran Church cannot be justly charged with schism in separating from Rome. We believe that before men and angels and God, she stands fully justified in her separate, distinct existence. She is not in the Roman Catholic Church because she could not remain there. She was thrust out, and obedience to conscience and the Word of God, demanded she should no longer submit to corruption and tyranny. We can endorse all that was said on this point thus far.

We can go a step further. We hold that the Augsburg Confession is truly a catholic and liberal Confession ; and interpreted as it was by its author, there would have been little excuse for the existence and multiplication of other Creeds and other denominations. With the due exercise of charity, the Augsburg Confession might have furnished the basis of a united Protestantism, as it has since been confessed by different nationalities and different denominations.

But the question I desire to ask is this : Has not the Lutheran Church, by the adoption of a very extended confessional system, including explanations of disputed points among evangelical Christians, and making a subscription to this system a condition of re-

---

expressly the privilege of improving them, of completing or of extending, as occasional necessity requires." Any number of authorities might be cited to the same purpose. It is a lame attempt to meet the plain question, to set up the plea that for an individual to object to the infallibility of the Confession, is to claim infallibility for himself, and to set up his individual infallibility against the infallibility of the Church. On this principle, no member of the Church of Rome would ever doubt the Papal infallibility— for to do so would be to assert his own.

maining in the Church, furnished other denominations a good and sufficient excuse for their separate organizations? Cannot other denominations plead the same excuse in justification for their existence outside of the Lutheran Church, that Lutherans plead against Rome? True, they may not have been thrust out, but was not their remaining in made impossible, except at the sacrifice of conscientious convictions of truth and duty?

We do not wish to quibble or to raise doubtful questions, but to deal with plain facts. Take as an illustration the action of the Lutheran Church in 1580, in adopting the entire Book of Concord. There were thousands and tens of thousands then and since, in and out of the Lutheran Church, who could not and would not subscribe this Book. There have been venerable men in the Ministerium of Pennsylvania, whose names have been mentioned with honor as Lutherans on the floor of this Diet, who have declared themselves willing to endure any sufferings rather than subscribe to everything in these Symbolical Books. There are things there which do not constitute any part of genuine Catholic Lutheranism, and yet which have been imposed, at some times and in some places, as a condition of remaining in the Lutheran Church. It cannot and will not be questioned in this Diet, that thousands and tens of thousands of as learned, honest, and godly men, as the Church has ever known in any age, have not found themselves able to accept the peculiarities of the Lutheran faith. It would be useless to call the roll of illustrious scholars, learned divines, devoted missionaries, and self-sacrificing laborers in every department, who have proved their sincerity and devotion to the cause of Christ, by evidence which challenges our admiration. No man can, without an audacity of which few are possessed, deny the intelligence, or learning, or piety, or sincerity, of the hosts of great and good men in the other denominations of Christendom. This is not even disputed by the most zealous advocates of Lutheranism.

Now, I ask if the exclusion of these men from the Lutheran

Church does not give them the same ground for a separate denominational existence, that we claim for ourselves? Cannot they, before men, and angels and God, justify themselves for not being in the Lutheran Church? Have we any right to set up a rule that excludes them, and then to condemn them because they do not choose to do violence to their consciences, and profess what they cannot believe? It is egregious trifling to say that they were not compelled to take a position outside of the Lutheran Church. If we admit their honesty, they simply acted as honest and God-fearing men. They have done what every man's conscience must approve. And they have not been left without evidence of favor and approval from above.

I have asked this question because it goes directly to the heart of this matter of denominationalism. It demands to know what share we have in this work, and whether the course some insist on as a test of genuine Lutheranism, is not fraught with all the evils of division and schism in the Lutheran Church and in the Church of Christ?

REMARKS OF REV. C. P. KRAUTH, D. D., LL. D. (*General Council.*)

Dr. Krauth said that the point made by Dr. Schaeffer, as against the position taken by Dr. Brown, is very important. Dr. Brown has totally failed to mark the real question, which is not, whether the Lutheran Church is infallible, for all admit that she is not, but whether she has in fact failed. An infallible rule does not make infallible interpreters, but it protects those who use it aright, from failure. It is not the infallibility of men, but the power of God's Word to produce clear, unmistaken convictions on the part of those who use it as it directs, on which we rest our claim that the Church may reach truth without any intermingling of error in faith; and by the comparison of our confessions with this Word, and by the conformity with the Word thus established, we reach the conclusion that she has not erred. Infallibility and failure are not the only suppositions possible. There is a third supposition—that though there be fallibility, there has not been actual failure.

In the minute method of marking wherein the infallibility of the original text consists, it might consistently have been added that the Rule of Faith is the Word, as written in the manuscripts of the sacred penmen. These manuscripts have vanished for ages. No copies known to us approach them by several centuries. The Word as the Holy Spirit gave it is infallible, but the transcribers, the printers, the editors, are not. In Dr. Brown's mode of construction we have not, in fact, an infallible rule of faith, but only fallible manuscripts of it, no two of which absolutely agree. Nor does he seem to realize the real dishonor put in terms of honor on the Word, which, infallible itself, is either the generator of constant failures, or fails, of necessity, to prevent them. That is an empty vine which brings forth fruit only for itself. It is, indeed, an extraordinary mode of defending the sufficiency of the Word, a book which, according to him, has an infallible sense, in which those who use it are infallibly mistaken, or at least can never be sure they are right, inasmuch as they are fallible themselves. Our Church holds that the very object of this infallible book, is to correct and to prevent the errors into which fallible men fall without it. It is an infallible book, meant to prevent failures. And as a rule is actualized only as men take its meaning into their minds and hearts, the truth infallible as it lies in the Word, is transmuted into possible error in the very act of reception by fallible man, alike in reading the originals, when he translates it himself, or in reading the translations of others. It is a view which annihilates all possibility of an assured faith, and is as conclusive against the certitude of the doctrines which Dr. Brown considers necessary, as against those he would leave open. It leaves all opinions, and allows of no faith.

Dr. Brown seems to confound those changes in creeds which amplify, and defend, and state more felicitously the faith, to prevent change in it or misunderstanding of it, with those whose object would be to deny faith once confessed. The faith confessed at Augsburg was fixed before the Diet was called. The abstract in the XVII Articles of Luther, which was laid as the basis of the doctrinal part of it, sets forth in all respects the same faith. All the labor of the Confession was directed to perfecting—not the doctrine, for that was fixed—but the form. Melanchthon was so great a precisian in style that he touched and retouched everything to the time of his death. There is no impossibility and no difficulty in determining what is the "true original Augsburg Confession," in any sense in which we are practically interested in it as a standard. In the Latin, there is the first edition of 1530, edited by Melanchthon himself, while the Diet was still sitting, and now incorporated in all editions of the Book of Concord. In German we have the first edition of the same year, edited by Melanchthon during the sitting of the Diet. There are nine known manuscripts of the Latin and twelve of the German, preserved in the archives of the Lutheran States and cities. The edition of the German in the Book of Concord, is from the Mentz copy in the Protocol of the Empire. Twenty-one manuscripts, seven unauthorized editions, one edition in each language by Melanchthon himself, all of the year 1530, are collated, and thus in the hands of scholars, to settle the precise text of the Augsburg Confession. We can ask with far more force, which among the various editions of the Greek New Testament is the true original New Testament? We have editions varying by many thousands of stylistic minutenesses, and we can only approximate the original text, which is the perfect, infallible Rule of faith. And yet one ignorant of the facts might suppose that we, who have no practical difficulty whatever about the Biblical text, are quite at sea about the Augsburg Confession, and that however willing we might be to accept it, no man can tell us where it is, or what it is; when in fact there is scarcely a great document of equal antiquity whose text we can settle by so many direct vouchers. We know that the faith of the Rule is so inwrought in the Rule, that the mere textual differences do not affect the result. The faith of the New Testament is the same in the Sinaitic Uncial and the latest Cursives, in the first of Erasmus, and the last of Tischendorf. And the faith of the Augsburg Confession is the same in every edition, Latin and German, which pretends to be the Confession as actually read June 25th, 1530. The deliberate changes or corruption of either the Rule or the Confession are very different, and when we see evidences of them, we should at once throw aside the whole book, whether it pretends to be Scripture or Confession.

Sectarianism, not satisfied with open warfare against our Church, endangered it yet more for political reasons, by pretences of conformity with the Augsburg Confession as "interpreted by its author," meaning Melanchthon, who yet was not its author in any respect which gave him a right to change it, and whose interpretation of the meaning of the Confession when in 1530 he composed it, differed in no respect from that of Luther. The meaning of the Augsburg Confession is that which those, who presented it in 1530 then designed, it to express; and any change from *that* meaning, by whomsoever made, is not an interpretation of the Confession, but a perversion of it.

The Formula of Concord grew out of the struggle of the Lutheran Church for her very life. So far from originating the divisions in Protestant Christendom, it came after the organization of all the Reformed Churches. *It* was not at Augsburg to frighten the Zwinglians and Tetrapolitans from union with us in 1530. The Basel Confession of 1534, the Helvetic of 1536, the Zurich of 1545, the Genevan Catechism of 1541, the Zurich Consensus of 1549, the French Confession of 1559, the Confession of the Netherlands of 1561, the Scotch of 1568, the Heidelberg Catechism of 1562, the Second Helvetic of 1566, the Thirty-Nine Articles of the Church of England of 1562— surely these, and the Churches which stood under them, did not owe their existence to the Formula of Concord, which did not appear till 1580. The doctrinal objections to the Formula of Concord are at their root always objections to the Augsburg Confession, as an intelligent *ex animo* reception of the Augsburg Confession is at its root always a virtual reception of the Formula of Concord. The Formula of Concord originated no sects. It saved the Lutheran Church and the Reformation from being swamped by them.

There is an extraordinary want of consistency in the opponents of the Book of Concord. Sometimes they talk as if the Lutheran Church were so rigidly bound to the Augsburg Confession exclusively, that the recognition of anything beside would be inconsistent. Yet when it suits them they claim the largest liberty for the Church to alter, cut down, add to, substitute—an illimitable right to make and change creeds. They make a fetich of the Augsburg Confession, idolizing it (in phrase) one day, and claiming the next day the right to a new fetich, whenever they want it, and to make any changes they please in the old one; and this, they tell us, is the Lutheran position in regard to our Church creeds. The denial of this they represent as Symbolism, the putting of the creed on the level of Scripture. But in this whole matter they start with confounding very distinct things—the faith itself, the divine doctrine, and the particular confessions of it in their individual style and method. A pure Church can have but one faith; that faith makes her pure; losing it she loses her purity, she loses herself; a pure faith once is a pure faith forever. The ages cannot touch it, nor change it. The Church may express that faith with greater clearness; she may withdraw what is less full, and substitute what is more full, or may add without withdrawing. She may give officially an explanation of a creed, to prevent mistake or correct misstatement, but the faith itself she cannot change. The faith is older than the creed. The pure creed is begotten of the pure faith. As the faith has life in itself, it gives to the creed to have life in itself. Hence a true creed once, is a true creed forever, and the Church can only substitute another for it, to express the faith of the old creed in a more perfect form. The new pure creed is then not the death of the old, but its resurrection—its glorification. But old or new, the true creed is not the rival of the Scriptures. All its glory is secondary and derivative. But because the Word is unmixed truth, the Confession, though men's hands have made it, may lift something which is most surely from that ocean and of it. The purest creed is not the ocean; it is but a golden bowl; but that which fills it comes from the ocean, and shares in the purity of its source.

REMARKS OF REV. J. A. SEISS, D. D. (*General Council.*)

Dr. Seiss said that he had no wish to protract the discussion, and would not enter upon the points suggested. He would only remark, respecting the questions of Dr. Brown, that if the several things stated in the Essay were carefully considered together, especially the statements in the concluding sections, he thought a sufficient answer, so far as he was concerned, could readily be deduced. He had given it as his belief that there were times and places in the general Lutheran household, in which attitudes were assumed which he did not undertake to justify, and exhibitions made, in opposite directions, which he considered misrepresentations. If the Lutheran cause were to be judged and rated after these, there would be more show for certain dissenting opponents and separatistic antagonisms. He had reasoned on the inner right of the thing, and fully admitted the modifying force of external facts and circumstances in some cases. The weaknesses of men are always present, and often have something of an excusing influence, even in unjustifiable proceedings; but temporary and provisional excusableness, is a different matter from a thorough, permanent, and justifiable principle. Many things may be, for the time and under the circumstances, excused, which in principle and right, especially if persevered in when the special stress has disappeared, cannot be justified, and are quite without any solid basis on which to rest. The Lutheran severance from Rome, so far as respected the Lutherans, was, and still is, fully justifiable, on the broadest and deepest principles of faith and righteousness; but the Lutheran churches, as a whole, or in any way to make them unitedly responsible, have never given cause for antagonizing communions, except in so far as those communions take from or add to the one only faith of the true Catholic Church. Adopting that with Lutherans, people become Lutherans, and are at fault for maintaining church opposition to Lutherans ; and in so far as people do not hold that faith with Lutherans, they are at fault as Christians, and are really errorists and sects, who elect to abide by their own opinions against the true Catholic Church. That they do it in honest sincerity, not rightly understanding what they do, may modify our judgment of their guilt, but not our judgment of their error.

FIFTH SESSION.

DECEMBER 29TH, 2:30 P. M.

Prayer by Rev. A. M. Whetstone, of Somerset. The eighth paper was then read.

THE CHARACTERISTICS OF THE AUGSBURG CONFESSION.

BY REV. F. W. CONRAD, D. D., PHILADELPHIA.

IN the ongoing of Providence and under the peculiar exigencies that have arisen in the Christian Church, creeds or confessions of faith have been originated, promulgated and adopted, by individuals, churches, cities, states and countries. These confessions are numerous, and differ from each other in their length, doctrinal statements, and ecclesiastical principles. These differences constitute the characteristics by which they are distinguished from each other, and furnish at the same time the basis for their division into general and particular classes. Some of these confessions are, however, so peculiarly constituted, that they form a class by themselves, and among such the Augsburg Confession stands pre-eminent. This will, we trust, become manifest from its characteristics, which we propose to present for your consideration, as the subject assigned us on this occasion.

In order, however, to understand the characteristics of the Augsburg Confession, it will be necessary to consider the character of the persons who took part in its formation, as well as the circumstances and influences under which it originated. The work to be accomplished was a momentous one. No general creed had been adopted for a thousand years. The historic sense of the Œcumenical creeds had been perverted, and they were made to bear witness to error. The exigencies of the Church called for the origination of a creed adapted to the crisis that had arisen in her history. And the Confessors of Augsburg were raised up and called by the Providence of God to bear witness to the truth, through the preparation and presentation of their great Confession.

A literary production receives its peculiarities from the ideal of its composer, and, in like manner, did the Augsburg Confession receive its characteristics from the theological opinions, the ecclesiastical principles, and the personal traits of character of its authors and signers. Our limits constrain us, however, to confine ourselves to a simple enumeration of the principal traits of character exhibited by the Confessors. They were distinguished by fervent piety, by heroic adherence to truth, by conscientious fidelity to their convictions, by a spirit of toleration, by moderate views respecting churchliness, and by sincere devotion to the preservation of the unity of the Church. In view of the significance and relative importance of the last-mentioned trait, we shall devote a little space to its presentation.

The Confessors accepted the articles of the Ecumenical creeds, declaring the existence and perpetuity of one holy catholic Church, consisting of the "body of true believers in all parts of the world, who have but one gospel, one Christ, the same Baptism and Holy Supper, and who are ruled by one Holy Spirit, although they have different ceremonies." In this Church they were born, baptized and confirmed, and in it they desired to live, labor and die. Dissensions had occurred in it; and they came to Augsburg to consult about the best manner of suppressing them. They foresaw the evils of schism, and labored to heal the breaches of Zion. They anticipated and deplored the consequences of separation, and left no means untried, consistent with the will of God and the dictates of conscience, to prevent it. They professed true loyalty to Christ, and claimed the rights conferred upon all believers by the Word of God. They were not schismatics nor separatists, but advocates of Christian and ecclesiastical union. They declared that they had neither formed a new sect nor left the Church, and protested, through their Confession, that they could not justly be condemned as errorists, nor excluded from the communion of the Holy Catholic Church. They were not ready to strike a truce with error, and extend the hand of fellowship to heretics. They realized the necessity as well as the duty of tolerating differences of opinion on minor points, and their Confession itself presents the basis upon which, in their judgment, church fellowship and co operation might be maintained. Indeed, to prevent the dismemberment of the Catholic and schism in the Evangelical Church, was the object of all their conferences and diets, colloquies and discussions with the Romanists in the earlier, and with their fellow Protestants in the later, periods of the Reformation. While, therefore, we are called upon to give due weight to the authority of the Confessors of Augsburg, we must not forget that they were human, possessed of like passions with ourselves, encompassed with peculiar temptations, perplexed with formidable difficulties, and liable to err in judgment, and to make mistakes in deciding the numerous and diversified questions submitted to them. Fallible themselves, human fallibility must necessarily attach to their Confession; but distinguished by the traits of character just enumerated, and directed by the Word, Spirit and Providence of God, they were delivered from the delusions of Romish error, and led to the discovery of "the truth as it is in Jesus," and to the confession of "the faith once delivered to the saints."

The Augsburg Confession did not, like Jonah's gourd, spring up in a night, but was the growth of an age. It appeared in the blade at Marburg, developed the stalk at Swabach and Torgau, and bore the full corn at Augsburg. It was not the work of a single individual, but the product of the joint efforts and common counsels of many The part taken in its preparation by some was more, and that of others less conspicuous and influential.

Luther was the chief among the Confessors. His leadership was recognized, and his influence was everywhere manifest in the work of the Reformation. This was strikingly illustrated at Augsburg. For personal and political reasons he remained at Coburg, but although absent from Augsburg in body, he was, nevertheless, present in spirit. He had written the Marburg, and taken the principal part in the preparation of the Swabach and Torgau articles, which served Melanchthon as a basis and model in the arrangement and composition of the Confession. Communication was established by couriers, between Coburg and Augsburg, and a correspondence conducted between Luther, Melanchthon and the Elector John, of Saxony. His opinions and advice were thus sought and given, in the determination of some of the perplexing questions submitted to the Confessors before and during the sessions of the Diet. On the 11th of May, the Confession itself, in the first draft of its completed form, was sent to him by the Elector, accompanied with a letter requesting him to give it a thorough examination and revision, and to return it with such changes and additions as he thought proper to make. He sent it back on the 15th of May, with the statement that he had read it from beginning to end, that it pleased him exceedingly well, and that he had made no changes in it because he did not know how he could improve it.

From the time the Confession was first sent to Luther on the 11th of May, until the time of its presentation to the Emperor on the 25th of June, it underwent many and various changes, and appeared in different forms of completeness in the successive stages of its composition. And in this improved form it was sent to Luther between the 22d of May and the 2d of June, and again received his unqualified approval.[1]

Melanchthon was the theologian of the Reformation and the teacher of Germany. He was selected by common consent to pre-

---

[1] The correctness of this statement was called into question at the Diet, and the authority on which it was based called for. We accordingly refer to the statements made by Melanchthon in his letter to Luther of May 22, and in the Preface to his Body of Christian Doctrine, and to Luther's letter to Melanchthon of June 3, as quoted by Dr. Krauth in his 'Conservative Reformation.'

According to the statement made above, the Augsburg Confession in the first draft of its completed form, left the hands of Luther on the 15th of May. On the 22d of May, Melanchthon wrote to Luther: "In the Apology, we daily change many things. * * * * * * I wish you would run over the Articles of Faith: if you think there is no defect in them, we will treat of the other points as we best may." *Con. Ref.*, p. 227.

On the 3d of June, Luther wrote to Melanchthon: "I yesterday (June 2) reread your Apology entire, with care, and it pleases me exceedingly." *Ib.*, p. 234.

In giving a history of the Augsburg Confession, in the Preface to his Body of Christian Doctrine, Melanchthon refers to the preparation and presentation of the complete form of the Confession as follows:

1. "I brought together the principal points of the Confession, embracing pretty nearly the sum of the doctrines of our Churches."

2. "I assumed nothing to myself, for in the presence of the Princes and other officials, and of the preachers, it was discussed and determined upon in regular course, sentence by sentence."

3. "The complete form of the Confession was subsequently sent to Luther, who wrote to the Princes, that he had read the Confession and approved it."

4. "After this, before the Emperor Charles, in a great assemblage of the Princes, this Confession was read." *Ib.*, p. 233.

In support of the truth of these statements, he added: "That these things were so done, the Princes, and other learned and honest men, *yet living*, well remember."

pare the declaration of the Protestants. For the accomplishment of this work, he was eminently qualified. He entered upon it with a realizing sense of its responsibilities, and under the divine guidance composed the great Confession. This was his symbolical masterpiece. In its style, statements and discussions, it bears the marks of his taste, learning and literary skill, and in its tone and spirit, it is pervaded by his constitutional amiability and kindness, as well as by his Christian moderation, forbearance and catholicity.

It is manifest, therefore, that the part taken by Melanchthon, in the preparation of the Augsburg Confession, was no less significant and valuable than that contributed by Luther. With respect to its matter, its authorship may be ascribed to Luther; determined by its form, it must be accredited to Melanchthon. It may, therefore, be justly divided between them—Melanchthon fashioned its body, Luther imparted to it its confessional soul.

The Evangelical Princes, with their councillors and theologians, were associated with Melanchthon, as representatives of the Protestant cause, and took a prominent part in the deliberations of the Protestants and the proceedings of the Diet. In the preparation of the Confession, the most difficult questions to be determined were not what doctrines must be declared, and what abuses ought to be corrected, but in what form shall these doctrines be stated, and in what manner shall these abuses be corrected. In this most difficult part of his task, Melanchthon did not rely upon his own judgment and that of Luther, but availed himself of the counsel and advice of his fellow Confessors. Although they were not equal in theological attainments and Biblical knowledge to Luther and Melanchthon, their individual counsels and collective judgment were sought, and proved of great value in deciding the different questions that arose during the preparation of the Confession.

From the representations just made, the respective parts taken by the several Confessors in the origination of the Confession may be determined. They were not, however, called upon to accomplish their work in ordinary times, untrammeled by diverse considerations, and unaffected by conflicting influences. But as the plant receives its peculiar properties from the formative influences of the germ of its particular species, so did the Augsburg Confession receive its distinguishing characteristics, through the numerous and diversified influences exerted upon the Confessors during the successive stages of its preparation. And to the presentation of the sources and character of these moulding influences, we now desire to call attention.

The Catholic princes, deputies, ambassadors and theologians, constituted the other prominent party at the Diet of Augsburg. Some of the theologians were distinguished for their theological attainments, others for their dialectic skill, others for their personal magnetism, and all alike for their devotion to the dogmas and usages of the Romish Church. The princes and deputies exerted a political, and the theologians an ecclesiastical influence upon the Emperor, as well as a corresponding influence upon the Protestant princes, councillors and theologians, in their consultations with them.

Zwingle, although not personally present, nevertheless made himself felt at Augsburg. He had, upon his own judgment, prepared and sent a confession to the Emperor. It set forth his views in explicit terms, but its form of expression was not happy, and its tone was rather repulsive than conciliatory. It lacked both prudence and moderation, and proved untimely and prejudicial to the cause of the Protestants.

There were ten cities represented at the Diet, two of which signed the Confession before its presentation, and four afterwards. The four remaining cities were Strasburg, Memmingen, Costnitz and Lindau. They were represented by Bucer and Capito. They agreed with the statements of the Confession on all points except those made in the Tenth Article; yet they did not, on the other hand, agree with the representations made on the subject of the Real Presence with Zwingle in his confession. They, therefore, had one prepared by Bucer, with the assistance of Capito and Hedio, and signed it as their own. It is known as the Tetrapolitana, the confession of the four cities, and it was presented to the Emperor on the 11th of July.

Charles V. did not fully comprehend the character of the religious agitations which were convulsing the empire. The mighty events of the previous decade seem to have taught him but little, and he appeared at Augsburg the same haughty tyrant and pliant vassal of the Church of Rome, as he proved himself to be by the issue of the Edict of Worms. He claimed, as Emperor, to be not only the Supreme Sovereign of the State, but also the Ruler of the Church. His legitimate authority in civil affairs the Protestants recognized; his right to decide ecclesiastical questions they denied. He presided at the Diet of the Empire. He was biased in favor of the Romanists, and prejudiced against the Protestants. While, therefore, the Protestants realized that the Emperor could not preside as an impartial judge between them and the Romanists, they, nevertheless, felt the influence he exerted upon the Diet, and duly considered it in the preparation of their Confession.

The object of the Diet, and the best means of attaining it, as set forth in the call of the Emperor, and explained in the preface to the Confession by Chancellor Brück, must also be considered. This was to harmonize and settle divergent opinions, to heal religious dissensions, to restore concord, and to establish ecclesiastical fellowship in the one Christian Church. The methods suggested for attaining these ends were a consultation, in which the opinions of the contending parties might be mutually expressed, explained and considered with moderation, mildness and affection among themselves, in the presence of the Emperor; and erroneous opinions abandoned or corrected, and an agreement secured, so far as it could be honorably done, between the Protestants and Catholics. The ultimate object of the Diet, thus set forth, exerted a decided influence upon the Confessors of Augsburg, and was kept constantly in view in the preparation of their Confession.

Besides the various influences exerted by the individuals and parties just named upon the Confessors, and through them upon the matter and form of their Confession, others of a more general character ought not to be overlooked. The political agitation of the Empire consequent upon the occurrence of war, the threatening aspects of the invasion by the Turks, the dissensions and controversies that had arisen in the Church between the Protestants and Romanists, and the differences between the Protestants themselves, must all be taken into consideration and their respective bearings determined. The exigencies that had arisen, in both Church and State, became invested with the force of circumstances and the pressure of the times, and exerted a corresponding influence upon the opinions, judgment and decisions of all persons and parties concerned in the deliberations of Augsburg To these influences the Confessors were constantly exposed, and under their moulding power their Confession received its distinguishing characteristics.

But in addition to all these influences, the Confessors were subjected to various others which were both powerful and perplexing. Some of them were temporary and others more permanent in their character, and the Confessors can never be said to have been altogether exempt from their pressure. And it is only by a careful consideration of all these influences and circumstances, which were more or less powerful at different times during the Diet, that the changes of sentiment and differences of doctrinal statement made by the Confessors before, after and during the Diet, can be properly understood. A few illustrations of this we subjoin.

At Augsburg, the condemnatory clause of the Tenth Article of the Confession ("the opposite doctrine is therefore rejected") was aimed at the doctrine on the Lord's Supper held by the Swiss; and yet Philip, the Landgrave of Hesse, who sympathized with the Zwinglian view, and objected to that set forth in the Tenth Article, was not only permitted but urged to sign the Confession.

At Marburg, Melanchthon met Bucer in conference; at Augsburg, he rejected all his overtures for a personal meeting; but at Cassel, in 1534, he engaged cordially in a religious consultation with him, which resulted in a better understanding between them, and in inducing the Strasburg divines to teach according to the Augsburg Confession.

In 1530, Melanchthon so stated the doctrine of the Real Presence in the Tenth Article, that the Romanists professed to approve of it, and the Swiss objected to it; in 1540, Melanchthon so changed the Tenth Article of the Confession, that the Swiss approved of it and the Romanists objected to it.[2]

In 1530, the Evangelical Princes adopted the original Augsburg

---

[2] The tenth article of the edition of 1530 reads thus: "Concerning the Lord's Supper, they teach that the body and blood of Christ are truly present and distributed to those who eat in the Lord's Supper; and they reject those who teach otherwise." In the edition of 1540, it reads thus: "Concerning the Lord's Supper, they teach that with the bread and wine, the body and blood of Christ are truly exhibited to those who eat in the Lord's Supper." But by making these changes in the phraseology of the Tenth Article, Melanchthon did not intend to change the doctrine set forth in it. He never adopted either the views of Zwingle or Calvin on the Lord's Supper but adhered to those of Luther until his death. He did, however, change his opinions concerning the relative importance of the difference between them, as well as the real character of both the Zwinglian and Calvinistic view of the Lord's Supper. He no longer regarded the difference as fundamental, and as forming a justifiable bar to Christian recognition and ecclesiastical fellowship.

Confession, and in their subsequent conferences with the Romanists at Worms and other places, made Melanchthon's edition of it the basis of their negotiations; after 1540, the Protestants made Melanchthon's edition of 1540 (the Variata) the basis of similar conferences with the Catholics; and in 1561, at Naumburg, the Evangelical Princes formally adopted both the altered and the unaltered edition of the Confession, and thereby recognized the substantial identity of their doctrinal statements, as well as the equality of their confessional significance and authority.

During the Diet of Augsburg, Bucer, convinced of the importance of securing a union among the Protestants, wrote to Luther, and afterwards visited him at Coburg; but Luther refused to answer his letter, and gave him little encouragement in his efforts to harmonize the differences between him and the Swiss; yet, under different circumstances, Luther subsequently wrote to Bucer, and expressed his views as follows: "I wish that this schism were put an end to, even if I had to give my life for it three times over, because I see how necessary your fellowship is for us, and how much inconvenience this disunion has occasioned to the Gospel, and still occasions; so that I am convinced that all the gates of hell, the Papacy, the Turk, the whole world, the flesh, and whatever evil thing there is, would not have been able to injure the Gospel so much, if we had remained at one."

In 1529, Luther disapproved the holding of the Marburg Conference with the Swiss, in the interest of union, and took part in it reluctantly; in 1536, he himself proposed the holding of the convenvention, for the promotion of Protestant union, at Wittenberg, which resulted in the adoption of the so-called Wittenberg Formula Concordiæ. In view of the modified positions set forth in the Concordia, Dörner says it "may, therefore, be regarded as a document which shows beforehand that a stand in the doctrine of the Supper, such as became afterwards, through Calvin, the ruling one in the Reformed churches, was acknowledged even by Luther himself to be one with which brotherly communion was Christianly lawful. And this historical judgment is not altered by the fact that seven years afterwards Luther suddenly broke out again in his *Kleine Bekenntniss vom Abendmahl* in violent ebullition against the Swiss, quite unexpectedly to all, except those who were envious of and hated Melanchthon, and who had goaded Luther on to this."

At Marburg, Luther, on the third day of the Conference, refused the proffered hand of Zwingle, and although he extended his hand to Zwingle on the fourth day, he nevertheless refused to acknowledge the Swiss as brethren; yet, after the Wittenberg Concord, he recognized and called the Swiss "our dear brethren in the Lord," and in answering a letter of inquiry addressed to him, concerning his views on the spiritual enjoyment of the body and blood of Christ, in the Lord's Supper, expressed his views in a letter to the Zurichers as follows: "We leave it in the hands of Omnipotence, *how* the body and blood of Christ are given us in the Supper. Where we have not entirely come to an understanding on this, it is best that we be friendly towards one another, and always expect the best of one another, until the mire and troubled water settle." In quoting the above testimony, Dörner says: "From this it is evident how Luther regards it as indispensable *that* the body and blood of Christ are given us in the Supper, but distinguishes from this the *how* and the connection with the elements," and consequently "the peace established between the two parties (at Wittenberg) was recognized to be rightful, if there was agreement in the chief matter, in the *what?*"

Having thus presented to our view the men who formed, and the circumstances and influences under which they formed and adopted the Augsburg Confession, we are prepared, in some measure, to consider and appreciate the characteristics of the great symbol of evangelical doctrine, which, after many difficulties, they completed and submitted to the Emperor, Charles V., at Augsburg, and to the judgment of the Christian world.

I. THE AUGSBURG CONFESSION IS PROTESTANT.

Charles V., the Emperor of Germany, was a haughty Spaniard, an imperious despot, and a religious persecutor. In 1521 he issued the Edict of Worms prepared by Aleander, the Pope's Nuncio, in which Luther is charged with blasphemy and heresy; with assailing the Church, defying all authority, destroying the Christian faith, and inciting to revolt, schism, war, murder, theft and incendiarism. He is declared to be "no man, but Satan, in the form of a man in a monk's hood; a madman, possessed of the devil." He was declared an outlaw, his followers placed under the ban of the empire, his writings ordered to be burned, and all efforts to propagate his doctrines, and make proselytes to his cause, forbidden as a crime.

subject to heavy penalties. The Edict of the first Diet of Spire (1526) repealed that of Worms, and granted to each State full liberty in religious matters. At the second Diet of Spire (1529) the Edict of the first was peremptorily repealed by Charles V., thereby depriving the disciples of Luther of religious liberty, exposing them to political disabilities and punishment, and restricting the promulgation of the Gospel. Unprepared for such a breach of faith, the Evangelical Princes were thunderstruck, and retired to an adjoining chamber for consultation. After due consideration, they came to the unanimous conclusion to reject the decree passed by the majority of the States and sanctioned by the Emperor, and to appeal to the decisions of a general council. They accordingly drew up a declaration, and headed by John, Elector of Saxony, presented their world-renowned *Protest* to the assembled Diet. From this Protest the followers of Luther were subsequently called Protestants. This Protest contains the politico-religious principles of Protestantism. It asserts the right of private judgment, the prerogatives of conscience, and the supreme authority of the Word of God; and protests against the claim of the civil power to regulate matters of religion, as well as against the arbitrary power of the Church to determine matters of faith.

The Augsburg Confession is a legitimate development of the Protest of Spire. Indeed, the Protestants of Spire were also the Confessors of Augsburg. The religious authority claimed over them by the Emperor at Spire, they repudiated before his face at Augsburg; the religious rights denied them at Spire, they asserted at Augsburg; and the principles contained in their Protest, they amplified and reiterated in their Confession. It may, therefore, be justly regarded, not only as the Confession of Faith of the Evangelical Princes, but also as their completed Protest against the usurpations of the State and the despotism of the Romish Church.

The term Protestant, in its strictly historic sense, is restricted to the subjects involved in civil and religious liberty. In its theologico-confessional sense, it designates the distinguishing differences in doctrine and usages between the Reformers and the Romanists. The object of the Confessors of Augsburg was to set forth these differences in their Confession. The doctrinal differences embrace the doctrine of justification by faith, new obedience, the office of the ministry, the real presence, the efficacy of the sacraments, auricular confession, repentance, good works, ecclesiastical rites, civil government, the Christian Church, the worship of saints, and the exclusive mediatorship of Jesus Christ. The ceremonial and practical differences include the communion in one kind, the celibacy of the priests, the mass, confession, human traditions, monastic vows, church power, and the jurisdiction of the bishops.

These distinguishing differences between Protestantism and Romanism take up the greater part of the entire Confession, and include not only the principles of Protestantism, in a politico-ecclesiastical sense, but also its doctrines, ecclesiastical principles and ceremonial usages, in its theologico-confessional sense. Thus, the Augsburg Confession defined and established the principles of Protestantism, by discriminating them from Romanism; and this is its first general and historic characteristic.

II. THE AUGSBURG CONFESSION IS EVANGELICAL.

In its literal sense the word Evangelical means "according to the gospel," but in its historic sense it signifies "salvation by grace." This signification it received during the Reformation, in consequence of the peculiarity of the religious controversy which then took place. The differences between the Protestants and Romanists were numerous and embraced both doctrine and practice. But while this was the case, it was manifest that most, if not all, these differences arose from the divergent views entertained by the contending parties on the doctrine of justification by faith. A term was therefore needed to express the distinguishing difference between the Romish and Protestant systems of doctrine, and the word Evangelical was chosen for this purpose. It expresses the generic conception of "salvation by grace" held by the Protestants, over against the legalistic conception of salvation by works, maintained by the Romanists. The Romish Church teaches "that, although a man is entitled in part to justification, through the merits of Christ, these are nevertheless not sufficient, and hence, he must earn the same for himself before his conversion by his own strength and good works. Thus he receives the first justification, *i. e.*, regeneration: and after this it becomes indispensable that man should continue to earn for himself the grace of God and eternal salvation, by keeping the commandments and doing other good works."

The Confession of Augsburg teaches, " That men cannot be justified before God by their own strength, merit or works, but that they are justified gratuitously for Christ's sake, through faith, when they believe that they are received into favor, and that their sins are remitted on account of Christ, who made satisfaction for our transgressions by His death. This faith God imputes to us as righteousness."

The relative importance and character of the article on Justification by Faith, are set forth by Melanchthon in the Apology. It is here declared that it constitutes "the principal and most important article of Christian doctrine," and the "only key to the whole Bible;" that it "contributes especially to a clear and correct apprehension of all the holy Scriptures;" that it "alone shows the way to the unspeakable treasure and the true knowledge of Christ, without which the poor conscience can have no true, invariable, fixed hope, nor conceive the riches of the grace of Christ."

This conception of justification by the unmerited grace of God, through faith alone in the merits of Christ, pervades the entire Confession. It is its very heart, sending forth its animating influence into every article and sentence, and rendering it in all its parts instinct with saving grace and quickening power. It annihilates all claims of merit, that man can set up to secure pardon and acceptance before God, whether based upon the cultivation of natural virtue, worldly morality, legalistic obedience, ceremonial performances or self-imposed penance, and declares directly and indirectly that justification, regeneration, sanctification and salvation, can only be obtained as the free gift of God, through faith in Jesus Christ. If the article on justification determines, as Luther said, "the character of a standing or falling Church," it determines also the character of the Augsburg Confession as pre-eminently Evangelical.

III. THE AUGSBURG CONFESSION IS ORTHODOX.

The Bible contains the revelation of God. Its authors were inspired by the Holy Ghost. It furnishes man with an infallible rule of faith and practice. It is placed in his hands and he is commanded to search it, believe its truths, and regulate his life according to its precepts. As a written directory its meaning is said to be so clear, that even the wayfaring man, with his minimum degree of knowledge, may find the way of life. And as an additional safeguard against the delusions of error, the Holy Spirit is given to aid man in the discovery, apprehension and practice of the truth which it reveals. Adequate provision has thus been made to guard the Church against the perversion of the Scriptures, and the promulgation of destructive error, and to secure from her, as the true witness of God, a faithful testimony of saving truth. Such a testimony is found in the Œcumenical Creeds, which have stood through ages as a barrier to heresy and a bulwark to the Christian faith.

The doctrines thus confessed by the Church catholic, either by formal statement or necessary implication, are: The Trinity of Persons in the Godhead, the Divinity of Christ, the vicarious nature of the atonement, the depravity of the human race, justification by faith alone, the necessity of regeneration by the Holy Ghost, the obligation to live a holy life, the appointment of the ministry, the institution of Baptism and the Lord's Supper as means of grace, the immortality of the soul, the resurrection of the body, the everlasting blessedness of the righteous, and the eternal damnation of the wicked.

The term "orthodox," which in its literal sense means "right in opinion," has been employed in ecclesiastical usage, to designate the truths above stated as the essential doctrines of the Christian system. These doctrines are inseparably connected and constitute a consistent whole. The denial of any one of them will impair the integrity of the system, and affect the genuineness of faith. The rejection of all of them, and the substitution of their opposites, would involve an utter perversion of the Scriptures, and the ruin of the Church.

The Augsburg Confession not only recognizes the symbolical character of the Œcumenical Creeds, but contains a consistent development and a fuller statement of the doctrines they contain, and it may therefore be justly designated as thoroughly orthodox.

IV. THE AUGSBURG CONFESSION IS LUTHERAN.

Luther was endowed with such rare natural and spiritual abilities by the Providence and grace of God, as to constitute him at once the leading reformer. He first discovered the Bible, detected the delusive errors of Rome, and promulgated the saving truths of the Gospel. He thus became the author of the Reformation, and as its master spirit directed its course. From his extraordinary theological and ecclesiastical resources he supplied its doctrinal, catechetical, liturgical and governmental principles, and stamped his own impress upon it. He translated the Bible into the vernacular tongue for the people. He prepared a catechism for the children, and provided a liturgy for the altar. He composed hymns and tunes for the service of song, and furnished the material for the preparation of the Augsburg Confession, as a symbolic standard for the Evangelical Church. In view, therefore, of the service rendered Melanchthon in the compilation and composition of the Confession by Luther, he could justly claim it as his own (which he did), and while Melanchthon could, with characteristic modesty, call it "the Confession of the revered Doctor Luther," Luther could in the same spirit return the compliment, and designate it as "the Apology of Master Philip."

The doctrines and ecclesiastical principles set forth in the Confession were those held and maintained by Luther. On this account, the Romanists applied the terms "Lutheran" and "Lutheranism" as epithets of reproach to the Church of the Augsburg Confession, and to the system of doctrine it contained; and they were accepted and employed by the Protestants, as a matter of convenience, in distinguishing the followers of Luther from the Romanists on the one hand, and from the Reformed on the other.

Other differences may be detected in the doctrinal statements made in the Reformed and Lutheran Confessions; but the principal differences have reference to the sacraments and confession. The Lutheran views on these subjects, as distinguished from those of the Reformed, are contained in the IX., X., XI. and XIII. Articles of the Confession, treating of Baptism, the Lord's Supper, the Use of the Sacraments, and Confession.

Article X.—*Of the Lord's Supper.*

"Concerning the Holy Supper of the Lord it is taught that the true body and blood of Christ are truly present, under the form of bread and wine, in the Lord's Supper, and are there administered and received. The opposite doctrine is, therefore, rejected."

In this article the Lutheran doctrine of the real presence of Christ in the Lord's Supper is presented. It is based upon the inseparable union of the human and divine natures in the constitution of the person of Christ (Art. III.), from which it necessarily follows that the person of Christ cannot be divided into two parts, and the divine nature, separated from the human, be present on earth and everywhere else; and the human nature, separated from the divine, be present in heaven and nowhere else; but that wherever and whenever Christ is present, whether at the right hand of God in heaven or in the Holy Supper on earth, He must be present in His whole person, constituted of natures both human and divine, indissolubly united. It is distinguished from the Romish doctrine of Transubstantiation, according to which the bread and wine are changed into the body and blood of Christ; and also from the extreme Zwinglian doctrine, according to which the supernatural presence and reception of the body and blood of Christ in the Lord's Supper are altogether denied, and its purely commemorative character alone affirmed. The mode of the presence and the manner of the reception of the body and blood of Christ in the Eucharist are not defined in the Article; but from the discriminating explanations given thereof by the Lutheran confessors and theologians, the candid inquirer may obtain correct apprehensions in regard to them.

Luther, in setting forth his views on this subject, says: "Christ's body has three modes of presence. First, the comprehensible, corporeal mode, such as He used when He was on earth, local. Secondly, in another, incomprehensible, spiritual mode, it can be present illocall. Moreover (thirdly) it can be present in a divine and heavenly mode, since it is one person with God." The Confessors, accordingly, denied that Christ's body was present locally in the Lord's Supper, and held that in that sense, as circumscribed in space, it was in heaven, and could not at the same time be present anywhere else. They also rejected *impanation*, that Christ is *in* the bread and wine—*subpanation*, that Christ is *under* the bread and wine—and *consubstantiation*, that the body and blood of Christ are changed into one substance *with* the bread and wine, as well as a local and physical conjunction of the body and blood of Christ with the bread and wine. They held the presence of the body and blood of Christ as true, real and substantial; the mode of their presence, as spiritual, supernatural and heavenly; and their reception, under the form of bread and wine, as mystical, sacramental and incomprehensible.

From these representations it is manifest that the Confessors discarded every physical and materialistic conception of the presence, as well as every species of a gross, carnal or Capernaitish eating of the body and drinking of the blood of Christ in the Holy Supper; and regarded it not only as a memorial and symbol through the observance of which they commemorated and showed forth His death, but also as a communion through the partaking of which the bread which they brake became "the communion of the body of Christ," and the cup of blessing. which they blessed, "the communion of the blood of Christ." And from the records of history, they asserted that the doctrine of the Real Presence was held in the primitive ages by the universal Church, that it was perverted by the Romish Church and transformed into transubstantiation, and that it was divested by them of its superstitious features, and reaffirmed and confessed in its scriptural purity.

Candor constrains us, however, to admit, that language was used, illustrations and arguments employed, and authorities cited, in the sacramental controversies that took place during the Reformation, which, when taken in their literal sense, and interpreted without any regard to their connection, or the disclaimers and explanations made by the Lutheran Confessors, have led to grave misconceptions, and gross misrepresentations of the Lutheran doctrine of the Real Presence of Christ in the Lord's Supper, not only by the rejectors of the doctrine but by Lutherans themselves.

Article IX.—Of Baptism.

"Concerning Baptism it is taught that it is necessary; and that children ought to be baptized, who are through such Baptism presented unto God, and become acceptable unto Him."

In this article the Lutheran doctrine of Baptism is set forth. From the declarations it contains, and the explanations made by the Confessors in their other confessional writings, their views in regard to Baptism may be learned from the following summary statement:

Baptism is a religious ordinance, instituted by Jesus Christ. Its constituent elements are water and the Word of God. Its administration consists in the application of water in the name of the Father, Son and Holy Ghost, by an authorized minister of the Gospel, either by sprinkling, pouring or immersion. Its subjects are adult believers and their children. Its validity is based upon its divine institution and observance according to the command of God, and not upon either the character of the administrator, the mode of applying the water, or the faith of the recipient. It is a sacrament, or "visible word;" an efficacious sign and seal of the promise of God; a sure testimony of His will toward us. It becomes efficacious, not *ex opere operato*, but through faith, apprehending the truths signified, and relying upon the promise made by it. It is a means of grace, through which God offers His grace and confers the Holy Spirit, who excites and confirms faith in those who use it aright, whereby they obtain the remission of sins, are born again, released from condemnation and eternal death, and are received and remain in God's favor, so long as they continue in a state of faith and bring forth good works; but to them who are destitute of faith it remains a fruitless sign and imparts no blessing; while those who misimprove their Baptism by a course of willful sin and wicked works, receive the grace of God in vain, grieve and lose the Holy Spirit, and fall into a state of condemnation, from which they cannot be recovered, except by true conversion, involving a renewal of the understanding, will and heart. Baptism ought also to be administered to children, who through it are offered to God, become acceptable to Him, and are received into his favor. It imposes the duty of Christian nurture upon parents and the Church, and finds its complement in Confirmation. It is ordinarily necessary, as a divinely appointed ordinance, but not absolutely essential to salvation. In these statements the Lutheran doctrine of "Baptismal Grace," as maintained by the Confessors, is comprehended. It was confessed by the primitive Church and defended by the Christian Fathers. It was perverted by the Romish Church and transformed into "Baptismal Regeneration," *ex opere operato*. It was drawn by the Confessors from the Holy Scriptures, sustained by the most learned and profound commentators of both ancient and modern times, and accepted by many Protestants of other denominations.

Article XIII.—*Of the Use of the Sacraments.*

"Concerning the use of the Sacraments, it is taught that they have been instituted, not only as tokens by which Christians may be known externally, but as signs and evidences of the divine will towards us, for the purpose of exciting and strengthening our faith; hence they also require faith, and they are properly used then only when received in faith, and when faith is strengthened by them."

The manner in which the sacraments become efficacious in excit ing and strengthening faith, is explained by Melanchthon in the Apology as follows: "The sacraments, as external signs, were instituted to move our hearts, namely, both by the word and the external signs, to believe when we are baptized, and when we receive the Lord's body, that God will be truly merciful to us, as Paul says, Rom. x: 17, Faith cometh by hearing." As the word enters our ears, so the external signs are placed before our eyes, inwardly to excite and move the heart to faith. The word and the external signs work the same thing in our hearts; as Augustin well says: "The sacrament is a visible word, for the external sign is like a picture, and signifies the same thing preached by the word; both, therefore, effect the same thing."

Article XI.—Of Confession.

"In reference to Confession, it is taught that private absolution ought to be retained in the Church and should not be discontinued. In Confession, however, it is unnecessary to enumerate all transgressions and sins, which, indeed, is not possible. Ps. xix: 12: Who can understand his errors?"

In this article the Confessors present the Lutheran view of Confession and Absolution. They retained, indeed, the words "confession" and "absolution," but they employed them in an evangelical sense. They rejected "auricular confession" and priestly absolution, as practiced by the Romish Church. They retained, however, private or individual confession and scriptural absolution, principally on account of the comfort thus afforded to penitent souls, in their approach to the Lord's Table. They did not regard confession as commanded by the Scriptures, and its practice as necessary, obligatory and unchangeable. They recognized it as a custom, established by the Church, in the exercise of her Christian liberty, and which might be either changed or abrogated. The practice of private individual confession has, accordingly, been discontinued in the Lutheran Church to a very great extent, and the custom of making a general confession of sin by the congregations collectively at the service preparatory to the Lord's Supper has been introduced in its stead.

The Scriptural interpretation of Absolution, in the evangelical sense, is given by Luther in his celebrated sermon on the remission of sins, as follows:

"The remission of sins is out of the power of the pope, bishop or priest, or any other man living, and rests solely on the Word of Christ and thine own faith. For if a simple believer say to thee, though a woman or a child, 'God pardon thy sins in the name of Jesus Christ,' and thou receive that word with strong faith, thou art absolved; but let faith in pardon through Christ hold the first place and command the whole field of your warfare."

Confession and Absolution, as thus explained by Luther, meant nothing more than the declaration of the promise of pardon made by God to the confessing, penitent and believing soul, whether uttered formally by the pastor at the preparatory service, or informally to the inquiring soul while engaged in his pastoral work, or declared in the public promulgation of the Gospel.

The doctrines concerning the Lord's Supper, Baptism and Confession, distinguish the Lutheran from the Reformed Churches. In these, as well as in some other doctrines, there are points of agreement and of difference, the specific presentation of which our limits forbid us to attempt. And as the doctrines held by Luther on the Sacraments and Confession are set forth in the Augsburg Confession, it may properly and truly be called *Lutheran*.

V. THE AUGSBURG CONFESSION IS CONSERVATIVE.

When the great religious movement of the sixteenth century was contemplated from the standpoint of church authority, it was called Protestant; when from that of doctrine, Evangelical, and when from that of morals, the Reformation. But reformation presupposes the prevalence of corruption. Such corruption had taken place in the Church of Rome. It was general, embracing doctrine and practice. Its existence had been acknowledged and its pernicious influence felt and lamented for ages. Wickliffe, Huss and Jerome had borne witness against it, and sealed their testimony with their blood. The most candid among the Romanists themselves, acknowledged the prevalence of error and advocated measures of reform; but their counsels were unheeded, and the tide of corruption continued to flow.

Thus, the unwillingness of the Church of Rome to correct her errors and reform her superstitious practices, became the occasion of the origination of the Augsburg Confession, and determined both its matter and form. In the first part, it presents the principles of reform, and in the second applies them to the correction of abuses. In the accomplishment of these ends, the Confessors did not invent novel instrumentalities and agencies of reform, but availed themselves of those which God had furnished ready to their hands. They relied upon the legitimate use of the divinely-appointed means of grace, the preaching of the Word, and the administration of the Sacraments. These are set forth in the articles on justification, the office of the ministry, new obedience, and the institution and efficacy of the sacraments.

In the prosecution of the work of reform, different principles and methods were adopted by the various contending parties in the Reformation. The Romanists, under the claim of papal infallibility, resisted all reform. The Anabaptists overturned all established religious institutions, and began to build anew from the very foundation. The Reformed rejected all forms, ceremonies and usages not commanded in the Scriptures, and the Lutherans discarded all practices clearly condemned by the Word of God, but retained such usages as were not contrary to the Scriptures, in the expectation that those customs which would prove unedifying and injurious, would, in due time, be either improved or abrogated.

This is true conservatism. It detects error and aims at correcting it; it recognizes evils, and tries to remove them; it is not afraid to pull down, but it anticipates the necessity, and makes timely and adequate preparation, for building up. In the accomplishment of its reformatory ends it takes wise counsel from experience, adopts Scriptural means, employs rational methods, and exhibits becoming patience under the inspiration of hope. And such conservatism is a leading characteristic of the great Confession of Augsburg.

VI. IT IS ALSO TRULY CATHOLIC.

The term *catholic*, in its literal sense, means *general*, and as such stands as the antithesis of *specific*. A confession may, therefore, be designated as catholic just in proportion as it states truth in a general or in a specific form. According to this criterion, the ancient creeds, although pre-eminently distinguished for their catholicity, differ in the degree in which they exhibit it. The Athanasian Creed is more specific and less catholic than the Nicene; and the Apostles' Creed is less specific than the Nicene, and the most catholic confession of Christendom. The Augsburg Confession does, indeed, embrace many more points of doctrine, and sets most of them forth in a more specific form than the Œcumenical Creeds; but it is, nevertheless, distinguished in these respects from many of the confessions subsequently adopted by the Lutheran, as well as the Reformed churches.

The Confessors expressly state that in presenting the Articles of Faith contained in their Confession, they had restricted themselves to the principal points and presented only "the sum of the doctrines held by them, and taught in their churches." They set forth the chief or fundamental articles of faith deemed necessary to exhibit their faith in the truth of the Gospel, and to furnish a basis of union and fellowship in the Christian Church. They abstained designedly from introducing many minor or non-essential points, as well as from stating the main or essential points in minute and extended detail. On the contrary, they satisfied themselves with originating but twenty-one articles of faith, and with declaring the truths they contain in brief general statements. And although for this reason the Augsburg Confession is less catholic than either of the Œcumenical Creeds, it nevertheless partakes more of their distinguishing characteristics than it does of those of the Thirty-nine Articles, the Westminster Confession, or the Form of Concord. And as the Œcumenical Creeds, because of their catholicity, proved themselves adapted to be the bond of union between the pure parts of the Church Catholic in primitive times, the Augsburg Confession, on account of its catholicity, is pre-eminently adapted to constitute the bond of union between the pure parts of the revived primitive and the reformed Protestant Church of modern times. This has been verified in its history. As modified and explained by Melanchthon, it has not only been adopted by all Lutheran, but also by many Reformed theologians and churches.

John Calvin was installed as pastor and professor of theology in the city of Strasburg in 1538, which in its collective capacity had signed the unaltered Augsburg Confession. He signed it himself in 1539, and appeared in the deliberations in 1541 at Worms and Ratisbon as a Lutheran theologian. In referring to this, Calvin said: "Nor do I repudiate the Augsburg Confession (which I long ago willingly and gladly signed) as explained by its author." It was also signed, says Dr. Schaff, by Farel and Beza at the conference at Worms, in 1557; by the Calvinists at Bremen, in 1562; by

Frederick III., the (Reformed) Elector of the Palatinate, at the convent of Princes, at Naumburg, in 1561; and again at the Diet of Augsburg, in 1566; and by John Sigismund, of Brandenburg, in 1614.

But the catholicity of the Augsburg Confession was not only recognized during the Reformation; it has also been illustrated in our day. In 1853, a church diet was held at Berlin, at which more than 1400 pastors, professors and theologians were present, representing the four grand divisions of Protestantism in Europe—the Lutherans, Reformed, the Evangelical Unionists, and the Moravians. It was deemed expedient to make a united confession of their faith as Protestants, and to deliver a united testimony against Roman Catholicism. They therefore acknowledged the Augustana as the true expression of their common Protestant faith, in the following words: "The members of the German Evangelical Church Diet hereby put on record, that they hold and profess with heart and mouth, the Confession delivered A. D. 1530, at the Diet of Augsburg, by the Evangelical Princes and States to the Emperor Charles V., and hereby publicly testify their agreement with it, as the oldest, simplest common document of publicly recognized Evangelical doctrine in Germany." It was, however, expressly understood that they did not thereby compromise their respective positions to the Tenth Article, and to the particular confessions of their respective ecclesiastical associations.

The Augsburg Confession in its catholicity has become a component confessional part of the Evangelical Church of Prussia during the last half century. In view of the facts just stated, and of its whole history, Dr. Schaff states that "Some German writers of the Evangelical Unionist school have based the hope, that the Augsburg Confession may one day become the united Confession or Œcumenical Creed of all the Evangelical Churches of Germany." This view is also expressed by Gieseler, the distinguished Reformed church historian. He says: "If the question be, which among all the Protestant Confessions is best adapted for forming the foundation of a union among Protestant churches, we declare ourselves unreservedly for the Augsburg Confession."

As thus distinguished, the Augsburg Confession may justly be regarded not only as the Œcumenical Creed of the Lutheran, but of the whole Protestant Church. Through its recognition of the Œcumenical Creeds, it reaches back and establishes a legitimate connection and ecclesiastical fellowship with the Holy Catholic Church of every age. For the Confessors of Augsburg expressly declared, that they had adopted no articles of faith, and introduced no ceremonies of religion, which were inconsistent with those of the Universal Christian Church. And this claim is established by its œcumenical characteristics, its adaptation for promoting Church union, and by the testimony of true witnesses, down to the apostolic age. And this characteristic of the Confession we hold to be the crown of its highest glory.

VII. THE AUGSBURG CONFESSION IS SCRIPTURAL.

The Confessors acknowledged the Canonical Scriptures to be the inspired Word of God, and the only infallible rule of faith and practice. They exalted the authority of the Scriptures above that of the fathers, the popes and the councils, and recognized them as the ultimate umpire by which all religious questions must be decided. They regarded the Word of God as the true source of all confessions, by which the correctness of their statements was to be tested. From the Holy Scriptures they drew their Confession, and to their unerring testimony they appealed for the verification of the declarations it contained.

In accordance with these positions, the Confessors, in presenting their Confession to the Emperor, declared that it was drawn in its present form from the Holy Scriptures; that in the Articles of Faith there is nothing taught contrary to the Holy Scriptures; that they were constrained to correct the abuses which existed in the Romish churches by the command of God; that the doctrines set forth in their Confession were clearly taught in the Holy Scriptures; and that they would not expose their own souls and consciences to the greatest danger before God, by misusing or abusing the Divine Name and Word, nor transmit to their children and followers any other doctrine than is consonant with the pure, Divine Word and Christian truth. And on these grounds they claimed that their Confession was both "Scriptural and Christian."

To this great work the Confessors were called in the Providence of God, and for its achievement they possessed the necessary qualifications. Luther stood pre-eminent as a Biblical scholar, and Melanchthon was the first theologian of his age. Most of the other theologians were distinguished for their theological attainments, and some of the Evangelical Princes were well versed in the knowledge of the Scriptures. During the preparation of the Confession, daily conferences were held by the Confessors, at which Melanchthon submitted the parts as they were finished. Every article was then compared with the Scriptures, sentence by sentence, and, after due examination, either accepted or modified, and then adopted as consonant with the Word of God. Luther, to whom it had been submitted, subjected it to a similar test. In referring to this he says: "I am occupied with the matter day and night, thinking over it, revolving it in my mind, arguing, searching the entire Scriptures; and there grows upon me constantly that fullness of assurance in this our doctrine, that is, in its Scriptural verity." Realizing their liability to err, and their dependence on divine direction, they prayed with one accord for the enlightening influences of the Holy Spirit, that He might guide them into the saving knowledge of the truth, and to preserve them from falling into error.

And in this aim and effort, the Confessors were successful. Notwithstanding the peculiar circumstances in which they were placed, and the various influences to which they were exposed, they were so directed and guarded by the Providence and grace of God, as to bring forth a Scriptural Confession. Some of its doctrinal statements they made in the language of the Scriptures, and others they sustained by relevant proof passages. It carried this conviction with it to candid minds at its first reading. It drew this acknowledgment from the Bishop of Augsburg: "All that the Lutherans have said is true, and we cannot deny it." When the Duke of Bavaria asked Eck, "Can you by sound reasons refute the Confession of the Elector and his allies?" he replied: "With the writings of the apostles and prophets, no; but with those of the fathers and councils, yes." His reply was: "I understand it. The Lutherans are in the Scriptures, and we are outside of them."

We do not, however, understand the Confessors as claiming a Scriptural origin for every word and phrase, statement and reference, in the Confession; for a careful examination proves that it contains philosophical statements, historical references, authoritative quotations, individual opinions, and incidental matters, drawn from other sources than the Scriptures. Nor would we make the impression that they were under a kind of semi-inspiration, rendering them for the time being infallible, and that in consequence of such extraordinary enlightenment, they expressed in every word and phrase employed by them the exact conception of the Holy Ghost; for this is more than can be justly claimed for any human production, and involves both inspiration and infallibility. But we maintain that in regard to all the great truths entering into the constitution of the Evangelical Lutheran system, and indispensable to the attainment of soundness in doctrine and purity in practice, they did succeed in discovering, and in expressing them correctly in their Confession.

Being eminently Scriptural, it has carried conviction to all unprejudiced minds, and made converts among pastors and churches, princes and nobles, kings and emperors. It has won allegiance from teachers and professors, and has transformed schools and universities. It has conquered cities and towns, kingdoms and empires. As the source whence it is drawn appears the more pure as the light by which it is examined increases, so does this Confession appear the more Scriptural, as the increased light of philology and exegesis has been thrown upon it. The profoundest Biblical scholars and the most diligent students of the Confession, have been the most fully convinced of its truthfulness, and became its most ardent admirers and defenders. It still throws its convincing sceptre over more than half the Protestant world, and through the testimony of millions of Christians in nearly all nations and climes, it vindicates the claim that it sets forth the most precious truths revealed in the Scriptures of God.

The Augsburg Confession was not originally prepared as a Church symbol. Its design was two-fold: first, to point out the doctrines and ceremonies in dispute between the Protestants and the Catholics; and secondly, to refute the slanders that had been circulated concerning the doctrines held by the Confessors. The Articles of Faith were accordingly presented in the form of a Confession, and the Abuses Corrected in that of an Apology. It was not regarded as complete in its original form, and hence it received many changes from the hand of Melanchthon in subsequent editions, culminating in that of 1540. These changes were intended by their author to be improvements, and were regarded as such by his contemporaries. Nor was the course pursued by Melanchthon in this respect singular. The Romanists made changes in their

Confutation after it was presented to the Diet. Melanchthon did the same with his Apology in reply to it; and Luther took the same liberty with the Smalcald Articles after their first presentation. From all of which it is manifest, that during the lives of Luther and Melanchthon, the formative period of the Reformation, the text of the original Confession was not regarded as sacred and unchangeable, and that the edition of 1530 had not yet been invested with any special confessional authority.

The statement made in the Confession, that it contained "about the sum of the doctrines," taught by the Protestant pastors in their churches, was true, but neither the pastors nor the churches had ever formally adopted or subscribed it. But when it became manifest that the questions at issue could not be satisfactorily settled; that a separation between the Protestants and Romanists was inevitable; and that necessity was laid upon Luther and his coadjutors to organize the Evangelical, as the revived primitive, Catholic Church, then a creed, to serve as a basis of organization and a bond of ecclesiastical union, became indispensable, and the Augsburg Confession was appropriated to this purpose by common consent. The edition selected was that of 1530, edited by Melanchthon himself. It is known as the *editio princeps*, and is universally recognized as the symbolic standard of the Lutheran Church.

The Augsburg Confession, as the mother symbol of the Reformation, has exerted a controlling influence in the preparation of a number of other Protestant confessions. It was selected by Zinzendorf as the doctrinal basis of the Moravian Church. It, together with the Wurtemberg Confession, furnished Cranmer with the matter for the compilation of the Thirty-Nine Articles of the Episcopal Church, which, with some modifications, have also become the doctrinal standard of the Methodist Episcopal Church. It also furnished Ursinus, a disciple of Melanchthon, and a co worker with Olevianus, a disciple of Calvin, in the preparation of the Heidelberg Catechism, the general symbol of the German and Dutch Reformed Churches. It has thus through its moulding influence stamped its impress, directly and indirectly, upon all branches of the Protestant Church.

The Augsburg Confession stands pre-eminent, not only among the Lutheran symbols, but among all the creeds of Christendom. This position is accorded to it, not alone by Lutheran, but also by distinguished Reformed witnesses.

Dr. Schaff says: "The Augsburg Confession is the fundamental and generally received Confession of the Lutheran Church. * * * It is inseparable from the theology and history of that denomination; it best exhibits the prevailing genius of the German Reformation. But its influence extends far beyond the Lutheran Church. It struck the key-note to other evangelical confessions, and strengthened the cause of the Reformation everywhere, and it will ever be cherished as one of the noblest monuments of faith from the Pentecostal period of Protestantism." Spalatin said "It is a Confession the like of which has not been promulgated for a thousand years." D'Aubigne, the distinguished Calvinistic historian of the Reformation, testifies: "This Confession of Augsburg will forever remain one of the master-pieces of the human mind, enlightened by the Spirit of God."

The influence and value of the Confession can scarcely be overestimated. As a Confession, it is a faithful witness of the truth, and bears unimpeachable testimony against error. As an Apology, it is a complete vindication of Protestantism and an unanswerable arraignment of Romanism. As Pro estant, it is the magna charta of liberty to the State, and a declaration of independence to the Church. As evangelical, it publishes the glad tidings of salvation by grace, through faith alone in Jesus Christ. As orthodox, it condemns heresy, and excludes heretics from its fellowship. As Lutheran, it sets forth the distinctive doctrines and principles of the Evangelical Lutheran Church. As conservative, it proves all things and holds fast that which is good. As catholic, it recognizes the priesthood of believers, and acknowledges their right to the communion of saints. And as Scriptural, it holds forth the Word of Life, as the only hope of salvation to a ruined world.

REMARKS OF REV. C. P. KRAUTH, D. D., LL. D. (*General Council.*)

Dr. Krauth said that various statements in the elaborate essay of Dr. Conrad needed further elucidation. Two lines of thinking ran through it, which did not always seem in perfect accord. Melanchthon was not strictly the author of the Confession, but rather its composer. As an official paper, it belongs to those who signed it, and gave it to the Emperor, and to those in whose name they were entitled to act. Once delivered, neither Melanchthon, nor the signers, had any moral right to set forth a changed document as the document laid before the Diet of the Empire. A Confession varied purely in verbal respects might be but a perilous impropriety, but a Confession varied in meaning would be a fraud and falsehood. Those who say that Melanchthon in the Variata introduced changes in doctrine, charge him with immorality of a gross kind, the charge being made more severe by the fact that he disavows having made any change whatever in the sense.

Zwingli's Fidei Ratio, which he sent to the Emperor, is dated July 3d, 1530, and could hardly have influenced the Augsburg Confession, which had been read the 25th of the month previous. The conception of influence which runs through part of the essay seems vague and conflicting. The doctrine was fixed before the Diet met, and embodied in Luther's Seventeen Articles, and as Dr. Conrad shows, was rightly fixed and rightly confessed.

Philip of Hesse was a blot on the whole fair fame of the Reformation—involving Luther in the only transaction of his life which requires a defence. Philip, a young man at the time of the Diet, was eager for political combination, and his zeal for or against the dividing doctrines of Luther and Zwingli was not very great. He insisted that Zwingli's deviation from Luther was verbal merely. Were it true that, although he rejected the Tenth Article, he was urged to sign the Confession, it might well be asked why the Zwinglians at large were excluded? why the Tetrapolitans were not included? But the facts are these: Philip was one of the Lutheran Princes. The Reformation in Hesse had been conducted in accordance with Melanchthon's counsel. The political Unionism of Philip, inspired however great hopes on the part of the Zwinglians, that negatively at least he would help them. Luther, at Melanchthon's urgent request, wrote to Philip to counteract this influence (May 20, 1530). Whatever sympathy Philip felt with the Zwinglians, when the time of signing the Confession approached, was secret.

Philip signed the Confession, and thus in the most solemn manner declared it to be his faith. If he was dissatisfied with the Tenth Article, on the ground that it was false doctrine, he made himself a perjured man in signing it. When, on June 23d, the Confession was read in full assembly of the orders for the very purpose of giving opportunity for any suggestion, it was approved by *all and each*—the Landgrave of Hesse included. When, on the 24th of June, the question was raised whether the request of the Emperor should be granted to have it merely handed to him in writing, the Landgrave led the opposition to his wish, and insisted that it should be read publicly before the Estates of the Realm, and it was so read the next day. And it is Erhard Schnepf, the Landgrave's court preacher, who was present through the whole, who says expressly, that *not one* of those who took part in the Augsburg Confession, and was admitted to the discussions, held the view of the Zwinglians. On the 25th of June, perhaps while the Confession was actually being read, Melanchthon wrote to Luther: "The Landgrave approves of our Confession, and has signed it." The day after, Melanchthon wrote to Vitus Theodorus: "The Landgrave has signed with us in the Confession, in which is also an Article on the Lord's Supper, in accordance with the judgment of Luther." He was not allowed to sign it with any expressed reservation as to doctrine, whatever.

The Wittenberg Concord hardly seems in place in a statement of the influences which shaped the Augsburg Confession, as it was not prepared till 1536. It is not a concession to Zwinglianism, nor Calvinism, but is a powerful rejection and exposure of it, from Luther's own hand. None but a Lutheran could sign it in good faith. Bucer in signing it professed to abandon the Zwinglian view, and to come over to Luther's. The honest Zwinglians rejected the Concord, and repelled Bucer when he attempted to bring them to accord with it, and treated him as an apostate. When Luther spoke of the Swiss as "dear brethren," it was under an impression easily made upon his guileless and loving nature, that they had actually come to the recognition of the truth, and his feeling that he had been deluded in this was the cause of his later bitterness.

It is not a correct statement that the Romanists did not object to the doctrine of the Tenth Article Dr. Krauth then read from the Romish Confutation, what is said on the Tenth Article, They object that it does not teach the doctrine of concomitance, by which the Romish Church justifies the Communion in one kind, and insists that it is extremely necessary to the Article, that the doctrine of Transubstantiation shall be added to it.

The Lutheran Church does not define the *mode* of presence; that is, does not attempt to solve to human reason *how* so great a thing can be; but the *kind* of presence she does define as real, supernatural, substantial presence, as against what is imaginary or subjective. She denies that it is in that sense spiritual, yet she holds that it is spiritual as against the carnal. If the mode of presence were a presence to memory or faith, there could be no difficulty in stating it. It is a deep and vital question, and the principles of interpretation are so far-reaching, that if our Church is wrong—if she holds that something is really Christ's body and blood, which He clearly teaches is no more than bread and wine— instead of standing up as a great witness for truth in the world, she should be willing to fall humbly at the feet of a little child which has the true mind of the Spirit, and ask that child to teach her. In regard to the Variata in the Lutheran Church, the truth is that Melanchthon constantly affirmed that its doctrine is the same as that of the Augsburg Confession; that after its appearance, he repeatedly, in solemn public testification, accepted the Unchanged Confession and the Apology, and rejected Zwinglianism in the strongest terms. So long as the Lutheran Church believed that there was no change of meaning, and solely because of this belief, the Variata was tolerated. In the Diet of the Princes, at Naumburg, 1561, the various later editions of the Confession were recognized, because of their greater explicitness against Romish errors, *but the original edition of 1530 alone was subscribed.* From the hour that the Variata began to be regarded as having changed the doctrine or rendered it ambiguous, all genuine Lutherans set themselves against it.

The Augsburg Confession offers a point of union for divided Protestantism, but union will be effected neither by Variatas in the Creed, which change the words, nor by Variatas in men, which keep the word, but change the sense or repudiate it. When men are agreed in a hearty and intelligent acceptance of the Augsburg Confession, the Formula of Concord will form no barrier between them. Dr. Conrad is an enthusiast for union in our Church, but there can be no union except in the unity of the truth. Till he realizes this, his toils will be in vain.

REMARKS OF REV. PROF. J. A. BROWN, D. D. (*General Synod.*)

We are a little surprised to find Dr. Conrad repeating the statement of the Augsburg Confession being sent to Luther "*between the 22d of May and the 2d of June, and again securing Luther's unqualified approval.*" We challenge the proof of this fact. We have a right to be furnished with the evidence on which it rests; and in the absence of any reliable testimony to the fact, we pronounce it a myth. We speak advisedly on this subject. We do not need to prove a negative, but we have asked, and now ask again, for any such proof as would satisfy an intelligent and impartial judge. If there is any such proof, let it be forthcoming, for we regard that usually adduced utterly unreliable and unsatisfactory. As Dr. Krauth has endorsed the statement of Dr. Conrad, we now, in the presence of this Diet, challenge them both to furnish, in the Church papers or elsewhere, such evidence as would be accepted in any court, or satisfy any impartial jury. We simply deny that they have given us any reliable evidence for their allegations, and we hold them to the proof.

A few questions were asked by Dr. Mann and answered by Dr. Conrad.

NOTE OF DR. KRAUTH IN ANSWER TO DR. BROWN'S CHALLENGE.

In the Conservative Reformation, p. 232, it is said that the Augsburg Confession "was sent as nearly as possible in its complete shape to Luther for a third time, before it was delivered, and was approved by him in what may probably be called its final form." This is the statement which we understood Dr. Conrad to endorse, and Dr. Brown to challenge. If the emphasis is on June 2*d*, we do not endorse Dr. Conrad, nor deny Dr. Brown's statement. It was the *third* sending in which we were interested, and of which we spoke.

1. The first sending of the Confession to Luther was May 11th, by the Elector; the second May 22d, by Melanchthon. These are undisputed. The question is, was there a later sending—that is, between May 22d and June 25th (*not* June 2*d*)—an interval of about five weeks.

2. The evidence relied upon is Melanchthon's own statement. It is found *i.*, in the preface to his Book of Christian Doctrine (Corpus Doctrinæ) 1560 and 1563; *ii.*, in the preface of the first volume of the Wittenberg Edition of his works, 1560 and 1601; *iii.*, in the Corpus Reformatorum, vol. ix., No. 6932—these are in Latin; *iv.*, the German Preface is found in the German Corpus, 1560. All these texts have been carefully compared.

I. In giving an account of the preparation of the Confession of what he styles "Luther's Doctrine," Melanchthon says that he does so "because it is necessary that posterity should know, that our Confession was not written as an individual matter. The princes and officials *whose names follow* the Confession, believed that it should be offered as evidence that they had not acted in levity, or impelled by any unlawful desire, but that for the glory of God and the salvation of their own souls, and the souls of many, they had embraced the purer doctrine."

II. "I brought together, therefore, in singleness of purpose, the principal points of the Confession, which is extant, embracing pretty nearly the sum of the doctrine of our Churches."

III. "I assumed nothing to myself. For in the presence of the Princes and other officials, and of the preachers, it was discussed and determined upon in regular course, sentence by sentence."

IV. "The complete form (*tota forma*) of the Confession was *subsequently* (*deinde*) sent to Luther, who wrote to the Princes that he had both read the (literally *this, hanc*) Confession, and approved it."

V. "That these things were so, the Princes and other honest and learned men, yet living, will remember."

VI. "*After this (postea)*, before the Emperor Charles, in a great assembly of the Princes, this Confession was read."

This passage of Melanchthon was adduced to confute the theory of Rückert, that the Augsburg Confession was meant to be a compromise with Rome, and was consequently kept back from Luther, for fear he would spoil the scheme. We think we may claim that the citations in the Conservative Reformation (228-232) have disposed of Rückert's theory. Those inclined to favor it have made a little battle on the point now before us, but if they could sustain their denial, so far as to throw it entirely out, they would simply remove it from an argument which is convincing without it. But it is evident, further, that the moral value of this citation, for its purpose, is by no means dependent on any question of date. If we were to grant that it does not prove a THIRD sending of the Confession to Luther, it yet proves that what Melanchthon identifies with the Augsburg Confession as delivered, was read and approved by Luther before it was presented. His whole statement is reduced to falsehood or nonsense on any other supposition.

The question of dates, then, becomes one simply of chronological interest, and here, if it be granted that Melanchthon is a competent witness, there is no great hazard in taking up the glove so dauntlessly thrown down, unless the *date*, June 2d, be the main point. Note then:

1. That what Luther passed upon is defined as the "Confession, now extant," which Melanchthon, quoting in substance its own phrase, characterizes as "embracing pretty nearly the sum of the doctrine of our churches."[1] This implies that the Confession, when Luther's judgment was given, was in such a state of substantial completeness as to make it *morally identical* with the one delivered.

2. It is expressly and emphatically said, so as to be essential to Melanchthon's whole argument, that the "*tota forma*"—the complete Confession—as contrasted with any earlier and imperfect form of the Confession, was sent to Luther.

3. It was sent *after* the *discussion* and *determination* of it, in regular order, article by article as it came, and sentence by sentence, before and by princes, officials and theologians.

4. It was returned by Luther with a letter to the Princes, saying that he approved it.

5. After this return of this Complete Confession, it was presented (June 25th) to Charles V.

Let us now see how these facts bear on the question of dates.

1. The endorsement of Luther, of which Melanchthon's Preface speaks, can not be of the Confession sent May 11th.[2] That was not the "*tota forma*," but relatively unfinished: that had not been discussed before the princes, officials and preachers, for they were not yet present. The Landgrave of Hesse came May 12; the Nurembergers May 15, and others still later. Nor was it then meant that the Confession should be made in the name of all the Evangelical States. It was to be limited to Saxony. The Elector wrote to Luther, May 11, sending him the Confession, treating it purely as a matter in his own hands, and the hands of his theologians, and

---

[1] In Melanchthon's Preface: Complexus paene summam doctrinæ Ecclesiarum nostrum. In the Confession (xxii.): Haec fere summa est doctrinæ apud nos; in the German: "in unserm Kirchen;" and again in the epilogue, doctrinæ summa.

[2] Melanchthon's Letter; Corpus Reformator., ii., No. 685. Coelestinus, ., 41 a.

giving Luther unlimited right to adapt it to his judgment of what was best.³ Luther's reply to this letter (May 15)¹ was not, and could not be, to the princes, but was to John of Saxony alone, who, up to May 11 (with his suite), was the only one of the princes at Augsburg, and who, as his letter shows, expected to deliver this very Confession of May 11 to the Emperor.

2. But neither can Melanchthon's words refer to the copy sent May 22d. George of Brandenburg did not come till May 24th. May 24th Pontanus, the Chancellor of Saxony, was taking part in finishing the Confession, as purely in the hands of Saxony.

May 28th, the Saxon theologians and counsellor were alone in examining the Confession. Up to June 8th the Confession had been worked upon exclusively in the name of the Elector of Saxony, and is styled the "*Saxon* Counsel" (Rathschlus) or Statement (Verzeichniss), and designated as the work of the "*Saxon* theologians," by the Nuremberg Legates, up to June 8,⁵ and retrospectively even up to June 15th.⁶

The movement was now made, that the entire body of the Protestants (Lutherans) should be conjoined with the Elector, in offering the Confession "in the name of all the United Lutheran Princes and Estates," requiring the substitution throughout of a general term, in place of the exclusive reference to Saxony.⁷ Not until *after* May 22d, therefore, could that conjoint discussion in the presence of the *Princes* and other officials have taken place, which Melanchthon declares *preceded* the sending to Luther of that *tota*

---

³ The Elector to Luther: Corpus Reformat., ii., No. 798. Luther's Werke Leipzig, xx., 173; Walch., xvi., 785.

⁴ Luther to the Elector; Briefe: De Witte., iv., 17. Werke: Leipzig, xx., p. 173. Walch. xvi., 786. Chytraeus Historia (German), xxviii, p. 30. In Latin, Coelestinus i., 40-42. Buddeus, 93.

⁵ Corpus Reformat., ii., No. 712, 715.

⁶ Do., No 723.

⁷ Do. do. See Libri Symbolic. Eccl. Luth., Ed. Francke, 1847. Prolegomena: xviii., No. 16.

forma, which he identifies with the Confession read before the Emperor and then extant.

Rev. Dr. Greenwald, the author of the next paper, was unable to be present. Rev. D. H. Geissinger appeared as his representative, with the essay that had been prepared. Owing to the necessity which would not allow the presence, beyond Friday evening, of several of the remaining essayists, the Diet, with great regret, suspended the regular order. It was hoped that time would still be found for Dr. Greenwald's essay, at a succeeding place. But as all the time of the Diet, up to the adjournment, was filled by the remaining essays, and it became manifest that an additional session could not be held on Saturday morning, it was resolved to print Dr. Greenwald's essay in the proceedings. It is accordingly given in the place where it properly belongs.

TRUE AND FALSE SPIRITUALITY IN THE LUTHERAN CHURCH.

BY REV. E. GREENWALD, D. D., LANCASTER, PA.

THE Apostle Paul describes sound Christians, as contradistinguished from others who are not sound, by applying to them the expression, "Ye which are spiritual." Gal. 6: 1.

Who are They That are Spiritual?

The word "spiritual" both in the original Greek and in our English translation is derived from the word that designates the Holy Ghost, the divine Author of spiritual life in the soul of man. It denotes the effects produced in the soul, by the gracious influences of the Holy Ghost. It means spiritual in opposition to carnal—heavenly-minded in distinction from worldly-minded—a devout, pious, godly spirit, the reverse of a prayerless, irreligious, sensual spirit. A spiritual man is a godly man; one who loves God, communes with God, bears the image of God, has the spirit of God. A spiritual man possesses deep spirituality, cultivates fervent devotion, and has the same mind in him that was in Christ. A spiritual man is a man of sound piety, relishes the presence of God, and walks in near and most intimate fellowship with God. A spiritual man has the mind of God, breathes the spirit of God, lives the life of God.

This spiritual nature results from the mystical union with Christ, which is effected by the grace of the Holy Spirit in His application of Christ's redemption to man. Union with God is the work of the Holy Ghost. By His mighty working in the heart of man, through the Word of God, which is spirit and life, through the Holy Sacrament of Baptism, by which Christ is put on and the man is made a partaker of Christ's life, and through the Holy Sacrament of the Lord's Supper, by which Christ's body and blood nourishes and develops and matures the divine life in the soul, this mystical union is brought about and continued. God dwells in the believer.

This union with Christ is directly taught in many passages of God's Word. Christ Himself says, John xiv: 23, "If a man love me he will keep my words, and my Father will love him, and we will come unto him and make our abode with him." Paul says, 1 Cor. vi: 15–17, "Know ye not that your bodies are the members of Christ?" "for two shall be one flesh. But he that is joined to the Lord is one spirit." Eph. v: 30: "For we are members of his body, of his flesh, and of his bones." Gal. ii: 20. "I am crucified with Christ, nevertheless I live; yet not I, but Christ liveth in me; and the life which I now live in the flesh, I live by the faith of the Son of God who loved me and gave himself for me." Peter says, 2 Peter i: 4, "Whereby are given unto us exceeding great and precious promises, that by these ye might be partakers of the divine nature." From these, and many other passages of like import, we learn the great doctrine of the mystical union of the believer with God. It is the source of all true spiritual life in him. He is "spiritual" because he sustains this relation to Christ, has this union with Him, and lives not his own life, but Christ's life in him.

By this indwelling of God in man, is meant more than the resemblance of man's spirit to God's spirit, or the conformity of man's will to the divine will. This, of course, exists in the case of all true believers in Christ. But the relation of regenerated man to God, and the nature of spiritual life in him, are more substantial and thorough than even this. It will be profitable to quote on this point, the matured sentiments of some of the old divines of our Church.

Says Quenstedt, that prince of theologians: "The mystical union does not consist merely in the harmony and tempering of the affections, as when the soul of Jonathan was knit with the soul of David, 1 Sam. xviii: 1, but in a true, real, literal, and most intimate union; for Christ uses the expression, 'as thou, Father, art in me, and I in thee, that they also may be one in us.' To be in some one, implies the real presence of the thing which is said to be in, not figuratively, as a lover in the beloved."

"The mystical union is the real and most intimate conjunction of the substance of the Sacred Trinity and the God-man Christ, with the substance of believers, effected by God Himself through the Gospel, the Sacraments, and faith by which, through a special approximation of His essence, and by a gracious operation, He is in them, just as also believers are in Him, that, by a mutual and reciprocal immanence, or indwelling, they may partake of His vivifying power, and all His mercies, become assured of the grace of God and eternal salvation, and preserve unity in the faith, and love, with all the other members of His mystical body."

Calovius, another of our old divines, says: "The mystical union of Christ with the believer, is a true, and real, and most intimate conjunction of the divine and human nature of the theanthropic Christ with a regenerated man, which is effected by the virtue of the merit of Christ through the Word and Sacraments; so that Christ constitutes a spiritual unit with the regenerated person, and operates in him, and through him; and those things which the believer does or suffers, He appropriates to Himself, so that the man does not live, as to his spiritual and divine life, of himself, but by the faith of the Son of God, until he is taken to heaven."

In the Formula of Concord, the assertion that " not God himself, but only the gifts of God, dwell in believers," is designated as false. It is further declared, that "the essence of the subjects to be united are on the one part, the divine substance of the whole Trinity, and the substance of the human nature of Christ. On the other part, the substance of believers, as to body and soul."

This mystical union with Christ, as thus described, being God dwelling in us, and united with us, a partaking of the divine nature, having the life of Christ living in us, so that the motions of godly living are not our own, but Christ's, who is our life—this union with Christ is the well spring of all our spiritual character. It is the source of its existence, and constitutes its peculiar nature. Christians are spiritual because God dwells in them, and the life they life in the flesh is not their own, but Christ's who liveth in them.

Concerning this union with Christ as the source and spring of our spiritual life, we remark several things:

1. *It is not Natural.*

The natural spirit, and disposition, and life, in man, are directly the reverse of this. Our natural birth is a birth in sin, with a depraved nature, and with a spirit that is carnal, sensual, worldly, and devilish. The natural mind receiveth not these things, is hostile to them; they are foolishness to it; and because they are spiritually discerned, it, not being spiritual, but carnal, cannot discern, or appreciate, or exercise them. That which is born of the flesh is flesh, that only which is born of the spirit is spirit.

2. *It is not the Result of Human Will, or Power, or Work.*

As it is a new or spiritual birth, in contradistinction to the natural birth, it is expressly declared by St. John to be a spiritual man, produced by "the power of God," and "born, not of blood, nor of the will of the flesh, nor of the will of man, but of God." It is a spiritual creation. Being the opposite of a human birth, it is necessarily a divine birth.

3. *It is the Work of the Holy Ghost.*

The divine agent that produces it, is the Spirit of God. He that works all our works in us, is the Holy Ghost. Being the spirit of *life*, He gives spiritual life to us,—as the *Holy* Ghost he sanctifies us—as the third Person of the *God*-head, He makes us partakers of the divine nature. What He does, God does, for the Holy Ghost is God.

4. *The Holy Ghost does this only through the Blessed Means of Grace, His Word and Sacraments.*

The Word is one of the means of grace, which "acts by a true, real, divine, and ineffable influx of its gracious power, so that it effectually and truly converts, illuminates and unites with Christ, the Holy Spirit operating in, with, and through it, thus constituting it a divine, and not a human word." Jesus himself says, "My words, they are spirit, and they are life." Baptism, which is a Sacrament, not of one element, water, only, but of two elements, water and the Holy Ghost, is another means of grace, through which grace is given; we are baptized into Christ, put on Christ, become children of God, and are made to partake of the divine nature, for Jesus expressly called it being "born again of water and of the Holy Ghost," John iii. 5; and St. Paul directly describes it as being the "washing of regeneration and the renewing of the Holy Ghost." The Lord's Supper, too, is a means of grace, and aids in promoting this union with Christ, and divine life in the soul, since Jesus, in obvious reference to this Sacrament, and to its spiritual effects, declares, "Except ye eat the flesh, and drink the blood of the Son of man, ye have no life in you." Here "spirit," "regeneration," "life," are asserted to be produced by the Holy Ghost, through these means of grace instituted for the purpose, and by which His operations in, and upon, the nature of man are wrought.

5. *This Spiritual Nature is a Divine Nature.*

Not that there is in regenerated man such a union of the two natures, as the union of the divine and human natures in Christ, constituting one person. "Nor," says Quenstedt, "does this union consist in transubstantiation, or the conversion of our substance into the substance of God and of Christ, or *vice versa*, as the rod of Moses was converted into a serpent. Nor in consubstantiation, so that of two united essences there is formed one substance." Says Hollazius, "(a) God dwells in us as in temples, by the favor of the mystical union, 1 Cor. iii. 16; but the habitation is not changed into the inhabitant, nor the inhabitant into the habitation. (b) By the mystical union we put on Christ, Gal. iii. 27; but the garment is not essentially one with the person who wears it. (c) The divine nature is very distinct from the human, although God comes to us and makes His abode with us, John xiv. 23, for He can depart from man to whom He has come." Whilst all these errors are carefully avoided, yet this union consists, says the Formula of Concord, "in a true, real, intrinsic, and most close conjunction of the substance of the believer with the substance of the Holy Trinity, and the flesh of Christ." "Two things, therefore, pertain to the *form* of the mystical union," says Calovius. "(1) A true and real *adiastasia*; a nearness, through the approximation of the divine essence to the believer, whereby the triune God comes to us and makes His abode with us, which is not then merely a naked operation without the approach of God, but a nearer access to us, or an advent, that He may be and remain in us, John xiv. 23. (2) A gracious energy or operation, whereby God comes to us and dwells in us, that He fills us with all the fullness of His spiritual wisdom, holiness, power (Eph. iii. 19), and other divine gifts (Ch. iv. 7); which denotes also the mystical *perichoresis*, whereby God is in us, and remains through grace; but we are in God, and adhere to Him in trust, so that nothing can separate us from God, who are united to Him through trust, Rom. viii. 38, *seq.*" It is really and truly, God dwelling in us, and we in God.

6. *It is a Genuine Spiritual Nature, as opposed to all False Spiritualism.*

There is a spiritualism that is not genuine spirituality. "Ye that are spiritual," in the mouth of a holy apostle, is a very different thing from that which is meant by many men who use the same words. There is a spiritualism that claims to be the highest spirituality, and that denies spirituality to anything else than itself, that is, in almost every respect, a very different thing from true spirituality. "*Sie haben einen anderen Geist*," said Luther, concerning a class of men in his time, who professed to be far more spiritual than himself, who even condemned his want of spirituality, and who pretended to divine inspiration, to visions, and to extraordinary fervor of devotion. This spiritualism is self-righteous, proud, censorious, extravagant, unsacramental, unchurchly, often sensual and lax in moral strictness, and often ends in an utter shipwreck of faith, and in the entire abandonment of the Church, and its holy Sacraments. This is necessarily a false and perverted spiritualism. It is an unhappy and deplorable development of the religious emotions. The Lutheran Church in this country has suffered from it in many places. The injurious effects of it have not yet wholly passed away. It needs to be strenuously guarded against and avoided, as a most insidious enemy to true and sound godliness.

7. *True Spirituality is in Entire Harmony with the Evangelical System of Doctrine, Duty, and Church Order.*

It is interesting and instructive to trace the contrast between true and false spirituality, in their relation to all that is true and sound in the doctrines of our holy Christianity. Such a tracing of the marks of contrast between the two, will enable us to have a just conception of both, and to distinguish between the one that is sound and the other that is unsound. Let me invite attention to such an examination.

(*a.*) *The relation of spirituality to our justification before God.*

Our justification is our judicial acquittal before God's judgment, of the charge of sin, and our release from condemnation, and the forgiveness of our sins on the ground of Christ's vicarious righteousness, appropriated by faith. The true and sound spiritual affections which this doctrine develops in the heart of a true believer, are humble trust in Christ, love to God for this unspeakable blessing, hearty gratitude, self renunciation, deep humiliation of soul, sincere sorrow for sin and hatred to it, and in general, a sense of utter unworthiness, and the disposition to place itself very low down at the foot of the cross. This abasement of soul, this renunciation of all merit or claim of any kind, this humble looking to Jesus alone for salvation and eternal life, draws the affections very near to a crucified Saviour, and brings them into very sweet communion with His spirit. There is also produced in the soul, an intense feeling of the odiousness of sin, and of hatred to it, on account of the great sufferings endured by the Saviour in order to redeem us from it. It therefore leads to true holiness of heart and life, moved thereto by the purest and best of all motives, the love of Jesus. The soul thus brought to the foot of the cross, stays there, and has no desire to get away from it. It does not "get through" any process of religious experience, by which it can now at length dispense with the blood of Jesus shed on the cross, constantly applied, for the remission of its sins. Its progress in holiness is rather the constant deepening of the consciousness that it daily needs the blood of Jesus Christ, to cleanse it from all sin. This feeling of humble, trustful, daily and hourly leaning upon Christ crucified, for mercy and grace, and for the hope of salvation and eternal life, is inexpressibly tender, precious and comforting to the soul. This is true, sound evangelical spirituality, in full harmony with the life of God in the soul, and is ardently cherished by every heart that is really spiritual after apostolic example.

In two essential points particularly, a false spiritualism differs from a true and sound spirituality, in its relation to the doctrine of Justification by Faith. The one is the claiming for itself a personal sinlessness that diminishes its estimate of the absolute and indispensable necessity of the vicarious merits of Jesus for its acceptance with God; and the other is the feeling that, however much it needed the atonement of Christ's blood for the forgiveness of the sins committed before its conversion, it can now, since its conversion, dispense largely, if not wholly, with the application of that blood, and can live so free from sin as not to need its daily and hourly virtue, to keep the soul clean from its defilement. It is remarkable how changed is, at once, the language of an individual who, from a true and sound position on the doctrine of Justification, is brought under the influence of an erroneous spiritualism. Instead of

Christ's redemption, His blood shed, His mercy offered, His obedience rendered, His righteousness imputed, His forgiveness extended, being the themes dearest to the heart and readiest in the discourse, the entire subject of thought and speech is, what the individual has felt, what raptures he has experienced, what readiness in prayer he enjoys, what freedom from sin he has attained, how earnestly he serves God, and the like feelings and expressions, all centering upon self, and glorifying, not the Saviour, but the man. From being at the foot of the cross, content to stay there and look with an humble and self-renouncing faith up to Christ on the cross, as all his righteousness, he seems to have climbed up until he has got above the cross and can dispense with the blood shed, the righteousness acquired, and the sacrifice offered on it by the Saviour. Such a spiritualism as this is self-righteous, vain, unevangelical, false, and exceedingly dangerous to the soul that cherishes it.

(*b*) *The relation of spirituality to the sacraments of the Church.*

The Sacraments are essential to both individual and Church Christian life. They meet the soul at the beginning of its spiritual life, and they attend it to the close, when God calls it to His everlasting kingdom. By a holy Sacrament the gracious germ-life is implanted, and by a holy Sacrament that growing life is nourished, and strengthened, and developed, and matured until it becomes ripe for heaven. True spirituality greatly values the Sacraments. It prepares for the reception of the Holy Communion, and the Holy Communion increases and strengthens it. Through the Lord's Supper the soul enjoys its nearest and sweetest communion with God. Its enjoyment is tender, subdued, self-renouncing, devout, holy. It is then nearer to Jesus than it can be at any other place or on any other occasion. It relishes this communion of spirit with Christ's spirit, this feeling of nearness to its Lord, this participation of Christ's most precious grace and blessing at the Lord's table, beyond the power of words to express it. It is never more truly spiritual, devout, and heavenly minded, than at the Communion Table. And this spiritual feeling is in its nature the purest, most god-like and heavenly, that can be conceived, because it flows out directly from the divine life in the soul, is in completest harmony with it, and is constituted by it what it is.

A false spirituality, on the contrary, depreciates the Sacraments, undervalues their necessity, takes from them their heavenly element, degrades them to the condition of mere rites and ceremonies, finds in them a chill, rather than an incitement to devotion, and in many instances, either defers them, or dispenses with them altogether. By such an erroneous spiritualism, they are put very far into the background. Other methods and instrumentalities, devised by human minds, seem much better adapted than they are to awaken devotion, to excite feeling, to kindle fervor, and to promote spiritual religion. They are regarded as mere outward forms that lead to formality, empty ceremonies that convey no grace, dampeners to rapturous emotion, and that produce in those who are not very much on their guard, a dead, godless, sacramental religion. According to this view of the relation of the Sacraments to spirituality, God's institutions have been found wanting, and man's inventions are much better adapted than they are, to promote vital godliness.

(c) The relation of spirituality to the doctrines of Christianity.

Sound doctrine is essential to sound Christianity. True practice must necessarily be founded upon true principles. The spirit of the mind is influenced and constituted by the governing principles entertained by the mind. Sound thinking, so far from being a hindrance to true devotion, aids and promotes it. An enlightened and safe judgment is essentially valuable as a regulator of the feelings, which are usually variable and impatient of control. There is no necessary antagonism between right thinking, right feeling, and right doing. Indeed, it is only when all these are well proportioned, and well balanced in any man, that he is the best specimen of what a man should be. A sound orthodox Christian is, and necessarily must be, a sound spiritual Christian. His orthodoxy helps his spirituality. His piety is sound because his faith is sound. His devout feelings are right, because his correct knowledge and enlightened judgment regulate them properly, and control them aright. He lays a sanctified intellect upon God's altar. His head, and heart, and life, present a well-proportioned and divinely symmetrical Christian. His devotions spring from his faith. Having the true Christian faith, he breathes the spirit of true Christian devotion. There is no conflict between his faith and his devotions, but as the one is pure, so the others are sound.

An erroneous spiritualism, on the contrary, has relaxed and easy notions about the faith. One of its ready maxims declares, "It matters not what a man's opinions are, so only his heart is converted, and his practice is right." It forgets that practice is governed by principles, and that as is the faith, such also are the devotions that spring from it. It is the faith of the Hindoo that produces the superstitious devotions of the Hindoo; it is Mohammedan faith that constitutes the peculiar religious spirit of the Moslem worshiper; and it is from the true faith of Christ that the intelligent, pure, and Christ-like spirit of the Christian's devotions springs. The spiritualism that undervalues sound doctrine, that confounds the true and the false, that exalts feeling above knowledge, that places practice in antagonism to principle, that sacrifices the faith in the interest of spirituality, and that considers it necessary to overthrow the pure faith of the Church in order to advance the cause of vital godliness in the Church, is a spiritualism that is erroneous, unsafe, and that needs to be carefully guarded against. However specious may be its pretensions, it is not the true spirituality of Christ and His apostles, or which will promote, in the end, the best and most enduring interests of Christianity, and the Christian Church. Let a man be alike sound in doctrine, devout in spirit, and holy in life, and we have in him the highest and best style of a Christian, after the pattern of Christ, of the Holy Apostles, and of the best and holiest men in all ages of the Christian Church.

(*d*) *The relation of spirituality to the order and service of the Church.*

The Church is the Body of Christ, and Christians are members of His Body. As the life of the body is the life of the members, and the members live because the body lives, so the life that lives and moves and acts in the hearts of Christians, is the life of the Son of God Himself. Our union with Christ, the Head, is through His Body, the Church. True evangelical spirituality is churchly—necessarily churchly. It is through the Church that we come to Christ, in the Church that we find Christ, and by means of the Church that we have the faith, and spirit, and life of Christ. In the Church we have the word of Christ, the ministry of Christ, the Sacraments of Christ, the worship of Christ, the service and obedience of Christ. All the means for the origination, the progress, and the perfection of spiritual life in the souls of men, are found in the Church. These means of grace produce the true spirit of devotion in the heart. They draw the soul into close and intimate communion and fellowship with God. The Christian comes very near to God in the reading and hearing of His Word, in the confession of sin, in the profession of faith, in the prayers offered, in the hymns sung. The spirit of devotion which is thereby produced is intelligent, reverent, solemn, pure. It is tender, delightful, holy. God is felt to be in the place, and the presence of God is inexpressibly dear to the soul. The forms of the Church service express the sentiments and feelings of the worshiper, and his holiest and happiest thoughts go along with them from the first silent prayer on entering, to the last silent prayer before leaving, the sanctuary. They are not barren, lifeless forms. They are used devoutly, and they foster in the breast the purest spirit of devotion.

A false spirituality overleaps the settled order and forms of Christianity, and is a wild and erratic law unto itself. It is the creature of impulse. Its action is spasmodic. It is wholly emotional. It feels so, and therefore it is right. It will not be restrained by forms, nor hampered by ceremony, nor controlled by rules of order. Like the untamed steed of the plains, it will rear, and plunge, and rush forward at its own sweet will. Said one of this class to me recently, "I have got above all churches." It chose its own way, and no longer needed God's way, or institutions, or sacraments, or Church, or help It had got above all these. It is not only restless under the restraints of the forms of a sound churchliness, but despises and denounces them as dead formalism, high churchism, a cold sacramental religion. Even when yielding to their observance, it has no reverence for them. Indeed, the spirit of irreverence in the Church, in the pew, in the pulpit, at prayer, at the Communion table, and at every part of divine service, is one of the most marked peculiarities of an erroneous spirituality. This spirit of irreverence in the most sacred places, and during the most solemn services, is shocking to a truly devout and spiritually minded Christian, and it is a sure evidence that the spirit that leads to it is unsound and false.

(*e*) *The relation of spirituality to the duty of prayer.*

A spiritual mind is a devout mind. The spirit of devotion is essential to spirituality. A pious mind is a mind imbued with the spirit of prayer. It delights in communion with God. The consciousness of God's presence with it, is very pleasing to a godly heart. It cherishes the thought that God is near it; it draws nigh in spirit to God's Spirit; it loves to feel that it is alone with God, in the closet and in other places of solitude; and the fellowship of soul with God, in all the public and private exercises of devotion, is very dear and precious. This spirit of devotion is subdued, tender, shrinking from observation, humble, self-abased, calm, pure. The best ideal I have before my mind is that of a sainted mother, as I often saw her in my childhood, sitting in her chamber, with her German Bible, or Arndt's Paradies-Gaertlein, or Stark's Handbuch before her. All was quiet around her; her own person was motionless, with her head resting on her hand, her face beamed forth seriousness, gentleness and peace; her eyes were fixed upon the page, and often the tear-drop swelled under the eyelid, coursed down her cheek, and fell on and wetted the page she was perusing. It was calm, subdued, tender, lowly, sincere, genuine, spiritual communion with God. It was spirituality of the old sort, without pretense, sound and holy, such as would necessarily proceed from the life of God in the soul. It was itself pure and holy, and it made its subject purer and holier.

In contradistinction to this, a false spirituality is bold, obtrusive, noisy, demonstrative, sensational, self-righteous, and relaxed in moral strictness. It seeks to work itself up to a high pitch of extravagant emotion, by the labored heaving of the breast, the affected tones of the voice, the violent rubbing together of the hands, and other bodily demonstrations, forced and unnatural. As of old, so now, it delights to display itself before the crowd, at the corners of the streets, and to gain the applause of men. It is proud of itself, condemnatory of another spirit better than itself, and passes easily from the most extravagant demonstrations of devoutness, to excessive lightness both of language and demeanor. Even when these objectionable traits exist in much less degree, it is still a spirit differing essentially from the genuine and holy spirituality which lived in the heart of Jesus, and because it lived there, lives also in the heart of all His faithful followers.

It now only remains for me to say that the Apostle's words, "Ye which are spiritual," should be descriptive of every human being. They should truly describe us as ministers and members here assembled. They should describe the entire Church of our Lord Jesus Christ, of which we are members and ministers, and which we love. The Church should never lack a sound and genuine spirituality. True spirituality should never be wanting, either by its place being usurped by a false spiritualism, or by the heart being sunk into a sad state of irreligiousness and want of fervent devotion. Let us carefully guard against the error of letting sound spirituality decline in our hearts, because others exhibit a spirituality that is unsound. Let the Church conscientiously cultivate the old devout spirit of the venerable fathers of the Reformation era. It is sometimes objected that the advocacy of the old faith of the Church, and of the old and wholesome Church service and Church order, is inconsistent with the maintenance of a high tone of spirituality in the Church. We believe the allegation to be false. We believe that a sound Lutheran faith, a wholesome Church order, and a high-toned spirituality, are not antagonistic, but exist necessarily together. Let all unite to prove, in our preaching, in our personal experience, and in the spirit prevalent in our congregations, that the true faith as held by the Church, is a living faith, that a wholesome Church service is the helper and not the enemy of fervent piety, and that the Word of God, as believed and preached by the fathers, has now, as then, the power to produce and maintain the sound godliness of the fathers. It is desirable that this spirit should pervade every part of the Church. It should be breathed in the pastor's sermons, in his catechetical lectures, in his private admonitions to the young and the old. It should be cherished in the hearts of ministers, in the breasts of our members, in the homes of our children, in the Sunday-school classes, in the chambers of the sick and dying. It should be impressed upon the hearts of all our theological students as they sit in the recitation rooms of our seminaries, and it ought to be earnestly cultivated by them not only in the morning and evening prayers in the chapel, but also in their study rooms, and in their retired chambers. The want of a sound spirit of devotion is a sad preparation for the active duties of the ministry. Let the spirit of devotion be cultivated by parents and children in all our families, by the regular morning and evening prayers, by the offering of grace at meat, by retired closet devotions, and in all suitable times and ways, in the sanctuary and out of it. Let us read God's Word devoutly, believe devoutly, pray devoutly, sing devoutly, preach devoutly, commune devoutly, live devoutly, animated and moved thereto by the life of God that dwells in us. We shall then be spiritual Christians after the pattern of Christ and His Apostles, of Luther and the Reformers, of the fathers of the Lutheran Church in this country, and of all, in every age, who truly believe in and love the name of our dear Lord Jesus Christ.

The regular order having been suspended, it was resolved to hear the essay of Dr. Stork next.

LITURGICAL FORMS IN WORSHIP.

BY REV. C. A. STORK, D. D., BALTIMORE, MD.

THE question of Liturgics is not a great question in Christianity, but it is one that can be solved only by an appeal to great Christian principle. The little finger is not a very important member, but its existence and function are determined by very important structural facts in the body.

How shall we worship God in public? Shall we trust for order and matter to the inspiration of the hour? Shall we prepare the order, and leave only the mode to the suggestion of the moment? Or, shall there be an established order, and a definite form of expression to be habitually observed?

It is unfortunate, that these questions have been discussed for several centuries, now, in an atmosphere clouded by strong partisan feeling; and that they have been determined, for the most part, by an appeal either to mere tradition or to individual taste. As for the disturbance of judgment, that arises from the vehemence with which the subject has been discussed, that we can in no wise escape, unless we are prepared to give up discussing all matters in which we have a present, practical interest. All questions become personal questions when they enter the arena of life: the *lumen siccum*, that dry light of reason, that impersonal atmosphere, in which Bacon thought it so desirable that all unsettled questions should be viewed, is possible only to those subjects in which human beings have no interest. Human feeling will mix with all earnest human thinking. We must, therefore, accept the disabilities of our diverse ways of looking at things, and allow for the refraction caused by this heated atmosphere of strife as best we can.

I do not think we can settle the question of Liturgics by a simple appeal to tradition. We may have the profoundest and tenderest reverence for antiquity, and yet find no reasonable vindication of a practice or belief in saying "Our fathers did so." We are continually revising the doings and beliefs of our fathers, summoning them to the bar of great principles; and irreverence towards the past lies not in revising its work, but in ignoring it, in refusing to consider it at all. So when it is said "Liturgic forms are the most adequate expression of public worship, because the Church has always used them," we are only summoned to review history and to ask, Has the Church always used them, and if so, why? The Past lands an immense cargo at our feet; some of it is gold, some silver, much rubbish. And in all open questions like this of the use of Liturgical forms, the business of a reasonable man is to inquire, what does antiquity in this case mean? That the Church has almost exclusively poured her devotions through them is a very serious call to the consideration of the meaning of such catholic consent. But that use has not been exclusive. If it were true that she had always done so, if it were not an *almost* but an *altogether*, if there were no break in the tradition, then we would not be discussing the matter to-day. An unbroken tradition calls for no discussion; the common consent is the voucher of the very truth. But here the Church divides; she has divided for two centuries or more. And unless we are of those who think the voice of the Church of importance only before the 18th century, and of none since, we must take this divided testimony into account.

As for the other, the purely modern, if I may so call it, the American method of determining the question by an appeal to individual taste, this, it seems to me, is the most futile, the most puerile of all. This subjects the solemn business of approaching God in the worship of the great congregation to a private fancy, to an irresponsible individual whim.

For a man to say "I will worship God with, or without, established forms, because I feel like it," is to say, "I will because I will," which has always been accounted a good feminine reason for conduct, but not one that commends itself to the rational, the masculine intellect. Acts of religion or worship that have no better reason for their performance than individual taste, are open to the objection that they are not worthy a rational creature to pay to a wise and holy God. If the only reason we can give for having prayers without a book is that we don't like a book, I am afraid, as those who have come to years of discretion, we shall have to give up our free forms. The reasoning of a great many good men *against* Liturgical forms in public worship, and of as many good men *for* Liturgical forms, viz., that they do, or do not, like them, has always seemed to me really childish.

But let us leave these reminiscences of battle, and approach the subject from what we may call the inside.

Public Worship: what are the elements of it? the formal elements, I mean. The matter, the substance of worship, is very simple: adoration, praise, confession, petition, these are its material elements; but the formal part, the mode of paying these, what is it? In private worship the formal element is very simple, too; whatever makes a bridge between the soul and its Creator (over which communication can pass), whatever opens a channel between the solitary soul and the Infinite Spirit, by which the two may mingle and commune,—this is all; and each man must determine that for himself. But add the word *public*, and immediately it becomes something quite different. It is changed by the introduction of two additional elements embraced in the word *public*. It is *associated* worship; the act of a united body. The race, as it were, appears before its Maker to confess and adore. It is no longer individual but corporate in its character, and hence invested with a solemnity, an august quality, such as cannot belong to the devotion of a solitary soul. With this goes also the indefinable sense of community, fellowship, the thrill of multitude, the harmony of souls uniting in the same act. Every one, I suppose, knows the difference between melody and harmony: there is in a harmonized chord, a something that never can be got out of a mere succession of notes, a melody. And so in the worship of the congregation, the rich, the poor, the high, the low, the little child, the old man, the sage, the peasant, there is a quality that is not the mere intensification of the individual's devotion; it is a new quality; it is "*the Communion of Saints.*"

If we keep these two elements in mind we shall see, I think, what change passes upon private worship in being made *public*.

The solemn official quality of the Church approaching her Sovereign, her Redeemer, her Head, must be there.

And the sense of fellowship, of communion, the feeling not only of the Great Head above bending down and receiving, but the touch of brother against brother, the almost actual sense of fellowship, the devout thrill making all one, that too is there.

Now it is these two elements, both present, both distinct, and yet blending into one in every act of public worship, it seems to me, that have determined the constant tendency in all religions to the use of Liturgical Forms. I take this stream of tendency for granted. It is found in all non-revealed religions. It is conspicuous in Judaism to the present day. In the early Christian Church it is too obvious to call for more than a mere passing notice. In the Mediæval Church it was exclusive. Even in the Protestant Churches it has predominated. And now in those very Churches, the non-liturgical, in which for generations it was resisted and apparently overcome, it is making itself increasingly felt. It is simply a natural current channeled in the very constitution of man's religious nature, and nothing can ever permanently intercept it, or make it other than it is. Of the meaning of the tendency to abandon old established forms which was developed at the time of the Reformation I shall speak presently. I believe it to have had a ground of reality: the repugnance to Liturgical Forms meant something. It is more than a revolt against forms too closely associated with corrupt doctrines. But of that farther on. But one thing is certain, that the dominant tendency in the Church Catholic in all ages has been to the use of Liturgical Forms. And that tendency, I repeat, is due to the influence of the two elements involved in the very idea of worship that is public. We will examine them separately.

1. *Public Service* is, in a very real sense, the worship of the race. It is, so to speak, an official act. It is humanity appearing before God. No man I think can help feeling that, when he joins an assembly of earnest men engaged in worship. When they stand up or kneel down to pray, when together they confess or praise, there is a quality of solemnity, as of the transaction of some august ceremony. The most violent defender of free prayer cannot escape the impression. Men may seek to root out the idea of ceremony as they will; they may abolish vestments and postures; they may pulverize orders of service and scatter the dust of them to the winds; but as the idea of ceremony does not inhere in these, but only uses them as instruments, as garments in which to clothe itself, it will still remain in the assembly as a spirit. That is, it will remain as long as it is a truly worshiping assembly, a body of men consciously paying devotion to their Creator. A great many religious assemblies are not worshiping at all; they are meetings for teaching, for social intercourse, for the comparison of experience, for the enjoyment of religious emotions; but as soon as they worship—when the prayer and praise, the adoration and confession

begin—then the spirit of ceremony must be present. How can it be otherwise? There is the throne and He that sits thereon, and here are the creatures bowed and paying their homage. Involuntarily the expression becomes stately, solemn, ceremonious; or if it does not, the common consciousness of the worshiper is disturbed; they revolt from the easy, familiar tone; they say "that prayer was irreverent."

The natural effect of such a feeling, is to invest the approach to God with safe-guards that shall secure it from what is common and familiar. The leader of devotion will check his utterance. He will remember the words of the Wise Man, "*God is in heaven, and thou upon earth: therefore let thy words be few.*" He will cut off rhetoric, and eschew hyperbole and extravagant expression. He becomes simple. Then, finding himself falling into faults of utterance from the hurry of the moment, he finds it necessary to choose his words before. You can follow out the process for yourself. It ends in the formation of a Liturgical Form. If a Church were to set out for itself *de novo*, with no knowledge and no prejudice drawn from the past, with only the Scriptures and the instincts of the religious nature for the constructive forces, it would in process of time have a liturgical form of its own making. It would make an order, it would fix certain phrases, it would continually tend to a more absolutely established form even of words. It would do this because the solemn atmosphere of worship would call for just such an order. The instinct for *Liturgical Forms*, then, is rooted in man's religious nature.

2. But there is another element in associated worship. Men do not worship together simply to make a public recognition of God, as an official act, so to speak. They worship together to satisfy the desire for fellowship. That desire is laid deep in human nature; and the revelation of a new fellowship in Christ makes it still deeper. "*We are all baptized into one body;*" and that is "*the body of Christ.*" And as members of that body we "*are members one of another.*" Now of this new fellowship public worship is perhaps the most vivid, palpable realization we can have. It is as old as the little company in the beginning of the Christian Church; it is as new as the last Church service in which together we adored our God. We know the power of that common stream of worship in which we are borne as on a mighty current into regions of holy

thoughts, and aspirations, and adorations, that we never reach alone.

But what has this to do with the use of Liturgical Forms? Would not the sense of fellowship be as vivid with a free prayer, a movable order?

I answer, Yes, and No.

Yes, so far as the Communion of Saints is expressed by that one assembly.

No, when we reflect that the Communion of Saints embraces not only the Present, but also the Past:

> "Part of the host have crossed the flood,
> And part are crossing now."

But it is one host, and the fellowship extends backward and upward, as well as to those on the earth with us now. This Communion with the Church of the past, is not so palpable a fact as the fellowship with the Church of the present. But it is nevertheless a fact; and the Church cannot with impunity ignore it. At times the Church has ignored it; and always to its great loss. Thus the non-liturgical Churches, in turning their backs on the past, have broken the continuity of the Church. In so far they have destroyed that sense of solidarity of which we hear so much in secular circles, but which is realized in its fullness only in the Christian body. They have done so in past generations; but they are awaking to recognize their loss. They will be non-historic no longer. They are knitting again the broken strands. They are claiming their place in the continuity. They are welcome. It was our loss as well as theirs that the solidarity was ever broken. But this return shows us something. Christianity is not a force that dies to-day to rise again in another form to-morrow. It is not an isolated flame burning in the solitary soul or congregation, and then kindled in another solitary soul, or isolated congregation. The body is one, and the spirit is one. It leaps over barriers of Space and Time; it diffuses itself through the long ranks of generations and centuries; it fuses even diverse theologies and forms; there is One Lord, One Faith, One Baptism.

Now we may regard this great fact simply as a theological dogma, and speculate upon it, define it, draw it out. And that is well. But the Church has done more than that; it has taken the fact up into its life. It has striven to bring it into more and more vivid and continual consciousness. It would not be a truth of doctrine if the Christian body had not verified it by making it a truth of life. And how has it been realized? Very largely by the use of Liturgical Forms. The Communion of Saints is brought to consciousness in one very intense way by the use in worship of the same order and forms; nay, the very words and cadences used by the generations of the saints before us. There is a power in words. They are "winged," in Homer's subtle phrase, with the swift motion and thrill of life. We know the power a word has to bring forth a vague thought, an elusive feeling: spoken, it is fixed, it comes forth out of the empty, the impalpable, into the concrete. We know, too, the power of old words; how a phrase, a cadence, a web of thought and feeling woven up in familiar expression, brings with it a power more than its own, a color, a fragrance, a warm breath, in which the dead words and phrases palpitate with a glow of life.

Now we may analyze all this and label it *association*. But putting a name on a great process of the human spirit does not dissolve its mystery, nor abridge its power. It *is* association; and that is just the secret of the power there lies in the use of an old Liturgy: the prayer, the praise, the confession, the adoration, are instinct with a life more than their own, the life of past generations, the life of the Church once breathed through them, and yet warm in them. It is a palpable, almost sensible realization of the mystic fellowship that runs through the Church universal. A prayer that has been prayed by my father, and before him by his father, and so for centuries backward gathers on its petitions the yearning breath of generation after generation, is a very different thing from the petition just made for me and uttered for the first time. Every word vibrates with the thrill of joys, sorrows, hopes, devout aspirations, once warm, and though past, not extinct. I feel in that vibration the harmony of the Christian fellowship through the ages, as in the sound of the voices praying or confessing by my side, I feel the harmony of the present communion of saints. So that our confessions and anthems, our collects and doxologies, do for the past what our public assembly and presence with each other do for the present—they make palpable, actual the Communion of Saints.

I know this view is open to the criticism that it is purely speculative; that, though it seems to be fact, it is not verifiable; that men do not feel so. But it is just this which is contended; that the reason the Church clings with such tenacity to its Liturgical Forms, is found in this sense of communion through them with the whole Church past and present.

This is the meaning of the peculiar power the Anglican Service exercises over those who use it. Men explain the charm of this service by its beautiful literary form, its fine old English. But that would explain its fascination over the more cultured, not its hold on the unlettered—on the many who are insensible to the charm of style, or the rhythm of old English. No; it is because it has been the channel of devotion for so many successive generations, that it takes such deep hold of men to-day. These ancient prayers and responses, like an old musical instrument, are full of echoes from strains played on them by past generations. A great writer describes a rustic going to the village church after the death of a beloved parent, and the effect the Liturgic service had upon him: "The Church Service was the best channel he could have found for his mingled regret, yearning and resignation; its interchange of beseeching cries for help, with outbursts of faith, and its recurrent responses and the familiar rhythm of its collects, seemed to speak for him as no other form of worship could have done." What was true of this sorrowing rustic is true of great bodies of men; no public prayer or acts of worship, made for the special occasion, can ever afford what the old forms offer. True Liturgical Forms cannot be made at all; they must grow. As each year adds another growth of branch to the tree, so wealth of fellowship accumulates generation by generation on the ancient prayer, confession, litany. They are no longer the voice of one man, the minister; they are not even the aggregated utterance of the present congregation only; they are full of echoes from the past; the Church of the Ages is heard praising, supplicating, adoring, through them.

At this point in the preparation of this paper my attention was arrested by a paragraph bearing on the subject, which occurs in the Yale lectures of that distinguished non-conformist, Dr. Dale. Speaking of the conduct of public worship, he says that for some time he had "a mistaken impression that extemporaneous prayer might include—in addition to its own excellence—the characteristic excellence of a liturgy. But," he goes on to say, "we must make our choice. In extemporaneous prayer, the stateliness, the majesty, the æsthetic beauty of such a service as that of the Anglican Episcopal Church, and the power which it derives from venerable associations, are impossible. We must be content with simplicity, directness, pathos, reverence, fervor; and, if we are less vividly conscious than those who use a Liturgy that we are walking in the footsteps of the saints of other centuries, we may find compensation in a closer and more direct relation to the actual life of the men, women, and children, who are waiting with ourselves for the mercy and help and pity of God. We lose less than we may gain." "You cannot have the venerable association," says the antagonist of Liturgical Forms; "but you may have something better, viz., the warmth and freedom of extemporaneous prayer." But is it better? If Dr. Dale and his friends would analyze what they mean by that vague generality, "venerable associations," they might find reason to change this comparative valuation. By "venerable associations" the non-liturgist means that pleasing sense of the picturesque which belongs to all that is past. It is put by him in the same category with old ruins, old family relics, mementos of distinguished persons of former ages. It belongs to the region of sentiment. It is classed along with "the stateliness, the majesty, the æsthetic beauty" of a Liturgy. They are all purely æsthetic qualities. But is that all that comes to us from the past? Is our connection with the Church of former ages only a matter of sentiment, of æsthetic feelings? It is a great deal more. It is really a connection of the same nature as that which binds us to the Church of the present. And the depth of solemnity, the awe, the thrill, the sense of sacredness that we cannot but feel as we use these anthems and prayers and confessions worn with the devotions of ages of worshipers, is nothing less than the solemn realization of the Communion of the Saints. If that is what is meant by "venerable associations," then I say no "closer relation to the actual life of men and women" about us can ever make good its loss. No fellowship of the Church now existent, though intensified to the highest degree, can ever make up for that which is lost by breaking the continuity with the Church of the past. The very fact that the members of that body are no longer on the earth, but in heaven, gives a color, a quality, a tone to the devotion that uses their ancient form, which nothing else can supply. As well say that the fellowship of brothers and sisters living with us can supply the loss of father and mother. Every such quality is unique:

it is itself and not another; and another cannot take its place, any more than a better quality of water will take the place of bread in supplying the wants of the body.

To break up the order, to have something novel, is in so far to break the continuity of the Church. The fellowship is narrowed down; the volume of worship is thinned; we are once more cut loose from " the goodly fellowship of the prophets, the noble army of the martyrs, the holy Church throughout the world, that doth acknowledge God."

That Public Worship will tend to make for itself an Established Liturgical Form, it seems to me, is one of those facts so deeply imbedded in our religious nature, that no revolt from it can ever be permanent. We are beginning to see the signs of a return from the great insurrection against form that marked the Puritan Revival. And now let us look at that revolt, and see what lesson it has for us.

3. That revolt againt forms of worship, which spread through so many religious bodies, and modified the habits of even the Liturgical bodies, was not, I am persuaded, merely a diseased growth. To think so would be a kind of treason to human nature; it would be of the nature of schism, dividing the body of Christ on a mere side issue. The hatred of the Puritan for the Prayer-Book was not merely a sympathetic irritation, extending itself from his abhorrence of Prelacy and Romanizing doctrine. The Wesleyan revival knew nothing of Prelacy or Romish errors; and the strong impulse of the Church in America to a free form of public worship surely could not be credited to a sympathy with Puritanism or Independency.

The revolt against Liturgical Forms was as really rooted in the religious nature as the tendency to establish forms. It was the form taken by the natural craving for a free prayer, the spontaneous uplifting of the soul to God on the need and impulse of the hour. Dr. Dale is right when he says that something must be given up if we are to confine ourselves exclusively to Liturgical Forms. Freedom must be given up; not the lawless license to do as one pleases, but the scope for those new creations of life that a Church if really living will put forth in the impulse of the worshiping hour. There grows a rigidity at last out of the exclusive use of these old established forms. Against this, human nature, when thoroughly alive, will revolt. It has revolted, and when it does not revolt, as, it may be urged, it did not for many ages in the Mediæval Church, it is because it falls exhausted, because it loses that peculiar mark of the Christian life, its elasticity, its spring, its unexpected putting forth of new shoots in directions never before dreamed of. This lack of vitality was the mark of the Church in the Middle Ages. It was not dead, as some Protestants delight to aver; but it certainly was oppressed with a fearful lassitude. It lived, but under oppression, without any power of initiation. It could only live; it could not originate any new life. But when the revival of the sixteenth and seventeenth centuries came, then the yoke that the Mediæval Church was too languid to feel oppressive, became intolerable. The young life beat itself against the bars of chant and confession and collect; it broke through. I do not blame it. It was inevitable. And it always will be inevitable. Life that has no scope for new expression, must struggle with a sense of imprisonment. And where there is life there will be new expression of it: the substance of the Christian life is, indeed, the same in all ages and in all men; yet in every soul, in every congregation, on almost every occasion, it will flame out in some special form. And if there is nothing but the iron uniformity of the established form, the soul will at last mutiny, and demand one utterance that shall be all its own. Give it vent; let the mood of sorrow, of hope, of special thanksgiving or supplication, go up to God in a fresh cry like no other cry before, and for the main of public worship the sense of the congregation will readily fall back on the fixed form. But shut it in, say—speak through these provided channels, or not at all—and there will be insurrection; you will have Puritanism with its stern hatred, its blind, bitter detestation, its total destruction of Liturgical Forms.

It has always seemed to me a mistake that the English Church gave no place for the spontaneous feeling of the hour, and men assembled for worship. To say that men do not need new forms of expression; that the old is better; that what was good enough for the fathers is good enough for us, is to say that the Unity of the Church in all ages is not a Unity, but a Uniformity. *"We are members one of another;"* but the very Unity which is constituted by the united members, requires that each member should have its own special life and function, unlike all others.

But, of course, no partisan of Liturgical Forms—no worshiper of the past, simply because it is the past—will see this, any more than the enemy of Liturgies can feel the need of fellowship with any age but his own. Some theologians seem to think that Church History stopped a couple of centuries ago, and that all we can do now is to reproduce the past in our churches, as we reproduce English history in our plays on the stage. The whole impulse of the exclusively liturgical body is to make the Christian life of to-day but a pale image of life centuries ago. This is to destroy, by our insistence on Liturgical Forms, the very basis on which alone they can reasonably be urged. If the life of the Church to-day is no real, original, creative power, but only a playing over on the barrel organ of archæology the tunes of the past, then there can be no fellowship with the past at all. Fellowship is possible only between living beings; and to say that the Church cannot strike out anything new—to brand all that is fresh and individual with the mark "*Nova, pulchra, falsa*"—is to say it has no life, only a galvanized simulacrum of life borrowed from what once lived. Do we not see that this is to cut up the fellowship of the saints from the roots? The Puritans of the sixteenth century and the Puritans of the nineteenth century would cut it up by breaking with the past; the exclusive Liturgical bodies would cut it up by breaking on the wheel the living, creative Church of to-day. But what profits it to discuss whether we shall hold by the communion of the past or that of the present? It is like asking, Shall we give up the head or the heart. It is only a question of what death we shall die.

We must remember then the two forces in the religious nature; that by which it holds by the past, and that by which it projects itself into the future. It is the problem of our age to reconcile the two. He who says—Give us the old Liturgical Forms and nothing else; the Church found them enough for ages, and so may we—he, I say, is blind and knows not whereof he affirms. He has one-half the problem: but that which solves only half a problem is no solution at all. And he who says, Away with forms; give us the free order; let us speak only as the spirit moves—he has the other half; and that, too, is no solution. Until we can make man in his religious nature to look only before him into the future, we cannot let go our Liturgical Forms; and until we have made him to look only after, backward to the past, we cannot give up free prayer.

Of course it is possible to deny this. Not only so, but what is worse, it is possible honestly not to see it. Do you say that the shouting Methodist, with his outspoken detestation of collects and confessions, is only a canting hypocrite? Or, on the other hand, that the churchly dignitary, who shudders at an extemporaneous prayer, is a pompous Pharisee who has the form of godliness without the power? Dismiss such easy solutions of the difficulty as these. If only it were so, that all the opposers of Liturgies were hypocrites, and all the defenders of them Pharisees, it would be easier to deal with this question. But they are only too honest. They speak just what they feel. You may persuade one who can but will not see, at last to see. But who will give sight to the blind? It is terribly possible to cultivate religious blindness. We may steadily cultivate one side of our religious nature till other parts shrivel and lose their sensibility; and then it will seem as if everything that appeals to other sensibilities than those left to us, were fantastic, unreal, a mere outburst of fanaticism or folly. One may so steadily look at the past that after awhile he has no eye for anything not cast in the old moulds; he has no life in himself that seeks new channels ; he becomes like the artist who copies the old master so long that at last his pencil refuses to draw any outline but Raphael's, to compose any subject but in the manner of Leonardo. Or we may insist so strenuously on our individual freedom, that at last the nerve of connection with the Church Universal is paralyzed, and we have no feeling for what is saintly or heroic in the old forms; the Church begins with us, extends as far as our circle of companions, and so ends. And so men can after awhile honestly wonder what any one can find in a Liturgy to satisfy his devotional longings; "It is so cold, so dead, so formal;" and to him it is: it has no life from the past in it for him, for to the past he is deaf, blind. But that is his loss; not the measure of what the Church needs, or what other men in a healthier state crave. And so another shudders at a free prayer ; "What is the use of it? it is so new, so strange." Yes, it is strange, for his life is all in the past ; he thinks and feels in the grooves of other men's spiritual movements; he has quelled all individual life of his own, until anything unwonted in worship seems a solecism, a piece of irreligion, a profanity. We do with ourselves in one direction of our spiritual life, just what we see very clearly the scientific investigator is apt to do with his whole spiritual being. We neglect it till it is shriveled and numb, and then, like the scientific skeptic, because our paralyzed sensibility in a certain direction reports nothing, nothing, we declare, is there. The skeptic loses the use of his spiritual nature, and then declares there is nothing spiritual. The modern religionist cuts himself loose from the Church Catholic, and then, grown insensible to any need of the Communion of Saints, asserts there is no such communion outside his little circle; and the Liturgical partisan, binding all his religious nature down to the Procrustean bed of an exclusive form, and in time fitted to that, is amazed that it should be possible for men to feel any devotional need not provided for in the collects or confessions.

But every man who knows something of the cunning tricks human nature plays, will be careful how he measures the Universe by the ten-inch rule of his own tastes and feelings. He will not insist that there is nothing in what a great part of the Christian body prizes and draws nutriment from, because it does not hit his fancy. If, when he looks steadily in the direction in which great bodies of other Christians are seeing visions, he discerns nothing, he will not at once cry out, "Stuff and nonsense; there is nothing there!" but ask whether possibly he may not be dull of vision.

I submit that the Liturgist is not all right, and the defender of a free order all wrong. Neither is the reverse the truth. They are both right positively; and both wrong negatively. The Liturgist is right in approving the power and fitness of the established and ancient order; and the defender of free prayer is right in his advocacy of spontaneous utterance in worship. The Liturgist is wrong when he says, "No free prayer;" and the opposer of Liturgies is wrong when he says, "No Liturgical Forms." They are the two halves of a divided sphere: each half by itself is false; join it to the other, and you have the round, completed truth.

I return to the words with which this paper begins: "The question of Liturgies is not a great question in Christianity, but it it one that can be solved only by appeal to great Christian principles." These principles are the freedom of the individual member, and the unity of the Christian body. They are the two great structural, or if we may speak Platonically, architectonic facts of the Christian life. Between them the Church for eighteen centuries has been oscillating, grasping now the one, and then the other, but never holding the two in completeness at once. Hold exclusively the one, the freedom of the individual, and you will have a free and shifting order; hold only the other, the unity of the body, and you will have a prescribed, unbroken Liturgical order. It is to be hoped the age will come when the Church will be strong enough and liberal enough to hold both at once; and then the Liturgical question will be settled forever.

From what has been said it will be seen at once that the perfect Liturgical Form is a growth: it cannot be made. We may construct an elaborate order; we may make it as august and stately as we will; but we cannot breathe into it the full vital sense, the glow, the flush, the vibrating harmony of the fellowship of the saints. Only the use of generations of worshiping men and women can do that.

The best approach to this ideal is to select only the old; not to attempt to make our Liturgical Forms *de novo*. It is the misfortune of the Lutheran Church that she has had so many Liturgies. She has changed them so often that no one order is venerable. The chord is always broken. But this we can do: We can compose an order to-day from material long used and resonant with the religious fervors, the penitence and aspiration of former ages. We have not the perfect instrument, but we can make an instrument from the mellow fragments of antiquity that lie all around, and the tones of the Past will reverberate through it.

And we can leave room for the spontaneous utterance of the Present. Some maintain that the day when a great Liturgical prayer, or chant, or confession, could be written, has passed away; that every age has its own peculiar gift, and that in former generations the Liturgical gift was rich and varied; that we have the gift of activity, not of lofty devotional utterance. It may be so. I think it more than probable. But be that as it may, the Church of to-day has its own peculiar life, solitary, the offspring of the hour. For this it finds no adequate utterance in the old forms: it craves a new voice. Let it have it.

As the result of the thoughts considered in this paper, I submit the following propositions:

1. That the Church for its public worship needs Liturgical Forms as an adequate expression of the solemnity of its united approach to the Creator.

2. That an established and venerable order most fully realizes the Communion of Saints.

3. That no order of public service can be considered complete which does not by some free prayer provide for the expression of the feeling peculiar to the time and circumstances.

4. That the ideal order cannot be made, but must grow by the use of generations of worshipers.

5. That any change of Liturgical Forms from the long-established order, except for doctrinal reasons, is to be deprecated as breaking the continuity of the fellowship of the Church in worship.

6. That in framing a Liturgy, if a Church is so unfortunate as not to have an established order, the various parts are to be chosen from Liturgies already consecrated by long use; and that collects, anthems, confessions, responsive orders, are not to be made *de novo*.

REMARKS OF REV. L. E. ALBERT, D. D. (*General Synod.*)

Dr. L. E. Albert said that he was glad to-day of his connection with the General Synod, because the principles of worship so ably and beautifully set forth in the paper of Dr. Stork, were the principles recognized in that body. Its order of service happily preserved the continuity of the past life of the Church with the present, in the adoption of forms sacred through long association, and in making provision at the same time for peculiar needs of the hour in unwritten prayers. The Liturgy which the Liturgical Committee, of which he was a member, were under orders to publish in its provisional form, fully embodied these principles and was adapted to give them effect.

REMARKS OF REV. F. W. CONRAD, D. D. (*General Synod.*)

I have listened with no ordinary interest to the paper just read. It treats of the subject of worship and discusses the best manner of performing it. Two modes of worship have prevailed in the Church—the liturgical and the spontaneous and free. God is Himself the author of liturgical forms of prayer and prescribed an order of service for the Jewish Church. But notwithstanding this, the spontaneous utterances of free prayer in secret, in social meetings, and on extraordinary occasions, were also called forth under the promptings of the Holy Spirit. Nor was it otherwise in the primitive Church. Christ furnished His disciples with a form of prayer and thus introduced the liturgical principle of worship into the Christian Church. The Apostles offered spontaneous supplications to God, and thus inaugurated free prayer as a component part of public worship. Both methods of worship have thus received the divine sanction, and both have been exemplified in the Mosaic and Christian dispensations.

The history of public worship proves that there is a felt want among Christians, both for the use of forms and for the utterance of spontaneous prayers. To supply these wants is the design of liturgical services and of free prayer. In the Jewish Church the liturgical method predominated; in the Primitive Church the use of free prayer predominated. The Romish Church gradually suppressed free prayer, and followed a long prescribed form of worship in an unknown tongue. The Protestant Church revived free prayer, and while it retained the most devotional forms of worship, shortened and purified the Church service.

Luther accepted the liturgical principle in worship as scriptural, and prepared several liturgies. The service of his last liturgy was shorter than that of the first. He had also prepared the outlines of a still more simple form of service before his death. Zwingli and Calvin also approved the use of liturgical forms in public worship. Hence, all the Churches of the Reformation—Lutheran, Zwinglian and Calvinistic—recognized the liturgical principle, not to the exclusion of, but as co-ordinate with, the use of free prayer.

Muhlenberg retained the principal parts of the simpler liturgical service prepared by Luther, and the first Lutheran churches in this country used liturgical services. But under the predominating influence of Puritanic opposition to all forms of prayer and liturgical services in public worship, the Puritanic method of worship by free prayer alone, was introduced into nearly all the Lutheran Churches of this country. A general reaction, however, against this Puritanic extreme has taken place during the last twenty years. Congregationalists themselves now confess that their fathers went too far in their exclusion of all liturgical forms, and now not a few of them use responsive readings of Scripture, the Creed and the Lord's Prayer in public worship. Similar sentiments are uttered and liturgical forms used among Presbyterians, Methodists and some other denominations in this country. Under the influence of this reaction, the Lutheran Church has gone back to her first principles, and furnished her churches with liturgical services, containing the purest and most devotional parts of worship, developed under religious experience, and the indicting influence of the Holy Spirit. Some of the Churches have adopted these liturgical forms exclusively, others continue to conduct public worship by free prayer alone, while others still combine both methods, using liturgical forms and spontaneous, free prayer in the religious services of the sanctuary. Not the body alone, to the exclusion of the soul—not the soul alone, to the exclusion of the body—but body and soul in organic unity, constitute the true type of humanity. In like manner, not liturgical forms alone to the exclusion of free prayer—nor free prayer alone to the exclusion of liturgical forms—but liturgical forms in connection with free prayer, constitute the true scriptural ideal of a devotional service for the worship of God in His sanctuary. The liturgical form supplies the general wants of the worshiper in his approach to God; free prayer supplies his peculiar wants, as they arise from time to time under the changing circumstances of life.

REMARKS OF REV. J. A. BROWN, D. D. (*General Synod.*)

There can be but one judgment in regard to the paper just read. It was marked by a sobriety of judgment, a clearness of discrimination, a hearty appreciation both of the importance and difficulty of the subject, and handled with a freshness and vigor, that must commend it to all sober and reflecting minds. It furnishes food for serious meditation in regard to our worship. This is no time or place to venture on an extemporaneous criticism of its literary character, but I think all were delighted with the style of it, and would agree that simply as an essay it possessed literary merits of a high order. I can only say that I was delighted, and, I believe, edified by the discussion.

Rev. G. F. Krotel, D. D., of New York, appointed to read the next paper, was prevented by indisposition both from preparing an essay, and from being present.

It was resolved that Rev. Dr. Mann occupy the vacant place.

The eleventh paper was then read.

THESES ON THE LUTHERANISM OF THE FATHERS OF THE CHURCH IN THIS COUNTRY.

BY REV. W. J. MANN, D. D.
Professor in the Evangelical Lutheran Theological Seminary, Philadelphia.

I. THE SUBJECT.

WE find, that in the presentation of the subject the expression, "Fathers of the Church," is used. We understand thereby, those men and their co-laborers, who were the founders of the Mother-Synod, and, consequently, the organizers of an independent, self-governing, Lutheran Church-body on this continent.

2. We have here before our mind, especially, the Rev. Dr. *H. M. Mühlenberg* and his associates, the Rev. Messrs. *Brunnholz, Heinzelmann, Handschuh, Kurz, Schulze* and others. We take the Rev. Dr. H. M. Mühlenberg as the most eminent type of their doctrinal position and practical principles.

3. There were Lutheran congregations established, and Lutheran pastors, of Dutch, Swedish and German origin, active in this country before the time of Mühlenberg. About their doctrinal views we can hardly entertain any doubt. We know that, on account of their Lutheran convictions, some of them had suffered persecution, and that one of them, the Rev. *Justus Falkner*, born in Zwickau, Saxony, who preached first in Montgomery county, Pa., and at a later period to Lutheran congregations at New York and Albany, published, A. D. 1708, a book which was undoubtedly called forth by his discussions with Calvinists, and which that last and venerable champion of the Lutheran Orthodoxy of the seventeenth century, *E. Valentine Loescher*, honors with the title of a "*Compendium Doctrinæ Anti-Calvinianum.*" The efforts of those congregations and of those men left, however, no distinguishable trace in the evolution and organization of the Lutheran Church in this country.

4. The history, not of the Lutherans, but of the organization of the Lutheran Church in this country, dates from the fifth decade of the last century, from the time of the arrival of H. M. Mühlenberg

on the western shore of the Atlantic, 1742, and from the formation of the first Synod, 1748. The inner history of the Church witnesses to a considerable deviation from the principles and the spirit of the Fathers, since the first decades of the present century. With the generation of the "Epigonoi," we have, however, nothing to do here.

5. The term Lutheranism, as used in connection with the subject-matter before us, refers not only to the doctrinal position, but also to its practical application, and, especially, to the principles and ways of pastoral life.

II. THE HISTORICAL CONNECTION.

1. When H. M. Mühlenberg was preparing himself for the ministry at Goettingen and Halle, the great crisis, through which orthodox Dogmatism in Germany was displaced by Pietism, on the one hand, and Rationalism on the other, was almost passed, but had produced its impression upon the religious mind of the age.

2. As there were "Pietists" even before Spener, though that appellation was then not used, so there were orthodox men among the Pietists, who had no sympathy with Rationalism, Unionism, Indifferentism. Whilst they opposed error, they were convinced that Lutheran Theology had something better to live on than bitter polemics against Christians of a different name, and had to show its strength also in other directions.

3. Spener's Pietism was not heterodox. Neither was it separatistic. It was not a revolution against the doctrinal basis of the Lutheran Church. Neither was it the establishment of a sect. But it was a reaction against that tendency, which often considered orthodoxy as the great end of Christianity, and forgot that it was the means to produce sound Christian faith and life.

4. Spener's Lutheranism was of a practical character. As such, it was true Christianity. Spener strove to excite the individuals to personal piety, and the Church to measures to promote that end. But he was very far from undervaluing the Means of Grace, or from thinking of them in an un-Lutheran way. The practical character combined with doctrinal decision and precision, which we see in the so-called Old-Lutherans, Missourians, Iowa-men, and others of our days, was the very Lutheranism of Spener's "Pia Desideria," save the acrimony and littleness often exhibited now.

5. The Lutheranism and Pietism of H. M. Mühlenberg, and of the other Fathers, was after the type of Spener. It was free from that indifference toward doctrinal landmarks and toward general literary and philosophical culture, which was observable in many Pietists; it was free from sickly sentimentalism and from hypocritical cant, both of which often serve as a substitute for religious fervor and moral energy.

6. Of other extravagancies also, which were peculiar to the Pietism, that, especially in the times of A .H. Francke, maintained at Halle and gave odium to a good cause, anxiety to the mind of Spener, and occasion for justifiable attacks on the part of E. Val. Loescher and others, we find no traces in the character of H. M. Mühlenberg, who, even as a student at Goettingen and Halle, proved himself a man of the right Christian practical character, by taking an active interest in the religious education and other necessities of neglected and needy children, and afterwards by accepting the call to labor among Lutherans in the far-off regions of the New World. His associates in the great work were men of similar character.

III. THE FIELD AND THE LABOR.

1. The social conditions which the Fathers found in this new field of the Church, were much at variance with those which they had left in Germany, a fact which well deserves to be noticed.

(*a*) In Germany, the people were living in congregations, which as such were identical with the local civil communalities. In this country, the people were dispersed over large territories and, even in larger towns, the organization of Lutheran congregations had hardly begun.

(*b*) In Germany, the people were in their respective localities a homogeneous mass as to ethnology, politics, language, habits, religious confession and forms of worship. In this country, the different elements from various parts of Europe, and also from various provinces of Germany, were promiscuously inter-located.

(*c*) In Germany, in the various localities, a system of religious instruction and a certain Church tradition had been established. Things were generally in a settled condition. In this country, the reverse of all this was prevalent, and out of the chaos the churchly cosmos had to be formed.

(*a*) In Germany, the lines separating the various denominations were well defined, and, in social life, well preserved. In this country, the various Christian parties were greatly intermixed with one another in all places; intermarriages between the adherents of the various confessions were the order of the day.

2. To the practical mind of the fathers, it appeared self-evident that these peculiar social conditions could not be changed; that to gather the Lutherans in separate localities, and there to organize them in congregations after the manner of Zinzendorf's Moravian Missions, was out of the question, and that any effort made in this direction, would, in the end, prove abortive.

3. There can be no doubt that Pietism—which was not under all circumstances a distortion of Christianity or of Lutheranism, but had in its best form been a healthful reaction of practical Christianity against ultra-theoretical, dogmatical orthodoxism, and an indispensable element in the progress of religious life in Germany— had done its share in preparing the Fathers for the work in store for them in the New World. Probably without Pietism they might never have crossed the ocean.

4. Under those peculiar circumstances, wherein they were placed and had to do the work of the Master, a sense of wisdom and duty directed them, in their pastoral activity and in preaching, to avoid offensive polemics, which would have produced strife in families and hatred among neighbors, without being convincing or conducive to practical piety.

5. Whilst the interests of the Lutheran Church and her peculiar features in doctrines and in forms of worship lay near to their heart, they acknowledged no barrier in the shape of language, nationality, color or social position.

6. They found it necessary for the promotion of the Church and her work, for the maintenance and well-being of her congregations and of her people, to bring about an organization of the Church on this new territory. To this organization they gave not the polity of the Presbyterian Church, but the essential features of a Presbyterian form of government, being convinced that under the circumstances with which they had to deal, such a form of government might be best calculated to promote the interests of the Church and to produce a desirable, active sympathy, between the pastors and the people. In this they made use of those liberal principles, peculiar to the Lutheran Church. And in this measure,

to bring the laity into active co-operation with the clergy in the government of Church and congregation, they carried out one of the "Pia Desideria" of Spener, one of the principles whereby the Evangelical Church opposes Romanism, and one of the features of Christianity as such.

7. That our Fathers' were far from radical ideas in the administration of Church-affairs, may be gathered also from this—that they carefully guarded against any obliteration of the distinction between the "ordo Clericus" and "ordo Laicus" and practically acknowledged, that the theologians and pastors of the Church had a sphere of duty peculiar to them, and that their special interests and rights should be properly taken care of. Therefore, also, special "Ministerial sessions" at the meetings of Synod.

8. The principle, that the Church has to exercise *discipline* toward her members, was not only theoretically acknowledged, but it was practically executed, a fact for which we could gather many striking proofs from the records of those times. The question of the incompatibility of Lutheran Church-membership with the membership of so-called secret societies, which now deservedly claims attention, was at that time not agitated, such societies then not prevailing as they now do.

9. The education of the children of the Church, and especially their proper religious instruction, was one of the great cares of those Fathers. They not only considered regular catechisation of the young as one of the most essential parts of pastoral activity, but they also endeavored to establish, wherever possible, parochial schools, and made the education of teachers one of their special cares. Schools from which religious instruction should be excluded, belonged to the things of which those godly men had no conception. The Sunday-schools of our times were not known then.

10. They considered it as essentially belonging to the pastoral office, to take a lively interest in the spiritual welfare of the individuals entrusted to their care. We see them not only in an edifying intercourse with the families and visiting the sick and the dying, but we also observe, that they endeavor to make themselves sure of the spiritual condition of every individual, especially before admission to the Lord's Supper. They deeply felt the responsibility of him who admits and of those who are admitted.

11. Of the character of the sermons of the Fathers the "Hallische

Nachrichten" give us sufficient information. There we find here and there introduced the leading thoughts, often the skeletons of sermons, preached at various occasions. We receive the impression that the preaching of those men was less doctrinal than practical; thoroughly biblical and calculated to edify the faithful and to lead sinners to repentance and to faith in Christ, whilst it was in strict harmony with the confessional character of our Church.

12. Much stress did the Fathers lay upon Pastoral Conferences, where they discussed biblical, doctrinal and practical questions, took counsel on difficult cases, appertaining to the pastoral office and experience, encouraged one another to faithfulness in the service, entrusted to them, and comforted one another under the heavy trials of their pastoral life. Those conferences they found excellent means to improve their own usefulness in the service of the Lord.

13. Taken all in all, those Fathers were very far from giving the Lutheran Church, as they organized it on this new field of labor, a form and character in any essential point different from what the Lutheran Church was in the Old World, and especially in Germany. They retained not only the old doctrinal standards, but also the old traditional elements and forms of worship; the Church-year with its great festivals, its Gospel and Epistle lessons, the Liturgy, the rite of Confirmation, preparatory service for the Lord's Supper, connected with the Confession of sins and with the Absolution.

14. It would be unjust, and would leave this short delineation of the Lutheranism of those founders of the Lutheran Church-organization in this country quite incomplete, if we would not refer to the manifestation of divine grace in their missionary spirit, personal devotion, energetic conscientiousness, self-sacrificing zeal and power of endurance, wherewith they gave themselves to the work to which Providence had called them. Of this their spiritual endowment the reports testify, which are embodied in the "Hallische Nachrichten," those invaluable annals of that great foundation period of the Lutheran Chnrch of this country. And to this, the Church itself, as they left it, when Christ called them to their eternal reward, stood as a lasting monument.

15. The founding and raising of our Church in this country was during the last century evidently a *missionary work*. Those Fathers were indeed Missionaries in the literal sense of the term. As such, they came from a far-off land and had to carry on their labors in

this new and extensive field, under very peculiar and trying circumstances. That this extraordinary state of things should have exercised no influence at all upon them, would seem very unnatural. They had to miss much which in their native country gave charms and strength to pastoral life. They felt the need of the sympathy of those also, who, though of another flock, served the same Master; and whilst never forgetting the distinctive character of Lutheranism, they cherished pleasant relations and intercourse here and there with pastors and laymen of other denominations, and at various and solemn occasions gave and received signs of mutual confidence and esteem. But they decisively and wisely resisted every undue influence from outside, by which Lutheranism might have been placed in jeopardy.

IV. CONCLUSION.

1. The doctrinal position of those Fathers was unmistakably *Lutheran*, in the sense in which Lutheranism is historically known, and is something individual and distinct, and as such stands in opposition to Romanism on the one hand, and to Zwingli, Calvin and all other so-called Protestant parties on the other.

2. To this testify among other things the following facts:

(*a*) Those Fathers were admitted to the ministry on condition of their own declaration that they were in harmony with the Confessio Augustana Invariata, and with all the other Symbolical Books of the Lutheran Church.

(*b*) They demanded of those whom they admitted to the sacred office, the same condition. The declaration had to be given in writing.

(*c*) They strenuously opposed any one who did not prove faithful to his given declaration, whilst being in the ministry.

(*d*) They allowed no organization or constitutions of congregations, without demanding the acknowledgment of all the Symbolical Books of the Lutheran Church as the doctrinal basis.

(*e*) They preached and prayed in harmony with the Standards of the Church, and based the religious instruction of the young upon them, and especially upon Luther's Smaller Catechism.

(*f*) They understood and interpreted these Standards in the sense in which the founders of the Lutheran Church in the Sixteenth Century understood them.

3. Their Lutheranism did not differ from the Lutheran Orthodoxy of the preceding period, in the *matter of doctrine*, but to an extent in the *manner of applying it*. It was orthodoxy practically vitalized. They were less theoretical and polemical, than preceding generations. Whilst tolerant toward those of other convictions, they were, however, neither indifferent nor unionistically inclined, and never conformed Lutheranism to any other form of Christianity, though in their days the pressure in this direction was heavy. They actualized their own Lutheran convictions through a noble, exemplary life and service. Their Pietism was truly Lutheran piety, a warm-hearted, devout, active, practical Lutheranism.

4. Keeping in view the circumstances under which they had to labor, we are persuaded that just such men, such Lutherans, such pastors, were the proper men for the work, to which in those times a wise Providence had called them, and that men of another type would never have accomplished what they accomplished. It is worth while to consider, whether any other manner of Lutheranism will ever perform greater things, and establish the Church on a more lasting basis in this country, and better serve the cause of Christ. Knowing that as men they could err and did err, we praise God that through His grace He kept them in the true faith, and made them instruments to do much good, and to lay the proper foundation for the Lutheran Church in this Western hemisphere.

REMARKS OF REV. J. G. MORRIS, D. D., LL.D. (*General Synod.*)

Dr. Morris expressed his gratification with the valuable paper of Dr. Mann; but remarked, that of necessity some points of interest connected with the Lutheranism of the Fathers of our Church in this country, were omitted. Dr. Mann could not have condensed more facts into the time which he occupied. There was one matter, however, concerning which he desired to make inquiry. Many years ago he had accompanied a venerable clergyman, of the Ministerium of Pennsylvania, to a preparatory service before communion, held in what was then one of the most secluded parts of the territory of that Synod, and in one of its oldest congregations. When the time came for the confessional prayer, the pastor called upon an old lady, who, in a peculiarly shrill and piping tone, said the prescribed form. He desired to know whether this was a usual practice among the Fathers of our Church, or one which was simply occasional, and confined to certain localities.

REMARKS BY REV. W. J. MANN. (*General Council.*)

Dr. Mann replied that he was under the impression that it was frequently employed. A former sexton of his church had often spoken of it, and told him that for many years he had been assigned this part. The design of the custom was to avoid the awkwardness attending the two-fold position which the minister has otherwise to assume, first as the representative of the congregation of sinners, and then immediately afterward as the representative of God, granting and announcing forgiveness.

REMARKS OF REV. J. A. BROWN, D. D. (*General Synod.*)

Dr. Brown asked whether it was in accordance with sound Lutheranism for a woman to thus lead a congregation in prayer, in the presence of the pastor, and if so, what warrant could be had for forbidding women to teach in the Church.

REMARKS OF REV. W. J. MANN, D. D. (*General Council.*)

Dr. Mann replied that it would be perfectly proper for a woman to lead in such a prayer, in case there were no man present willing to do so. The case of teaching was not parallel. In the one case, the woman would stand in the place of the sinner, and as the representative of sinners, begging God for forgiveness; in the other, she would act as the mouth-piece of God.

REMARKS OF REV. J. G. MORRIS, D. D., LL.D. (*General Synod.*)

Dr. Morris said that there was another point to which he desired to refer. He would have been pleased to have heard something in Dr. Mann's paper, concerning the exchange of pulpits practiced by Mühlenberg, and some of the other Fathers, with ministers of the various English denominations.

The discussion that followed was almost conversational in form, and was participated in by Drs. Mann, Spaeth, Krauth, Brown, Seiss and Rev. Welden. It was argued, on the one side, that the preaching of Whitefield, and Rev. Peters of the Church of England, in Zion's Church, Philadelphia, was not to be understood as pulpit fellowship; that they did not preach by invitation of Lutheran ministers to Lutheran congregations, but that the church-edifice was simply granted them to conduct in it their own services for their own people. On the other side, it was urged that this explanation was not sufficient.

The remarks handed in by the speakers are as follows:

REMARKS OF REV. PROF. C. P. KRAUTH, D. D., LL.D.
(*General Council.*)

Dr. Krauth said that Dr. Mann had very properly said nothing of the "exchange of pulpits" the reciprocal giving and taking on the part of our Lutheran Fathers, as nothing equivalent to what now passes under that title was practiced by them. The Agenda shows beyond dispute that the Rule was that Lutheran altars were open to Lutheran communicants only. And the history of the time shows that the Rule, both theoretical and practical, was that Lutheran pulpits are for Lutheran ministers only. The exceptions were rare, were confined to extraordinary cases, and were believed to be in harmony with the Rule, as consistent, or, if you please, rigid Lutherans define it.

REMARKS OF REV. J. A. BROWN, D. D. (*General Synod.*)

The facts as they exist, and have in part been stated by Dr. Mann and the speakers who have followed him, leave no room to question that the early founders of Lutheranism in this country did cherish a liberal spirit and cultivate friendly relations with other evangelical denominations. There was an interchange of pulpits, and of other ministerial and ecclesiastical courtesies, which show that they recognized each other as belonging to the one "Holy Catholic Church." It is unnecessary to cite facts or to multiply proofs of this general statement. Take the case just mentioned of Rev. Peters of the Episcopal Church, officiating regularly on the day of the dedication of Zion Church, in that church; or of Rev. Whitefield, by invitation of the Ministerium, addressing the children in the Lutheran Church. It is simply ridiculous to say that the Church was given as a matter of courtesy for them to hold a service for themselves, but that it was no recognition or endorsement of their ministry. Would the advocates of exclusivism do the same thing to-day? or, if the friends of a more liberal and catholic policy were to repeat such acts of Muhlenberg and the Ministerium of Pennsylvania a century and a third ago, would they not be branded as unionistic, or wanting in loyalty to genuine Lutheranism? Were not complaints presented at the last meeting of the General Council for substantially the same conduct? Is it not well known that there is a sentiment prevailing in some quarters utterly adverse to any such recognition by the Lutheran Church of other denominations? There can be no difficulty, we think, in determining on which side Muhlenberg and his co-laborers are to be reckoned. Right or wrong, they are on the side of the liberal and tolerant Lutheranism, and those who seek to claim them as supporters of an exclusive and illiberal sectarianism can do so only by ignoring or denying the plainest and best authenticated facts. They were sound, conscientious, decided Lutherans—but did not refuse to recognize in a practical way others as brethren in the Lord and brethren in the ministry.

REMARKS OF REV. J. A. SEISS, D. D. (*General Council.*)

There is no advantage in slurring over facts. There were very great favors shown by the Patriarch Muhlenberg and his associates, to the celebrated Whitefield while in Philadelphia. He had invited that eminent minister to address the children of his congregation, which he also did in the presence of Muhlenberg and the Ministerium of Pennsylvania. The statement of the personal friendship and mutual regard between Muhlenberg and Rev. Mr. Peters of the

Episcopal Church, did not give the whole case. It is a matter of record that during the solemnities of the consecration of Zion Church, in this city, Rev. Peters was invited by the authorities of said church to occupy the pulpit, and to preach one of the sermons. Rev. Peters not only accepted the invitation, but his sermon was requested for publication, and officially given to the public in printed form by the officers of Zion Church. The speaker had himself seen and read a copy of it. If not mistaken in his recollection, he had recently also read a note of these facts in the "Hallische Nachrichten." These were circumstances of some moment, and should be distinctly brought out as they were.[1]

---

[1] "Hallische Nachrichten," p. 1122: "Oct. 15th, the clergy and deputies to Synod began to assemble. In the afternoon arrangements were made, etc., and it was also considered whether we should not invite Mr. Whitefield, and the two friendly ministers of the Episcopal Church, to be present on Monday and Tuesday, at the examination of the children of the Church. In the evening, Dr. Wrangel and I called on Mr. Whitefield *and invited him in the name of the Ministerium*, and also the rector of the High (Episcopal) Church, who was present with Mr. Whitefield."

Idem, p. 1128: "Oct. 18th, at 10 o'clock in the morning, we went to the church, and took the children with us. By degrees the following named persons arrived: Duchee and Inglis, of the Episcopal Church, Dr. Finley, President of the Presbyterian College in Jersey; the Elder Tennant, a Presbyterian minister from Newark; also Mr. Whitefield, and a large number of English friends. Mr. Whitefield ascended the pulpit, made a powerful prayer, turned to the children, and made a discourse about the pious children in the Old and New Testaments, and some later examples in his own experience, and then spoke to parents on their duties. The children were then examined by Dr. Wrangel and myself, and we closed with a church song. The preachers and deputies dined in the school-house, and the elder Mr. Tennant presided, and gratified us with edifying discourse. After dinner the Ministerium proceeded with its business."

Idem, p. 850: "On the 9th and 10th of August, I had a visit in Providence from the Rev. Mr. Richard Peters. In the morning he attended our German service, and expressed himself much pleased, and in the afternoon he preached an English sermon, very sound and edifying, to a large audience."

Idem, p. 908: "Friday, the 21st of May, I set out early on my journey to Philadelphia. About noon I reached Mr. R., who joyfully told me, how yesterday, Ascension Day, the Rev. Provost Wrangel, and the new Swedish minister, Mr. Wicksel, and the Reformed minister, Mr. Slatter, had preached in German and English in the new church, to large congregations, excellent and

REMARKS OF REV. C. F. WELDEN. (*General Council.*)

The invitation to Dr. Peters to preach in Zion's Church, and the special recognition of the sermon by the corporation of the Church, do not warrant the inference either of indifference to pure and wholesome doctrine, as set forth in our confessions, or of a weak and subservient policy, on the part of the Fathers of our Church in America, to the leading denominations around them. The Dr. Peters referred to, and so highly respected by our Fathers, was then a rector, not of the modern Protestant Episcopal, but of the Anglican Protestant Church, under the colonial government of Great Britain. The Anglican Church in Pennsylvania, under the supremacy of the Georges of Hanover, assumed and professed that there existed no difference between it and the Lutheran Churches of Germany, of Denmark, and of Sweden, save the differences of nationality and language; and this profession was believed and accepted by our Lutheran Fathers. The Fathers of the Lutheran Church in America cannot therefore be chargeable with looseness or inconsistency, as regards the standards of truth confessed and practiced by the Lutheran Church; much less can the proceedings in Zion's German Evangelical Lutheran Church on the occasion

---

edifying sermons. I arrived in Philadelphia in the evening at 6 o'clock, having baptized several children on the way."

Idem, pp. 1247-48: In the account of the consecration of Zion's Church, which occurred on the occasion of the meeting of the Synod, it is recorded, that in consideration of favors received from the English Academy, "the Church council resolved to invite the Rev. Richard Peters, commissioner of the High (Episcopal) Church and president of the Academy, who had always proved himself a friend of the Lutheran preachers and congregations, to preach an English sermon in Zion's Church on Monday, June 26, at which the Governor, the whole of the clergy of the High (Episcopal) Church, with their vestryman, etc., were present as invited guests. Mr. Duchee opened by reading the English prayers, the Pro-rector of the Academy made a suitable prayer for the occasion, the commissioner Peters delivered an excellent sermon on the Angels' Song, Luke ii. In conclusion Mr. Muhlenberg, in the English language, in the name of the congregation, thanked the honorable assemblage for their friendship and good will, and for doing the newly-erected church the honor to conduct a service in it."

referred to, be construed as favoring the loose and almost indiscriminate interchange of pulpits with divergent denominations, now prevalent in Protestant sects.

In evidence of this, let it be remembered, that never having had a resident bishop in North America, this branch of the Anglican Church becoming widowed, and being unable to maintain her organization of Episcopal Government without a bishop, in consequence of the rupture with the mother country, looked wistfully to the Lutheran Church in Denmark for the consecration of a bishop for the United States. Further, that until a much later period the same professions continued to be made on the part of Episcopalians, and that under these representations all of the Swedish Lutheran Churches of Pennsylvania and Delaware have become absorbed in what has now come to be the modern Protestant Episcopal Church in the United States.

DR. KRAUTH'S REMARKS AND NOTE.

In connection with Dr. Seiss's statement, Dr. Krauth said that he was entirely familiar with the general facts of the case, and that on that knowledge he based and repeated his assertion that there was nothing in the early practice of our fathers in this country fairly parallel with or justifying what is now carried on under the name of "Exchange of pulpits."

In explanation of his meaning he would here add

(*i*.) That the relations between the Lutheran Church and the Church of England were exceptional, and that the idea prevailed upon both sides, and was sustained by a great number of acts on the part of both, that the two churches were in fundamental accord. The conviction was general, and was acted on, that there was no difference but that of language. Rev. Peter Muhlenberg was ordained to the Lutheran ministry, by an English Bishop. Many things showed—as Prof. Jacobs has demonstrated by his Article read before the Diet—that our Church looked to a probable absorption into the Episcopal, as it passed out of its German life.

(*ii.*) The official invitations noted in the "Hallische Nachrichten" were very few, were confined to clergymen of the Church of England, and were given under very peculiar circumstances. The very care and solemnity of the invitations, mark the fact that they were exceptional. Whitefield was a clergyman of the Church of England, in some respects an evangelist of forgotten or ignored doctrines of the gospel, a witness excluded from many pulpits of his own Church because of his earnestness in preaching the truth, in some sense a martyr. This invested him with interest in the eyes of our Fathers, and his love to the Lutheran Church, and his services to it, made him very dear. Dr. Peters, a clergyman also of the Church of England, had shown great interest in our Church, and had aided it with his influence; the service which he held was the Episcopal service, and the whole occasion one in which the English community had an opening for showing its interest in our Church. It was no case of "exchange of pulpits," between denominations regarded as antagonistic, but a recognition of special favors granted and of special love shown by those who were believed to differ from us in little but language. That the sermon was published simply strengthens this view of the case.

(*iii.*) The allowing of the use of a building, when Lutherans did not use it, at a period especially when both buildings and preaching were rare, to those who had helped to erect it, or the use at different hours of the day of the pulpits of Union churches, does not involve the principle here in discussion.

Despair before the English had quite as much to do as obstinacy about the German, with some of the most fatal experiences of our Church in America. The conviction that our Church differed in little but language from the Episcopal, that it needed no future in English, led, as it became Anglicized, to a large absorption of it into the Episcopal Church. Had there been no fresh immigrations, our Church would have been lost in America. As it was, the honest fallacy about the two Churches robbed us of vitality and hope, and cost us hundreds of thousands of members. It led to a torpor in the matter of language on the English side, which, with the persistence in the matter of language on the German side, would, but for God's gracious providence, have left us no future in America. It swept away the posterity of our pilgrim fathers, whose toils and blood had been designed to open a new home for the Church they loved; it took away our churches; it obliterated the traces of one of our noblest nationalities, and made over some of our grandest historic treasures, to form part of the theatrical properties of the so-called "Swedish (Episcopal) Churches." We, who are in what was the future of that past, dare not read back into it, what only the future could reveal, and make our knowledge a ground for condemning our fathers. They acted in the light of their own time, soberly and prayerfully; and it is an insult, without excuse, to their memory, to quote them as helping to support that loose, sectarian practice, so popular in our land, and in our time, under the name of "exchange of pulpits."

Adjourned.

SIXTH SESSION.

DECEMBER 28TH, 1877, 7½ P. M.

After prayer by the Rev. F. C. C. Kaehler, of Phœnixville, Pa., at the request of the author, the President of the Diet read the next paper.

THE DIVINE AND HUMAN FACTORS IN THE CALL TO THE MINISTERIAL OFFICE, ACCORDING TO THE OLDER LUTHERAN AUTHORITIES.

BY REV. G. DIEHL, D. D., FREDERICK, MD.

Augsburg Confession, Article V. "For the obtaining of this Faith, the ministry of teaching the Gospel, and the administering of Sacraments, was instituted." Augsburg Confession, Article XIV. "Concerning Ecclesiastical Orders (Church Government), they teach that no man should publicly in the Church, teach, or administer the Sacraments, except he be regularly called (without a regular call)."

THE ministry of the Word and Sacraments is a distinct office in the Church, instituted by God Himself; and not a merely human regulation.

As such it is separate from the universal priesthood of believers. The opponents of Luther charged him with teaching in his writings, on the priesthood of believers, that all Christians had a commission publicly to teach the Gospel; and thus doing away with the ministerial office. In entering on our subject, it may contribute to a clearer view of the scriptural doctrine concerning the pastoral office, to define the universal priesthood of believers.

The passages bearing most directly on this point, are, 1 Peter ii. 9, "Ye are a chosen generation, a royal priesthood, an holy nation, a peculiar people; that ye should show forth the praises of Him who hath called you out of darkness into His marvellous light," and Rev. i. 5, 6, "Unto Him that loved us, and washed us from our sins in His own blood, and hath made us kings and priests unto God and His Father; to Him be glory and dominion forever and ever. Amen."

Taking the term priesthood to indicate the teaching of divine truth, and the offering of sacrifices—its usual sense—there is no difficulty in its application to all believers. Christians are commissioned and required to impart religious instruction to those around them, and to offer spiritual sacrifices to God. Every pious man is to teach in his own house the Word of God to his children, according to the divine command, given by Moses (Deut. vi. 7), "Thou shalt teach them diligently unto thy children." The apostle says (1 Peter ii. 5), "Ye are built up a spiritual house, a holy priesthood, to offer up spiritual sacrifices acceptable to God by Jesus Christ."

These sacrifices consist in prayer, thanksgiving, beneficence, the devotion of the entire person to Christ with the crucifixion of our evil nature, and the offering up of life in martyrdom.

That prayer is, in the scriptural sense, a spiritual sacrifice, is evident from such declarations as (Ps. cxli. 2) "Let my prayer be set forth before Thee as incense, and the lifting up of my hands as the evening sacrifice;" (Rev. v. 8) "Golden vials full of odors, which are the prayers of saints;" (Rev. viii. 4) "And the smoke of the incense, which came with the prayers of the saints, ascended up before God out of the angel's hand."

Thanksgiving is set down among spiritual sacrifices in Heb. xiii. 15, "By him, therefore, let us offer the sacrifice of praise to God continually, the fruit of our lips, giving thanks to His name." Beneficence is so represented in Phil. iv. 18, "I am full, having received the things which were sent by you, an odor of a sweet smell, a sacrifice acceptable, well pleasing to God." Again in Heb. xiii. 16, "But to do good and to communicate forget not; for with such sacrifices God is well pleased." The devotion of the energies of the entire person with the crucifixion of the body of sin is represented as a spiritual offering by Paul in Rom. xii. 1, "Present your bodies a living sacrifice, holy, acceptable unto God, which is your reasonable service." And the confession of Christ in martyrdom is so viewed by the apostle in Phil. ii. 17, "If I be offered upon the sacrifice of your faith;" and in 2 Tim. iv. 6, "I am now ready to be offered." Thus all true Christians are spiritual priests, offering the spiritual sacrifices of praise, prayers and holy living.

Augustine in commenting on Psalm xciv., says: "If we are the temple of God, our souls are *the altar* of God. What is the *sacrifice?* We lay the offering on the altar when we praise God."

In addition to teaching the truths of religion in conversations with neighbors, and in family instruction, the offerings of prayer, thanksgiving, alms-deeds, the devotion of all talents and energies to the divine service, and the confessing of Christ in martyrdom, there is on the part of all believers, who through baptism have been brought into covenant relations with God and sacramentally sealed, a capacity, capability, or eligibility (fähigkeit, Luther calls it), to the pastoral office. But this eligibility gives no authority to discharge the functions of the office until one is regularly called of God and invested with the ministry by the Church. As the eligibility of all native-born male citizens of the United States over forty years of age to the office of President guaranteed by the constitution, gives no American the right to the honor and power of that office, unless elected to the same by the people, so the "fähigkeit" of all baptized believers contended for by Luther, gives to no one a commission to teach publicly in the assemblies of God's people and administer the Sacraments, unless he be also called of God and chosen by the Church.

That the public preaching of the Gospel and the administering of the Sacraments is not entrusted to all pious members of the Church is manifest from the words of the apostle, "Are *all* apostles? Are *all* prophets? Are *all* teachers?" (1 Cor. xii. 29.)

We must ever distinguish between the ministry of the Word and Sacraments, and the universal commission which all the pious receive in their admission to the communion of the Church, by which it is demanded that they should bring to God the devotion of their persons and the offerings of worship; to take care the Word of God dwell richly among them (Col. iii. 16); that they teach and admonish one another in psalms, hymns and spiritual songs with grace in their hearts to the Lord (Eph. v. 19); and that they comfort one another with these words (1 Thes. iv. 18). The one is a specific office ordained of God. The other is a universal privilege and duty. To the one certain persons are regularly called and formally invested. The other is the common right and obligation of all Christians.

The Divine Factor in Conferring the Office.

As God Himself has ordained a specific office for the preaching of His word and the administration of His Sacraments, so *He calls* those who are to be entrusted with the commission.

Jehovah Himself at first discharged the functions of religious teacher, when He proclaimed to Adam and Eve the law forbidding them to eat of the tree of the knowledge of good and evil (Gen. ii. 17), and when He proclaimed the promise of salvation to the disconsolate spirits of that fallen pair, in the prediction that the seed of the woman should bruise the serpent's head (Gen. iii. 15).

He then transferred the teaching office to men; to Adam first, and then to the patriarchs. These were the teachers and priests of the Church when the Church was confined to a single household, to a tribe, or to several tribes. He afterwards called Moses to the work of the ministry; and ordained the Aaronic and Levitical priesthood, through which, for many centuries, under the old covenant, He perpetuated the sacred office. Under the Mosaic dispensation He sent also many prophets, each one receiving his call and commission directly from heaven.

In ushering in the New Dispensation this great office devolved upon the eternal Son. "God, who at sundry times and in divers manners spake in time past unto the fathers by the prophets, hath in these last days spoken unto us by His Son, whom He hath appointed heir of all things, by whom also He made the worlds" (Heb. i. 1, 2); Christ the Eternal Word (John i. 1); the Light of the World (John viii. 12); the Way, the Truth and the Life (John xiv. 6); the Prophet promised, when the Father said, "I will put my words in His mouth, and He shall speak unto them all that I shall command" (Deut. xviii. 18, 19); to Whom Peter said, "Lord, to whom shall we go? Thou hast the words of eternal life" (John vi. 68, 69); Christ the Eternal Word, for the space of three years, discharged the functions of the holy ministry, as it had never been before, and has not since. "Never man spake like this man" (John vii. 46).

The twelve apostles and the seventy who were sent forth to teach, (Matt. x) were selected by Christ Himself through a special, distinct and personal call. This was the beginning of the fulfillment of the promise that shepherds and teachers should be given to the New Testament Church: "The Lord gave the word; great was the company of those that published it" (Ps. lxviii. 11); "And I will give you pastors according to Mine heart, which shall feed you with knowledge and understanding" (Jer. iii. 15).

When Christ commissioned the apostles and their successors He said : " All power is given unto Me in heaven and in earth. Go ye therefore and teach all nations, baptizing them in the name of the Father, and of the Son, and of the Holy Ghost; teaching them to observe all things whatsoever I have commanded you (Matt. xxviii. 18–20).

That ministers are called into the sacred office and clothed with pastoral functions by God is affirmed by the apostles. "God hath set some in the church, first apostles, secondarily prophets, thirdly teachers, after that miracles; then gifts of healings, helps, governments, diversities of tongues" (1 Cor. xii. 28). God hath given to us the ministry of reconciliation (2 Cor. v. 18). "And He gave some, apostles; and some, prophets ; and some, evangelists; and some, pastors and teachers, for the perfecting of the saints, for the work of the ministry, for the edifying of the body of Christ: till we all come in the unity of the faith, and of the knowledge of the Son of God, unto a perfect man, unto the measure of the stature of the fullness of Christ" (Eph. iv. 11, 13).

From these passages it is clear that the commission comes from Christ. The message to be delivered is His. The overture to be made by these ambassadors is His ; and He selects the agents or instruments by whom his law is to be explained, His ordinances administered and His redemption offered to men.

The fact that the public teachers of the Christian religion are directly called and commissioned from heaven, is set forth in those parables of the Saviour which describe the work of the servants of the Great Householder—the royal Lord of the kingdom of heaven. In the parable of the tares, *the Lord* commanded the servants not " to gather up the tares," lest they " root up also the wheat with them" (Matt. xiii. 29). The commission here is directly from the Master. In the parable of the laborers in the vineyard, *the Lord* of the vineyard went out early in the morning, and repeatedly at different hours, " to hire laborers into his vineyard" (Matt xx. 1). This call was personal, distinct, special. In the parable of the Great Householder, who let out to husbandmen his vineyard, planted and hedged, with its tower and winepress, it was *the Lord* who sent his servants to receive a rental of fruit from the tenants. The agents were selected, commissioned, and sent by the Proprietor. (Matt. xxi. 33-37.) In the parable of the fruitless fig tree, the dresser of the vineyard is clothed with the authority and functions of his office immediately by the Lord. (Luke xiii. 6-8.)

That ministers are called of God and equipped from above, is implied in the exhortation of the Saviour to His followers to pray for them. "Pray ye, therefore, the Lord of the harvest that he will send forth laborers into his harvest" (Matt. ix. 38).

We read in the Acts of the Apostles that when the first ministers, after those selected by Christ Himself, were to be chosen in the Christian Church, the assembled congregation besought the Lord to guide them in making the selection, thus recognizing the necessity of a call from above to the investiture of a genuine minister. In filling the vacancy in the apostolic college caused by the apostasy of Judas, the Church "prayed, and said, Thou Lord which knowest the hearts of all men, show us whether of these two *Thou* hast chosen, that he may take part of this ministry and apostleship" (Acts i. 24, 25). To ascertain the divine choice "they gave forth their lots: and the lot fell upon Matthias." The divine response to the prayer was unmistakable. The call of the Apostle Paul was still more strikingly from the Master. It was by an audible voice, in a direct personal address, amid supernatural appearances and a distinct announcement that the One who spoke and called His servant into the ministry was Christ the Lord.

This truth that men can be scripturally invested with the ministerial office only by God and Christ is distinctly and forcibly stated by the recognized early Lutheran authorities. It is taught at least by implication in the Smalcald Articles. Luther says: "At first the apostles were chosen, not through human instrumentality, but directly by Jesus Christ and God. Others were called into the pastoral office by God, but through men" (Kirchenpost, St. Andrew's day). Again: "I hope that all believers, and all who call themselves Christians, will certainly know that the ministerial state was instituted and established by God" (Sermon on educating children). Again: "The laying on of hands is not a human statute, but God makes and ordains ministers, and it is not the priest (pfarrherr) who absolves thee, but the mouth and hand of the minister is the mouth and hand of God" (Com. Gen. xxviii. 17). By laying on of hands, Luther here evidently means investing a man with the holy office. He elsewhere says repeatedly, that the laying on of hands is merely a Church usage and not indispensable to ordination. For instance, "while the ceremony of laying on of hands is something (impressive and proper), it is only a customary usage to call persons into the ministry of the Church." In saying, therefore, that the laying on of hands is not a human statute (menschensatzung), he merely affirms the divine institution and ordination of the ministry; the ceremony uniformly practiced, although not essential to the validity of the office, being substituted, by a figure of speech, for the creation of the office itself. Again Luther says, after quoting Titus i. 5-7, "Whoever believes that the Holy Spirit here speaks through Paul, must know that this is a divine appointment and ordinance, that in every city or town, there should be one or more pastors" (Disc. on Abuses of the Mass, 1522). Chemnitz says: "That the ministry of the Word and Sacraments was instituted by the Son of God, is established beyond doubt. This is evident from the promise that God would approve the appointment of those who are called through the voice of the Church; being made overseers over the flock by the Holy Ghost (Acts xx. 28); and from the promise that God would bestow His grace and gifts to those called, whereby they should be able righty to fulfill the functions of the office; breathing upon them the Holy Ghost (John xx. 22); giving them understanding of the Scripture; abiding with them (Matt. xxviii. 20); giving them mouth and wisdom (Luke xxi. 15); the spirit of the Father speaking through them (Matt. x. 19, 20). It is proven also by the promise that increase shall be given to the planting and watering by pastors, which will result in the calling and enlightening, the repentance and faith, the conversion and sanctification of the believers."

In perfect accord with these statements are the declarations of Gerhard and others. On this point the testimony of Lutheran theologians is uniform. Not a dissenting voice is heard.

The divine agency in the calling of men is thus so fully set forth in Scripture and so distinctly recognized in the standard authorities of the Church, that we can appreciate the force of the language when God in addressing the incumbents of the sacred office says, "I have given the priest's office unto you, as a gift of the Lord to do service" (Num. xviii. 6). Not only is the office given but the men are chosen. "He separated the tribe of Levi to bear the ark of the covenant of Jehovah and to stand before Him and minister unto Him." To the prophet He said, "I have made thee a watchman unto Israel, therefore hear the word at My mouth and give them warning." "Thou shalt stand before Me. And if thou take forth the precious from the vile, thou shalt be as My mouth. And I will make thee unto this people a fenced brasen wall. For I am with thee to save thee and to deliver thee, saith the Lord" (Jer. xv. 19-20). "I have set watchmen upon thy walls, O Jerusalem, which shall never hold their peace" (Isa. lxii. 6). "I have ordained thee a prophet unto the nations" (Jer. i. 5). In the intercession with which the Saviour closed His ministry on the earth, He said, "As thou hast sent Me, so have I also sent them into the world" (John xvii. 18). He said also to His ministers, "I have chosen you." And the great Apostle said, "Let a man so account of us as the ministers of Christ, and stewards of the mysteries of God" (1 Cor. iv. 1). "No man taketh this honor unto himself but he that is called of God, as was Aaron" (Heb. v. 4).

The language of the poet is not therefore extravagant:

> "He alone his office holds
> Immediately from God; from God receives
> Authority, and is to none but God
> Amenable * * * his call,
> His consecration, his anointing, all
> Are inward; in the conscience heard and felt,
> Thus by Jehovah chosen and ordained,
> To take into his charge the souls of men;
> And for his trust to answer at the day
> Of Judgment—great plenipotent of Heaven
> And representative of God on earth.
> * * * Burning with love to souls
> Unquenchable, and mindful still of his
> Great charge and vast responsibility,
> High in the temple of the living God,
> He stands amidst the people and declares
> Aloud the truth, the whole revealed truth,
> Ready to seal it with his blood."

The Human Factor.

The divine agency in investing men with the sacred office, since the age of miracles is past, although as real, is not so immediate and direct as it was in the call of the prophets. The manner and circumstances are different now. No angelic appearance in the flame; no burning bush; no heavenly voice from the midst of the flame of fire, calling the subject by name; no audible utterance, "thou shalt say unto the children of Israel, I AM hath sent me unto you" (Ex. iii. 14); not as Moses was called; not as Paul was; not as Isaiah and Jeremiah and Ezekiel and Daniel and Elijah. God does not now speak in audible sounds to those who are called. He does not call them by name. He employs no miraculous circumstances. There is no communication by angels; no supernatural visions; no heaven-inspired dreams by which men are clearly informed of the divine vocation. They are called and clothed with the functions of the ministry by other means. The call comes from heaven but it must be recognized by the Church. By the Divine Spirit the Church is moved to ratify the work of heaven. The Church in the organization of a single congregation, or in an association of individual congregations, in a Synod, Council or Conference, must consent to clothe the candidate with ministerial functions. The flock must call him before he can feed the flock.

In the human portion of the work there are two parties. It is not supposable that the Holy Spirit would work conviction in the minds of the members of a Church, that a particular person is divinely called to preach the Gospel without operating at the same time upon the mind of the subject of that call, producing a similar conviction that he is designated by the Great Head of the Church to be a religious teacher. The same divine agent that called the prophets in ways so manifest, and by speech so distinct, as to produce absolute certainty in their convictions, does now, in ways less marvellous, and circumstances less imposing, produce a similar conviction in the mind of every man whose ministry heaven has authenticated.

The instrument employed by the spirit of God in the calling ministers, as in conversion and sanctification, is the truth. Some portion of divine truth, or some aspects of the great Christian system, are vividly impressed on the soul. It may be that the youth who is about to be divinely invested with the high functions of the holy office, is led by the illumination of the Spirit to view the great harvest field, ripe for the sickle, and an overpowering impression rests on his soul that he should enter as one of the reapers. He may have so vivid a view of the millions who are perishing for lack of knowledge, as to lead him to the resolution to become to some of those millions a religious guide. The truth impressed by the divine spirit on the mind may be the value of the soul;—honors, riches, power, all the treasures of earth, are nothing in comparison, and the young man is moved by that consideration to devote his life and energies to the work of saving souls. In looking at Gethsemane and Calvary, his mind may be so illumined as to see something of that unspeakable love and mercy, until all his faculties are moved, his heart melted, his soul roused, and the resolution rises up to spend all his energies in proclaiming a Saviour's love. Whatever portion of truth, or whatever aspect of it, is employed by God as the instrument of the illumination, the conviction and the resolution, it is in this way that men are called. It is by a voice in the soul. God speaks; but it is to the inner spirit. It is a direct transaction between Christ and a redeemed man.

But when the candidate for holy orders gives expression to his convictions, and announces to others his inner call, the Church must be satisfied that there is no delusion in his mind; that it is not a fanatical impulse or transient emotion; that it is not the promptings of selfish ambition; but that the call is genuine, that it is a voice from heaven. The motives prompting the youth to make application for ordination must be inquired into, and the character of the feelings he has expressed. Other things must also be learned with reference to his fitness for the office. Has he the essential qualifications? Is he really pious? Has he good sense, sound judgment, correct taste? Is he possessed of gentlemanly instincts and a high sense of honor? Is he gifted with intellect and power of emotion? Has he the requisite physical constitution and a good personal presence? Has he voice and elocution? Has he mental training and stores of knowledge? Has he sobriety of character and dignity of demeanor? Has he such social qualities as will fit him for pastoral relations and pastoral work?

The investigation and decision of these questions is a part of the Church's work. In no service should the Church more fervently implore the divine guidance, than in deciding the question, whether an applicant for ministerial authority has been called by the Holy Spirit to preach the Gospel. A satisfactory conclusion having been reached that the candidate has the higher spiritual and divine credentials, his own deep impressions being corroborated by the possession of the essential qualifications for the office, the Church has a divine commission to invest him with ministerial functions.

This authority is involved in the Church's spiritual priesthood, and in the possession of the keys of the kingdom of heaven. (Matt. xvi. 19, 20.)

The Smalcald Articles teach, "The keys are an office and power of the Church given by Christ to bind and to loose sins, not only enormous and manifest, but also subtle and secret sins." Art. VII.

"For wherever the Church is, there indeed is the command to preach the Gospel. For this reason the churches must retain the authority to call, to elect and ordain ministers. And this authority is a privilege which God has given especially to the Church; and it cannot be taken away from the Church by any human power, as Paul testifies (Eph. iv. 8, 11, 12), "When He ascended up on high, He led captivity captive, and gave gifts unto men." And among these gifts, which belong to the Church, he enumerates pastors and teachers; and adds that these were given for the edifying of the Church. Wherefore it follows that wherever there is a true Church there is also the power to elect and ordain ministers." "To this point the declarations of Christ pertain, which show that the keys were given to the whole Church, and not to some particular persons; as the Scripture saith, 'Where two or three are gathered together in My name, there am I in the midst of them' (Matt. xviii. 20)."

"Finally this is also confirmed by the declaration of Peter, 'Ye are a royal priesthood" (1 Peter ii. 9). These words relate specially to the true Church, which, because it alone has the priesthood, must also have the power to choose and ordain ministers."

"The common usages of the Church likewise prove this; for in former times the people elected clergymen and bishops; then the bishops living in or near the same place came and confirmed the elected bishop, by the laying on of hands; and at that time, the ordination was nothing else but this approbation." (Appendix to Smalcald Articles.)

Melanchthon says: "God instituted and commanded the pastoral office, and annexed to it glorious promises; 'The Gospel is the power of God unto salvation to all that believe' (Rom. i. 16). 'My word that goeth forth out of my mouth shall not return unto me void, but shall accomplish that which I please'" (Isaiah lv. 11).

"The Church has the command of God to appoint preachers and deacons. While this is very precious, we know that God will preach and work through men, and those who have been elected by man" (Apol., Art. 13).

The Augsburg Confession says, "This power of the keys is put in execution only by teaching or preaching the Gospel, and administering the Sacraments, either to many or to single individuals, in accordance with their call; for thereby not only corporal things, but eternal, are granted, as an eternal righteousness, the Holy Ghost, life everlasting. These things cannot be got but by the ministry of the Word and the Sacraments" (Art. 28).

Luther says, "It is God's will that we go and hear the Gospel from those who preach it."

Chemnitz says, "It is true that God begins, works, increases and carries forward, by His power, operation, incitement, and inspiration, whatever appertains to calling, enlightening, conversion, repentance, faith, renewal, in short, whatever belongs to the work of our salvation; but God had determined, according to His declared counsel, that He will accomplish this, not by the infusion of new and special revelations, enlightenments and movements (tractatibus) in the souls of men, without the use of means, but through the external ministry of the Word. This office, however, He did not entrust to angels, that the appearance of them should be sought and expected; but to men did He commit the ministry of reconciliation; and He wills that through these ministers the voice of the Gospel shall be sounded. Not every believer is allowed to take upon himself the office of publicly preaching the Word and administering the Sacraments, but only those who have received from God a genuine call; and this occurs either immediately or through means. And the right and authentic way of such a divine call is by the voice of the Church."

The investing of men with the functions of the ministerial office, is clearly entrusted by God to the Church. To the full constitution of the Church there must be pastors as well as a flock, for the Gospel must be preached and the Sacraments administered. The Church, necessarily, whether by the ministry alone, or by the combined action of clergy and laity, must perpetuate the sacred office, by calling, electing, and ordaining those who are publicly to teach the Word and administer the Sacraments. The procedure of calling the first minister by the Church, is stated in the Acts of the Apostles. In the choice of Matthias to the high office of the apostleship, not only the eleven, but the whole multitude of assembled disciples took part. It would be a violent and unauthorized construction to assume that the one hundred and twenty were all ministers (Acts i. 15-26). The choice, however, was not definite. They appointed two men, and then invoked God to decide by lot which of the two He had chosen. When, at the suggestion of Peter, deacons were chosen, the election was made by the whole multitude of disciples (Acts vi. 1-6). But there remains a question to be settled as to the office then instituted, whether its functions were limited to the temporalities of the Church, or embraced the commission which at least two of them, Stephen and Philip, afterwards executed, in preaching and baptizing. Luther says, "A whole congregation or church shall have power to elect and install a pastor."

While it is distinctly stated that Paul and Barnabas "ordained them elders in every church" (Acts xiv: 23) planted in their first missionary tour, we are not informed as to the part taken in the choice of the persons to be made pastors, by the people. Some maintain that the great apostle and his missionary fellow-laborer, regulated this according to their own judgment. Others affirm that we have no right to assume that the congregation did not in every case acquiesce, and virtually elect their religious instructors by designating the men to be ordained. Where Scripture is silent, it is as easy to affirm one thing as the other. It is impossible to decide, beyond all doubt, in the absence of Scripture statements, whether the people did or did not take part. The early Lutheran authorities, however, have very generally maintained that the congregations did either indicate or endorse the selections made by the Apostles. It can scarcely be questioned that the people gave at least tacit acquiescence. Even if the apostles did, under the authority and wisdom of their higher inspiration, regulate exclusively the choice of pastors for the newly-organized churches, this would not settle the question as to the course to be pursued after apostolic times, when special inspiration was no longer vouchsafed to the ministry.

John Wigand says, "The Church in every place, that is, the whole assembly, both laity and clergy, jointly have the power to elect suitable ministers, to call and ordain them; also to expel and depose false teachers, and those who by scandalous and immoral lives would injure the cause of piety."

The Wittenberg theologians say, "We do not say that the Romish method of calling pastors is in every particular wrong, in that the bishops ordain ministers; but we cannot approve their course in placing pastors over churches without the knowledge or consent of the people, because according to the old saying (aussage) 'The calling of a pastor, without the consent of the people, is null and void.'"

Chemnitz says: "Here it may be asked, who are they by whose voice the sanction and call of ministers is to take place, so that it may be regarded a divine appointment, that is, that God by that instrument is calling and sending the laborers into His harvest? For deciding this point we find certain clear examples in the Scriptures. When an apostle was to be chosen in place of Judas, Peter laid the matter not before the apostles alone, but before all the assembled disciples, the number being one hundred and twenty. (Acts i. 15.) He showed from the Scriptures how such a choice was to be made, and from among whom to select, and commands were annexed (adjunguntur orationes). The lot was used, because being the choice of an apostle, it should not be entirely by human instrumentality, (quia non debeat esse simpliciter mediata sed apostolica vocatio), but afterward in the calling of ministers the lot was not used. When deacons were to be called and elected, the apostles would not claim the right of making the choice alone, but called the congregation together. Yet they did not surrender the calling of ministers entirely, and entrust it to the blind and ungoverned willfulness of the people or the multitude; but took the direction and control of the choice into their own hands. They gave instruction and regulations as to whom they should elect, and how. Thus the elected were placed before the apostles, that by their judgment it should be decided whether the election was a proper one and had been rightly made. The apostles ratified the election by the laying on of hands and by prayer. Paul and Barnabas ordained elders in every church established by them. (Acts xiv. 23.) But they did not assume the right and authority exclusively of electing and installing pastors; but Luke uses the word χειροτονήσαντες, which (2 Cor. viii. 19) is used concerning the election, which took place by the vote of the congregation; the same being taken from a Greek usage, giving their votes by stretching forth the hand, and signifies the investing of some one with the office by votes, to designate him or give their consent. Paul and Barnabas, therefore, did not impose presbyters on the Church against the will of the people, without seeking their consent. And when men were to be chosen who should be sent to convey to the Church at Antioch the charge or decision of the Church, Luke says: 'It pleased the apostles, and elders, and the whole Church, to send chosen men of their own company to Antioch with Paul and Barnabas' (Acts xv. 22). It is necessary to observe in the history of the apostles, that sometimes the ministers and the rest of the congregation jointly elected whom they thought worthy of the sacred office. (Acts i. 23.) Sometimes the congregation made the choice, and submitted it to the judgment of the apostles, whether the election should be ratified. (Acts vi. 5, 6.) Often the apostles, who were the best judges of the fitness of men, proposed to the Church whom they thought worthy of the ministry, and when the consent and suffrage of the people was added, the call was consummated. So Paul sent Timothy, Titus, Sylvanus, etc., to the churches. So, in Acts xiv., twenty-three elders were selected, to whom the Church per χειροτονίαν, had given their consent. In the meantime, some offered themselves to the Church. (1 Tim. iii. 1.) 'If a man desire the office of a bishop, he desireth a good work.' Yet, always in apostolic times, in every case of the regular investiture of men with the pastoral office, both the consent of the congregation and the approval and ratification of the ministerium were given. Thus was Titus sent to Crete to direct and control the election of elders, that it should be done in a proper manner, and that the rightly-conducted election should be approved and ratified by ordination. Therefore, Paul, Titus i. 5, concerning the investiture of men with the office of elder, employs the same word which occurs Acts xiv. 23, where at the same time he mentions also χειροτονίας, and the ordination of elders. So he instructs Titus that he should sharply reprove those who are not sound in doctrine, nor in what they ought to teach. And this he says clearly (1 Tim. v. 22), 'Lay hands suddenly on no man, neither be partaker of other men's sins,' namely, by ratifying a call which was not rightly made. These examples from apostolic history show clearly, that the election or calling belongs to the whole Church in a specific way, so that in the election or calling the ministerium have their part and the people have their part. And this apostolic method of choosing and calling into the ministerial office was retained in the Church later. When afterwards emperors and kings embraced the Christian religion, their wish, judgment and authority began to be sought and required, which was proper, as they were the foster-parents of the Church. This was the sentiment of the apostolic, primitive and ancient Church, concerning the legitimate election and calling of men into the ministry of the Word and Sacraments, which sentiment appertains to those Churches which are already established by the word of God, embracing a ministry sound in doctrine, a Christian government, and a pious people, well indoctrinated in the truth."

John Gerhard says, "To the Church belongs the pastoral office. 1 Cor. viii. 21: 'All things are yours whether Paul, or Apollos, or Cephas.' Therefore, the Church has a delegated right to appoint worthy teachers of the Word, and God desires to be served by the calling of pious men into the ministry."

His train of argument is somewhat similar to that of Chemnitz. He reduces the work of making ministers into a systematic division. He says: "Although no specific rule can be prescribed for every individual case, yet if we would give a comprehensive portraiture, we would say, to the ministerium belong the examination, ordination and installation; to the Christian government, the nomination, the presentation, and the confirmation; and to the congregation, the consent, the election, the approval, or according to circumstances, the petitioning (postulatio)."

Many Lutheran theologians of the present day have not adopted the construction put upon some of the passages of Scripture quoted by Chemnitz and Gerhard. The former affirm that in the appointment of Matthias there was no election; that the appeal was to God, who decided the choice by lot; that the deacons appointed by the multitude (Acts vi.) were not ministers, but lay-officers to manage the temporalities of the congregation; that Titus was left in Crete to ordain ministers, and no intimation is given that the congregations took any part in the election; that when Paul and Barnabas ordained elders for the newly planted churches in Asia Minor, the congregations took no part in the transaction.

A different view from this was taken by the earlier theologians of the Church, as was noticed in the passages cited from Chemnitz and

Gerhard. These affirm that there was an election or selection by the whole congregation of one hundred and twenty to fill the vacancy in the apostolic college; that the election was as real as any could be, only not definite, that is, they elected two, and then called on God to decide which of two He had chosen. So far as this election went, laity and clergy took equal part, and being the first instance in the calling of a minister in which the Church was one of the factors and God the other, the rule of lay-participation was established. They also hold that the deacons chosen (Acts vi.) were not merely temporal officers, to secure a just and impartial distribution of the charities of the Church; that their first work was the control of these temporalities, but that without any additional commission (so far as the history shows), beyond the diaconate, several are presented to us as performing ministerial acts (certainly one) both preaching and baptizing.

They further hold that, the principle once laid down that the entire Church, clerical and lay, should take part in the investiture of men with the sacred office, these first transactions flash light through all subsequent ordinations mentioned in the New Testament; that an apostolic principle cannot be controvened by the apostles themselves; that inspired men would not adopt one rule at Jerusalem, and another in Crete; that the practice pursued twice by the Mother Church at Jerusalem under apostolic guidance, would certainly be followed by Paul and Barnabas in Asia Minor and by Titus in Crete.

By a process of reasoning in this way the great theologians of the Church immediately after the Reformation, came to adopt the theory above stated.

In the proper treatment of my subject it is not necessary to settle the question of difference on this point. The general position laid down in this essay, viz.: that the Church is one of the factors in the calling and ordination of ministers is fully endorsed by all Lutheran theologians.

What must be the dignity of an office which the everlasting Father and the eternal Son once filled, and which in the present dispensation of the Spirit, God and the Church unite in laying on men? How carefully should the candidate inquire into the genuineness of his call. How strictly should the Church heed the admonition, "Lay hands suddenly on no man."

If there be two factors in the making of a minister, can the one party without clear authority from the other undo the work? Can the Church scripturally and rightfully depose a minister except for soul-destroying heresy, or for flagrant immorality, unquestionably proven in a fair trial?

Can a minister demit the holy office without direct authority from heaven and the full consent of the Church? And what should be regarded as adequate proof that God has authorized the demission?

Some points presented in this paper were discussed by Rev. N. M. Price, Dr. Mann, Dr. Brown and Dr. Conrad.

REMARKS OF REV. N. M. PRICE. (*General Synod.*)

Rev. Price did not agree with the sentiment advanced in the essay, that God does not call men by an audible voice, or by supernatural means. He believed that some men are called in these marvellous ways. Luther was called by a clap of thunder and a flash of lightning killing Alexis his college friend. God's power to work wonders has not ceased.

REMARKS OF REV. W. J. MANN, D. D. (*General Council.*)

Dr. Mann remarked that, in his judgment, the views advanced by Dr. Diehl in the essay, and the point raised by Mr. Price, could be harmonized. He supposed the author of the essay would admit that God might work miracles in this age, if there were any necessity for it; but the paper read merely affirmed that God does not call men now by a voice from heaven, or a burning bush, or visions of angels.

REMARKS OF REV. J. A. BROWN, D. D. (*General Synod.*)

Dr. Brown would be surprised if any one in this nineteenth century, and in this Diet, should indorse the construction put upon some of the Scripture passages cited, which, indeed, the early Lutheran theologians did so interpret. But there is no truth in it. There was no election in the call of Matthias—merely a decision by lot.

The deacons were not ministers, but lay officers. Not a word is said in Scripture about Paul, and Barnabas, and Titus, calling the congregations together to get their vote. It is all groundless assumption.

Having been informed that the essayist cited those texts only in quotations from Chemnitz and Gerhard to set forth their views and the arguments by which they sustained them, the subject assigned him being the divine and human factors in the call into the ministry as held by Lutheran authorities, Dr. Brown said that for that purpose it was perfectly legitimate. The theory of those older Lutherans was correctly stated, and the citation of their arguments faithfully made. Yet their interpretations on those points were untenable.

REMARKS OF REV. F. W. CONRAD, D. D. (*General Synod.*)

I do not agree with some of the representations concerning the call to the ministry, just read. According to a general notion, the call to the ministry comes directly from God, is addressed to particular individuals, and is revealed to them by the Holy Spirit in an extra ordinary manner. Prompted by the conviction thus produced, the subject of it makes known his call and the Church is expected to endorse it, and to aid him in preparing for the ministry. Thus the question is not decided by self-knowledge and adaptation for the work, but by an impulse, desire, impression, or notion entertained by the individual. The Church is not called upon to exercise her judgment in regard to the existence of the necessary qualifications, as the indispensable marks of a true call to the ministry, but to take it for granted that the person presenting himself is truly called. She is accordingly expected to furnish him the necessary aid in the expectation that the qualifications necessary for the successful prosecution of the ministry, will be developed in the applicant in due time.

I hold on the contrary, that the true call to the ministry involves the following characteristics: The natural constitutional capacities conferred by creation ; true piety, or the spiritual qualifications bestowed through redemption ; the conscious obligation to devote life to the glory of God ; the conviction, based upon self-knowledge, that he possesses the necessary natural and spiritual qualifications ; and the further conviction, wrought by the ordinary influences of the Holy Spirit through the truth, that in the ministry he could, in the highest degree, glorify God in the service of the Church to which he belongs.

These characteristics will not develop themselves, but must be cultivated by the Church, in order to develop the conviction of a call to the ministry in the candidate, corroborated by the facts in his case. The natural faculties must be developed by education ; the spiritual qualifications by the means of grace ; the obligation to make the glory of God the supreme object of life, by special instruction ; and the conviction that through the vocation of the ministry the highest usefulness could be attained by self-examination, consultation and study. In thus developing the call to the ministry, parents, teachers, professors, pastors, and members of the Church, should all take part. To the ministry alone is entrusted the decision of the possession of the qualifications necessary to constitute a true call, and the introduction into the office by licensure and ordination ; and to the laity alone, the election of the candidate, to the pastorship of the congregation in which he is thus authorized to exercise the functions of his office.

The informing idea of a call to the ministry is that of adaptation to the successful prosecution of the work, and the attainment of highest usefulness. By this judgment the Father was governed in calling the Son to the work of redemption; Christ in calling the seventy disciples and the twelve apostles ; the apostles in selecting elders to become pastors of the churches, and the churches in choosing deacons and deaconesses. In no case did the individual present himself, and reveal the fact that he was called to this or that special work, based upon his own impression, notion, or judgment. In each case, on the contrary, the judgment of others was brought into requisition, in looking out for those possessed of the required qualifications for the service needed, and by revealing such judgment to the persons interested, awakening the conviction of the call of duty, and leading them to respond to it, by entering upon, and prosecuting, the special work pointed out to them.

Every theory must, in order to maintain its verity, interpret all the facts pertaining to its sphere. The ordinary theory of the call to the ministry cannot meet this requisition in a single case, while the theory whose characteristics I have endeavored to present, accords with all the passages of Scripture bearing on the subject, and its truthfulness is further illustrated by every example of a call to the ministry given in the New Testament.

REMARKS OF REV. W. J. MANN, D. D. (*General Council.*)

Dr. Mann differed from Dr. Conrad. He would like to know whether Dr. Conrad was called by his parents or religious instructors seeking him out and telling him he had a call to preach, or whether he was moved by the Spirit in his soul.

REMARKS OF REV. J. A. BROWN, D. D. (*General Synod.*)

Dr. Brown dissented from the views expressed by Dr. Conrad. That process would be no call from God. He believed the divine Spirit operates in the soul of the subject and leads him to seek the ministry. The call is subjective. The conviction of its being a duty to preach the Gospel is wrought by God. As "the spirit of the prophets is subject to the prophets," this inward call and conviction must be submitted to the judgment and decision of the Church, properly exercised. Parents, teachers, pastors, may be instruments, but the *divine agent* in the call is the Holy Ghost.[1]

The last paper was then read.

---

[1] Discussion, with exception of Dr. Conrad's remarks, reported by Dr. Diehl.

THE EDUCATIONAL AND SACRAMENTAL IDEAS OF THE LUTHERAN CHURCH IN RELATION TO PRACTICAL PIETY.

BY REV. A. C. WEDEKIND, D. D., NEW YORK.

BEYOND all controversy, God has given His Holy Word as the principal means of grace. In it He does not only reveal His adorable nature and character, but He sets forth, specifically, His benevolent purpose to redeem man; pointing out to him clearly what he is to know and to believe, to experience and to practice; and then graciously proffers him the aids through which he can yield compliance with these holy demands. The sacred Scriptures, therefore, are designed to be, to man's believing apprehension, both the power and the wisdom of God unto salvation.

Beyond all controversy, too, the centre of this Divine Revelation, in both the Old and the New Testaments, is the Lord Jesus Christ. The law, ceremonies, and types of the Old Testament, as they are related to man's recovery, pointed like so many finger-boards to the coming Messiah, as the hope of Israel; whilst the New Testament sets him forth as the One, who, "in the fullness of time," actually appeared, and who is thenceforward the eternally present help and hope of man. Christ, then, is at once the embodiment and fulfillment of the law, as well as the living, incarnate Gospel. "He is the end of the law for righteousness," as well as the only perfect type and pattern of it. He alone is "the Way, the Truth, and the Life," through whom man can come to the Father. As the God-man, uniting in Himself personally Deity and humanity, he has effectively, through His righteousness, suffering and death, expiated all human guilt. Hence, whosoever hears, believes and trusts His Word, without the ability or opportunity to attend to any other means of grace, will be saved.

This disposes of the twaddle, so frequently indulged in when the nature and efficacy of the Sacraments are considered, in reference to the thief on the cross, to whom Christ opened the gates of Paradise ; and of Mary Magdalene, whom He sent away " in peace," as a freely forgiven sinner.

But this divinely inspired Word, "which is able to save our souls" (James i. 21); "which is the incorruptible seed of which we are born again" (1 Peter i. 23); through which we are "built up and have an inheritance among them that are sanctified" (Acts xx. 32); which gives us "a good hope through grace" (2 Thess. ii. 14-16); this blessed Word, to which the Lutheran Church, amidst all changes and vicissitudes, lapses of men and alterations of opinions, has so steadfastly adhered, adding nothing, subtracting nothing, altering nothing; this unchanging and unchangeable Word, reveals to us that God in mercy and great condescension has established and ordained certain Rites and Ordinances, called in the Church *Sacraments*, for high and holy purposes in relation to man's recovery from the thralldom of sin, and his introduction and support in the kingdom of grace. It is my delightful theme to show you the *Educational and Sacramental Ideas of the Lutheran Church in Relation to Practical Piety.*

Or in other words: What relation do these holy Rites or Ordinances sustain in the divine economy, to secure the gracious ends proposed, according to Lutheran views? There are two distinct branches of my subject—the Educational and the Sacramental. The former, in its positive aspect, will meet us further on ; but it may be brought into essential unity with the latter through the incidental educational effect upon the Church at large, resulting from the discussions of the Sacraments themselves. And these effects are in every way important, as they set men to thinking, to compare views and ideas with counter views and ideas, thus leading her members, like the "more noble Bereans, to search and see whether these things be so." A world of good has thus been done by our theologians—however much abused for it—who, in the spirit of true churchliness and Lutheran orthodoxy, have devoted themselves so largely to the setting forth the Church's views upon these doctrines. As the two Sacraments, Baptism and the Lord's Supper, may be regarded as a mirror in which the whole of Christianity is reflected as in a miniature portrait, every *minutia* in regard to them becomes important. Hence the dispassionate, didactic discussion of them cannot but be beneficial. As a historical fact, of great significance in this connection, it may be mentioned that in the dreary period of *Rationalism*, when piety was banished from the domain of learning, and had to seek her retreat in the cottages of the humble and the lowly, such discussions were "like angel visits, few and far between." They were sneered at with supercilious *hauteur*, as belonging to the swaddling clothes of an infantile age of the Church, which the boasted age of reason had fully outgrown. And it may further be mentioned, that with the revival of these discussions came the revival of genuine piety. Indeed, how could it be otherwise? When the divinely appointed means of grace were lightly esteemed, how could grace itself grow? How could true godliness flourish, when men knew not how to advance in it; when human notions, bald and shallow, were substituted for Christ's teachings and Christ's mysteries?

Nor was the case very much different with the Church here in this western world, in the days of her sifting; when in a false spirit of accommodation she was rapidly losing her identity, becoming the common hunting ground for every ism by which she was surrounded; when her inner glory was concealed, her gold became dim, and the seamless robe which her Master had put upon her was covered by the cast-off rags, either of frigid formalism on the one hand, or of wild fanaticism on the other: in both those periods the earnest voice or forceful pen seldom set forth her distinctive doctrines of the means of grace, and in both periods "the logic of events" tended alike to her ultimate extinction. It was with the revival of searching, exhaustive discussion of these things, that her true life-blood filled again her arteries with vigorous and healthy progress. It is, therefore, no longer an open question that her *Educational Ideas* in this direction tended to practical piety; that piety, we mean, which is rooted and grounded in the positive doctrines and institutions of God's Word; which is above the tide-mark of strait-laced formalism, or effervescent emotionalism, but which is a real product and growth of divine truth, embraced and enshrouded by the heart's holiest affections.

We see, of course, a good deal yet of the retiring spray of the storms that have passed over the Church, in the loose and unscriptural views that still linger in her ranks. The heaving billows are not yet fully at rest, as every pastor knows whose eyes and ears are open to the things that transpire around him. To many of his members the external ceremonies of the Sacraments only remain, and they attend to them as mere matters of form, transmitted to them from a former generation. Baptism, e. g., in many families, has no higher significance than that the child gets a name; in others it is the occasion of a joyous family feast, sometimes followed with music and dance. With others still, it is a sort of "Mrs. Winslow's Soothing Syrup." The child is cross; the mother tired; and the rite of Baptism is called in to quiet the infant and give the mother rest. Not unfrequently when a pastor comes into the house of a parishioner, a child is brought to him with the remark: "This is the man that put water on your head;" or "This is the man that gave you a name!!" Of the sublime mysteries connected with that event they are as profoundly ignorant as though they were Hottentots.

This brings to view, then, the main point of my theme, viz., THE SACRAMENTAL IDEAS OF THE LUTHERAN CHURCH, IN RELATION TO PRACTICAL PIETY.

Now, to graduate their effect, we must first know what those ideas are. Of course this necessitates the placing before you the doctrines of the Lutheran Church with regard to the Sacraments. It is a grand theme, second to none in importance, of the mighty and timely topics that have already been discussed, or that may yet follow. And from my heart do I wish that abler hands had been employed to handle it, for it involves the very centre around which nearly all the confessional divergencies revolve. In approaching it, methinks I hear the divine injunction: "Take the shoes from off thy feet, for the ground whereon thou standest is holy ground." May Isaiah's blessing be mine, and Cornelius' grace be yours!

WHAT, THEN, IS A SACRAMENT?

It is an institution, not of man's devising, but of God's ordaining. It is not a human invention, but a divine appointment. No human authority can make Sacraments in the Evangelical sense of that term. No Church can do it; and the authority claimed to establish seven, might, with equal propriety, have designated twenty. God, and God only, can do this.

"A Sacrament," says Schmid in his Evangelische Dogmatik, "is a holy rite, appointed by God, through which, by means of an external and visible sign, saving grace is imparted to a man, or if he already possess it, is assured to him. The Evangelical Church enumerates two such rites, Baptism and the Lord's Supper; for only through these two rites, in accordance with the direction of Christ, is such saving grace imparted; and among all the sacred ordinances prescribed in the Scriptures, it is only in these two that these distinguishing characteristics are combined, viz.: (1) A special, divine purpose, in accordance with which, in the sacred rite, an external element is to be thus employed; and (2) the promise given in the divine Word, that by the application of this element, Evangelical saving grace shall be imparted." The usual definition that *"a Sacrament is a visible sign of invisible grace"* is only half true; and the more important half of the truth is not even intimated in the definition, as will appear when we consider

THE DESIGNS OF THE SACRAMENTS.

These are various, though unique, all aiming at man's highest spiritual interest. The time allowed me in this paper precludes, of course, any other than a mere indication of each.

(1) As churchly transactions, Sacraments are first *confessional*. In and through them the subject of them confesses himself to be a disciple of Christ, and therefore a member of His Church. The very term Sacrament implies "to consecrate," "to vow allegiance to." Sacraments are, therefore, in this sense, badges of Christian discipleship. "Go ye into all the world and make disciples of all nations, baptizing them," was the Lord's own command. "The cup of blessing which we bless," etc., "For we being many are one bread, and *one body*, for we are all partakers of that one bread," is St. Paul's statement. In both, the individual participant declares himself to be a member of the "sacramental host of the Lord;" a member of that mystical body of which Christ Himself is the all-glorious head: under the most solemn obligation of fidelity "*to Him who is God over all, blessed forevermore.*"

The practical tendency of this design of the holy Sacraments can hardly be overestimated. As every Roman soldier who deserted his standard was not only thereby disgraced, but also liable to the severest punishment, so the church-member who violates his sacramental covenant with God, who fails to "come up to the help of the Lord, to the help of the Lord against the mighty," exposes himself to the sorest displeasure of King Emmanuel. And one reason why there are so many *tepid Christians* in the Church—lukewarm disciples—is that they are so rarely reminded that their names stand on the muster-roll of Christ's army; that He " has need of them" and expects them to do their whole duty in the mighty conflict waging against sin and the devil. Each Roman soldier who had taken the "*sacramentum*" regarded the honor and success of the whole army as committed to his individual care and keeping, and this conviction made him a veritable hero. He stood like a rock in in the day of trial, as is so beautifully illustrated in "*The Last Days of Pompeii.*" The tremendous deluge of fire is sweeping towards the doomed city, and its various inmates, following the bent of their minds, seek the things most prized by them; some, as the late excavations so strikingly illustrate, have their hands on their money-drawers—others are collecting their jewels—others still are gathering around them their loved ones—whilst the Roman soldier, halberd in hand, covered with ashes, soot and scoria, is found standing at his post of duty at one of the city's gates, a monument of fidelity to his *sacramental* obligation.

(2) Another design of the Sacraments is that they are signs and seals of spiritual blessings. Man cannot promise divine grace; neither can he put a seal to a divine promise, with which to authenticate it. Such a transaction would be a stupendous fraud. Sacraments are therefore not human works which men originate, but divine institutions of mercy, of which men are the objects and recipients. They are indissolubly connected with the Word, without which they are nothing and profit nothing. Hence they are, as already mentioned, in themselves a miniature gospel, and are, therefore, sometimes called the "*visible Word*," through which the Holy Ghost especially exhibits and seals the general promises of gospel grace to the believer; assuring him thus, in the most impressive and solemn manner, of the blessings of the covenant of grace. In human transactions a seal is attached to a document, not to add to the contents of that document, but to attest its binding force and irreversible nature. So God has not only promised purity, pardon and peace, but remembering our weakness, and how strongly we are impressed by sensible objects, He has appointed these ordinances as seals or pledges of His promises. "The simple assurance given to Noah that the earth should not a second time be destroyed by a deluge, might have been a sufficient foundation for confidence; bu

God saw fit to appoint the rainbow to be a perpetual confirmation of His covenant; and through all generations, when the bow appears, men feel that it is not merely a sign of the returning sun, but a divinely appointed pledge of the promise of God." So, too, the promise of deliverance from Egyptian bondage, given to the Israelites, was in itself sufficient to assure them that, in the accomplishment of His promise, the destroying angel should pass over their houses without disturbing any of their inmates; yet it pleased Him to appoint the blood of the paschal lamb as the sign and seal of this covenant. In like manner, God, willing more abundantly to show unto His people the immutability of His promise, has confirmed it by these seals, to assure them that, as certainly as they receive the signs of the blessings of the covenant, so certainly shall they receive the blessings themselves.

(3) And this brings to view the primary design of the Sacraments, viz.: "The offering, conferring and applying, as well as sealing of gospel grace." "Gospel grace is offered to all who use the Sacraments; it is conferred on all who worthily use them; it is applied and sealed to adult believers." Sacraments are, therefore, channels through which the covenanted blessings are conveyed to the worthy recipient of them. The testamentary parchment that contains the friendly bequest of a large fortune to me, is not simply the sign or the seal of my inheritance, but the instrument that conveys it to me. It would be a poor satisfaction, indeed, to be content with the paper as the mere sign of the kind intention of the testator, whilst the rich contents remained unappropriated. The value and importance of the paper consist in the fortune it conveys to me.

So our blessed Lord, whose "unsearchable riches" have been bequeathed to his followers in express terms of "*the New Testament in His blood*," has clearly stated. As the divine Word is endowed with supernatural efficacy to produce regenerating, renewing and sanctifying effects on the minds of men, when, through the Divine Spirit, it is believingly apprehended, so the Sacraments, which are the *visible Word*, communicate, through the same holy agency, what the gracious Lord Himself has put into them. They are His appointed channels to confer and apply His *general* promises of grace, specifically and especially to their worthy individual recipients. Nothing less than this can satisfy the strong language of the Scriptures on this subject, or the experience of God's people. When baptism is called the washing of regeneration (Titus iii. 5), when it is said to unite us to Christ (Gal. iii. 27), to make us partakers of His death and life (Rom. vi. 4, 5), to wash away our sins, (Acts xxii. 16), to save the soul (1 Pet. iii. 21); and when the bread and wine in the Lord's Supper are said to be the body and the blood of Christ, the partaking of which secures union with Christ, and participation of the merits of His death (1 Cor. x. 16, 17), it is the merest, sheerest, baldest logomachy, as well as the most unenviable piety, to fritter away such *unqualified* declarations of the Holy Ghost, into mere hyperboles, or simple signs and symbols. We ask with great emphasis, where is there anything of this sort in the bond? Is it there? No? Then by what authority do you put it there? Who gave *you* the authority to amend the teachings of the Holy Ghost? Ten thousand times shame on your wicked presumption! Would you have ever dreamed of it had not Rome in her frenzy taught the *ex opere operato* theory? No? Then why do you suppose that two wrongs will make a right? Has the Lutheran Church ever taught you any such notion? Far from it. She teaches you most explicitly that faith is necessarily required in order to the reception of the salutary efficacy of the Sacraments. If the Sacraments are the visible rosy-red hand of God's mercy in which He offers the richest boons of His grace; she teaches her children that a trusting, confiding hand on their part is necessary to secure them. Whilst she undoubtedly teaches—and I personally thank God for it—that in infants the Holy Spirit kindles faith by the Sacrament of initiation, by which they receive the grace of the covenant (if they receive not that, what do they receive?) she, with equal clearness, announces to those of riper years, that the Sacraments confer no grace on adults, unless, when offered, they receive them by true faith, which must exist in their hearts previously.

Shielded thus against all misapprehension and false application, it will not be difficult to set forth the Lutheran views of each of the Sacraments separately. We of course commence with

BAPTISM.

This was instituted by Christ Himself, and has the promise of salvation. It makes its subject God's child—the greatest blessing of man on earth. It introduces him to God's covenant, and secures for him all God's covenanted mercies. It is administered in the name of the Father, Son and Holy Ghost, to show not only the intense solemnity of the transaction, but to pledge us at the same time the Father's love, the Son's righteousness, and the Spirit's comfort and communion. There is in this ordinance a deep mystery which transcends all human ken, and demands an unreserved, child-like and entire faith and confidence in the words and promise of Christ and His apostles. To me its profound spiritual meaning seems typified by the several external events that transpired at Christ's own baptism. It is stated that on that occasion Jesus saw "heaven opened;" typifying, I think, that Baptism opens to us the kingdom of heaven; next, the Father's voice is heard saying, "This is My beloved Son in whom I am well pleased;" announcing to us the fact that in Baptism we are sealed as the Father's dear children; and finally, the Spirit of God is seen, in dove-like form, to hover over this deeply mysterious and "all-righteousness fulfilling" transaction, indicating the design, that in Baptism the spirit of love, of purity, and of dove like innocence, shall descend into the heart of the baptized person.

The main reason why so many pastors know not what position to assign to this blessed ordinance, is the confusion of ideas in the "Order of Salvation," and the interchange, as synonymous terms, of regeneration and conversion. In Baptism the former is effected, and the right of the latter secured. In the *initiative* ordinance man becomes God's child, and the divine life in its germinal character is implanted in his soul, which lies in the heart, not like a concealed stone, but like a good seed in the garden, or like a noble scion grafted on a wild stem, and not like a dead nail driven into the trunk. The very term, "conversion," implies that the man has gone *from* something good, and in "turning round"—which is the meaning of the word "conversion"—he is to go back to "that good thing committed to him."

The objection here urged is, that if conversion is necessary, then what practical benefit is regeneration? Answer: If he remains faithful in his baptismal covenant, growing "up in the nurture and admonition of the Lord," like John the Baptist, the baptized child will be "sanctified from his mother's womb." That this *can be*, no believer in the Bible, who is acquainted with the history of a Samuel, a John, or a Timothy, will question. That it *ought* to be,

St. Paul's language, quoted above, sufficiently indicates. That it *is* not, proves nothing against God's Word, nor the doctrine of our Church, but only shows that there is a fearful delinquency somewhere; and where that is we shall see by and by. It is, alas! but too true, as every pastor knows, that not all who have been baptized continue in their baptismal grace and covenant, and live as it becomes God's children; yea, some live as if there were no God to fear and no hell to dread. They "put asunder what God has joined together"—FAITH AND BAPTISM. To secure salvation, both are necessary. " He that believeth *and* is baptized, shall be saved; he that believeth not shall be damned." If faith, therefore, is not added to baptism; if the stupid theory of *ex opere operato* is consciously or unconsciously relied on, then unbelief will drag after it its own legitimate fruit—damnation. But, says the objector, if Faith does the work, what use is there of Baptism? "Much every way." First, because *God has so ordained*. From this statement there can be no appeal. In reference to it, we can only say: "Even so, Lord, for so it seemeth good in Thy sight." Nothing but the baldest infidelity, or the most supercilious conceit, can set this fact aside. Then, too, the relation established through this ordinance between God and the baptized person is a most sacred one—that of childhood of God. Now a child that *has* a father can seek him again even if he has gone astray; he who has a father's house to go to, can always return, though like the Prodigal, he " has gone into a far country." This is the prerogative which Baptism secures to God's erring child. How is it with an earthly father, whose prodigal son has most grievously wronged him, when that son, after long wanderings, returns, though in the dead hour of midnight, and, with tearful eye and choked voice, knocks at the paternal door, begging: Father, open unto me! thy child, weary, naked and desolate, stands here, freezing in the cold of winter, and perishing with hunger and thirst in this merciless world;—what, think you, would that father do? And will not our compassionate Father in heaven open mercy's door to His returning prodigal child, and thus save him from despair? I tell you, yea, for He has made a covenant with him in Baptism, " well ordered in all things and sure ;" and though man may violate it again and again, God never. "He cannot deny Himself." He will continue his Father, even should the child at last be lost. O! there is in this holy Sacrament, depth of mercy which no human plummet has ever yet sounded.

And what an ocean of comfort there lies in this doctrine of our Church for practical piety. Man's utter impotence is learned nowhere so thoroughly as where his love nestles most warmly. A mother[1] in tears sits by the cradle of an ailing child sobbing: 'My darling is very ill;' but she is thrice blessed, if, when bowing before her Maker in prayer, she can say: 'Father, Thy child is sick.' Or the father notices with deep sorrow and grief, how unruly passions and sinful desires develop themselves in his child, which he cannot eradicate; but thrice happy is he when he can look up to God and say: 'Behold, Father, Thy child is tempted of the flesh, the world, and the devil; Thou hast conquered these foes, Thou canst shield and succor Thy child.' The eyes of father and mother can't see very far, nor can their hands reach at a great distance, and when their child leaves the parental roof to try the slippery paths of a corrupt and corrupting world, they look after him with deep anxiety; but how blessed are they to know that their loved one is accompanied by another Father, whose eye never slumbers and whose mighty arm is round and about him in all his wanderings. And when at last the father's eye breaks and the mother's hand grows cold, and the final struggle comes to tear their hearts loose from the child that stands weeping at their death-bed, how comforting for them to know that He never dies "who is the true Father of all them that are called children." How truly poor is that household in which the faith in the unspeakable blessings of the baptismal covenant has become extinct! How have the children been robbed of their holiest attire, their chief jewel! And what deep anxiety and discomfort must those parents feel when their natural attachment for their offspring arouses their hearts' deepest concern for their temporal and eternal welfare!

Bear with me, then, brethren, if I seem unnecessarily lengthy on this subject. Above all others, this demands chief attention just now. You, as well as I, have noticed that almost every district conference in our Church is debating some aspect or other of this ordinance, indicating not only that this a living question, but that there is a painful unfixedness of views, as well as a general feeling after the truth. If this paper shall call special attention to the proper study

---

[1] Büchsel's "*Erinnerungen*," to which I am indebted for many of these thoughts.

of this subject, its principal aim will be attained. I go on, therefore, and say:

That another difficulty in the way of assigning the proper position to this Sacrament is the inadequate conception in many minds of the deep depravity of the human heart. They fail to grasp the Bible idea of what is meant by man being "conceived in sin and shapen in iniquity;" that "he is unrighteous before God;" that he "is of the earth, earthy;" that "what is born of the flesh, is flesh;" that "the whole head is sick, and the whole heart faint;" that this moral disease has infected his whole being, lying within his very centre like the seed of the deadly night-shade, that will grow with his growth, and strengthen with his strength; and that unless God in His infinite mercy change that nature, it will and must develop into a child of wrath. Hence the blessed Saviour so explicitly teaches, John iii. 5, "Except any one be born again of water and of the Spirit, he cannot see God." But now, "It is not the will of your heavenly Father that any of these little ones should perish;" therefore He meets them at the very entrance of life with the moral antidote to the moral disease, and that not only in a purely spiritual and invisible way, but also in the visible sign and pledge of holy Baptism. The child is thus early placed in the hands of the Holy Ghost as its spiritual physician. This assigns to this ordinance a definite, most gracious, and most positive position. It makes something more of it than a mere venerable and ancient custom, which at most can do no harm, and which by some, indeed, is regarded as "being honored more in the breach than in the observance." We speak not unadvisedly on this subject; nor are we to be considered as false accusers of brethren when we affirm that there are Synods in our Church, which, according to the last General Synod's Report, do not average two infant baptisms a year in each of their thirty-four congregations! Is it supposable that in such localities the doctrine of the heart's moral disease, and its divine antidote, are fully comprehended? Is there no urgent need of calling special attention to this subject?

But in this covenant of Baptism, there are other parties besides the Holy God and the feeble child. And here "*The Educational Ideas of the Lutheran Church*" *come in.* Parents have assumed the weighty responsibilities of Christian nurture in reference to their children; and their children have the unquestioned and unquestionable claim to it. And woe be to them who neglect it! They become not only "covenant breakers," but the neglecters, if not the destroyers, of the highest interests of their offspring. Here is the last answer in the baptismal formula of our Church: "Do you desire that this child shall be baptized into the Christian faith: and are you *resolved* to *instruct him carefully in the gospel of our Lord Jesus Christ, and to teach him to walk according to its holy commandments? Answer*, YES." In the baptismal covenant the parents have become God's messengers to these little immortals; His co-workers for their religious training; yea, His substitutes, doing as He would do, were He visibly present to manage this momentous work! To Him, therefore, they are responsible for every step they take in this important matter. They are vital factors in this gracious plan and purpose of the Almighty. So God teaches; so our Church believes. Hence Luther prepared his *Small Catechism*, primarily for the family; heading each division thus: "*Quomodo pater-familias (id.) suæ familiæ simplicissime tradere debeat.*" But alas! as in so many other instances, so also here; there is a heaven-wide difference between precept and practice, between plan and execution! How many children are denied this wholesome spiritual food! How many grow up, even in nominally Christian families, without prayer, without instruction, without the simple knowledge even that they stand in God's covenant, without ever so much as having seen a catechism until they are sent to the pastor for instruction! And yet, just from such sources come the objections to the Church's doctrine on this subject, as many pastors present, as well as absent, can abundantly testify. But is it a wonder that the Divine purpose in this holy covenant is so largely neutralized, seeing the conditions from the human side, so recklessly neglected if not positively ignored? Can we expect to "gather grapes from thorns, or figs from thistles?" Will "a bitter fountain send forth sweet water?" Yet this is the sad condition in thousands of our families.[2] Of course, man cannot see what

---

[2] During my present course of catechetical instruction, four lads in my class, when questioned on this subject (they are not the children of my flock) acknowledged that they had never read two chapters in the Bible, though each was over fifteen years of age! One had never read a single verse at home! The other thought that perhaps they might have read from ten verses to two chapters, *but certainly not more!* Neither of them knew whether he was baptized!!

the Holy Spirit is doing all this while in the youthful heart; how He is fanning the gentle flame to keep it alive, so that, as in nature, when the frost of winter is thawed by the warming rays and showers of spring, and the superincumbent ice and snow melt, and "the storms are over and gone," the little sprig of the planted seed springs forth despite the unpromising antecedents. One thing is sure, and we wish to score it, that no greater earthly blessing can come to a child than to unfold its being in the sacred precincts of a Christian family, where it is enfolded in the warm embrace of sanctified maternal love, and where its tiny hand is laid, into that of a pious, God-fearing father for guidance and direction. No inheritance, however vast, is comparable to this. No world-wide renown, however brilliant, can bless a child one tithe as much as the simple and ineffaceable remembrance of a Christ-loving father and mother. Well did Richard Baxter say, that if parents would do their duty, more would be savingly called in the family than in the sanctuary. God fill our churches with such parents!

But in this baptismal covenant the CHURCH as well as the family, has an important part to perform. She is not only the divinely appointed almoner of God's mercies and mysteries: she is an essential factor in the development of the gracious purposes designed to be accomplished in Baptism. As an agency co-ordinate with the family, in this direction, she is to give "line upon line," etc., in the education of the lambs of the flock. To her the blessed Master said, through Peter: "Feed *My* lambs." What the parents are designed to commence, the Church is commanded to carry forward and complete. From the family into school; from the school into Church, from the Church into heaven, is her theory. Accordingly the children are sent to the pastor for "instruction" in the doctrines of religion and the duties of life. In no department of the pastor's work can he make himself more lastingly and more beneficially felt than in these hours. Here was the secret spring of that pietistic movement, so much lauded but so little understood, of Philip Jacob Spener. If conscientious and faithful in the catechetical class, the pastor will have comfort and joy in all his congregational work. At no other time and in no other place can he approach the heart nearer, or convey a knowledge of Christianity to the comprehension of the youthful mind clearer, than in the catechetical system of the Church. It is a shame, therefore, that this glorious system should have ever been suffered to degenerate into a mere humdrum-like perfunctory performance, resembling the Hindoo's praying machine placed by the stream to be turned by the flowing water, soulless, aimless, senseless; or to be supplanted altogether by a system which, whilst it may have the glare and furor of a prairie fire, is as destructive too. These *Educational Ideas of the Church*, or catechetical instructions, where the meetings are but once a week, should extend, at least, through one whole year. They are, of course, preparatory to the solemn rite of *Confirmation*, which is the connecting link between the two Sacraments, or the bridge by which we pass from the one over to the other. Confirmation, which has come to us from the apostolic age, is a personal ratification of the baptismal covenant, and an individual assumption of all its conditions and responsibilities. It is followed by the first reception of the Lord's Supper, and unites thus in itself, as in the focal point of the Christian life, all the means of grace: the Word, through the preceding instruction; Baptism, through the renewal of the covenant, and the Holy Supper, through the first participation of it. What a day! How glad, how sad! How full of holy reminiscences! How big with hopes and fears! Its salutary influences are designed to extend through the whole life.

We are now brought to consider the second Sacrament of the Church:

THE LORD'S SUPPER.

As in the *initiative* ordinance the divine life in the soul has its beginning, so the *confirmative* Supper is designed to nourish and strengthen it; but as in the world this spiritual life is often depressed and weakened, this means of reviving it is to be frequently repeated. This was the case in the primitive Church, and also in the Reformation period. It is, therefore, a matter of deep regret that the un-Lutheran custom obtains so extensively throughout our Church, of celebrating this ordinance but once or twice, or at most four times a year. May the day soon come when our congregations will make arrangements that the Lord's table shall be spread once a month!

In this holy ordinance, instituted by Christ Himself, "on the night in which He was betrayed," He gives us, through the visible elements of bread and wine, all the blessings of the Gospel, as these blessings are all embodied in Himself: for He gives us Himself; as the words of the institution so emphatically declare: "This is My body;" "This is My blood." It is Myself; let each one of you, believingly, appropriate Myself to himself

In this Sacrament, even more than in the first, the Lutheran Church differs from all other Protestants, as well as from all Romanists. She utterly rejects the Tridentine doctrine of *transubstantiation;* and with equal energy and emphasis she rejects the mere mnemonic notions of Zwingle. She does, indeed, not ignore the *memorial feature* of this holy ordinance; for her Lord has said: "Do this in remembrance of Me," and she has the utmost regard and reverence for His words. As the paschal lamb, eaten at the same table at which the holy Supper was instituted, should perpetuate from generation to generation the remembrance of Israel's wonderful deliverance from Egyptian bondage; so Jesus desired that His holy Supper should remind His followers through all time to come of their great redemption from the thralldom of sin and Satan through His innocent sufferings and death. Our Church teaches her children devoutly to call to mind Christ's agony in Gethsemane, His indignities at Pilate's bar, and His unutterable sufferings on Golgatha. They remember His sweat as it falls like great drops of blood to the ground; they think of the horrible scourgings, the cruel mockings, and the piercing cry: "My God, my God, why hast Thou forsaken Me." All these things, endured by the Son of God for the redemption of man, pass like a living panorama before us as we stand or kneel around the Lord's table. Yes, the Lutheran Church teaches, and all her children believe, the memorial feature of the holy Supper.

But with equal fervor and unquestioned confidence she teaches, and her children believe, every other statement made by the blessed Lord and His inspired apostles in reference to this holy ordinance. Accordingly she finds in it unspeakably more than the mere memorial feature. If it be no more than a simple mnemonic rite, then a "crucifix" or an "Ecce Homo" painting, would much better accomplish that end than a piece of bread and a little wine. And, therefore, the Lutheran Church teaches, and her children believe, that the Lord's Supper is not only a visible gospel that recalls to mind the most stupendous facts in the history of redemption, but that it carries and communicates to the humble, penitent, believing participant, all that it objectively sets forth, as indicated by the Saviour's language, "broken for you," and "shed for the remission of sin." And this she teaches, and they believe, not because she has fathomed, and they have encompassed, the mighty mystery involved in His holy ordinance, but upon the sole declaration of the blessed Lord Himself. And thus trusting with childlike simplicity her loving Lord, she is fully persuaded that He will not tantalize or deceive her. When He says, "This is my body," "this is my blood," "take and eat," "drink ye all of it," He does not offer us a *myth* instead. He offers us Himself, as the soul-food of all His followers. Hence He says, "He that eateth My flesh and drinketh My blood, dwelleth in Me, and I in him." "As the living Father hath sent Me, and I live by the Father, so he that eateth Me, even he shall live by Me." Language could not be plainer. The words and things chosen set forth this gracious, ennobling, soul supporting union and communion with Him.

It requires only an entrance into, and a full realization of the circumstances of the institution of this sacrament, to apprehend in some humble measure the profound purposes of its divine Author. He had announced to His disciples the withdrawal of His visible presence from them. This announcement filled them with undisguised sorrow. "Their hearts were troubled." He deeply sympathized with them. "Having loved His own, He loved them unto the end." And to assure them of this unfailing and undiminished love, and setting aside all known laws of human language, He says to them, in the overflow of His love: Here, take Me; take My whole self—"My body and blood;" feast upon Me, and let this be your soul-food for evermore!

Does any one now say, with the murmuring Jews: "How can this man give us His flesh to eat?" We answer: Jesus never asserted, our Church never taught, and her children never believed, any such gross, *Capernaitish* idea or view. What we believe the Saviour to have taught is that, with the external signs of bread and wine which remain unchanged in all respects, the Lord Jesus Christ in a *supernatural* and to us *incomprehensible way*, communicates Himself with, in and under the form of bread and wine, to the believing communicant, with all the effects of His glorious redemption work; that He unites Himself *mystically* but really with them; conformably to the teachings of the Holy Ghost, 1 Cor. x, 16.

22

"The cup of blessing which we bless, is it not the communion of the blood of Christ? The bread which we break, is it not the communion of the body of Christ?" As certainly, therefore, as we have in the Holy Supper real bread and real wine, not the semblance of bread nor the semblance of wine, so have we in it the real presence of Christ, and not an *imaginary, inferential* or *mythical* presence. Else how could the holy Apostle Paul say: "Whosoever shall eat this bread and drink this cup of the Lord unworthily, shall be guilty of the body and blood of the Lord." "For he that eateth and drinketh unworthily, eateth and drinketh damnation to himself, *not discerning the Lord's body.*"

The theological and practical bearings of this Sacrament, as held by the Lutheran Church, are of incalculable moment. We cannot now even enumerate them, for this paper is already much beyond the prescribed limit. But incidentally it may be mentioned that the doctrine of the person of Christ is essentially involved in it. In it, too, centers the Christian's joy, comfort, hope and happiness. Hence he derives the full assurance of his glorious immortality. Here he sees, as nowhere else, that purity of heart and holiness of life are possible for him only as he abides in Christ, and Christ in him; so that he can adopt the triumphant language of St. Paul: "I live, yet not I, but Christ liveth in me; and the life which I now live in the flesh, I live by the faith of the Son of God, who loved me and gave Himself for me."

This ordinance emphasizes the doctrine of the "*Communion of Saints.*" Around the sacramental board we proclaim ourselves members of one holy family, whose father is God and whose elder brother is Christ, the Lord. Hence says the Apostle Paul, "We, being many, are one body, for we are all partakers of that one bread." And as an experimental fact, it may be mentioned that at no other time, and on no other occasion, are Christian hearts so united, their sympathies so active, their interests so mutual, their affections so cordial, their forgivenesses so free, their criminations so few, and their generosities so unrestrained, as when they kneel around the communion altar. The *sanctifying* influences of this holy ordinance can easily be inferred, but not here discussed.

Such, then, are the Educational and Sacramental Ideas of the Lutheran Church. They lead, as you perceive, not only into the outer courts of God's sanctuary, but into the holy of holies. They kindle a divine glow and ardor which thaw all world-frost and spiritual torpor that threaten incessantly to chill the life of Christ in the soul. Naturalists inform us that the deeper we descend into the earth, the warmer it becomes. How true this maxim is we cannot say; for they have not gone deep enough to determine. Like many others of their maxims, it rests on assumption. But this we can positively affirm, that the deeper we go into these sacred mysteries the warmer it becomes, for they enfold the very heart of Christ. They deliver from that legalism which keeps the believer in the mere vestibule of this holy sanctuary, where the winds are cold, coming as they do from the icy tops of Sinai, and bringing nothing but death and destruction. But entering by faith into this holy tabernacle of the Lord, we have all the riches which the Father's infinite love and compassion have devised for His children: which the Eternal Son has procured for them by His innocent sufferings and death, and which the Holy Ghost is offering and is ready to make over to them. Here the table is spread with "milk and wine," with "marrow and fatness;" and the invitation is: "Eat, O friends; drink, yea, drink abundantly, O beloved."

The lateness of the hour prevented any discussion.

Dr. Seiss moved that the hearty thanks of this Diet be extended to the pastor and congregation of St. Matthew's church for their kindness to the Diet. Adopted.

Dr. Seiss moved that the Secretaries be directed to procure the papers read, and to make provision, if possible, for their publication. Adopted.

The subject of making provision for another Diet was then introduced as follows:

REMARKS OF REV. J. A. SEISS, D. D. (*General Council.*)

Mr. President: As there is a disposition to adjourn finally tonight, and members are beginning to retire, I have a matter of business which I should like to bring forward before our numbers are further diminished.

We have had a Diet. What was doubtful and uncertain a few

days ago, has become fixed, and passed into history. We now have some practical idea of a free congress in the Lutheran Church. It is a matter of some worth that such a convention could be organized and successfuly carried through. It is a point gained for our common cause. And it seems to be conceded that good has been accomplished by our coming together in this way. Separated for a decade of years, it has been a pleasant thing to see each other's faces, hear each other's voices, grasp each other's hands, and make a little comparison of views on given topics. Though not one in all things, the meeting has been something of an event to be remembered. If it has not been to the full what might have been desired, I have heard but one sentiment concerning it, and that is one of gratification and pleasure. The nature of the transactions, what has been read and said, the questions which have been asked and answered, the searchings for truth that have been evinced, and the patient and friendly manner in which matters of great moment have been presented and talked over, must serve to lift us in each other's esteem, to reflect credit upon our Church, to sow seeds of good in the minds and hearts of those in attendance, and to effect quiet plantings here and there which will grow, and bloom, and bring forth their fruits of blessing in after days.

The attempt to form and carry through this Diet, was something of a novelty and an experiment. It involved matters of difficulty and delicacy. It necessarily had to be on a limited scale, embracing only the most accessible men, to be assigned prominent parts. That there are many good and able men whom it would have been a pleasure to hear, is frankly admitted; but a selection had to be made, and that selection was prudentially limited to a territory not exceeding 300 miles. The best was done which, under all the circumstances, was thought most sure of making the attempt successful. The result has been what we may now pronounce a success. So far as I have learned, there is a common agreement that this Diet has been a good thing.

It has therefore occurred to me that it would perhaps be well, before finally adjourning, to give some expression, and to make some incipient provision, respecting a repetition, on a wider scale, at some future time, of what we have here had. I have thought that we might at least designate a committee to arrange for another Diet, on the same general plan as this; leaving it to them to determine as best they can, by conference with men in different sections of the Church, and by watching the indications, when, where, and how, it shall be held, and also to make up for it a full programme in advance. I would make a motion to this effect, save that I do not wish to press the suggestion if there is not a general sentiment in favor of it. To make it, only to be resisted and broken down, would be worse than not to have it made at all. I would, therefore, with the permission of the chair, very much like to have some informal expression of opinion on the subject; feeling, for my own part, that it would be eminently proper for us, here and now, before separating, unitedly to take the initiative for another Diet, say in the course of a year or so, and thus give the impulse for a succession of Diets, in which to dig after a right understanding of the truth, for the general upbuilding of ourselves and churches in the knowledge of our doctrines and of each other, and of those strong foundations on which our cause rests.

As there were calls from all sides that the suggestion accorded with the feeling of those present, it was moved by Dr. Seiss, and seconded by Dr. Brown, that a committee be appointed to make provision for another Diet. Adopted unanimously.

After some discussion as to how the committee should be constituted, it was finally resolved that the committee consist of Drs. Morris and Seiss, with power to add a third.

Dr. Conrad moved that the thanks of the Diet be returned to the reporters of the city papers. Adopted.

Dr. Brown moved that the thanks of the Diet be returned to its officers. Adopted.

REMARKS OF REV. F. W. CONRAD, D. D. (*General Synod.*)

Mr. President: Before we separate, I feel impelled to give expression to the impressions made upon me during the sessions of this Diet. When it was first broached, I doubted whether it would be held; when I was requested, months ago, to read a paper before it, I consented with no little hesitancy, and when at last the time and place of its meeting were announced, I feared that it might prove a failure. But the Diet has been held and is about to adjourn, and I desire to confess that my doubts and fears have been dispelled, and that the expectations of the most sanguine have been fully realized. From the evidence furnished by its proceedings and attendance from day to day, it must be pronounced a success, and I congratulate you, Mr. President, as its projector, and your worthy colleague, upon its character and results.

The importance of the subjects treated and discussed; the learning, research and ability displayed; the courtesy extended; the Christian spirit manifested, and the fraternal greetings exchanged, reflected credit upon all who participated in it, and could not fail to make a favorable impression upon those who attended its sessions.

Some of those present I have known many years, with others I have been upon the most intimate terms of friendship, and the privilege of meeting and taking counsel with them in this Diet, has been to me a source of no ordinary gratification. Notwithstanding the separation which left some of us in the General Synod, and led others into the General Council, our differences have not wholly schismatized our hearts, which are still bound together by the tie of a common ecclesiastical lineage, and a common Christian faith. There is yet a goodly number in both bodies, who fully realize that "we be brethren," and who, in obedience to the apostolic injunction: "Let brotherly love continue," still love one another with pure hearts fervently.

The Diet was a voluntary and unrepresentative assemblage of Lutheran ministers. Each one was at full liberty to utter his sentiments, for which he alone is responsible. It was not proposed to present the points of difference between us, and in so far as such points were introduced in the discussions, they were merely incidental. Nor was it designed for the promotion of organic union in the Lutheran Church, and hence that subject was neither assigned to a reader nor introduced into the discussions. But if the breaches in the walls of Zion are ever to be closed, and its divided parts united in "one fold" under "one Shepherd," it will be indispensable that the divisions now existing in the different Christian denominations be first healed, before a general union between them can take place. The harmonizing of the differences dividing the Lutheran Church, becomes, therefore, the pre-requisite to the union of the Protestant Churches, and the union of Protestantism will be the precursor of the consolidation of Christendom.

The divisions in the Lutheran Church of America have had their occasions and their causes, and her union, whenever it may occur, will also have its occasions and causes. And while the signs in the ecclesiastical heavens may not augur that the "set time" for the inauguration of a movement to unite the different parts in this country has come, may we not cherish the hope that the holding of this Diet will prove at least an occasion which may lead, in due time, to the adoption of such means and measures as shall, with God's blessing, eventually culminate in the organic union of the Lutheran Church in the United States of America?

A few remarks were then made by Dr. Brown.

The President announced that a motion to adjourn was in order. After a long pause, the motion was at length made and adopted; and the first Free Diet of the Lutheran Church in America, adjourned *sine die* after prayer by its President.

H. E. JACOBS.
W. M. BAUM.
Secretaries.

INDEX OF PERSONS.

Acrelius, I., 107, 110.
Albert, L. E., 77, 171, 178, 272.
Albert, Prince, 184.
Alexandra, Princess, 184.
Anstadt, P., 119.
Arndt, J., 95, 129, 133, 254.
Augustine, 224, 293.

Bacon, 257.
Baetes, W., 115.
Bager, J. G., 43, 135.
Baird, R., 125.
Baker, J. C., 115.
Bancroft, G., 113.
Baum, W. M., 9, 10, 11, 335.
Baumgarten, 65.
Baxter, 129, 326.
Bergman, C. F., 113.
Bergman, J. E., 113.
Bernheim, G. D., 107.
Beza, 15, 227.
Billican, 38.
Bolzius, J. M., 113.
Bossuet, 185.
Boyer, S. R., 77.
Brentz, 20.
Brobst, S. K., 119.
Brodhead, J. R., 108.
Brown, J. A., 9, 73, 79, 80, 104, 139, 195, 237, 274, 284, 285, 309, 312, 333.
Brück, Chancellor, 212.
Brunnholtz, P., 113, 114, 276.
Bucer, 21, 38, 211, 213, 214.
Büchsel, 323.
Bull, Bishop, 24.
Bunyan, 129.
Butler, J. G., Sr., 114, 115.

Calixtus, 40, 95, 193.
Calovius, 95, 245, 247.
Calvin, 15, 18, 38, 213 sq., 227, 273, 282.
Campanius, 110.
Capito, 211.
Cardwell, 24.
Carlstadt, 35, 38.
Cassander, 40.

Castellio, 38.
Charles V., 209, 211, 215, 239, 240.
Chemnitz, 298, 303, 305, 307, 310.
Chytraeus, 241.
Coelestinus, 240.
Cook, H. S., 177.
Conrad, F. W., 9, 72, 99, 137, 206, 272, 309, 310, 333, 334.
Conrad, V. L., 97, 99.
Cranmer, 18, 19, 20, 23, 232.

Dale, R. W., 264.
D'Aubigne, 63, 232.
Diehl, G., 10, 292, 312.
Doddridge, 129.
Dörer, 215.
Dreier, 193.
Drisius, 109.
Duchee, 287, 288.
Duraeus, 40.
Dylander, 110.

Eck, 230.
Edwards, 129.
Eichelberger, L., 118.
Eliot, 110.
Emery, W. S., 103.
Endress, C., 115.
Erasmus, 40, 202.

Falkner, Justus, 110, 111, 112, 276.
Farel, 15, 227.
Fink, R. A., 102.
Finley, Pres't, 287.
Flacius, 95.
Francis, J. W., 115.
Francke, A. H., 95, 278.
Frederick III., Elector, 15, 228.
Frick, W. K., 163.

Geissenhainer, F. W., Sr., 114.
Geissinger, D. H., 242.
George of Brandenburg, 240.
Gerhard, John, 55, 129, 298, 307, 310.
Giessler, 228.

(337)

INDEX OF PERSONS.

Goering, J., 43, 114, 115.
Goetwater, J. E., 109.
Graeber, J. G., 113.
Greenwald, E., 9, 118, 242, 243.
Grob, J., 114.
Gronau, I. C., 113.

Hallam, 182.
Hamilton, 182.
Handschuh, J. F., 113, 114, 276.
Hardwick, 21.
Hare, 183.
Hartwig, J. C., 114, 158.
Hazelius, E. L., 45, 107, 117, 119, 130.
Hedio, 211.
Heintzelmann, J. D. M., 113, 276.
Helmuth, J. C. F., 43, 108, 113, 114, 115, 118, 135.
Henry VIII., 17.
Henkel, P. 115.
Herberger, 129.
Herbst, J., 118.
Hollazius, 247.
Hontheim, 40.
Hooker, 184.
Horneius, 193.

Inglis, 287.

Jacobs, H. E., 9, 10, 107, 289, 335.
John, Elector, 216, 240.
John, Sigismund, 15, 228.
Jonas, Justus, 18, 22, 23.
Junius, Francis, 40.

Kaehler, F. C. C., 292.
King, Lord Chancellor, 65.
Kirk, E. N., 28.
Klinefelter, F., 77.
Knoll, 112.
Kocherthal, 112.
Köstering, J. F., 125.
Kohler, J. 174.
Krauth, C. P. Sr., 141.
Krauth, C. P., 9, 27, 77, 141, 199, 209, 233, 238, 285, 289.
Krotel, G. F., 10, 176, 275.
Kunze, J. C., 43, 44, 114, 115, 135, 168.
Kurtz, B. 125, 137.
Kurtz, J. D., 43, 114, 116.
Kurtz, J. N., 43, 113, 114, 276.
Kurtz, W., 43, 111.

Laud, 31.
Latermann, 193.
Laurence, 16, 17, 20.
Lintner, G. A., 113.
Lochman, G., 114, 115, 116, 134.

Löhe, 126.
Löscher, 276, 278.
Luther, D., 162, 165, 177.
Luther, Dr. Martin, 16, 17, 21, 22, 35, *sqq*., 63, 72, 74, 94, 95, 96, 98, 180, 182, 183, 184, 193, 201, 206 *sqq*., 214 *sq*., 220, 229 *sq*., 235, 238 *sqq*., 248, 2, 3, 292, 294, 297, 298, 303, 304.

Mann, W. J., 10, 96, 98, 176, 178, 237, 275, 276, 284, 265, 309, 312.
Martin, J. N., 115.
Mason, J. M., 40.
Megapolensis, 109.
Melanchthon, 16, 17, 19 *sqq*., 94, 95, 180, 193, 196, 201, 202, 206 *sqq*., 213, 218, 220, 223, 229 *sq*., 233, 236, 238 *sq*., 302,
Melsheimer, 115.
Miller, J, 115.
Miller, R. J., 127.
Miller, S., 115.
Moehler, 185.
Morris, J. G, 9, 10, 13, 15, 118, 283, 284.
Müller, H. (Germany), 129.
Müller, H. (America), 114.
Müller, J. T., 196.
Muhlenberg, H. E., 43, 114, 115.
Muhlenberg, H. M., 43, 95, 100, 111, 113, 132, 163, 273, 276, 277, 278, 286.
Muhlenberg, P., 115, 289.

Nyberg, 111.

Œcolampadius, 34.
Olevianus, 232.

Pallavicini, 182.
Palmer, 185.
Parker, 24.
Passavant, W. A., 118.
Penn, William, 110, 166.
Peters, R., 286, 287, 288, 290.
Pfaff, 40.
Philip of Hesse, 213, 234, 240.
Plitt, J. K., 172.
Pohlman, H. N., 113.
Pontanus, 240.
Price, N. M., 309.
Proctor, 20.
Pusey, 182.

Quenstedt, 244, 247.

Rath, J. B., 172.
Reinmund, J. F., 107, 163.
Repass, S. A., 9, 162.
Reynolds, W. M., 107, 108.
Romeyn, J. B., 40.
Rosenmiller, D. P., 70, 96, 144.

INDEX OF PERSONS.

Rückert, 239.
Rudman, 110.

Sadtler, B., 70, 176.
Sandin, 114.
Schaeffer, C. W., 14, 70, 107, 194, 199.
Schaeffer, D. F. 108, 118.
Schaeffer, F. D., 114.
Schaff, P., 15, 20, 25, 183, 192, 227, 228, 233.
Schaum, J. H., 113, 114, 132.
Schlatter, 287.
Schmid, H. 316.
Schmidt, F., 119.
Schmidt, J. F., 43, 113, 114, 115, 118, 135.
Schmucker, J. G., 114, 115, 118.
Schmucker, S. S., 107, 118, 119, 127.
Schnepf, 235.
Schultze, E., 113, 276.
Scriver, 129.
Seckendorf, 22.
Seiss, J. A., 9, 26, 162, 180, 264, 286, 331, 333.
Short, 23.
Spaeth, A., 163, 176, 285.
Spalatin, 232.
Spener, 95, 193, 277, 280, 326.
Sprague, W. B., 108, 114, 115.
Sprecher, S., 99.
Stark, 254.
Steinhoefer, 30.
Stoever, M. L., 107.
Stork, C. A., 10, 163, 257.

Stork, C. A. G., 115.
Strebeck, G., 44, 115, 134.
Streit, C., 43, 114.
Strobel, P. A., 107.

Tennant, 287.
Tetzel, 35.
Tischendorf, 202.
Torkillus, R., 110.
Turretin, 40.

Ursinus, 232.

Valentine, M., 9, 145, 163, 164.
Victoria, Queen, 184.
Vitus, Theodorus, 235.

Walker, F., 113.
Wedekind, A. C., 10, 101, 313.
Welden, C. F., 288.
Wesley, 29, 129.
Weyl, C., 119.
Whetstone, A. M., 206.
Whitefield, 29, 286, 287, 290.
Whittingham, 25.
Wicel, 40.
Wicksel, 281.
Wigand, 304.
Wildbahn, C. F., 114, 136.
Wrangle, Von, 110, 111, 287.

Zinzendorf, 30, 111, 232, 279.
Zwingli, 35, *sqq*, 202, 211, 213, 215, 234, 273, 282, 328.

INDEX OF SUBJECTS AND PLACES.

Absolution, 224, 281.
Academies, Church, 161.
Agnosticism, 60.
Agreement among Christians, 81.
               among Lutherans in America, 82, 97, 102, 105.
Albany, N. Y., 110, 276.
Altar Fellowship, 48, 73, 76.
               Principles of, 50.
America, Social Condition of, 278.
Anglican Church,
     Book of Common Prayer, 16, 21, 184, 264.
     Homilies of, 16.
     Thirty-nine Articles of, 15 *sqq.*, 184, 202, 227, 232.
Apology of Augsburg Confession, 131, 324.
Arminianism, 30.
Articles, Edwardine, 21 *sqq.*
         Thirty-nine, see Anglican Church,
         Twenty-five of, Methodists, 26, 232.
Associate Reformed, 40.
Augsburg Confession,
     Invariata, 282.
     Variata, 213, 231, 234, 236.
     Oldest of Modern Confessions, 85.
     Relation to Œcumenical Creeds, 207.
     Characteristics of, 206 *sqq.*
     Relation of Luther to, 208 *sqq.*, 230.
               of Melanchthon to, 209 *sqq.*, 233.
     Correspondence concerning, 209, 237, 238,
     Changes in, 196, 201.
     Interpretation of, 96.
     Subscription to, 86, 96, 103, 126 *sq.*, 196, 202, 282.
     Amer. Recension of, 128, 132.
     and the Thirty-nine Articles, 15 *sqq.*
     The Confession of the Reformed and Union Churches of Germany, 15.
     On Ministry, 292.
     On Power of Keys, 303.

Baltimore, Md., 114.
Baptism, Age of Subjects of, 135.
         Lutheran Doctrine of, 192, 227, 246, 320 *sqq.*

Baptist Churches, 29, 49.
     Reformed, 31.
Bethlehem, Pa., 172, 177.
Book of Common Prayer, 21, 23.
Book of Concord, 131, 198, 201, 203.

Call to the Ministry, 292 *sqq.*, 309 *sqq.*
Calvinists, 54, 55.
Carolinas, Lutherans in, 113, 114.
Catechetical Instruction, 88, 130, 163, 177, 280, 325.
Catechism, Luther's Small, 88, 96, 130, 163, 177, 282, 325.
Catechism, Heidelberg, 202, 232.
Catholic, the term defined, 226.
Catholic Church not visible, 59.
Catholicity of Augsburg Confession, 226 *sqq.*
Charleston, S. C., 115.
Chillicothe, O., 117.
Christianity and Science, 146.
Church, Ancient, and Close Communion, 65.
Church, Catholic or Invisible, 55.
Church, Anglican, 15 *sqq.*, 29, 110, 112, 184, 285 *sqq.*
     Baptist, 29.
     Calvinistic-Reformed, 29.
     Congregational, 29, 49, 189.
     Cumberland Presbyterian, 29.
     Dutch Reformed, 29.
     Evangelical Lutheran, 28.
     French Reformed, 29.
     Friends, 31.
     German Reformed, 29.
     Greek Orthodox, 28.
     Independents, 29.
     Mennonite, 29.
     Methodist, 30.
     Moravian, 30.
     Roman Catholic, 28.
Church Order and Spirituality, 259.
Church-Year, 135.
"*Churchmen*," 42, 183 *sq.*, 197.
Coburg, 208.
Colleges, Lutheran, by Nationalities, 151.
         Multiplication of, 152.
         Relation of, to Theological Seminaries, 154.
Columbia College, 114.

Communion, Close, 64 *sqq.*
          Interdenominational, 43 *sqq.*, 71.
          Unionistic, 40.
Communion of Saints, 259, 262, 330.
Conferences, Pastoral, 281.
Confession, Augsburg, see Augsburg Confession.
          Basle, 202.
          French, 202.
          Helvetic, 202.
          Netherlands, 202.
          Second Helvetic, 202.
          Tetrapolitan, 202, 211.
          Zurich, 202.
          Zwingli's, 38, 202, 211, 234.
Confession before Communion, 43, 280 *sq.*
Confession, Private, 224, 280.
Confessional Position of Lutheran Church, 47, 194.
          In America, 130.
Confirmation, 88, 281, 327.
Confutation, Romish, of Augsburg Confession, 232, 236.
Congregational Churches, 29, 49, 189.
Consecration of Bishops, 289
Consensus Repetitus, 193.
Conservatism, True, 228.
          Ultra, of Rome, 34.
Constitution, Church, 132, 279.
Consubstantiation, 192, 221.
Conversion, 321.
Co-operation, Ecclesiastical, 90 *sqq.*
Council of Trent, Decrees of, 85.
Creed, Relation of to Faith, 203.
Creeds (Ecumenical and Augsburg Confession, 207, 219, 227.

Danish Immigration, 124.
Decorah, Ia., 126.
Denmark, Lutheran Churches in, 288.
Denominations, Definition of, 27.
          Classification of, 28.
          Names of, 31.
          Discrimination between, 33, 52.
Denominations, Evangelical, 49.
          True churches, 73.
          "Other," 74, 77.
          Christian zeal in, 74, 77, 78, 198.
          Responsibility for, 189, 197, 203, 204.
          in Germany and America in 18th Century, 273.
Denominationalism, Origin of, 34.
          Fruits of, 41.
Depravity, Total, 324.

Development of Lutheran church in America, 124.
Dickinson College, 115, 155.
Diet, Call for, 9.
          Members of, 11.
          Opening of, 13.
          Provision for Second, 333.
          Adjournment of, 335.
Discipline, Church, 280.
Divisions, Ecclesiastical, Responsibility for 66, 73, 198, 203, 204.
Doctrinal Position of Lutherans in America, 126 *sq.*, 282.
Doctrine and Spirituality, 248, 251.
          Unity in, essential to Church Union, 51, 63, 172, 177.
Donatism, charge of, 62 *sq*
Dort, Synod of, Decrees, 108.
Dutch Lutherans, 108 *sq.*, 124, 126, 276.

Easton, Pa., 172.
Ebenezer, Ga., 113, 115.
Education, in Lutheran Church in the United States, 145 *sq.*
       , Secularization of, 149.
       True Standard of, 150.
       , and Church Growth, 156.
       , Theological, 156 *sqq.*
       , Female, 160.
       and the State, 161.
       , of Children of Church, 113, 114, 116, 163, 280, 325 *sq.*
Educational Idea of Lutheran Church 313 *sqq.*
English Congregations formed, 115.
English Language and Lutheran church, 68, 167.
       , introduced into Church Service, 111, 115, 167 *sq.*, 173, 174.
Episcopacy, Lutheran, 187.
Episcopalians, 29, 49, 92, 111, 115, 127, 175, 189, 289, *sqq.*
Epistle for the Day, 133, 134, 281.
Evangelical Alliance, 41.
Evangelical Denominations, 49.
Exclusiveness, Charge of, 63.

Faith, Rule of, 47, 200.
Fallibility and Failure distinguished, 56, 199.
Fanaticism, 34.
Fathers of Lutheran Church in America, 276.
Fellowship, Interdenominational, 39, 73, 76.
       , Official, Results of, 67.
Foreign Missions, Co-operation in, 92.
Forms, Liturgical, 257 *sqq.*
       , Dissimilarity in, no hindrance to Church Union, 89, 177.
       Uniformity of, desirable, 175.

INDEX OF SUBJECTS AND PLACES. 343

Forms, in Lutheran Church in United States, 87, 132, 278 *sq.*, 281.
Formula of Concord, 89, 97, 131, 202, 227, 237.
Franklin College, 115, 151.
Friends, 31, 39.
Ft. Wayne, Ind., 99, 121, 122, 138, 144.
General Council, 80, 99, 122, 138, 286, 334.
General Synod, 80, 117, 120, 137, 140, 141, 143, 157, 158, 272, 324, 334.
General Synod (South), 80, 99, 122, 158.
Georgia, Lutheran Church in, 132, 133, 135.
German Immigration, 112, 124, 125, 151, 166, 276.
German Language, and English, 63, 116, 167, *sqq.*
Germany, Social Condition of, 278.
Germantown, Pa., 110, 114.
Gettysburg, Pa., 114, 118, 156.
Goettingen, University of, 277.
Gospel for the Day, 133, 134, 281.
Government, Church, Forms of, 181.
Gown, Clerical, 178.
Greek Orthodox Church, 28, 85.

Hagerstown, Md., 114, 117.
Halle Records, 107 *sqq.*, 280, 281, 287, 290.
Halle, University of, 192, 277.
Hanover, Pa., 115.
Harrisburg, Pa., 114.
Hartwick Seminary, 117, 151.
Harvard College, 155.
Helmstaedt, University of, 192.
Heresy, 64.
Herrnhuthers, 30.
High Church Anglicans, 31, 42, 183 *sq.*, 188, 197.
High Mass, 132.
Hymn-Books, English, 134.

Immigration, Statistics of, 124.
Impanation, 221.
Independents, 29, 39.
Indifferentism, 41, 42, 188, 277.
Infallibility, Charge of, 55 *sq.*, 195 *sq.*, 199.

Jansenists, 31.
Jesuits, 31.
Judgment, Private, Right of, 35.
Justification by Faith, Endangered by Unionism, 48.
———, Held by all Lutherans, 86.
———, Repudiated by High Churchmen, 184, 185.
——— Renounced by False Spirituality, 249.
———, As set forth in Augsburg Confession, 218.

Keys, Power of, 302.

Laity, Education of, 162.
———, Part of, in Call of Minister, 304, 306, 307.
Lancaster, Pa., 110, 111, 114, 157, 170.
Language and Faith, 68, 116.
———, in Lutheran Church in America, 68, 116, 165 *sqq*, 279, 291.
———, Separation on Basis of, 163 *sqq.*, 171.
Latitudinarianism, 42.
Laying on of Hands, 297.
Lay Reading, 127.
Lebanon, Pa., 114, 172.
Lebanon, O., 117.
Leipsic, University of, 193.
Life, as a Test of Faith, 74, 78.
Littlestown, Pa., 136.
Liturgical Forms, See Forms.
Liturgies, 43-5, 132-4, 272, See also Orders of Service.
Loonenburgh, N. Y., 113.
Lord's Supper, 36 *sqq.*, 53 *sq.*, 327 *sqq.*
———, Doctrine of, Fundamental, 53, 98, 213.
———, Lutheran Doctrine of, 71, 97, 220, 246, 328.
———, Lutheran Doctrine of, Misrepresented, 189, 192, 320.
———, Doctrine of Denominations, 71, 72.
———, Agreement concerning, 97, 102.
———, Condemning clause of Augsburg Confession concerning, 213.
———, Romish view of Augsburg Confession on, 213, 236.
———, Swiss view of Augsburg Confession on, 213.
———, Analogy between, and Baptism, 76, 79.
Losses, Annual, of Lutheran Church, 125.
Lutheran, the Name, 70, 82.
Lutheran Catechism in England, 18, 21.
Lutheran Church, Centre of, 28.
———, De Facto, 41 *sqq.*
———, De Jure, 46 *sqq.*
———, a Biblical Church, 47.
———, the Church of Faith, 47.
———, Confessional Position of, 47.
———, Divine Origin and Necessity of, 48.
———, Objections against, answered, 51 *sqq.*
———, an Educating Church, 148, 324 *sqq.*

Lutheran Church, not a Sect, 188, 207.
———, older than the Denominations, 189.
———, Truth fully taught by, 186, 191.
———, a true Church, 186, 191.
———, Organization of in America, 276.
——— and Christian Union, 335.
Lutheran Forms of Church Government, 181.
Lutheranism not co-extensive with Christianity, 84.
———, Degrees of, 83.
———, Defined, 277.
———, of Fathers, 276 *sqq*.
———, Decline of, 128, 277, 315.
———, Revival of, 130, 164, 315.
Lutherans, in America, Agreement among, 81, 100-103.
———, and Nationality, 83.
———, Diversity among, 88.
———, Origin of, 188.
———, Relation to Martin Luther, 182 *sq*.
———, not guilty of Schism, 186, 194, 197, 207.
———, not Heretics, 186, 194.
———, not a Sect, 188, 207.
———, Efforts of, to preserve External Unity, 186, 207.

Maine, Lutherans in, 113.
Marburg Articles, 208.
———, Conference, 35, 214, 215.
Marshal, Wis., 158.
Maryland, Lutherans in, 113.
Means of Grace, 192, 246, 277, 313.
Mendota, Ill., 158.
Mennonites, 29.
Ministerial Sessions, 280.
Ministerium, see Synod.
Ministry, Divine Institution of, 87, 295 *sqq*.
———, Call to, 292 *sqq*.
———, Defined, 292.
———, Distinguished from Spiritual Priesthood, 294.
———, Demission of, 309.
———, Deposition from, 309.
Missions, 117, 281.
Montgomery county, Pa., 111, 112, 114, 276.
Montgomery county, O., 117.
Moravians, 30, 228, 232.
Muhlenberg College, 70.
Mystical Union, 243 *sqq*.

Nantes, Edict of, 165.
Nationality and Faith, 83 *sqq*.
Newbern, N. C., 112.
Newburgh, N. Y., 112.

New Hanover, 113.
New Market, Va., 117.
New Measures, 88, 129.
New York, Lutherans in, 108, 109, 111, 112, 114 *sq*., 124, 276.
North Carolina, 115.

Old Lutherans, 277.
Orders of Service, 129, 133, 134.
Ordination, 298, 302.
———, administered by Swedish pastors, 111.
Organization of Lutheran Church in America, 132, 276, 279.
Orthodox, Defined, 219.
———, and Spirituality, 252.
Orthodoxism, 279, 283.

Pennsylvania, first Lutheran Church in, 110.
———, Germans in, 113.
See Synods.
Pennsylvania College, 107, 135, 145, 151.
Philadelphia, Pa., 9, 10, 111, 113, 114, 115, 132, 285, 286.
Pietism, 29, 128, 277, 279, 283.
Piety, 313 *sqq*.
Pittsburgh, Pa., 122.
Prayer, a Spiritual Sacrifice, 293.
———, and Spirituality, 253.
———, Extemporanous, 265, 267, 273.
———, Forms of, 258, 273. See Forms and Orders of Service.
———, Public, of Women, 284.
Preaching, of the Fathers, 135, 279, 280.
Presbyterian Form of Government, 279.
Presbyterians, 29, 49, 93, 175, 189, 274.
Press, Lutheran, in America, 118 *sq*.
Priesthood, 293.
———, of Believers, 87, 294.
Princeton College, 287.
Providence, Pa., 113.
Public Worship, 132, 259 *sqq*., 273.
Pulpit Fellowship, 48, 50, 73, 76, 111, 284 *sqq*.
Pulpits, Exchange of, 284 *sqq*.
Puritans and Liturgical Forms, 266 *sq*., 273.

Radicalism, 34.
———, and the Sacraments, 315.
Rationalism, 42, 277.
———, and the Sacraments, 315.
Reading, Pa., 114, 172, 174.
Reformed, 75, 108, 109, 128, 226, 228, 287.
See also German, Dutch, French, etc.
———, Episcopalians, 32.
———, Presbyterians, 32.
Regeneration, 321.
Revival Movements, 115.
Rochester, N. Y., 122.
Rochester, Pa., 120.

INDEX OF SUBJECTS AND PLACES. 345

Rock Island, Ill., 126.
Romanism in Protestantism, 59.
Roman Catholics, 28, 77, 86, 94, 149, 187 *sqq.*, 226.

Sacraments, Defined, 316.
——, Design of, 317 *sqq.*
——, Lutheran Doctrine of, 228, 250, 314 *sqq.*
——, and False Spirituality, 250.
See also Radicalism.
Sacramental Ideas of Lutheran Church, 313 *sqq.*
Sacrifices, Spiritual, 293.
Salzburgers, 113.
Savannah, Ga., 115.
Scandinavian Immigration, 124.
Schism, 27, 186, 190, 197, 215.
Schools, Common, 163, 164.
——, Parochial, 164.
Schoharie, N. Y., 112.
Schwabach Articles, 201, 208, 234.
Science and Christianity, 146.
Secret Societies, 280.
Sect and Sectarianism, 7, 33, 66, 67, 77–79, 188, 190, 202, 207.
Sensationalism, 254.
Separation and Language, 169 *sqq.*
Sermons of Fathers, 135; see Preaching.
Smalcald Articles, 131, 232, 297, 302.
Socinianism, 29, 31, 39, 67, 131.
—— in Lutheran Church, 42.
South Carolina, Lutherans in, 109. See Carolinas, and Synods.
Spires, Edict of, 216.
Spirituality, True and False, 243 *sqq.*
State and Education, 149, 161.
State Universities, 149.
St. Bartholomew, Massacre of, 165.
Statistics, 114, 118, 121–125, 151, 156, 158.
Subpanation, 221.
"*Substantially*," 103, 104.
Sunday-schools, 129, 280.
Swatara, Lutherans on the, 113.
Sweden, Lutheran Church in, 181, 288.
Swedish Immigration, 124.
——, Lutherans on the Delaware, 110 *sqq.*
Symbolical Books, 126, 282. See Book of Concord.
Syncretism, 42.
Synod, Alleghany, 120.
——, Ansgari, 120.
——, Augsburg, 120.
——, Augustana, Swedish, 122, 126.
——, Augustana, Nor.-Danish, 122, 158.
——, Canada, 122.
——, Central Pennsylvania, 120.

Synod, East Pennsylvania, 120.
——, English Conference of Mo., 122.
——, English District, of Ohio, 120, 122.
——, English, O., 120, 121, 122.
——, Franckean, 99, 120, 121, 137, 140, 141.
——, Georgia, 122.
——, German Maryland, 120.
——, Hartwick, 120.
——, Holston, 122.
——, Illinois, 120, 121, 122.
——, Indiana, 122.
——, Iowa (English), 120.
——, Iowa (German), 122, 158, 277.
——, Kansas, 120.
——, Kentucky, 120.
——, Maryland, 117.
——, Melanchthon, 120, 140, 142.
——, Miami, 120.
——, Michigan, 122.
——, Minnesota, 120, 121, 122.
——, Mississippi, 122.
——, Missouri, 122, 125, 164, 277.
——, New Jersey, 120.
——, New York, 44, 114, 116, 117, 120, 122. 126, 138.
——, North Carolina, 114, 117, 120, 122, 127
——, North Illinois, 120.
——, North Indiana, 120.
——, Norwegian, 122, 126.
——, Ohio, 45, 117, 122, 126.
——, Olive Branch, 120.
——, Pennsylvania, 44, 45, 113, 116, 117, 120, 122, 128, 132, 138, 144, 198.
——, Pittsburg, 120, 121, 122, 138, 143.
——, South Carolina, 45, 118, 120.
——, South-west, 120.
——, S. W. Virginia, 120, 122.
——, S. Illinois, 120.
——, Susquehanna, 120.
——, Tennessee, 117, 127.
——, Texas, 120, 121, 122.
——, Virginia, 120, 122.
——, Wartburg, 120.
——, West, 120.
——, Wisconsin, 122.
——, Wittenberg, 120.
Synodical Conference, 80, 122, 124, 131.
Tennessee, 114.
Testimony of General Synod, 158.
Tests for Fellowship, 64, 65, 71, 73, 79.
Theological Education, 157 *sqq.*
Theological Seminary, Columbus, O., 118.
——, Gettysburg, Pa., 80, 118, 125, 158.
——, Hartwick, N. Y., 117, 158.
——, Lexington, S. C., 118.

INDEX OF SUBJECTS AND PLACES.

Theological Seminary, Newberry, S. C., 118.
———, Philadelphia, Pa., 25, 115, 173, 276.
———, Salem, Va., 118.
Torgau Articles, 208.
Tractarians, 42, 183 *sq.*, 188, 197.
Tradition and Liturgies, 257.
Transubstantiation, 192, 328.
Trinity, Doctrine of, 180.
Tulpehocken, Lutherans on, 113.

Unionism, 34, 39 *sqq.*, 94, 188, 277.
Union Prayer Meetings, 41.
    Revivals, 41.
    Sunday-schools, 41.
    Tract, 41.
Universalism, 42.
University, a Lutheran, 93.
University of Pennsylvania, 114, 115.

Unity, Pre-requisites to, 172.
Urlsperger Records, 107.
Virginia, Lutherans in, 113, 116.
West Virginia, 114.
Wilmington, Del., 114.
Winchester, Va., 114.
Wittenberg, Formula Concordiæ, 214, 215, 235.
———, University of, 148, 193, 305.
Worms, Edict of, 215.
Worship, in Lutheran Church, in United States, 87, 132, 273 *sqq.*, 281.
———, Liturgical Forms in, 237 *sqq.*, 273 *sq.*
———, Uniformity of, 87, 172, 175. See Public Worship.
York, Pa., 110, 114, 138, 143, 144.
Young Men's Christian Associations, 41.
Zwinglians, 54, 270.

www.ingramcontent.com/pod-product-compliance
Lightning Source LLC
Chambersburg PA
CBHW030000240426
43672CB00007B/766